Maimonides in His World

JEWS, CHRISTIANS, AND MUSLIMS FROM THE ANCIENT TO THE MODERN WORLD

Edited by Michael Cook, William Chester Jordan, and Peter Schäfer

Imperialism and Jewish Society, 200 B.C.E. *to 640* C.E.
by Seth Schwartz

A Shared World: Christians and Muslims in the Early Modern Mediterranean
by Molly Greene

Beautiful Death: Jewish Poetry and Martyrdom in Medieval France
by Susan L. Einbinder

Power in the Portrayal: Representations of Jews and Muslims in Eleventh- and Twelfth-Century Islamic Spain
by Ross Brann

Mirrors of His Beauty: Feminine Images of God from the Bible to the Early Kabbalah
by Peter Schäfer

In the Shadow of the Virgin: Inquisitors, Friars, and Conversos *in Guadalupe, Spain*
by Gretchen D. Starr-LeBeau

The Curse of Ham: Race and Slavery in Early Judaism, Christianity, and Islam
by David M. Goldenberg

Resisting History: Historicism and Its Discontents in German-Jewish Thought
by David N. Myers

Mothers and Children: Jewish Family Life in Medieval Europe
by Elisheva Baumgarten

A Jewish Renaissance in Fifteenth-Century Spain
by Mark D. Meyerson

The Handless Maiden: Moriscos and the Politics of Religion in Early Modern Spain
by Mary Elizabeth Perry

Poverty and Charity in the Jewish Community of Medieval Egypt
by Mark R. Cohen

Reckless Rites: Purim and the Legacy of Jewish Violence
by Elliott Horowitz

Living Together, Living Apart: Rethinking Jewish-Christian Relations in the Middle Ages
by Jonathan Elukin

The Church in the Shadow of the Mosque: Christians and Muslims in the World of Islam
by Sidney H. Griffith

The Religious Enlightenment: Protestants, Catholics, Jews and Reasonable Belief, London to Vienna
by David Sorkin

American Evangelicals in Egypt: Missionary Encounters in an Age of Empire
by Heather J. Sharkey

Maimonides in His World: Portrait of a Mediterranean Thinker
by Sarah Stroumsa

Maimonides in His World

PORTRAIT OF A MEDITERRANEAN THINKER

Sarah Stroumsa

PRINCETON UNIVERSITY PRESS
PRINCETON AND OXFORD

Published by Princeton University Press, 41 William Street, Princeton, New Jersey 08540
In the United Kingdom: Princeton University Press, 6 Oxford Street, Woodstock, Oxfordshire OX20 1TW

Library of Congress Cataloging-in-Publication Data

Stroumsa, Sarah.
Maimonides in his world : portrait of a Mediterranean thinker / Sarah Stroumsa.
p. cm. — (Jews, Christians, and Muslims from the ancient to the modern world)
Includes bibliographical references and index.
ISBN 978-0-691-13763-6 (alk. paper)
1. Maimonides, Moses, 1135-1204. 2. Philosophy, Medieval. 3. Intellectual life—History. I. Title.
B759.M34S77 2009
181'.06—dc22

2009004666

British Library Cataloging-in-Publication Data is available

This book has been composed in Sabon

Printed on acid-free paper. ∞

press.princeton.edu

Printed in the United States of America

10 9 8 7 6 5 4 3 2

In loving memory of my parents

Zvi Avraham Wallach
Zoshka Wallach née Ludmer

CONTENTS

Preface	xi
Acknowledgments	xvii
Abbreviations	xix
Chapter One Maimonides and Mediterranean Culture	1
Mediterranean Cultures	3
Maimonides as a Mediterranean Thinker	6
Horizons	13
Transformations in the Jewish World	18
Maimonides and Saadia	22
Chapter Two The Theological Context of Maimonides' Thought	24
Islamic Theology	24
Heresies, Jewish and Muslim	38
Chapter Three An Almohad "Fundamentalist"?	53
Almohads	53
Maimonides and the Almohads	59
Legal Aspects	61
Theology	70
Exegesis and Political Philosophy	73
Philosophy and Astronomy	80
Conclusion	82
Chapter Four *La Longue Durée*: Maimonides as a Phenomenologist of Religion	84
Sabians	84
Maimonides as an Historian of Religion	106
"A Wise and Understanding People?": The Religion of the People	111

Chapter Five
A Critical Mind: Maimonides as Scientist 125
Medicine and Science 125
"Ravings": Maimonides' Concept of Pseudo-Science 138

Chapter Six
"From Moses to Moses": Maimonides' Vision of Perfection 153
"True Felicity": The Hereafter in Maimonides' Thought 153
Issues of Life and Death: The Controversy Regarding Resurrection 165
"Gates for the Righteous Nation": The Philosopher as Leader 183

Conclusion 189

Bibliography 193

Index 219

PREFACE

THE PRESENT BOOK is dedicated to one major medieval thinker, Moses Maimonides (d. 1204), and to the examination of his thought in its historical and cultural context. The description of Maimonides as a thinker (rather than a philosopher, for instance) follows from his own definition of thinking:

> Thought (*fikra*) is one of the properties of a human being that are consequent upon his form.[1]

As these carefully chosen words indicate, for Maimonides thinking in itself is not identical with human perfection, nor does it guarantee the achievement of this perfection. Thinking is relevant at all levels of the theoretical as well as the practical domain, and it can even be corrupted and turned to vile things.[2] When the process of thinking is interrupted "at first thought" (*bi-awwal fikra*) it is likely to produce unripe, erroneous, or harmful ideas.[3] When, however, it is used as befits the human form, it prepares the human being to become human in all endeavors: individual or collective, corporeal or intellectual. Maimonides wrote on philosophy and on theology, on medicine and on Jewish law, and he was a community leader and a practicing physician. In all these activities he was driven by the same yearning to think correctly, and to direct his thoughts upwards. To understand him, we must therefore approach his thought in its entirety, as reflecting different aspects of one and the same thinker.

This book does not provide a full picture of Maimonides' thought, nor does it aspire to do so. There are many books that offer a synthesis of our knowledge regarding Maimonides: some are the fruit of joint efforts, presented as collections of articles; others are monographs; and some of them are impressively learned and penetrating. A huge literature exists also on specific important questions in Maimonides' thought. His positions on such fundamental philosophical and religious issues as creation ex nihilo, prophecy, or predestination have been analyzed and debated, with new and interesting studies still appearing. The present book touches on these issues only occasionally and briefly. It is also not a book dedicated

[1] *Guide* 3.8 (*Dalāla,* 313:5–6; Pines, 434–35).
[2] On the human being's ability to "direct his thoughts" (*an yattajiha bi-fikrihi*) to both sublime and mean objects, see *Guide* 1.10 (*Dalāla*, 24:13–14; Pines, 36).
[3] *Guide* 1.26 (*Dalāla*, 37:20–22; Pines, 434–35).

to one particular subfield of Maimonidean scholarship: philosophy, or law (*halacha*), or science. On each of these topics, there exists a vast and rapidly growing literature. Furthermore, only a fraction of this scholarly literature appears in the notes to the present book. The footnotes are meant to acknowledge my intellectual and scholarly debt, and to point to the diversity of possible interpretations. This book does not aspire to summarize Maimonides' place in any of these subfields, nor does it purport to update Maimonides' biography or intellectual biography. Instead, it seeks to offer what one might call "a cultural biography":[4] Maimonides' interaction with his multifaceted historical and cultural legacy, and how this cultural context affected him and shaped his thought.

This approach has also determined my use of sources. Whereas some modern Maimonides scholars tend to evaluate non-Jewish sources as secondary, auxiliary, or irrelevant sources,[5] these sources are taken here to be of primary importance for appreciating Maimonides' work. Their intrinsic value is judged, as is that of the Jewish sources, according to the topic at hand and the quality of each particular source.

Moreover, regarding Maimonides' own sources, some scholars adopt a rigorous approach, which is in effect a minimalist one. For them, suggestions that Maimonides might have had access to a specific non-Jewish source encounter resistance and are expected to be accompanied by a positive proof that this was indeed the case.[6] My own working hypothesis is that Maimonides, who only rarely cited his sources, read all he could find, and that he had no qualms about perusing the theological or legal works of non-Jews, and even less so when he respected their author. A priori, therefore, and until proven otherwise, my assumption is that he was generally familiar with major books of his period, both those that circulated in the West and those he could read in Egypt. As the following pages will show, this assumption in itself allows us to uncover places where Maimonides' statements indeed reveal his familiarity with these works.

That, with the exception of Philo, Jewish systematic philosophy emerged under Islam, and the crucial importance of the Islamic context for understanding the flourishing of Judaeo-Arabic philosophy, have long been

[4] I am indebted to Mark Silk for suggesting this term.

[5] See, for example, H. A. Davidson, *Moses Maimonides, The Man and His Works* (Oxford 2005), 17–18, and 517n137 (regarding Ibn al-Qifṭī).

[6] See, for example A. Ivry, "Maimonides' Relation to the Teachings of Averroes," *Sefunot*, n.s. 8 (2003): 62; and Pines, "Translator's Introduction: The Philosophic Sources of the *Guide of the Perplexed*," in Moses Maimonides, *The Guide of the Perplexed,* trans. by Pines (Chicago and London 1963), cviii (regarding Ibn Rushd's independent works); and, see, chap. 2, note 3, below; and chap. 3, note 85 ff.

acknowledged. As already stated succinctly by Shlomo Pines, "in the sphere of philosophical literature . . . Jewish thinkers had recourse primarily to the books of their Moslem counterparts," whereas "rare and of secondary significance is that relationship to the teaching of their Jewish predecessors."[7] This assessment has been fully adopted in this book. Moreover, its adoption in the realm of philosophy also entails a change of perspective in other domains. A philosopher who was so fully immersed in Islamic philosophy and used it to shape his own could not disengage himself from Islamic culture when he delved into other kinds of intellectual activity, be it exegesis, theology, or polemics. My assumption is therefore that, in writing on Jewish law, for example, Maimonides was not only toeing the line of Rabbinic, Gaonic tradition, but also bringing to bear the influence of his non-Jewish cultural context.

Tracing influences is often frowned upon in modern scholarship. Many feel that *Quellenforschung*, which highlights the separate components of a given system, devalues the originality of this system and diverts scholarly attention from contents and ideas to the history of their transmission. When the previous life of ideas must be recognized, scholars nowadays prefer to concentrate on the mechanisms of their appropriation, and the word "influence" is often placed, with a skeptical grin, between quotation marks. The present study regards the detection of hitherto unrecognized direct influences as an indispensable tool for the historian of ideas and of mentalities. The identification of influences is critical in our attempt to gauge the depth of a thinker's attachment to his milieu. It enables us to transform this milieu from a scenic background into the pulsating world in which the thinker lived. In the case of Maimonides, far from obfuscating his originality, the identification of influences allows us to flesh out the person, his way of thinking, and his creative genius in recognizing the potential of the available crude material and in using it.

A central idea informing this book is the belief in the capital importance of the multifocal approach to intellectual history in the world of medieval Islam. An examination that focuses on the output of only one religious community, with an occasional dutiful nod to the rest of the religious puzzle, is similar to examination with a single eye, and is likely to produce a flat, two-dimensional picture. Reading Jewish and Muslim intellectual history together is a sine qua non condition if we strive to achieve a correct, well-rounded picture of this history. Generally speaking, for a truly three-dimensional picture, what is required is actually a trifocal approach that also takes the Christians into account. Although in the intellectual history of al-Andalus (Muslim Spain) the role played

[7] Pines, "Scholasticism after Thomas Aquinas and the Teachings of Ḥasdai Crescas and his Predecessors," *Proceedings of the Israel Academy of Science and Humanities* 1.10 (1967): 1.

by Christians was relatively marginal, they nevertheless represent a crucial piece in the puzzle of the development of this culture. One should emphasize that, for a correct application of the multifocal approach, a parallel but separate study of the different communities will not suffice. Furthermore, in this complex intellectual world the ideas flow into each other, brazenly oblivious to communal barriers. The flow of ideas was never unilateral or linear, but rather went back and forth, creating what I propose to call a "whirlpool effect," where, when an idea falls, like a drop of colored liquid, into the turbulence, it eventually colors the whole body of water. In order to follow the course of these ideas, and to see how a particular thinker contributed to their flow, a full picture must be obtained.

This whirlpool metaphor may also convey some of the difficulties involved in our approach. It is much easier to trace the course of neatly divided currents and trends than to reconstruct the way in which they contributed to the whirlpool. When first thinking of this book, I had planned to treat the material that fed into Maimonides' thought according to its origin in different communities. This would have implied, for example, writing a separate section on Muslim *kalām*, another on Jewish *kalām*, and yet another on Christian theology. The original plan, however, proved impossible to carry out: Maimonides' attitude to Jewish *kalām* cannot be treated separately from Muslim or Christian *kalām*.

The first chapter of this book serves as an introduction: it discusses the notion of the designation "Mediterranean" and its applicability and usefulness for the study of Maimonides. It also presents a "Mediterranean biography" of Maimonides, setting the ground for the following chapters, which can be seen as case studies touching upon cardinal points in Maimonides' thought. Chapter 2 is dedicated to the world of theology as Maimonides lived it: Jewish, Christian, and Muslim orthodox theology on the one hand, and heresies on the other. Chapter 3 focuses on the particular brand of theology that was the backdrop for the formative period of Maimonides' life: the Almohads, and their unacknowledged but immense impact on Maimonides's thought in all realms. Chapter 4 examines Maimonides' approach to religion: beginning with his analysis of the Sabians and idolatry, continuing with his view of the history of Islam, and concluding with his attitude to the various shades of popular religiosity. Chapter 5 studies Maimonides' scientific approach as it is reflected in his medical practice, on the one hand, and in his attitude to pseudo-science, on the other. Chapter 6 endeavors to examine various aspects of Maimonides' vision of human perfection: beyond this life (in the world to come or after the resurrection) or, within it, as part of society. The conclusion will briefly present the implications of these case studies for the study of Maimonides in particular and of Jewish and Islamic thought in general.

The present book grew, as books do, out of my work over several years, both in teaching and in writing. While some of the material it contains is published here for the first time, parts of it are based on previous publications. These publications treated specific aspects of Maimonides' thought, and the picture they offered was necessarily limited in scope. By their integration into a full portrait I hope to show that the traits they point to in Maimonides' thought were not just episodes, moments, or flashes in Maimonides' thinking. This was indeed his world.

ACKNOWLEDGMENTS

THE DECISION to write the present book was made in 2006, when I was enjoying a sabbatical year as a Fellow at the Center for Advanced Judaic Studies at the University of Pennsylvania. The CAJS provided ideal working conditions, a supportive staff, and a wonderful group of colleagues. Without all these, this book would have waited seven more years, if not more. In particular, I wish to thank the Center's Director, Professor David Ruderman, for his kind support; Etty Lassman, whose resourcefulness and dedication allowed me to move, with my antique files, into the twenty-first century; and the library staff—in particular, Dr. Arthur Kiron, Dr. Seth Dershowitz, Judith Halper, and Joseph Gulka—who painstakingly retrieved books and articles and shared my enthusiasm for their content.

A previous Sabbatical allowed me to spend, in 2000, a wonderful six months in Madrid. The scholars of the *Instituto des Estudios Arabes* at the Consejo Superior de Investigaciones Científicas welcomed me, with their customary warmth, to the world of al-Andalus, and shared with me their erudition. For this experience of true *convivencia* I am grateful to them, and in particular to Maribel Fierro, Mercedes García-Arenal, and Cristina de la Puente.

If I count the landmarks in the production of this book in terms of sabbaticals, this is due to the liberality of The Hebrew University of Jerusalem. In a world where the patience for academic *scholē* is growing thin, the Hebrew University continues to recognize the importance of scholarly mobility and international exposure and to support it generously. My foremost debt to the Hebrew University, however, is for the constant experience of intellectual challenge it provides. As a member of two of its departments (the Department of Arabic Language and Literature and the Department of Jewish Thought) I was introduced to a double share of its intellectual riches. I wish to take this opportunity to thank my friends at the Hebrew University—teachers, colleagues, and students—for their erudition, intellectual curiosity, friendly criticism, and kind encouragement that have inspired and sustained me over the years.

In writing about Maimonides, the memory of two of my teachers accompanies my every word: my high school teacher Yaacov Meir, whose classes vibrated with the moral and intellectual relevance of the *Eight Chapters*; and Shlomo Pines, the unassuming mentor, the critical thinker of philosophy in context. For the privilege of their inspiration I am forever grateful.

I wish to thank Fred Appel, the Senior Editor in Religion and Anthropology at Princeton University Press, for his gentle coaching and professional advice. I am grateful to Jon Munk, who copyedited the manuscript, and to Heath Renfroe, the production editor, for their competent and forthcoming help. The two anonymous readers have been extremely generous with their time and scholarship, and I am thankful for their meticulous reading and detailed, penetrating comments.

The etiquette of acknowledgments requires that family be relegated to the end, so it is at the end that I put Guy first: he was the first to suggest that I write this book, and as always, accompanied this book and me with relentless criticism and boundless encouragement. His friendship surpasses the one that the protagonist of the present book valued as perfect.[1]

[1] See Maimonides, *Commentary on the Mishna*, *Neziqin*, 411–12 (commentary on *Avot* 1.6).

ABBREVIATIONS

Works of Maimonides

Commentary on the Aphorisms of Hippocrates, = *Moshe ben Maimon: Commentary on the Aphorisms of Hippocrates*, ed. Suessmann Muntner, Hebrew trans. Moshe Ibn Tibbon (Maimonides, *Medical Works*, III) (Jerusalem: Mosad Harav Kook, 1961).

Commentary on the Mishnah = *Mishnah ʿim Perush Rabbenu Moshe ben Maimon*, ed. J. Kapaḥ (Jerusalem, 1965).

Dalāla = Mūsā ben Maymūn, *Dalālat al-ḥāʾirīn*, ed. S. Munk and I. Yoel (Jerusalem, 1931).

Epistulae = Moshe ben Maimon, *Epistulae*, ed. D. H. Baneth (Jerusalem, 1946).

Epistles = *Iggerot ha-Rambam*, ed. I. Shailat, 2 vols (Jerusalem: *Maʿaliyot*, 1987–88).

The Guide of the Perplexed: References to the *Guide* indicate part and chapter, with a following reference, respectively, to Munk-Joel's edition of the Judaeo-Arabic text (page and line) and to Pines's English translation. For example, *Guide*, 3.27 (*Dalāla*, 371:17; Pines, 510), indicates *The Guide of the Perplexed,* Part 3, chapter 27 (page 371, line 17, in Munk-Joel's edition; page 510 in Pines's translation).

Letters = Rabbi Moshe Ben Maimon, *Iggerot: Letters,* ed. and trans. J. Kafih (Jerusalem, 1987).

Medical Aphorisms = Maimonides, *Medical Aphorisms*, Treatises 1–5 *(Kitāb al-fuṣūl fīʾl-ṭibb*). ed., trans. and annotated by Gerrit Bos (The Medical Works of Moses Maimonides) (Provo: Brigham Young University Press, 2004).

Medical Aphorisms (*Pirqei Moshe*), ed. Seussmann Muntner (Jerusalem, 1959).

Mishneh Torah = Moshe ben Maimon, *Mishneh Torah* (Jerusalem, 1965).

On Asthma = *Maimonides On Asthma* (*maqāla fīʾl-rabwi*), ed., trans. and annotated by Gerrit Bos. (The Complete Medical Works of Moses Maimonides, vol. 1) (Provo: Brigham Young University 2002).

Pines = Moses Maimonides, *The Guide of the Perplexed.* Trans. with an Introduction and Notes by Shlomo Pines (Chicago and London: University of Chicago Press, 1963).

Responsa = Moshe ben Maimon, *Responsa*, ed. J. Blau. 4 vols. (Jerusalem, 1986).

Sefer ha-mitzvot = Moshe ben Maimon, *Sefer ha-mitzvot*, ed. J. Qafīḥ (Jerusalem, 1971).

Treatise on Resurrection = *Maimonides' Treatise on Resurrection* (*Maqāla fī teḥiyyat ha-metim*), ed. J. Finkel *PAAJR* 9 (New York: American Academy for Jewish Research, 1939).

Other Works

BT	Babylonian Talmud
BSOAS	*Bulletin of the School of Oriental and African Studies*
EI	*The Encyclopaedia of Islam*, New Edition (Leiden, Brill, 1986–2002).
IAU	Ibn Abī Uṣaybiʿa, *'Uyūn al-anbā' fī ṭabaqāt al-aṭibbā'*. ed. Nizār Riḍā (Beirut: *Maktabat al-ḥayāt*, n.d.).
IOS	*Israel Oriental Studies*
IQ	Ibn al-Qifṭī, *Ta'rikh al-ḥukamā*, ed. I. Lippert (Leipzig, 1903).
JQR	*Jewish Quarterly Review*
JAOS	*Journal of the American Oriental Society*
JSAI	*Jerusalem Studies in Arabic and Islam*
PAAJR	*Proceedings of the American Academy for Jewish Research*
ZDMG	*Zeitschrift der Morgendländer Gesselschaft*

Citations in Arabic or in Hebrew are in italics. Citations in Judaeo-Arabic are in italics, with the Hebrew words in bold characters. Translations from the Arabic or Hebrew, when no other translation is indicated, are my own.

Maimonides in His World

Chapter One

Maimonides and Mediterranean Culture

FROM THE MANY HONORIFIC TITLES appended to Maimonides' name, "The Great Eagle" has come to be identified as his particular, personal title. This biblical sobriquet (from Ezekiel 17: 3) was meant, no doubt, to underline his regal position in the Jewish community. At the same time, the imagery of the wide-spread wings does justice not only to the breadth of Maimonides' intellectual horizons, but also to the scope of his impact, which extended across the Mediterranean, and beyond it to Christian Europe.

To the extent that the quantity of scholarly studies about an author is a criterion for either importance or fame, Moses Maimonides (1138–1204) stands among the most prominent figures in Jewish history, and certainly the most famous medieval Jewish thinker.[1] The continuous stream of publications dedicated to Maimonides is, however, often characterized by overspecification. Following what appears to be a division in Maimonides' own literary output, scholars usually focus on a particular section of his work—philosophy, medicine, religious law, or community leadership—complementing it by forays into other domains. Each such subject creates its own context: the intellectual or historical environment that we reconstruct in our attempts to understand Maimonides' treatment of a certain topic.

The prevalent tendency to overemphasize disciplinary partitions within Maimonides' own work reinforces, in turn, another already existing tendency: to overemphasize the distinction between Maimonides the Jewish leader and Maimonides the Islamic thinker.[2] Although Maimonides, like many great thinkers, defies categorization, we are prone to search for familiar tags, convenient pigeon-holes in which we can neatly classify his

[1]To illustrate this point, one example may suffice: a search in RAMBI, The Index of Articles in Jewish Studies, published by the Jewish National and University Library at Jerusalem (http://jnul.huji.ac.il/rambi/) lists, as articles with "Maimonides" as a key-word in the title, 243 entries published between 2000 and 2007 (and this number does not include Hebrew articles in the same category). On the inflation in Maimonidean scholarship, see also P. Bouretz, "A la recherche des lumières médiévales: la leçon de Maïmonide," *Critique* 64 (Jan-Feb. 2008), 29. Several comprehensive books on Maimonides came out when the manuscript of the present book was already completed, and could not be cited extensively.

[2]For an example of such a distinction, see chap. 5, below, *apud* notes 18–20.

work. The ensuing scholarly result does not do justice to Maimonides. The image it paints resembles Maimonides' famous, very late portrait: imposing and yet flat and two-dimensional. In particular, it depreciates Maimonides' participation in the cultural world of Medieval Islam. In the realms of philosophy and science, and in these realms alone, Maimonides' connection to the Islamic world has been duly and universally recognized. Most (although by no means all) of the scholarly works treating his philosophy are based on his original Arabic works, which are analyzed in the context of contemporary Muslim philosophy. Even in the study of philosophy, however, where Maimonides is recognized as "a disciple of al-Fārābī,"[3] his contribution is seldom fully integrated into the picture of medieval Islamic philosophy. Studies that offer a panoramic view of a particular philosophic issue in the medieval Islamic world would thus, more often than not, fail to make use of the evidence provided by Maimonides. In the study of other aspects of Maimonides' activity, it is mostly the Jewish context that is brought to bear, whereas the Islamic world recedes into the background. Maimonides' legal works are thus studied mostly by students of Jewish law, many of whom treat their subject as if it can be isolated from parallel intellectual developments in the Islamic world. Even the study of Maimonides' communal activity, based on his (usually Judaeo-Arabic) correspondence, tends to paint the Muslim world as a mere background to the life of the Jewish community (rather than seeing it as the larger frame of which the Jewish community was an integral part). At the same time, all too often this Judaeo-Arabic material remains ignored by scholars of Islamic history and society.[4] Maimonides is thus widely recognized as a giant figure of Jewish history, but remains of almost anecdotal significance for the study of the Islamic world.

The aim of the present book is to present an integrative intellectual profile of Maimonides in his world, the world of Mediterranean culture. This world, broadly defined, also supplies the sources for the book. Only by reading Maimonides' own writings *in light of the information gleaned from other sources* can we hope to paint a well-rounded profile, and to instill life in it.[5]

[3] L. Berman, "Maimonides the Disciple of al-Fārābī," *IOS* 4 (1974): 154–78.

[4] In this context one can understand Mark Cohen's earnest plea, "The time has arrived to integrate the Cairo Geniza, alongside Islamic genizas, into the canon of Islamic studies"; see M. C. Cohen, "Geniza for Islamicists, Islamic Geniza, and 'the New Cairo Geniza,'" *Harvard Middle Eastern and Islamic Review* 7 (2006): 141.

[5] Compare, for example, Davidson's approach, for whom "the only way to assess [Maimonides'] training in rabbinics and philosophy, and for that matter in medicine as well, is to examine his writings and discover through them the works he read, studied and utilized." See H. A. Davidson, *Moses Maimonides: The Man and His Works* (Oxford 2005), 80; and

Mediterranean Cultures

The historical reflection on the cultural role of the Mediterranean, as a unifying principle of culture, began already with Henri Pirenne's groundbreaking *Mohammed and Charlemagne*.[6] Shortly thereafter Fernand Braudel, in his pioneering work on the Mediterranean world in the time of Philip II, argued that only a comprehensive approach that treats the Mediterranean as a single unit can enable the historian to understand local developments properly and to evaluate correctly their ramifications and implications.[7] Around the same time that Braudel's book appeared, Shlomo Dov Goitein was working on his magnum opus, the multivolume *A Mediterranean Society: The Jewish Communities of the Arab World as Portrayed in the Documents of the Cairo Geniza*.[8] Like Braudel, Goitein believed that our sources require that we constantly bear in mind the close interconnections and interdependence of the various parts of the Mediterranean. The fragments of the Cairo Geniza—the hoard of manuscripts discovered at the end of the nineteenth century in the Ben Ezra synagogue in Cairo—reflected, like so many snapshots, the life of the Jewish community in Cairo from the tenth century up to modern times.[9] Goitein skillfully brought these snapshots to life, reconstructing the web of economic alliances across the Mediterranean and beyond it, the political and personal ties between the individual writers, and their religious and cultural concerns.

Although Braudel and Goitein did not belong to the same circle of historians, for a half-century following them "Mediterraneanism" became very much in vogue. References to the Mediterranean appeared in titles of many works, and provided a conceptual frame for others.[10] The

---

see chap. 2, note 3, below. Compare, for example, Joel L. Kraemer, *Maimonides: The Life and World of One of Civilization's Greatest Minds* (New York, 2008), 14–15. Kraemer's overall approach in this matter is very similar to the one proposed in the present book.

[6] H. Pirenne, *Mahomet et Charlemagne* (Bruxelles, 1922).

[7] F. Braudel, *La Méditerranée et le monde méditerranéen à l'époque de Philippe II* (Paris, 1949); [=idem, *The Mediterranean and the Mediterranean World in the Age of Philip* II, trans. S. Reynolds (New York, 1976)].

[8] S. D. Goitein, *A Mediterranean Society: the Jewish Communities of the Arab World as Portrayed in the Documents of the Cairo Geniza* (Berkeley, 1967), 6 v. According to Goitein's own testimony (5:497), he began his work independently of Braudel and read the latter's work only when he was already writing the last volumes of his own.

[9] See Stefan C. Reif, *A Jewish Archive from Old Cairo: the History of Cambridge University's Genizah Collection* (Richmond and Surrey, 2000); ibid., *The Cambridge Genizah Collections: Their Contents and Significance* (Cambridge, 2002).

[10] See, by way of an example, M. J. Chiat and K. L. Reyerson, eds., *The Medieval Mediterranean: Cross-Cultural Contacts* (St. Cloud, Minn., 1988); R. Arnzen and J. Thielmann, eds., *Words, Texts and Concepts Cruising the Mediterranean Sea: Studies on the Sources,*

awareness of the concept's popularity led to a conscious attempt to examine its validity. Peregrine Horden and Nicholas Purcell, in their dramatically titled monumental work *The Corrupting Sea*, thus embarked on an analysis (and defense) of Mediterraneanism.[11]

But what is "the Mediterranean" for the historian? Unlike the well-defined geographical boundaries of the Mediterranean Sea, the cultural boundaries of "the Mediterranean world" are surprisingly flexible, and at times reach impressive dimensions. The center of gravity of Braudel's Mediterranean lies in its western and northwestern part: Spain, the Maghreb, and Italy, whereas Palestine and Egypt play a relatively minor role in his study—smaller, in fact, than the role accorded to decidedly non-Mediterranean countries such as the Netherlands. Beyond the geographical confines of the Mediterranean stretched Braudel's "greater" or "global Mediterranean," which he described as "a Mediterranean with the dimensions of history."[12] For the sixteenth century, these dimensions expanded to include the Atlantic shores as well as the Portuguese, Spanish, French, and English colonies in the Americas.[13] By contrast, the Mediterranean society described by Goitein on the basis of the documents or the Cairo Geniza tilted toward the east and south. Moreover, it occupied not only the shores of the Mediterranean, but also those areas defined today as the Near East, and its "global" or "historical" dimensions stretched eastward, as far as India.

The term "Mediterranean" is problematic not only because of its geographical inaccuracy. In recent years, the usefulness of treating the Mediterranean as an historical, anthropological, or economic unit has been increasingly questioned. In an interesting volume of essays dedicated to the examination of the thesis of Horden and Purcell, the classical scholar William Harris, for example, cites the definition of "Mediterraneanism" as "the doctrine that there are distinctive characteristics which the cultures of the Mediterranean have, or have had, in common."[14] He notes "the fact that Mediterraneanism is often nowadays little more than a reflex" and adds that "the Mediterranean seems somehow peculiarly vul-

---

Contents and Influences of Islamic Civilization and Arabic Philosophy and Science Dedicated to Gerhard Endress on His Sixty-Fifth Birthday (Leuven, 2004).

[11] P. Horden and N. Purcell, *The Corrupting Sea: A Study of Mediterranean History* (Oxford, 2000); and see Adnan A. Husain and K. E. Fleming, eds., *A Faithful Sea: The Religious Cultures of the Mediterranean, 1200–1700* (Oxford, 2007), 4–7.

[12] Braudel, *The Mediterranean and the Mediterranean World*, 153, 155. Cf. also R. Brague, *Au moyen du Moyen Age: Philosophies médievales en chrétienté, judaïsme et islam* (Chatou, 2006), 241.

[13] Ibid., pt. 2, chap. 4.

[14] W. Harris, "The Mediterranean and Ancient History," in W. V. Harris, ed., *Rethinking the Mediterranean* (Oxford and New York, 2000), 38.

nerable to misuse." As noted by Harris, "for many scholars Mediterranean unity has meant . . . primarily or indeed exclusively *cultural* unity."[15] These scholars, he says, were looking for "the basic homogeneity of Mediterranean civilization," a homogeneity the existence of which Harris then proceeds to disprove.

From various angles scholars now question not only the existence of enough unifying criteria for either the coastland or the deeper littoral countries, but also the existence of criteria sufficient to distinguish these countries from others. Even those who continue to use the term "Mediterranean" do so with an acute awareness of its shortcomings. The Arabist Gerhard Endress, for instance, seems to be addressing the abovementioned questions when he asserts that, in the Mediterranean world of the Islamic middle ages, "Business interactions, the exchange of goods and books, practical science and intellectual disputes, come together to make a multi-faceted picture; a picture which is in no way that unified, but in which one can recognize many surprising aspects of unity."[16] For Rémi Brague, "The Mediterranean played a role only when there was a single culture around its shores. This was achieved only with the Roman empire." Reluctant to abandon the concept altogether, however, Brague counts the world of medieval Islam as an expansion ("une sortie") of the Mediterranean toward the Indian Ocean.[17]

Regarding the place of the religious minorities in the Islamic world, adherence to "Mediterraneanism" introduces yet another set of problems: that of anachronistic value judgments. In his attempt to capture the place of the Jewish community within the fabric of the wider Mediterranean society, Goitein used the term "symbiosis," which he borrowed from the field of biology, to illustrate the separate identity that Jews managed to preserve within the dominant Muslim culture, while still being full participants in it.[18] Subsequent discussions of this topic, however, tend to highlight the comfortable, irenic aspects of symbiosis. This tendency is particularly pronounced regarding Maimonides' birthplace, al-Andalus (Islamic Spain) where the relations between the religious communities are

[15]Ibid., 26 (italics in the original). Cf. also Brague, *Au moyen du Moyen Age*, 240.

[16]G. Endress, "Der Islam und die Einheit des mediterraneen Kulturraums in Mittelalter," in Claus Rozen, ed., *Das Mittelmeer—die Wiege der europaeischen Kultur* (Bonn, 1998), 270.

[17]Brague, *Au moyen du Moyen Age*, 240–41. Brague's perception of the Mediterranean informs also S. Guguenheim, *Aristote au mont Saint-Michel: Les racines greques de l'Europe chrétienne* (Paris, 2008), 170–72.

[18]S. D. Goitein, *Jews and Arabs: Their Contacts Through the Ages* (New York, 1964), 11, 127. Goitein's magisterial *Mediterranean Society* dealt mostly with social and economic aspects of this symbiosis, and less with the history of ideas; cf. S. M. Wasserstrom, *Between Muslim and Jew: the Problem of Symbiosis under Early Islam* (Princeton, 1995), 3–12.

described in terms of *convivencia*, in which *las tres culturas* (Islam, Christianity, and Judaism) enjoyed a parallel golden age.[19] Such presentations play down the political, legal, and social differences between the ruling Muslims, on the one hand, and, on the other hand, the Christian and Jewish minorities living under Islamic rule, and present their interconnections in anachronistic terms of universalism and tolerance.[20]

In treating Maimonides as a Mediterranean thinker I seek to study the relative intellectual openness of his world, not to promote its tolerant image. From the religious point of view, this world presented what Thomas Burman, in his study of the Christians in Islamic Spain, judiciously called "pluralistic circumstances."[21] Whether or not these pluralistic circumstances also entailed religious tolerance is a different issue, which will be discussed in its proper context.[22]

Maimonides as a Mediterranean Thinker

Like Braudel, Goitein was interested in human rather than in physical geography. Although the bulk of his *Mediterranean Society* deals with social and economic history, already in the introduction to this work Goitein clearly defined the focus of his interest: "The subject that interests us most: the mind of the Geniza people, the things they believed in and stood for."[23] In its fifth and last volume, titled *The Individual*, Goitein included portraits of seven prominent intellectuals, as they emerge from their own writings as well as from the documents of the Geniza. Indeed, Goitein's original intention was to dedicate the last two volumes of his work to what he called "Mediterranean people," the individuals whose mind and intellectual creativity were shaped by the Mediterranean society in which they lived.

One should note that the Mediterranean basin did not provide group identity to its inhabitants. In all likelihood none of the persons described by Goitein as "Mediterranean" would have chosen this description for himself, and the same holds true for Maimonides. Born in Cordoba, he

[19] A down-to-earth rendering of what the term intends to convey is given by L. P. Harvey, *Muslims in Spain: 1500 to 1614* (Chicago and London, 2005), 44. Harvey sums it up as "the necessary live-and-let-live of the Iberian Peninsula in the days before the keys of the Alhambra were handed over in January 1492." On the contemporary, often politically loaded usage of this and related terms, see H. D. Aidi, "The Interference of al-Andalus: Spain, Islam, and the West," *Social Text* 87 (2006): 67–88, esp. 70 and 78.

[20] See, for instance, M. R. Menocal, *The Ornament of the World: How Muslims, Jews, and Christians Created a Culture of Tolerance in Medieval Spain* (Boston, 2002).

[21] T. E. Burman, *Religious Polemic and the Intellectual History of the Mozarabs, c.1050–1200* (Leiden and New York, 1994), 2.

[22] See chap. 3, below.

[23] Goitein, *A Mediterranean Society,* 1: 82.

saw himself throughout his life as an Andalusian, and identified himself as such by signing his name in Hebrew as "Moshe ben Maimon *ha-Sefaradi*" ("the Spaniard," or, in less anachronistic terms, "al-Andalusī").[24] For that reason, it probably would never have occurred to me to describe Maimonides as "a Mediterranean thinker" were it not for Goitein's insistence on calling the Geniza society "Mediterranean."

In so far as my choice of calling Maimonides "a Mediterranean thinker" depends on Goitein, it is open to all the criticisms of Mediterraneanism mentioned above. In the case of Maimonides' thought, however, the term is appropriate in ways that do not apply to the society as a whole. Maimonides' life circled the Mediterranean basin. The cultures that fed into his thought were, by and large, those of the wider Mediterranean littoral. Those cultures that came from outside this region reached him only to the extent that they were translated into Arabic and thus became part and parcel of the culture of the Islamic Mediterranean.

Furthermore, in contradistinction to the historians who, in choosing this term, have sought to underline the Mediterranean's distinctive unity, I employ it precisely in order to highlight the diversity within it. Maimonides is a Mediterranean thinker in the sense that he is more than a Jewish thinker, or more than an Islamic philosopher (that is to say, a philosopher pertaining to the world of Islam).[25] In modern parlance, he could perhaps be called "cosmopolitan," that is, a person who belongs to more than one of the subcultures that together form the world in which he lives. This last term grates, however, because of its crude anachronism as well as because of its (equally anachronistic) secular overtones.

The personal life-cycle of Moses Maimonides remained close to the shores of the Mediterranean, but the main events that affected his life occurred

[24] J. Blau, "'At Our Place in al-Andalus,' 'At Our Place in the Maghreb,'" in J. L. Kraemer, ed., *Perspectives on Maimonides: Philosophical and Historical Studies* (Oxford, 1991), 293–94; G. Anidjar, *"Our Place in al-Andalus": Kabbalah, Philosophy, Literature in Arab Jewish Letters* (Stanford, 2002). See, for instance, Maimonides, *On Asthma*, 21–22, where the need to prescribe dietary instructions give Maimonides the excuse to recall with nostalgia the tastes of the dishes of the Maghreb and al-Andalus. Regarding the philosophical tradition, see also chap. 4, note 52, below.

[25] On the term "Islamic," see J. L. Kraemer, "The Islamic Context of Medieval Jewish Philosophy," in D. H. Frank and O. Leaman, eds., *The Cambridge Companion to Medieval Jewish Philosophy* (Cambridge, 2003), 62 and note 5; O. Leaman, "Introduction," in Seyyed Hossein Nasr and O. Leaman, eds., *History of Islamic Philosophy* (London and New York, 1996), 1–5; H. Ben-Shammai, "Maimonides and Creation *Ex Nihilo* in the Tradition of Islamic Philosophy," in C. del Valle et al., eds., *Maimónides y su época* (Madrid, 2007), 103. Throughout the present book, I use "Muslim" to denote that which belongs specifically to the religion of Islam or to the believers of that religion, whereas "Islamic" denotes the culture developed in the world of Islam, by Muslims as well as by others.

in a much larger area, stretching from the Iberian peninsula to the Indian subcontinent.[26] The Islamic polity that Maimonides encountered during his lifetime was not made of one cloth, and his life was spent in no less than four major political entities:

1. From his birth in 1138 in Cordoba until 1148, Maimonides lived under the rule of the Berber dynasty of the *Murābiṭūn* (or Almoravids, according to their Latinized name) in al-Andalus. In the Cordoba of his childhood, ruled by the Almoravids, the Jewish (and Christian) communities were relatively protected, as decreed by Muslim law.[27]

2. In 1148 Cordoba was captured by another Berber dynasty, that of the *Muwaḥḥidūn* (or Almohads), whose highly idiosyncratic interpretation of Muslim law deprived the religious minorities of their traditional protected status. Almohad persecution forced Maimonides' family out of Cordoba, and their whereabouts in the following few years are unclear; they may have taken refuge in northern, Christian Spain (as others, like the Jewish philosopher Abraham Ibn Daud, did), or they may have spent some time in Seville.[28] At any rate, in 1160, when Maimonides was in his early twenties, the family moved to Fez, close to the North African capital of the Almohads, where it remained for about five years.[29]

3. Around 1165 the family left Fez for Palestine, which was then controlled by the Crusaders, and then finally settled down in Fāṭimid Egypt.[30] There, Maimonides became involved in the trade of precious stones, but

[26] For a detailed description of Maimonides' biography, see Davidson, *Moses Maimonides*, esp. chap. 1; J .L. Kraemer, "Moses Maimonides: An Intellectual Portrait," in K. Seeskin, ed., *The Cambridge Companion to Maimonides* (Cambridge, 2005), 10–57; idem, *Maimonides: The Life and World of One of Civilization's Greatest Minds*.

[27] On the status of the minorities in Islam, see A. Fattal, *Le statut légal des non-musulmans en pays d'Islam* (Beirut, 1995); Y. Friedmann, *Tolerance and Coercion in Islam: Interfaith Relations in the Muslim Tradition* (Cambridge and New York, 2003). On their status in the *Maghreb*, see H. R. Idris, "Les tributaires en occident musulman médiéval d'aprés le 'Miʿyār' d'al-Wanšarīsī," in P. Salmon, ed., *Mélanges d'islamologie: Volume dédié à la mémoire d'Armand Abel par ses collègues, ses élèves et ses amis* (Leiden, 1974), 172–96.

[28] See Maimonides' reference to the ships loading oil at Seville and sailing on the Guadalquivir to Alexandria; *Responsa* 2: 576. See also his autobiographical note in *Guide* 2.9 (*Dalāla*, 187; Pines, 269), according to which he has met the son of Ibn al-Aflaḥ of Seville. There is, however, no positive proof for the assertion that he sojourned all this time (about twelve years) in southern Spain; compare Bos's "Translator's Introduction," in Maimonides, *Medical Aphorisms*, xix.

[29] The question of how they lived, as forced converts, under the Almohads is connected to the issue of forced conversions, on which see chap. 3, below.

[30] S.V. Fāṭimids, M. Canard, *EI*, 2: 850–62; see also M. Ben-Sasson, "Maimonides in Egypt: The First Stage," *Maimonidean Studies* 2 (1991): 3–30; J. L. Kraemer, "Maimonides' Intellectual Milieu in Cairo," in T. Lévy and R. Rashed, eds., *Maïmonide: philosophe et savant* (Leuven, 2004), 1–37.

he was mainly supported by his brother David, until David's drowning in the Indian Ocean.[31]

4. Egypt was conquered by the Ayyūbids in 1171, and it is under their rule that Maimonides lived until his death in 1204.[32] The premature death of his brother forced Maimonides to seek another source of income, and he worked as a court-physician to the Ayyūbids in Fusṭāṭ (old Cairo).

Each of these political entities is closely associated with a specific school of Muslim law (*madhhab*), and, to some extent, it is also associated with a particular school of thought. The Almoravids are identified with Mālikī law, and typically (or stereotypically) described as opposed to rational speculation in all its forms. An extreme manifestation of this attitude was the public burning of the books of Abū Ḥāmid al-Ghazālī (d. 1111) in the Maghreb in 1109, during the reign of ʿAlī b. Yūsuf b. Tāshufīn (d. 1143).[33]

Like the Almoravids, the Ayyūbids were Sunni Muslims; they, however, followed Shāfiʿite law, and adopted Ashʿarite *kalām* or speculative theology.[34]

The Fāṭimids, Ismāʿīlī Shiʿites, developed their own system of jurisprudence, based on Qāḍī al-Nuʿmān's "Pillars of Islam." The Ismāʿīlī "external" law, accessible to all people, served as the legal basis for daily life, while its "internal" part was preached, on different levels, in the Friday *Majālis* and to the initiates. Their theology was shaped by a thorough adoption of Neoplatonic philosophy.[35]

And last, the Almohads were Sunni Muslims who developed their own legal system, although this system cannot properly be called a school.[36]

[31] See IQ, 318; S. D. Goitein, *Letters of Medieval Jewish Traders* (Princeton, 1974), 207–8.

[32] On the Ayyūbids, see Cl. Cahen, *EI*, 1: 796–807 (s.v.). On Maimonides' life in Ayyūbid Egypt, see M. R. Cohen, "Maimonides' Egypt," in E. L. Ormsby, ed., *Moses Maimonides and His Time* (Washington, 1989), 21–34; J. Drory, "The Early Decades of Ayyūbid Rule," in Kraemer, *Perspectives on Maimonides*, 295–302; A. S. Ehrenkreutz, "Saladin's Egypt and Maimonides," in Kraemer, *Perspectives on Maimonides,* 303–7; M. Winter, "Saladin's Religious Personality, Policy and Image," in Kraemer, *Perspectives on Maimonides,* 309–22.

[33] See P. Chalmeta, "The Almoravids in Spain," in *EI*, 7: 589–91, (s.v. *Al-Murābiṭūn*); Jamil M. Abun Nasr, *A History of the Maghrib in the Islamic Period* (Cambridge, 1987), 84. On the opposition to al-Ghazālī under the Almoravids, see K. Garden, *Al-Ghazālī's Contested Revival: "Iḥyā' ʿulūm al-dīn" and Its Critics in Khorasan and the Maghrib* (Ph.D. diss., University of Chicago, 2005), 155–89.

[34] See J. Drory, "The Early Decades of Ayyūbid Rule," esp. 296.

[35] See, for example, F. Daftary, *The Ismāʿīlīs—Their History and Doctrines* (Cambridge, 1990), esp. 144–255; H. Halm, *The Fatimids and Their Traditions of Learning* (London, 1997), esp. 28, 30–45. On their possible influence on Maimonides, see chap. 4, note 61, below.

[36] See, for example, M. Fierro, "The Legal Policies of the Almohad Caliphs and Ibn Rushd's *Bidāyat al-Mujtahid*," *Journal of Islamic Studies* 10 (1999): 226–48.

Their jurisprudence, based on Mālikī law, reveals some affinity with the Ẓāhirī school (although it cannot be identified as Ẓāhirī).[37] They also developed their own particular theologico-philosophical stance. Regarding theology, they are associated mostly with Ghazālī (that is, with Ashʿarite *kalām*), but some of the Arab historiographers also associate them with the Muʿtazila school of *kalām*, while others connect them (probably with much exaggeration) to Aristotelian philosophy.[38]

Still wider than the parameters of Maimonides' biography are the geographical parameters outlined by his literary output. In particular, his correspondence demonstrates a concern with a Jewish society that stretched across the cultural Mediterranean world, from southern France (known in medieval Jewish texts as "Provence") to Baghdad, and as far south as the Yemen. It seems that in 1174 Maimonides was appointed head of the Jewish community of Cairo (*raʾīs al-yahūd*), an appointment that gave an official administrative frame to his authority among the Jews of Egypt as well as over the Jewish communities of Palestine and the Yemen.[39]

The particular, often difficult circumstances of his life—exile, forced conversion to Islam, and years of wandering in search of a safe haven—gave Maimonides opportunities to encounter a particularly variegated list of political systems, cultural trends, and systems of thought. It would be incorrect, however, to perceive his intellectual breadth only as an inadvertent result of his being what John Matthews has called "an involuntary traveler."[40] His extraordinary personality and his insatiable intellectual curiosity drove him to make full and conscious use of life's opportunities.

In the above-mentioned discussions regarding the usefulness of the term "Mediterranean," historians ponder the existence of a cultural continuity in the Mediterranean region. For Maimonides, this continuity seems to have been an undisputed fact. Some of the philosophical and religious traditions that shaped Maimonides' thought belonged to his contemporary world, where they all existed side by side and in continuous exchange and debate. Other formative traditions were part of the past history of

[37] On the Ẓāhirīs, see I. Goldziher, *The Ẓāhirīs: Their Doctrine and Their History: A Contribution to the History of Islamic Theology*, trans. W. Behn (Leiden, 1971).

[38] Cf. M. Fletcher, "Ibn Tūmart's Teachers: The Relationship with al-Ghazālī," *Al-Qanṭara* 18 (1997): 305–30.; M. Geoffroy, "L'almohadisme théologique d'Averroès (Ibn Rushd)," *Archives d'Histoire Doctrinale et Littéraire du Moyen Age* 66 (1999): 9–47; and see chap. 3, below.

[39] See chap. 2, note 57, below.

[40] John F. Matthews, "Hostages, Philosophers, Pilgrims, and the Diffusion of Ideas in the Late Roman Mediterranean and Near East," in F. M. Clover and R. S. Humprheys, eds., *Tradition and Innovation in Late Antiquity* (London, 1989), 29.

the Mediterranean, where they succeeded one another, the latecomers conversing with previous ones, transmitting their ideas, polemicizing with them and building on their legacy. Whereas some medieval thinkers tried to ignore past layers of this continuum and to silence them, Maimonides stands out as an avid archaeologist of ideas, a passionate advocate for keeping the memory of the past alive and for the dialectic discourse with this memory.

In an oft-quoted passage in his *Commentary on the Mishnah*, Maimonides draws his readers' attention to his lack of originality in this text. The Mishnaic tractate *Avot* ("The Fathers") is a collection of the Sages' aphorisms, to the commentary on which Maimonides appends an introduction on ethics, known as "Eight Chapters." Introducing this ethical preamble, Maimonides notes the fact that people tend to judge a saying by its author rather than by its contents. The uninitiated is especially prone to reject anything attributed to a suspicious authority. Maimonides adjusted his style of writing to his audience, and since he expected to have the philosophically uninitiated among the readers of his *Commentary on the Mishnah*, he refrained in this text from quoting his philosophical sources in detail.[41] Nevertheless, he could not forgo the opportunity to indicate these sources in a general way, and to admonish:

> Know that what I say in these Chapters . . . does not represent ideas which I invented of my own accord, nor original interpretations. Rather, they are ideas gleaned from what the Sages say—in the *Midrashim*, in the Talmud and elsewhere in their compositions—from what the philosophers, both ancient and modern, say; as well as from the compositions of many other people: and you should listen to the truth, whoever may have said it.[42]

Notwithstanding the texts' brevity, the *Commentary* points unambiguously to the identity of the potentially suspect sources: non-Jewish philosophers, both ancient (that is to say, Hellenistic), and modern (that is

[41] By contrast, in his medical writings (and unlike most of his colleagues) he provides references to the sources he quotes; see *Medical Aphorisms,* xxiv–xxv; E. Lieber, "The Medical Works of Maimonides: A Reappraisal," in F. Rosner and S. S. Kottek, eds., *Moses Maimonides: Physician, Scientist, and Philosopher* (North Vale, N.J., 1993), 20.

[42] "*Isma' al-ḥaqq mi-man qālahu*" (literally, "Listen to the truth from he who says it," that is, regardless of the identity of the speaker. See *Commentary on the Mishnah, Neziqin,* 372–73; *The Eight Chapters of Maimonides on Ethics (Shemonah Perakim): A Psychological and Ethical Treatise*, ed. and trans. Joseph I. Gorfinkle (New York, 1966), 6, and cf. his translation, 35–36; R. L. Weiss and Ch. E. Butterworth, *Ethical Writings of Maimonides* (New York, 1975), 60; *Maïmonide, Traité d'éthique—"Huit chapitres,"* trans. R. Brague (Paris, 2001), 31–33.

to say, Muslims). The need to justify the use of Greek philosophy was felt by other medieval philosophers. For instance, another, not less famous "apologia" can be seen in the words of philosopher al-Kindī (d. 870), who admonishes the Caliph al-Muʿtaṣim, attributing to Aristotle the following saying: "We ought not to be ashamed of appreciating the truth and of acquiring it wherever it comes from, even if it comes from races distant and nations different from us. For the seeker of truth nothing takes precedence over the truth."[43]

Maimonides' admonition thus follows an established philosophical tradition, and one has no difficulty in assuming that he might even have read Kindī. It is, however, less expected to find in his formulation the imprint of another, nonphilosophical source. Kindī's contemporary Ibn Qutayba (d. 889), a traditional Muslim scholar, wrote an anthology of edifying material for the state secretaries, in the introduction to which we find him quoting the Prophet Muhammad's learned cousin, Ibn ʿAbbās, who had said: "Take wisdom from whomever you may hear it, for wisdom can come from the non-wise."[44] As the examples presented above indicate, the idea itself was, by that time, a commonplace among the learned, and Jewish scholars were no exception. It is interesting to note, however, that Maimonides does not support this idea with rabbinic prooftexts, as one could expect him to do in an introduction to a commentary on a Mishnaic text. The similarity of Maimonides' admonition, in both content and structure, to Ibn ʿAbbās's saying raises the possibility that he was familiar with it. If so, there would be a shade of irony in his allusion to a Muslim tradition in the advice "to listen to the truth, *whoever* may have said it." Whether or not Maimonides was indeed familiar (through Ibn Qutayba or through another source) with Ibn ʿAbbās's formulation of this idea is less significant than the idea they both espouse: the clearly stated methodological principle of reaching out for knowledge, whatever its source might have been.

[43] A.L. Ivry, *Al-Kindī's Metaphysics* (Albany, 1974), 58; *Kitāb al-Kindī ilā al-Muʿtaṣim bi'llāh fī'l-falsafa al-ūlā*, in *Œuvres philosophiques et scientifiques d'al-Kindī*, ed. R. Rashed and J. Jolivet, vol. 2, *Métaphysique et cosmologie* (Leiden, 1998), 13; cf. D. Gutas, *Greek Thought, Arabic Culture: the Graeco-Arabic Translation Movement in Baghdad and Early ʿAbbāsid Society (2nd–4th/8th–10th centuries)*, (London and New York, 1998), 158–59; S. Stroumsa, "Philosophy as Wisdom: On the Christians' Role in the Translation of Philosophical Material to Arabic," in H. Ben-Shammai et al., eds., *Exchange and Transmission across Cultural Boundaries: Philosophy and Science in the Mediterranean (Proceedings of a Workshop in Memory of Prof. Shlomo Pines: the Institute for Advanced Studies, Jerusalem (28 February–2 March 2005)* (Jerusalem, forthcoming).

[44] Ibn Qutayba, *ʿUyūn al-akhbār*, ed. C. Brockelmann (Berlin, 1900), 11, lines 5–7. Cf. Gutas, *Greek Thought*, 159; Brague, *Maïmonide, Traité d'éthique*, 32, note 25.

HORIZONS

Like Goitein's Mediterranean society, Maimonides' cultural Mediterranean encompassed the legacy of other religious communities. His world included the cultures of the various communities in the Mediterranean basin of his days: Muslims, Jews, and Christians, with their various denominations and sectarian disagreements. He read their books, including their religious scholarship. He was familiar with their philosophical and religious traditions, and with the mental world, the *imaginaire*, of both educated and simple people. His world also included past and extinct communities, previous layers of the Mediterranean palimpsest, whose imprints were left in Arabic literature. Maimonides fully lived and breathed the culture of his time, including the impact of contemporary culture, as well as sediments of previous cultures like the "Sabians." In Arabic medieval literature, the Sabians are presented as the heirs of ancient paganism, the practitioners of ancient occult sciences as well as the transmitters of philosophy. They are usually associated with the area of Ḥarrān, but most of the books cited by Maimonides were works that circulated in his native Andalus and in North Africa. Maimonides believed that these writings consisted in Arabic translations of authentic ancient Egyptian and Mesopotamian texts, and he wholeheartedly, consciously, and repeatedly admonished his disciple to study them.[45] The integration of this multilayered, multifaceted Mediterranean legacy into all his works is at the core of Maimonides' originality in all his endeavors. It is the prism through which all his works, in all domains, should be read, and we would be missing his originality by examining his activity according to neatly arranged fields.

An exemplary case can be seen in Maimonides' writings on Jewish law (*halacha*), the modern study of which is focused largely on his Hebrew works, and remains the domain of scholars of Judaism. The prevalent tendency in this field is to view Maimonides as one link in the unbroken chain of Rabbinic scholars. The assumption is therefore that, in halachic matters, his source of inspiration must have been solely his predecessors, previous halachic authorities. This approach leaves many of Maimonides' legal innovations unexplained. An integrative approach, on the other hand, would treat all of Maimonides' readings and encounters, Jewish or

[45] See *Guide* 3.29 (and chap. 4, below), but compare *Mishneh Torah*, *Hilkhot avodat kokhavim* 2:2: "Idolaters have composed many books about their cult . . . ; God has commanded us not to read these books at all." Maimonides explicitly notes the distinction between his disciple, who is well prepared for coping with "the fables of the Sabians and the ravings of the Chasdeans and Chaldeans," and other potential readers; see *Guide* 3.29 (*Dalāla*, 380:5–9; Pines, 520).

otherwise, as relevant, indeed essential, for understanding his legal thought. Maimonides' theory of religion was profoundly affected by his uncensored reading in what he believed to be authentic ancient pagan writings. His interpretation of biblical precepts was the result of discoveries he believed himself to have made in the course of these readings. Furthermore, his legal methodology was conditioned by his immersion in the Almohad society, and by his encounter with Muslim law (*fiqh*) in general and with Almohad law in particular. To fully understand Maimonides' legal writings and to duly appreciate his tremendous contribution to the development of Jewish law, all these elements, seemingly external to the Jewish legacy, must be taken into account.

What holds true for *halacha*, the supposedly exclusive domain of Jewish life, is even truer in other domains: political thought, philosophy, science. As succinctly stated by Pines, "Maimonides considered that philosophy transcended religious or national distinctions" and that "[*q*]*ua* philosopher he had the possibility to consider Judaism from the outside."[46] The Greek philosophical tradition, as interpreted and elaborated by philosophers from the Islamic East and from al-Andalus, formed the foundation of his philosophical world, and his writings reflect the various shades and nuances that this philosophy acquired over the centuries. Maimonides is commonly categorized as a *faylasūf*, that is, an Aristotelian philosopher, and indeed, he himself indicates in various ways his identification with the legacy of the Aristotelian school, or *falsafa*. In his correspondence with his disciple Joseph Ibn Shimʿon (d. 1226) and with Samuel Ibn Tibbon (d. 1230), the Hebrew translator of the *Guide of the Perplexed*, Maimonides gives them instructions for their reading, and indicates to them the authoritative texts of Aristotle and his commentators.[47] He gives precedence to Aristotle over his teacher Plato, but he warns his translator not to attempt to read Aristotle alone, and insists that Aristotle must be read together with his authoritative commentators: Alexander of Aphrodisias (early third century), Themistius (d. ca. 387) or Ibn Rushd (Latin, Averroes, d. 1198). These instructions reflect the time-honored school curriculum, as developed in Alexandria and Baghdad, and further cultivated in al-Andalus.[48] In another instance he takes pains, almost pedantically, to note his own credentials: he read texts under the guidance of a pupil of one of the contemporary masters

[46] Pines, "Translator's Introduction," *Guide*, cxxxiv.

[47] See A. Marx, "Texts by and about Maimonides," *JQR* n.s. 25 (1934–35): 374–81; on this letter, see chap. 2, below. See also Pines, "Translator's Introduction"; *Epistles*, 552–54.

[48] See *Epistles*, 552; and see A. Guidi, A. "L'obscurité intentionnelle du philosophe: thèmes néoplatoniciens et Farabiens chez Maïmonide," *Revue des études juives* 166 (2007): 129–45.

of philosophy, Ibn Bājja (d. 1138), and he met the son of the astronomer Ibn al-Aflaḥ (d. ca. 1150).[49] The urge to declare his personal contacts with these masters is another indication of Maimonides' identification with the school tradition. This identification with a school of thought is quite atypical for Jewish medieval thinkers, who, although often classified by modern scholars as belonging to a certain school, do not identify explicitly as followers of that school (for example, by explicit quotations of the canonical works of the school), nor are they quoted in the school's listing of its followers.[50]

The Arabic Aristotelian tradition blended Platonic political philosophy and Plotinian metaphysics with the logic and physics of Aristotle. This blend reflects the metamorphosis of the school tradition as it traveled—through the efforts of Zoroastrian, Christian, and Muslim translators—from Athens to Alexandria, Nisibis, Gundishapur, and Baghdad, and was translated from Greek to Syriac, Persian, and Arabic.

Maimonides' philosophical frame of reference faithfully reflects this legacy. In the same letter to Samuel Ibn Tibbon, Maimonides refers to the great luminaries of philosophy, and although he probably did not intend this letter to offer a list of recommended readings, it mirrors his perception of the landmarks of philosophy. This letter, complemented by occasional remarks culled from Maimonides' other writings, presents a picture of a well-stocked philosophical bookshelf. The basis of this bookshelf is Greek philosophy: first and foremost Aristotle, while Plato, too, is mentioned, although with a certain reluctance and reserve. The philosophical tradition of Late Antiquity is represented by Alexander of Aphrodisias and Themistius, whose works were already part of the teaching in Alexandria. Not surprisingly, the name of Plotinus is never mentioned by Maimonides; this omission is in line with the Arab Aristotelian tradition, where a paraphrase of Plotinus's *Enneads* circulated under the title "The Theology of Aristotle" or as the sayings of "the Greek Sage." The role of the Christians in the transmission of Aristotelianism is also acknowledged by Maimonides, although he had little respect for the Christian theologians as philosophers. Both the sixth-century Alexandrian Christian philosopher John Philoponus and the tenth-century Christian Arab philosopher Yaḥyā b. ʿAdī receive from him only pejorative remarks.

[49] *Guide* 2.9 (*Dalāla*, 187; Pines, 269); and see J. Kraemer, "Maimonides and the Spanish Aristotelian Tradition," in M. M. Meyerson and E. D. English, eds., *Christians, Muslims and Jews in Medieval and Early Modern Spain—Interaction and Cultural Change* (Notre Dame, Ind., 1999), 40–68. On the possible circumstances of these meetings, see note 28, above.

[50] See S. Stroumsa, "The Muslim Context of Medieval Jewish Philosophy," in S. Nadler and T. Rudavsky, eds., *The Cambridge History of Jewish Philosophy: From Antiquity through the Seventeenth Century* (Cambridge, 2009), 39–59.

The final layer constituting Maimonides' philosophical heritage is that of the Arab-Muslim world: the tenth-century thinker Abū Naṣr al-Fārābī, who lived in Baghdad, Aleppo, and Damascus (d. 951); Ibn Sīnā (Latin, Avicenna, d. 1037), who lived in Iran; and the twelfth-century Andalusian philosophers Ibn Bājja, Ibn Ṭufayl (d. 1185), and Averroes.

Sciences—astronomy, medicine, and mathematics—were part and parcel of the philosopher's education, and in Maimonides' references to the sciences we find the same multilayered legacy revealed in his philosophy, beginning with the Stagirite and Hippocrates, through the Hellenistic culture of Late Antiquity (Ptolemy and Galen), to the "modern" Muslim contributions from the East—the tenth-century freethinker Abū-Bakr al-Rāzī (the Latin Rhazes)—and from the West (Ibn al-Aflaḥ).

In addition to this philosophical and scientific "core curriculum," Maimonides' intellectual world included other philosophical traditions, which, although he rejected them, undoubtedly had a profound influence on his thought. Maimonides boasts of his vast reading, including the study of the so-called Sabian literature. He derides the Sabian lore of magic, alchemy, and astronomy, which he considered to be nothing but "ravings," the pejorative term he employed to denote their pseudo-science. Nevertheless, he took great pains to collect their books and to study them, before setting off to refute their claims.[51]

The richness and diversity that is unveiled in examining the philosophical tradition that Maimonides inherited from his predecessors are further confirmed and enriched when we examine the profile of his contemporaneous culture. Al-Andalus and the Maghreb were ruled by the Almohads, Sunni Muslims with a rather idiosyncratic theology and law. One of their (still not fully understood) idiosyncrasies involved the forced conversion of what used to be "protected minorities" (*ahl al-dhimma*) and it seems probable that under this law Maimonides' family had to convert (albeit only overtly) to Islam. According to Muslim sources, the Almohads suspected the external nature of such forced conversions. Nevertheless, they expected putative converts to conform to Muslim law and to educate their children accordingly. With this background, it is not surprising to find in Maimonides' theological and legal writings some innovative ideas, which may well reflect the innovations of what has been called the "Almohad revolution."[52]

When Maimonides finally arrived in Egypt, around 1165, it was still ruled by the Fāṭimids. Like other Ismāʿīlī Shiʿites, the Fāṭimids adopted Neoplatonic philosophy as part of their religious doctrine. The Ismāʿīlī predilection for the occult sciences received from Maimonides the same

[51] See chap. 4, below.
[52] See chap. 3, below.

harsh remarks as did Sabian science. He also squarely rejected their allegorical hermeneutics.[53] Nevertheless, their particular brand of Neoplatonism seems to have left its mark on his own philosophy, either directly or through the works of Jewish Neoplatonists. As examples of such influence one may cite Maimonides' concept of divine volition,[54] or his use of the concept of the two graded "intentions" as part of the divine economy of salvation.[55]

Maimonides' Neoplatonism also reflects the impact of Sufism (that is, Islamic mysticism). By the twelfth century, largely owing to the impact of Ghazālī, the influence of Sufism had become widespread across the Mediterranean, from Khorasān to al-Andalus. Already in Maimonides' *Guide of the Perplexed*, shaped by Neoplatonized Aristotelianism, one can detect strong mystical overtones.[56] But it remained to Maimonides' descendants to cultivate and develop the Jewish-Sufi trend, and to establish a pietistic, mystical school in Egypt.[57]

In 1171 Egypt was conquered by the Ayyūbids, Sunni Muslims who had adopted strict Ashʿarite theology. Maimonides was very familiar with the intricacies of Islamic theology (*kalām*), and is known to have participated in theological discussions with Muslims.[58] But he had little respect for the *kalām*, both in its earlier Muʿtazilite form and in its contemporary dominant Ashʿarite version. In the former case, the Jewish context may explain the vehemence of Maimonides' reaction: during the ninth and early tenth centuries, the Geonim (the heads of the *Yeshivot*, or talmudic schools, of Baghdad) had been greatly influenced by Muʿtazilite *kalām*. This holds true also for the Karaite Jews, whose intellectual center was in Jerusalem, and who had practically adopted the theology of the Baṣra school of the Muʿtazila. In Maimonides' lifetime, the intellectual challenge of the Karaites had become much less of a threat for the Rabbanite community, and Baghdad was no longer the undisputed center of the Jewish world. Nevertheless, *kalām* continued to play an important role in Jewish intellectual discourse.

53 See *Guide* 2.25 (*Dalāla*, 229:25–26; Pines, 328); and see chap. 5, *apud* note 117, below.

54 As argued by A. L. Ivry, "Neoplatonic Currents in Maimonides' Thought," in Kraemer, *Perspectives on Maimonides*, 115–40.

55 See chap. 4, *apud* notes 57–59, below.

56 See, for instance, D. R. Blumenthal, "Maimonides: Prayer, Worship and Mysticism," in D. R. Blumenthal, ed., *Approaches to Judaism in Medieval Times*, vol. 3 (Atlanta, 1988).

57 See P. Fenton, *Obadiah ben Abraham Maimonides: The Treatise of the Pool=al-Maqāla al-Ḥawḍiyya* (London, 1981); ibid., *Deux traités de mystique juive: Obadyah b. Abraham b. Moïse Maïmonide (Le traité du puits=al-Maqāla al-Ḥawḍiyya); David b. Josué, dernier des Maïmonides (Le guide du détachement=al-Murshid ilā t-Tafarrud)* (Lagrasse, 1987).

58 See S. D. Goitein, "The Moses Maimonides—Ibn Sanāʾ al-Mulk Circle (a Deathbed Declaration from March 1182)," in M. Sharon, ed., *Studies in Islamic History and Civilization, in Honour of Professor David Ayalon* (Jerusalem, 1986), 399–405.

The last few years of Maimonides' life were troubled by an ongoing controversy with the Gaon of Baghdad, Samuel ben ʿEli. The main issue of the controversy was theological: the resurrection of the dead and its meaning. Characteristically, the discussion meandered between various bodies of texts, changing methods according to the context. On both sides, biblical and Rabbinic quotations were brought to bear, employing commonly used exegetical techniques. Both sides also quoted the philosophers: the Muslim Avicenna and the Jewish philosopher Abū al-Barakāt al-Baghdādī (d. ca. 1164), the use of whose names reflect the culture of the educated elite. But it was mainly *kalām* arguments that provided the Gaon with the necessary intellectual varnish. From the testimony of Maimonides' disciple Joseph Ibn Shimʿon we know that the Gaon also introduced into the discussion the culture of the common people: divination techniques that were an integral and important part of their religiosity.[59] This kind of popular religiosity was strongly criticized by Maimonides. He regarded it as superstitious, and his aversion to it is expressed not only in his rejection of its practical applications, but also in his scornful criticism of popular sermons. Nevertheless, this popular culture, which, just like the philosophers' highbrow culture, crossed religious boundaries, was an integral part of Mediterranean culture, and Maimonides' *responsa* testify to the fact that these practices were a fact with which he had to contend.[60]

Transformations in the Jewish World

Maimonides' intellectual horizons were restricted neither by his time and place nor by his religious denomination. Nevertheless, the center of his intellectual endeavor was undoubtedly the Jewish world. During his lifetime, the Jewish community underwent several significant changes. As mentioned above, Maimonides' most famous controversy with the Gaon revolved around the issue of the resurrection of the dead. Other disputed issues regarded some of Maimonides' rulings in his *Mishneh Torah*. The subtext of the controversy, however, was neither theological nor legal, but political. As mentioned above, twelfth-century Baghdad was no longer the center of hegemony for Jewish communities. With Maimonides' stature, Egypt overshadowed Baghdad, and the Gaon was fighting to preserve his authority.[61]

[59] See chap. 6, note 62, below.
[60] See chap. 4, below.
[61] See chap. 6, below.

The real rising force, however, was not Egypt. Although Maimonides contributed significantly to the development of the Cairene Jewish center, the balance of forces was tipping more and more toward Europe: Catalonia, southern France, and Ashkenaz (northeastern France and the Rhine Valley). Although the rise of Christian Europe as a political power played a major role in this change, in the present context I shall focus on its narrow Jewish intellectual aspects.[62] In the tenth century, Jews from around the Mediterranean would turn to Baghdad for halachic rulings, and to Arabic culture for philosophy and science. The Jewish communities of southern France had been translating Judaeo-Arabic and Arabic works into Hebrew since the eleventh century. They corresponded with Maimonides, presented questions regarding the translation of his work, and he patiently answered their queries. In the following centuries, the "translation movement" from Arabic into Hebrew gained momentum, and eventually came to include much of the philosophical and scientific Arabic library. Through such translations, the world of Islamic science and philosophy was transferred to Italy, France, and Christian Spain. And it is through such translations, in fact, that European Jews became gradually independent of the knowledge and libraries of their co-religionists in Islamic countries. Maimonides, Avicenna, and Averroes were thus transplanted into non-Arabic, non-Islamic ground, where they continued to play a central role long after the decline of Mediterranean Islamic philosophy.

Like other Jews in his milieu, Maimonides' language was Arabic, or, to be precise, Judaeo-Arabic.[63] He wrote in a relatively high register of middle-Arabic (that is to say, mixing high classical Arabic with the vernacular), laced with Hebrew words and citations and written in Hebrew characters. This was the language in which he wrote on all subject matters: philosophy, science, and *halacha*.[64] His choice of Hebrew characters was not intended to protect his writings from critical Muslim eyes, as

[62]This changing map of the Jewish world should of course be seen in the context of the transformations of the balance of power between Christian Europe and the Islamic Lands. The two processes, however, do not develop synchronically, and the question deserves to be studied separately.

[63]On written medieval Judaeo-Arabic, and on its relation to the spoken dialects, on the one hand, and classical Arabic, on the other, see J. Blau, *The Emergence and Linguistic Background of Judaeo-Arabic : a Study of the Origins of Middle Arabic* (Jerusalem, 1981), chap. 1; and see S. Hopkins, "The Languages of Maimonides," in G. Tamer, ed., *The Trias of Maimonides: Jewish, Arabic and Ancient Cultures of Knowledge* (Berlin, 2005), 85–106. Compare George Saliba, *Islamic Science and the Making of the European Renaissance*, (Cambridge, Mass. and London, 2007).

[64]See Hopkins, "The Languages of Maimonides," 97; and cf. Saliba, *Islamic Science and the Making of the European Renaissance*, 3, who wrongly assumes that for writing on Jewish law Maimonides chose Hebrew.

suggested by his contemporary Muslim scholar ʿAbd al-Laṭīf al-Baghdādī.[65] Quite rightly, Maimonides did not believe that the different script would prevent curious Muslims from getting to know the contents of his work. For this reason, when he was worried about the adverse repercussions that the dissemination of his work might cause, he urged his addressee to be discreet.[66] He wrote in Judaeo-Arabic even when polemicizing against Islam, pleading with his correspondents to be extremely careful in disseminating the work.[67] Writing in Judaeo-Arabic was for him the default option, from which he departed only when there was a specific reason to do so. His medical treatises, composed for his princely Muslim patrons, were probably copied into Arabic characters by a scribe.[68] And he wrote in Hebrew when the recipients knew only, or preferred, that language.[69] For writing the *Mishneh Torah* (redacted around 1178), Maimonides chose Mishnaic Hebrew, as a clear indication of his aspirations to follow the example of Rabbi Judah "the Prince."[70]

His philosophical work, the *Guide of the Perplexed*, was thus written in Judaeo-Arabic, too. When, however, he was asked to translate it into Hebrew, he was happy for the suggestion that the book be translated, apologizing for his inability to do the work himself, and making excuses for having written the book in Arabic "in the language of Qedar, whose light had now dimmed—for I have dwelt in their tents."[71] It is interesting to compare Maimonides' patient cooperation with the translation of the *Guide* into Hebrew with his reaction concerning a request to translate the *Mishneh Torah* into Arabic. This last request was made by a certain Joseph Ibn Jābir, a Jewish merchant from Baghdad, who confessed his

[65] See IAU, 687; B. D. Lewis, "Jews and Judaism in Arab sources," *Metsudah* 3–4 (1945): 176; and see Hopkins, "The Languages of Maimonides," 91.

[66] See, for instance, *Epistles*, 298, and 311n5 (probably regarding the chapters of the *Guide* that criticize Muslim *kalām*).

[67] See "Epistle to Yemen," *Epistles,* 112; A. I. Halkin, *Igeret Teman* (New York 1952); Davidson, *Moses Maimonides*, 487.

[68] See Davidson, *Moses Maimonides*, 434; G. Schwarb, "Die Rezeption Maimonides' in christlisch-arabischen Literature," *Judaica* 63 (2007): 4, and note 12; Bos, *Maimonides on Asthma*, xxxix; and cf. M. Meyerhof, "The Medical Works of Maimonides," in S. W. Baron, ed., *Essays on Maimonides: An Octocentennial Volume* (New York, 1941), 272; but cf. T. Y. Langermann, "Arabic Writings in Hebrew Manuscripts: A Preliminary Listing," *Arabic Science and Philosophy* 6 (1996): 139; Bos, *Medical Aphorisms*, xxxi.

[69] As in his correspondence with the Jews of Southern France, or his response to Obadiah the proselyte; see *Epistles*, 233–41.

[70] And not just because Mishnaic Hebrew is more accessible, as Maimonides explains in his Introduction to the *Book of Commandments*. See also Hopkins, "The Languages of Maimonides," 97–99, 101.

[71] "Epistle to Lunel", *Epistles*, 558. I take the description of Qedar to be factual, although theoretically it may be a calque on the Arabic usage of past tense for blessings and cursing (in which case, one would translate, "Qedar, may its sun be dimmed").

difficulty in reading Hebrew, and pleaded with Maimonides to translate his legal code into Arabic. Maimonides, who some thirty years previously had written his *Commentary on the Mishnah* in Judaeo-Arabic, now turned this request down kindly but firmly. In his justification for the refusal, he insisted on the importance of acquiring a good knowledge of the Hebrew language. Not only does he refuse to translate the *Mishneh Torah*, "for this will spoil its melody," but he also informs his correspondent of his plans to translate into Hebrew both the *Commentary on the Mishnah* and the *Book of Commandments*.[72] One suspects, however, that Maimonides' objection to an Arabic translation of his work reflects also the changing linguistic scene of the Jewish world. Indeed, on another occasion Maimonides expresses his regret at having written the *Book of Commandments* in Arabic, "since this is a book that everyone needs" (the implication being that "everyone's" language is now Hebrew).[73] During Maimonides' lifetime, Judaeo-Arabic had rapidly moved from being the almost universal lingua franca, for both daily communication and intellectual exchange among the Jewish communities around the Mediterranean (in its Geniza-defined borders), to becoming the specific language of the so called "oriental" Jewish communities. The shift in Maimonides' linguistic preferences (from Judaeo-Arabic to Hebrew) reflects his awareness of these developments. By urging an interested, passably educated merchant to cultivate his Hebrew, Maimonides seems to respond to linguistic developments as a result of which, he realized, the Jews of Baghdad might find themselves cut off from the rest of the Jewish world.

The change that Maimonides detected was not merely linguistic: in a letter to the Jewish community of Lunel in southern France he gives a poignant overview of the Jewish world in the last years of his life.

> Most large communities[74] are dead, the rest are moribund, and the remaining three or four places are ailing. In Palestine and the whole of Syria only a single city, Aleppo, has a few wise men who study the Torah, but they do not fully dedicate themselves to it. Only two

[72] *Epistles*, 409; on this correspondence, see chap. 4, note 126, and chap. 6, note 94, below. The *Commentary on the Mishnah* was translated into Hebrew during the thirteenth century; see Davidson, *Moses Maimonides*, 166. On the other hand, parts of the *Mishneh Torah* may also have been translated into Arabic: see G. Schwarb, "Die Rezeption Maimonides' in der christlich-arabischen Literatur," 3 and note 11; idem, "ʿAlī Ibn Ṭaybughā's Commentary on Maimonides' *Mishneh Torah, Sefer Ha-Madaʿ, Hilkhot Yesodei Ha-Torah* 1–4: *A Philosophical 'Encyclopaedia' of the 14th Century*" (forthcoming). I wish to thank Gregor Schwarb for allowing me to read this article before publication.

[73] *Responsa*, 335; *Epistles*, 223; S. Rawidowicz, "Maimonides' *Sefer Ha-mitswoth* and *Sefer Ha-maddaʿ*," *Metsudah* 3–4 (1945): 185 [Hebrew].

[74] literally: cities.

> or three grains can be found in the whole of Babylon and Persia. In all the cities of Yemen and in all the Arab cities, a few people study the Talmud, but they do so only in a mercenary way, looking for gain. . . . The Jews who live in India do not know the scriptures, and their only religious mark is that they keep the Sabbath and circumcise their sons on the eighth day. In the Muslim Persian cities[75] they read the scriptures literally.[76] As to the cities in the Maghreb—we already know the decrees that befell them.[77] You, brothers, are our only [hope] for help.[78]

Not only the language, but also the content of the *Mishneh Torah* betrays Maimonides' awareness that times have changed. The book includes many rulings that one would not expect to find in a practical, everyday halachic guide book. The main explanation for the ambitious scope of the book is to be found in Maimonides' desire to replace the scattered and fragmented oral law with a single concise and comprehensive treatise. Nevertheless, it is noteworthy that Maimonides' idea of what belongs in such a compendium seems to follow the Provençal rather than the Andalusian model. The Jewish leaders of al-Andalus had indeed limited their halachic compositions to the practical needs of the community, such as contracts and dietary laws, whereas the center in Provence had developed a reputation for a scholarly theoretical interest.[79] The fact that Maimonides included in the *Mishneh Torah* the whole range of halachic lore, practical and not-so-practical, bespeaks his determination to present an authoritative learned work for the whole Jewish world. It testifies to his ability to realize the significance of the shift from the Judaeo-Arabic Mediterranean to the Hebrew-speaking Jewish world of Christian Europe, and to adjust to it.

Maimonides and Saadia

This rapid panorama of Maimonides' activity gives a foretaste of his broad spectrum: Maimonides the philosopher, the erudite, the man of law, the leader of the community. His own towering personality was, no

[75] *ʿilgim* is a literal translation of *ʿajam*; cf. Shelat, *Epistles*, note 45.

[76] This does not seem to allude to Karaites, but rather to the paucity of Talmudic erudition or to the lack of sophisticated understanding in these Rabbanite communities.

[77] A reference to the Almohads' forced conversion; see further chap. 3, *apud* note 37, below.

[78] *Epistles*, 559.

[79] See B. Z. Benedict, "On the History of the Torah Center in Provence," *Tarbiz* 22 (1951): 92–93 [Hebrew].

doubt, the leading force behind this astounding versatility. At the same time, we must not forget that the historical context has its share in shaping a person. In the case of Maimonides, the great diversity of this context, and what this diversity entails, still remains to be fully appreciated. For example, had the indigenous culture of al-Andalus remained isolated, restricted to "this peninsula," as the Andalusians sometimes referred to their country, it would probably not have been able to produce a Maimonides. It is the integration of al-Andalus within the Mediterranean world, the close connections of the Andalusian Jewish community with other, Jewish and non-Jewish, communities, and Maimonides' own Mediterranean biography that combined to shape the whole stature of "the Great Eagle."

The "Mediterranean culture" that shaped Maimonides had, of course, produced other Jewish leaders and scholars. It is interesting to compare Maimonides to another "Mediterranean thinker" of impressive stature, Saʿadia ben Yosef Fayyūmī, alias Saadia Gaon (d. 942).[80] Like Maimonides', Saadia's thought was shaped by his education, travels, readings, and personal encounters, and included the legacy of different schools and religious communities. Like Maimonides', Saadia's originality lies in his ability to integrate these diverse sources of influence into a coherent Jewish thought, speaking the universal cultural language of his time while yet remaining entirely Jewish. The differences between the tenth-century Saadia and the twelfth-century Maimonides are not only differences of personality. The distinctive characters of their respective "cultural Mediterraneans" reflect the turning point in the twelfth century. Both Saadia and Maimonides can be seen as high-water marks of the Jewish Mediterranean society. Saadia, in the tenth century, marks the consolidation and coming of age of the Judaeo-Arabic Mediterranean culture. Maimonides, at the close of the twelfth century, marks the turning of the tide, the end of an era: the beginning of the waning of Islamic culture, the rise of European intellectual power, and, as part of this process, the great shift occurring within the Jewish world.

[80] See S. Stroumsa, *Saadia Gaon: A Jewish Thinker in a Mediterranean Society* (Tel-Aviv, 2001) [Hebrew].

Chapter Two

The Theological Context of Maimonides' Thought

Islamic Theology

Scrupulous footnoting, which we nowadays regard as essential to scientific publications, was not part of the ethos of medieval authors.[1] Medieval writers often quote without indicating their source, and they regularly present their thought without mentioning previous authors who inspired them (unless, of course, they want to present themselves as following a school tradition). An investigation that aspires to draw the parameters of Maimonides' cultural world necessarily requires the identification of his sources. This, however, turns out to be in many ways a task for the detective, who must keep alert for unexpected discoveries.

In seeking to identify the philosophical sources for Maimonides' *Guide of the Perplexed*, Shlomo Pines relied first and foremost upon Maimonides' explicit statements. Only few thinkers are mentioned by name in the *Guide*. Some additional information can be culled from Maimonides' letter to Samuel Ibn Tibbon. In writing this letter, however, Maimonides probably did not intend to compose an exhaustive annotated list of his readings. It is more likely that Ibn Tibbon, in a letter that is no longer extant, inquired concerning certain authors whose books were in his own library, and that Maimonides responded in his letter to this inquiry.[2] Like the *Guide*, then, the letter to Ibn Tibbon also does not exhaust the names of authors whom Maimonides read, to whom he reacted, or to the discussion of whose thought he attached particular importance. Maimonides' philosophical erudition was no doubt far broader than would seem to be the case only on the basis of his explicit references.[3] We must

[1] See F. Rosenthal, *The Technique and Approach of Muslim Scholarship* (Rome, 1947), esp. 41; S. Stroumsa, "Citation Traditions: On Explicit and Hidden Citations in Judaeo-Arabic Philosophical Literature," in J. Blau and D. Doron, eds., *Heritage and Innovation in Medieval Judaeo-Arabic Culture* (Ramat-Gan, 2000), 167–78 [Hebrew].

[2] See Marx, "Texts by and about Maimonides," 378; *Epistles*, 552–53; and see below, *apud* note 12.

[3] This working hypothesis is now widely accepted; see, for instance, the *Bulletin de philosophie medieval* 46 (2004): 283–87. Nevertheless, it still seems to be diametrically op-

therefore be alert to the possibility that Maimonides' words reflect, whether by way of acceptance or by way of reaction and criticism, his knowledge of the works of thinkers whose names are not explicitly mentioned. Judah Halevi (d. 1141), for instance, is not mentioned by Maimonides, yet it is very likely that Maimonides' remarks, in several places in the *Guide*, reflect acquaintance with Halevi's *Kuzari*.[4]

Another example is the Muslim theologian Ghazālī, whose name is also never mentioned by Maimonides. Pines had argued that Maimonides must have been familiar with Ghazālī's work, because "no philosopher who wishes to keep abreast of the intellectual debate of this period could have afforded not to have done so; and such a lacuna in Maimonides' knowledge of Arabic theological literature would have been most uncharacteristic."[5] Indeed, as several scholars have been able to show in the years that passed since Pines introduced his hypothesis, Maimonides' acquaintance with the writings of Ghazālī is obvious in his writings.[6] Avner Gilʿadi has suggested that even the title of Maimonides' philosophical book is inspired by this great Muslim thinker. Gilʿadi pointed out that at least twice in his *Iḥyāʾ ʿulūm al-dīn* Ghazālī referes to God as "Guide of the Perplexed" (*dalīl al-mutaḥayyirīn*), and suggested that Maimonides derived the title of his noted philosophic work from this usage of Ghazālī's. Gilʿadi also suggested that, being "most careful to avoid an exact identification between the Divine attribute and the title" of his own work, Maimonides changed it to *Dalālat al-ḥāʾirīn*.[7] An even clearer borrowing of Ghazālī's usage of divine attributes is found in Maimonides' "Epistle to Yemen," where he describes the Torah as God's book, "which guides us, and which delivers us from error (*al-munqidh lanā min al-ḍalāla*) and from erroneous opinions."[8] This formulation echoes, in all likelihood, the title of Ghazālī's spiritual autobiography, *al-Munqidh min*

---

posed to the one adopted by Davidson, who systematically regards anything that is not positively attested as just that: unattested. See, for instance, *Moses Maimonides*, 80.

[4] See Pines, "Translator's Introduction," cxxxiii; idem, "Shiʿite Terms and Conceptions in Judah Halevi's Kuzari," *JSAI* 2 (1980), appendix vii; and see H. Kreisel, "Judah Halevi's Influence on Maimonides: A Preliminary Appraisal," *Maimonidean Studies* 2 (1991): 95–121.

[5] Pines, "Translator's Introduction," cxxvii.

[6] See H. Lazarus-Yaffeh, "Was Maimonides Influenced by al-Ghazālī?" in M. Cogan et al., eds., *Tehillah le-Moshe*: *Biblical and Judaic Studies in Honor of Moshe Greenberg* (Winona Lake, 1997), 163–93; A. Eran, "Al-Ghazālī and Maimonides on the World to Come and Spiritual Pleasures," *JQR* 8 (2001): 137–66; A. L. Ivry, "The *Guide* and Maimonides' Philosophical Sources," in Seeskin, *The Cambridge Companion to Maimonides*, 68–70; and see chap. 3, note 71, below.

[7] See A. Gil'adi, "A Short Note on the Possible Origin of the Title *Moreh Ha-Nevukhim*," *Tarbiz* 48 (1979): 346–47 [Hebrew].

[8] *Epistles*, 103.

al-ḍalāl, and although Maimonides probably neither intended nor expected his Yemenite readers to recognize the allusion, it does betray his own familiarity with this work.

Unlike individual theologians, who are not mentioned by name, Muslim theology as a whole is discussed by Maimonides at length. Theology (*kalām*)—Muʿtazila and Ashʿariyya, Jewish (both Rabbanite and Karaite), and Muslim—was sharply criticized by Maimonides. His particular interest in rebuffing the *kalām*, together with the above mentioned general methodological assumption (namely, that Maimonides had read more than he quotes) support the now widely accepted assumption that Maimonides was well versed in Muslim theological literature.

Kalām: *Christian, Muslim, Jewish*

In chapter 71 of the first part of his *Guide of the Perplexed* Maimonides expounds his view on the beginning of Jewish philosophy. According to him, the components of his own philosophy are all to be found in the Jewish heritage, both biblical and Talmudic. He opens chapter 71 with some rather apologetic words: "Know that the many sciences devoted to establishing the truth in these matters [*scil.* physics and metaphysics] that have existed in our religious community, have perished."[9] Maimonides thus insists on the existence of scientific and philosophical knowledge in ancient Judaism, but he is also aware of the absence of any systematic philosophical writings from the ancient period to substantiate his claim.[10] He then argues that, because of the oral transmission of these sciences and because of the conditions of exile, this knowledge has perished. His own philosophy is therefore, from his own viewpoint, not a continuation but rather a rediscovery, a re-creation of that lost ancient lore.

In some ways, one can say that Maimonides' presentation, which acknowledges the emergence under Islam of a new kind of Jewish thought, corresponds to the standard view of early Jewish thought in modern scholarship. According to this standard view, Jewish systematic philosophy emerged in the ninth and tenth centuries under Islamic rule and was shaped by the influence of Islamic thought. For Maimonides, however, the nonphilosophical period of Jewish thought extends later than it does for modern scholarship. For him, the period devoid of Jewish philosophy stretches up to his own days. Maimonides does not seem to consider the

[9] *Dalāla*, 121:9–10; Pines, 175. Maimonides repeats this claim in other contexts, for example in *Mishneh Torah, hilkhot qiddush ha-ḥodesh*, 17:24 (regarding lost astronomical works from the times of the prophets).

[10] Philo, the only premedieval Jewish thinker to have offered a systematic philosophical thought, strongly influenced Christian thought, but had no direct impact on Jewish thought and remained, on the whole, unfamiliar to medieval Jewish thinkers.

Jewish thinkers who preceded him to be philosophers. No Jewish philosopher is mentioned by name in the *Guide*. In Maimonides' "Epistle to Yemen" Saadya's name appears only in order to make excuse for Saadya's lapse in his attempt to calculate the time of the advent of the Messiah.[11] Most notably, in his above mentioned letter to his Hebrew translator, Samuel Ibn Tibbon, Maimonides offers his evaluation of several books and philosophers. Only two Jewish philosophers are mentioned there (probably because Ibn Tibbon had only asked about these two), and Maimonides dismisses both of them with scathing contempt. Isaac Israeli (d. ca. 950) is put down as having been "only a physician", whereas Joseph Ibn Ñadiq (d. 1148), who wrote under the influence of the Neoplatonizing Pure Brethren (*Ikhwān al-ṣafāʾ*), is brushed aside with a biblical quotation that implies that he was a fool.[12]

Nevertheless, Maimonides cannot ignore the bulk of writings by previous Jewish thinkers, and in the same chapter 71 of the *Guide* he offers a remarkable analysis of where this kind of Jewish thought originated. According to him, the encounter of Christianity with Greek philosophy during the first Christian centuries forced the Christians to formulate an apologetic theology, for which they had to acquire philosophical tools. When Christianity became the religion of the empire, this apologetic philosophy was reinforced by the power of the state.

> Inasmuch as the Christian community came to include those communities [that is, the Greeks and the Syrians] . . . and inasmuch as the opinions of the philosophers were widely accepted in those communities in which philosophy had first arisen, and inasmuch as kings arose who protected religion, the learned of those periods from among the Greeks and Syrians saw that those preachings were greatly and clearly opposed to the philosophic opinions. Thus there arose among them the science of the *kalām*. They started to establish premises that would be useful to them with regard to their belief and to refute those opinions that ruined the foundations of their law.[13]

For Maimonides, then, the Christian philosophical tradition was nothing more than *kalām*—that is to say, theology. For him, this meant that "[the Christians] did not conform in their premises to the appearance of that which exists, but considered how being ought to be in order that it should furnish a proof for the correctness of a particular opinion, or at

[11] *Epistles*, 99–100 [Arabic], 142–44 [Hebrew].

[12] See Marx, "Texts by and about Maimonides," 378; *Epistles*, 552; and see Pines, "Translator's Introduction," cxxxii–iv; S. Stroumsa, "A Note on Maimonides' Attitude to Joseph Ibn Ṣadīq," *Shlomo Pines Jubilee Volume*, Part 2 (*Jerusalem Studies in Jewish Thought* 8 [1990]): 210–15 [Hebrew].

[13] *Dalāla*, 122; Pines, 177.

least should not refute it."[14] In other words, instead of directing their thoughts toward the quest for truth, these early Christian *mutakallimūn* harnessed the truth to their theology, and still worse, to their polity.

Maimonides' criticism of the use made of Greek philosophy by the Christians applies not only to what is admittedly and openly Christian theology, but also to what we generally designate as "Christian Philosophy." He specifically mentions John Philoponus, who had come to personify the Christianization of the Alexandrian schoo1.[15] A sharp critique of Philoponus was part of Fārābī's book *On the Changing Beings,* a work with which Maimonides was familiar:[16] hence the possibility, suggested by Pines, that in this historical sketch Maimonides was dependent on Fārābī.[17] Pines's suggestion is strengthened if we examine a short text preserved by Ibn Abī Uṣaybiʿa, who, in his *Classes of Physicians,* includes "a discourse" in which Fārābī outlined his views "concerning the emergence of Philosophy."[18]

A comparison of Fārābī's *Discourse* with the passage from Maimonides' *Guide* reveals a striking similarity. Ibn Abī Uṣaybiʿa concentrates

[14] *Dalāla,* 122; Pines, 178.

[15] This, despite the fact that Philoponus "the Grammarian" "never held a chair of philosophy in Alexandria," and that "at the time there was no synthesis of Aristotelianism and Christianity within the school" (A. Cameron, "The Last Days of the Academy at Athens," *Proceedings of the Cambridge Philological Society* 195 [n.s. 15; 1969], 36); and see M. Mahdi, "Alfarabi against Philoponus," *Journal of Near Eastern Studies* 26 (1967), 235; K. Verrycken, "The Development of Philoponus' Thought and its Chronology," in R. R. K. Sorabji, ed., *Aristotle Transformed* (London, 1990), 233–74. E. J. Watts, *City and School in Late Antique Athens and Alexandria* (Berkeley, 2006), 252–53. On Philoponus's combination of philosophy and theology see, for instance, R. Walzer, *Greek into Arabic* (Oxford, 1962), 4; and see M. Mahdi, "The Arabic Text of Alfarabi's Against John the Grammarian," in S. A. Hanna, ed., *Medieval and Middle Eastern Studies in Honor of Aziz Suryal Atiya* (Leiden, 1972), 277, and Mahdi's translation, on 257; ʿA. Badawī, *Rasāʾil falsafiyya li'l-Kindī wa'l-Fārābī wa-ibn Bājja wa-ibn ʿAdī* (Benghazi, 1973), 111. For the actual role that Philoponus may have played in reconciling the Christian authorities to the teaching of philosophy by pagans, see H.-D. Safrey, "Le Chrétien Jean Philopon et la survivance de l'école d'Alexandrie au VIe siècle," *Revue des Etudes Grecques* 67 (1954), 407–8; Mahdi, "Alfarabi against Philoponus," 234–35; and L. G. Westernick, *Anonymous Prolegomena to Platonic Philosophy* (Amsterdam, 1962), xii.

[16] See *Guide* 1.74 (*Dalāla,* 156:1–3; Pines, 222).

[17] Pines, "Translator's Introduction," lxxxvi.

[18] IAU, 604. This text was first published in M. Steinschneider, *al-Farabi (Alfarabius): Des arabischen Philosophen Leben und Schriften* (St. Petersburg, 1869), 211–13. An English translation and an analysis of this text are offered in N. Rescher, "Al-Farabi on Logical Tradition," *Journal of the History of Ideas* 24 (1963): 127–32, reprinted in his *Studies in the History of Arabic Logic* (Pittsburgh, 1963), 13–27. See also F. Rosenthal, *The Classical Heritage in Islam* (Berkeley and Los Angeles, 1975), 50; G. Strohmaier, "Von Alexandrien nach Baghdad - eine fiktive Schultradition," in J. Weisner, ed., *Aristoteles, Werk und Wirkung, Paul Moreaux gewidmet* (Berlin, 1987), 2:382; Mahdi, "Alfarabi against Philoponus," 233n1.

on the content of the curriculum, whereas Maimonides' text is more phenomenological and more outspokenly judgmental. But both advance the view that, in shaping the Christian approach to philosophy, religious considerations were predominant. Both also suggest that these Christian religious considerations were closely related to political ones, and that such scholarly-religious decisions were manipulated by "Christian kings," that is, the state. Although Maimonides speaks of both Syriac and Greek Christianity, the special place he grants John Philoponus is in line with Fārābī's concentration on the Alexandrian Academy.[19]

As Dimitri Gutas has shown, Fārābī's *Discourse* is related to a complex of other, longer summaries that tell the story of the crystallization of the medical curriculum in Alexandria.[20] In Fārābī's *Discourse*, however, there is a significant shift in the text's tenor. What Gutas describes as Fārābī's "fine-tuning the transmitted or translated texts to make them more explicit," is in fact the point where Fārābī introduced his anti-Christian bias into the received narrative. Maimonides belongs in this complex precisely because he distills Fārābī's "philosophical" narrative of its original medical context, thus allowing us a clearer view of its anti-Christian tenor.[21]

According to Maimonides, the Christians continued to exert their influence on the study of philosophy after the Muslim conquest:

> When thereupon the community of Islam arrived and the books of philosophers were transmitted to it, then were transmitted to it those refutations composed against the philosophers. Thus they found the *kalām* of John Philoponus, of Ibn ʿAdī and of others with regard to these notions, held on to it, and were victorious in their own opinion in a great task they sought to accomplish.[22]

The Christian philosopher Yaḥyā ibn ʿAdī (d. 974) appears in this passage, like John Philoponus, as a Christian *mutakallim* who had an unhealthy influence on the emergence of Muslim *kalām*. The sentence as it is includes a flagrant anachronism; living in the fourth Islamic century,

[19] Fārābī reacted particularly against Philoponus's proofs for the creation of the world. See Mahdi, "Alfarabi against Philoponus," esp. 233–36; Badawi, *Rasāʾil falsafiyya,* 17; see also Pines, "Translator's Introduction," lxxxv. Beyond this specific point, however, Fārābī saw Philoponus's very approach to philosophy as dangerous.

[20] D. Gutas, "The 'Alexandria to Baghdad' Complex of Narratives: A Contribution to the Study of Philosophical and Medical Historiography among the Arabs," *Documenti e studi sulla tradizione filosofica medievale* 10 (1999): 186–87.

[21] See S. Stroumsa, "Al-Fārābī and Maimonides on the Christian Philosophical Tradition: a Re-evaluation," *Der Islam* 68 (1991): 263–87; and compare Gutas, "The 'Alexandria to Baghdad' Complex," esp. note 6.

[22] *Guide* 1.71 (*Dalāla,* 122; Pines, 177–78).

Ibn ʿAdī could not have influenced the *emergence* of Muslim *kalām*. It seems that this error of Maimonides' resulted from the similarity between Yaḥyā ibn ʿAdī's given name and that of "the Grammarian" John Philoponus (in Arabic: Yaḥyā *al-naḥwī*).[23] But is it *only* an error?

Maimonides mentions Yaḥyā ibn ʿAdī in his letter to Samuel Ibn Tibbon, where he dedicates a separate paragraph to three Christian philosophers: Ibn al-Ṭayyib (d. 1063), Yaḥyā ibn ʿAdī, and Yaḥyā al-Biṭrīq (early ninth century).[24] Their renderings of the Aristotelian texts, says Maimonides, attempt to be servile and are ipso facto seriously flawed.[25]

This passage indicates, first of all, that Maimonides was familiar with Ibn ʿAdī's milieu. The fact that he refers to these three Arab Christians together suggests that he regarded the flaws in Ibn ʿAdī's writings as typical of Christian works. And the fact that Maimonides mentions Ibn ʿAdī with two other Christians who lived under Islam also suggests that he knew his correct chronological setting. If so, his embarrassing mistake in the *Guide* cannot be said to "make evident a glaring lacuna in his knowledge of the history of philosophy,"[26] and we must seek another explanation for it.

Maimonides' anachronism in the *Guide* appears to be more than a meaningless confusion of similar names. He mentions Ibn ʿAdī and John Philoponus while discussing the historical background to Jewish *kalām*, thus committing an obvious chronological error, but the context suggests that his primary association of these two Christian theologians with *kalām*

[23] As was first pointed out by Pines; see his translation of Maimonides' *Guide*, 178, note 19; idem, "Translator's Introduction," cxxvi and note 112.

[24] This last author is mentioned again by Maimonides in the course of his correspondence with Ibn Tibbon. Maimonides recommends an idiomatic translation, one that captures sense rather than etymology. This, he says, was Ḥunain ibn Isḥāq's way of translating philosophical texts, whereas al-Biṭrīq strived for a literal translation, the result being incomprehensible and incorrect. (*Epistles*, 532–33; I. Sonne, "Maimonides's Epistle to Samuel ibn Tibbon," *Tarbiz* 10 [1939]: 135–54 [Hebrew]).Opinions about the quality of Yaḥyā ibn ʿAdī's translations varied: Abū Ḥayyān al-Tawḥīdī considered these translations inelegant; see *Kitāb al-imtāʿ wa'l-mu'ānasa,* ed. Aḥmad Amīn and Aḥmad al-Zayn. (Beirut, n.d.), 37. Ibn Abī Uṣaybiʿa, on the other hand, thought highly of them. See also G. Bergsträsser, "Ḥunain ibn Isḥāq über die syrischen und arabischen Galen-Übersetzungen," *Abhandlungen für die Kunde des Morgenlandes* 17 (Leipzig 1925): 711–12; E. Booth, *Aristotelian Aporetic Ontology in Islamic and Christian Thinkers* (Cambridge, 1983), 89n202. On the various methods of translation, see S. Brock, "Aspects of Translation Technique in Antiquity," *Greek, Roman and Byzantine Studies* 26 (1979): 69–89.

[25] Marx, "Texts by and about Maimonides," 380; *Epistles*, 532. The Arabic original of this part of the letter is not extant. The Hebrew medieval translation speaks of the way al-Biṭrīq "used to explain (*haya mefaresh*) the books of Aristotle and of Galen," but from the context it is evident that this refers to the translations (perhaps rendering "*tafsīr*" in the sense of translation).

[26] Pines, "Translator's Introduction," cxxvi n112.

was phenomenological. For Maimonides, Yaḥyā ibn ʿAdī, like John Philoponus before him, was part of the tradition of Christian *kalām,* the tradition of harnessing philosophy to the needs of religion.

In other words, Maimonides was aware of a group of people like Yaḥyā ibn ʿAdī, that is, Arab Christians whose occupation was *falsafa.* He, however, considered them worthless as a school of philosophy. For him, they were only a modern version of the Christian *mutakallimūn.*

Yaḥyā ibn ʿAdī did not shun theology, and his contribution to Christian theology in Arabic is significant, but he was also a student of Fārābī, and certainly did not regard himself as a *mutakallim*: in fact, his depiction of the *mutakallimūn* is as scathing as that of Maimonides.[27] Fārābī's relations with his Christian colleagues in Baghdad, however, were complex, and there are reasons to believe that he left Baghdad because of the tension between them.[28] As we have seen above, Maimonides probably drew his view of pre-Islamic Christian philosophy and its influence on Muslim *kalām* from the writings of Fārābī. It is quite possible that in his attitude to contemporaneous Arab Christian philosophy Maimonides is also dependent on Fārābī, although, on this point, the scarcity of the evidence precludes any definite conclusion.

According to Maimonides, with the spread of Islam, the Muslims, too, in their turn, adopted philosophical tools and endeavored to give a philosophical garb to their religion. We should also note Maimonides' conviction that

> all the statements that the men of Islam—both the Muʿtazila and the Ashʿariyya—have made concerning these notions are all of them opinions founded upon premises that are taken over from the books of the Greeks and the Syrians who wished to disagree with the opinions of the philosophers.[29]

According to Maimonides, then, it was Christian *kalām* that fathered Muslim *kalām.* To Christian *kalām* the Muslims added their own touch

[27] See Abū Ḥayyān at-Tawḥīdī, *al-Muqābasāt,* ed. Ḥasan al-Sandūbī (Cairo, 1929), 224. On Yaḥyā ibn ʿAdī, see J. L. Kraemer, *Humanism in the Renaissance of Islam: The Cultural Revival during the Buyid Age* (Leiden, New York and Köln, 1992), 104–39; S. H. Griffith, *The Church in the Shadow of the Mosque: Christians and Muslims in the World of Islam* (Princeton and Oxford, 2007), 122–25.

[28] This point was convincingly argued by Muhsin Mahdi, in an unpublished lecture titled "Al-Fārābī and ʿAbbāsid Political Order." The lecture was delivered in March 1995 at the Israel Academy of Sciences in Jerusalem, as the annual Shlomo Pines Memorial Lecture. See also E. K. Rowson, *A Muslim Philosopher on the Soul and Its Fate: Al-ʿĀmirī's Kitāb al-Amad ʿalā l-abad* (New Haven, 1988), 2.

[29] *Guide* 1.71 (*Dalāla,* 122; cf. Pines, 176).

(which they then passed on to the Jews). In Maimonides' view, philosophy, twice harnessed in this manner to religion, was much the worse. From the search for truth it was transformed into a system for arbitrary distortion of the truth.

Maimonides' main concern, however, was neither the Christians nor the Muslims but his own co-religionist theologians, whose opinions he tried to discredit. He therefore continues his historical sketch so as to include also the Jews:

> As for that scanty bit of *kalām* regarding the notion of the unity of God and regarding what depends on this notion, which you will find in the writings of some Gaonim and in those of the Karaites, it should be noted that the subject matter of this *kalām* was taken over by them from the *Mutakallimūn* of Islam.

Muslim scholastic theology was thus, according to Maimonides, copied by Jewish scholars in the East, both Rabbanites—the Gaonim—and Karaites. He does not credit them with fashioning their thought to fit the size of Judaism, as Muslims and Christians before them had adopted philosophy for their needs. He does not credit them with any kind of discernment or choice. According to him, since the first Muslim theological school happened to be the *Muʿtazila*, it was this version of theology that was cloned by the Jewish thinkers: "This was not because they preferred the first opinion [i.e., that of the *Muʿtazila*] to the second [i.e., the *Ashʿariyya*], but because they had taken over and adopted the first opinion and considered it a matter proven by demonstration."[30] Maimonides then proceeds to offer a lengthy criticism of *kalām*, a system that he presents as a degradation and abuse of philosophy. In his writings, he rarely misses an opportunity for an aside to the *mutakallimūn*, whom he does not regard as engaged in the same endeavor as he is.

Despite its obvious flaws, Maimonides' outline is, on the whole, strikingly perceptive. The role of oriental Christians in translating and transmitting Hellenic culture to the Arabs has been long recognized, although the current "wisdom in the field" favors a revised evaluation of this role.[31] Maimonides' writings offer an interesting angle to this question: he grudg-

[30] *Guide* 1.71 *(Dalāla,* 122; Pines, 177). On the different schools of *kalām*, see, for instance, L. Gardet and M.-M. Anawati, *Introduction à la théologie musulmane: essai de théologie comparée* (Paris, 1981), 46–67; J. van Ess, *Theologie und Gesellschaft im 2. und 3. Jahrhundert Hidschra: Eine Geschichte des religiösen Denkens im frühen Islam*, five vols. (Berlin and New York, 1991–97).

[31] See D. Gutas, *Greek Thought, Arabic Culture: The Graeco-Arabic Translation Movement in Baghdad and Early ʿAbbāsid Society (2nd–4th/8th–10th centuries)* (London and New York, 1998); Stroumsa, "Philosophy as Wisdom: on the Christians' Role in the Translation of Philosophical Material to Arabic."

ingly recognizes the part that the Christian theological tradition played in the translation of scientific and philosophical texts, and he admits that they exerted a crucial influence on the formation of Islamic thought, but his appreciation of this influence is thoroughly negative.

His awareness of the force of encounter of different cultures and of the influence exercised by one culture upon another is remarkable. There is little to correct in his appraisal of the influence of Greek philosophy on the Church Fathers, although, under Fārābī's influence, he overrates the role played by the political power of the Christian empire in the crystallization of Christian theology. And Maimonides' description of the emergence of Muslim *kalām* stresses its indebtedness to its Christian predecessors, a point noted also by modern scholars.[32]

As for Maimonides' view of the origins of Jewish *kalām*, it also largely corresponds to the one adopted by modern scholars. Moritz Steinschneider, Isaac Husik, Jacob Guttmann, and Salo W. Baron, to mention only a few, all agree in regarding Jewish *kalām* as molded under the influence of Islam. The details of this influence were studied by scholars such as Harry Austryn Wolfson and Georges Vajda, and their seminal works have contributed to our understanding of Jewish *kalām* and its relations to Muslim *kalām*.[33] Admittedly, Jewish systematic philosophy developed, for the main part, under Islam and reflects the strong influence of Islamic philosophy.

Other parts of Maimonides' outline, however, have been disputed and corrected. Maimonides develops Fārābī's brief sketch and includes in it Jewish thought as another link in the same transmission chain. The encounter of Christianity with Greek philosophy generated the theology of the Church Fathers. The encounter of Islam with Christianity engendered Muslim *kalām*. Finally, the encounter of Judaism (both Rabbanite and that of the Karaites) with Muslim *kalām* fathered Jewish *kalām*. Maimonides' outline, however, is skewed in that it ignores the multicultural nature of early Islamic society. Contacts in such a society are never neatly arranged in pairs, and influences do not travel on a single linear track. There is no reason to assume, a priori, that, while Muslims were meeting

[32] See, for instance, M. Cook, "The Origins of Kalam", *BSOAS* 43 (1980): 32–43; S. Pines, "Some Traits of Christian Theological Writing in Relation to Muslim Kalām and to Jewish Thought," *Proceedings of the Israel Academy of Sciences and Humanities* 5 (1976): 104–25 (reprinted in "*The Collected Works of Shlomo Pines, 3*: *Studies in the History of Arabic Philosophy*, ed. S. Stroumsa [Jerusalem, 1996] 79–99).

[33] See, for example, H. A. Wolfson, *The Philosophy of the kalam* (Cambridge, Mass., 1976); idem, *Repercussions of the Kalam in Jewish Philosophy* (Cambridge, Mass., 1979); G. Vajda, "Le '*kalām*' dans la pensée reliegieuse juive du Moyen Age," *Revue de l'histoire des religions* 183 (1973): 160–63, as well as Vajda's numerous articles regarding Muqammaṣ, Qirqisānī, Saadya, or Yūsuf al-Baṣīr.

with Christians and were being exposed to their theology, their Jewish contemporaries were waiting patiently on the side until Muslims had developed their own theology, in order to then meet with Muslims alone. A more convincing working hypothesis postulates that, once the gates of communication were open, due to the unifying political and linguistic setting, Jews entered the arena along with everybody else.

Maimonides' evaluation of Jewish *kalām* as a servile, indiscriminate adoption of Muʿtazilite positions is clearly incorrect, and his sweeping evaluations must be challenged on several accounts. Early Jewish thinkers did not adopt Muʿtazilite ideas blindly, as Maimonides claimed, but rather selectively, as evidenced by their occasional dissent from these ideas. Nor did they follow the Muʿtazila exclusively, and other influences must be taken into account in the study of early Jewish philosophy.

There is ample evidence for direct Christian influence on the development of Jewish *kalām*, through the first Jewish medieval thinker, Dāwūd al-Muqammaṣ (in the first half of the ninth century) as well as through second-generation authors like Saadia and Qirqisānī.[34] Maimonides may not have been aware of the direct contacts between Jews and Christians in the ninth and tenth centuries, but it is also possible that, consciously or semiconsciously, he was willing to sacrifice historical precision in order to simplify the historical schema. Presenting Muslim *kalām* as the sole source of Jewish *kalām* makes it easier for him to present the Jewish *mutakallimūn* as servile imitators of their source of inspiration—a clearly incorrect presentation. Muqammaṣ, who studied for many years in Nisibis, was thoroughly influenced by his Christian teachers, as demonstrated by his sometimes wooden adaptations of their arguments to Jewish theology. To the extent that his writings also reflect direct contacts with Muslim theology, this testifies not to servile imitation but rather to his independent mind, and his attempts to look beyond his Christian schooling. It is also noteworthy that Muqammaṣ's exposure to the theological concerns of Muslim *kalām* went hand in hand with simultaneous exposure to philosophical, Aristotelian material. Already at this early stage, the Aristotelian corpus seems to have been accessible in some form in Arabic. Jewish *kalām* was thus not a pre-philosophical, primitive stage in the development of Jewish philosophy, but the result of a choice between several available intellectual options.[35] Saadya, a contemporary of Ashʿarī, was cognizant of theories that came to be identified with the Ashʿariyya.

[34] See S. Stroumsa, "Maimonides' Auffassung vom jüdischen *Kalām*: sein Wahrheitsgehalt und seine geschichtliche Wirkung," *Judaica* 61 (2005): 289–309; idem, "The Impact of Syriac Tradition on Early Judaeo-Arabic Bible Exegesis," *Aram* 3 (1991): 83–96.

[35] See S. Stroumsa, "Soul-searching at the Dawn of Jewish Philosophy: A Hitherto Lost Fragment of al-Muqammaṣ's *Twenty Chapters*," *Ginzei Qedem* 3 (2007): 143–44.

To the extent that he adopted Muʿtazilite rather than Ashaʿrite views, this was most probably not a result of mere chance or of blind following, but reflected his deliberate choice. The same holds true for Saadya's Karaite contemporary, Qirqisānī, whose theology is indeed close to that of the Muʿtazila. Qirqisānī's discussion of divine attributes includes a detailed refutation of the position of Ashʿarī's precursor Ibn-Kullāb. This refutation testifies to the choice Qirqisānī exercised when following the Muʿtazila.[36] Even in the work of the Karaite Yūsuf al-Baṣīr, who was deeply influenced by the Muʿtazilite ʿAbd al-Jabbār, one can see clearly that the dependence on the Muʿtazila was far from being automatic, but rather measured and carefully thought out.[37]

As is his wont, Maimonides makes a point of telling his reader that his analysis of the *kalām* does not rely on hearsay, but rather on his own readings. Michael Schwarz has pointed out the discrepancy between Maimonides' description of the *kalām* system and what we know of the Muʿtazila or the Ashʿariyya of the tenth century. Schwarz was able to demonstrate that Maimonides' detailed analysis of the *kalām* reflects extensive readings of the later *mutakallimūn*, with whose system it agrees to a great extent. Maimonides, however, presents his schema as valid for any *kalām* work: "When I studied the books of these *mutakallimūn*, as far as I had the opportunity . . . I found that the method of all the *mutakallimūn* was one and the same."[38] It is of course possible that this is the *kalām* with which Maimonides was familiar, and that he was ignorant of the differences between schools and the nuances that distinguished individual authors, or that his memory failed him, or that he reported not what he had read but what he had extrapolated.[39] Neither of these possibilities seems to me to square with Maimonides' personality. To some extent, he may have simplified the picture intentionally, drawing a caricature in order to facilitate his task of polemicist. In this as in other matters, however, one can also recognize Maimonides' phenomenological drive: to gloss over the differences and to paint with large strokes of the brush, which will allow him to make sense of the resulting picture.

[36]See H. Ben-Shammai, "Major Trends in Karaite Philosophy and Polemics in the Tenth and Eleventh Centuries," in M. Polliack, ed., *Karaite Judaism: A Guide to its History and Literary* Sources (Leiden, 2003), 339–62.

[37]See *Al-Kitāb al-Muḥtawī de Yūsuf al-Baṣīr*, G. Vajda and D. Blumenthal, eds. (Leiden, 1985), 152.

[38]*Guide* 1.71 (*Dalāla,* 123–24; Pines, 179); and see M. Schwarz, "Who Were Maimonides' *Mutakallimūn*? Some Remarks on *Guide of the Perplexed* Part I, Chapter 73," *Maimonidean Studies* 1 (1991): 159–209; 3 (1992–93): 143–72; Ivry, "The *Guide* and Maimonides' Philosophical Sources," in Seeskin, *The Cambridge Companion to Maimonides*, 71–75.

[39]Davidson, *Moses Maimonides*, 90.

In addition to presenting a simplified schema of the history of *kalām*, Maimonides also attempts to describe its geographic boundaries, saying: "As for the Andalusians among the people of our nation, all of them cling to the affirmations of the philosophers and incline to their opinions, in so far as these do not ruin the foundation of the Law. You will not find them in any way taking the paths of the *mutakallimūn*."[40]

One recognizes in these lines a certain Andalusian local-patriotism, discernible also in the works of Maimonides' Muslim compatriots.[41] It is indeed true that the *kalām*—and the Muʿtazila in particular—had few followers in al-Andalus.[42] Among the Jews, however, the reality is again less neat than Maimonides would have it. Although Rabbanite authors from the Islamic West—such as Judah Halevi, Joseph Ibn Ñadiq, and Dunash ben Tamīm—were no *mutakallimūn*, *kalām* is very present in their discussions of such issues as creation of the world in time or the divine attributes. Even Abraham Ibn Daud, Maimonides' Andalusian precursor in presenting a Jewish Aristotelian thought, does not hesitate to heap praises upon Saadya's *Book of Beliefs*. Maimonides does not want to admit the possibility of a complex, ambivalent (let alone a favorite) attitude toward *kalām* among Andalusian Jews, because this would imply that the *kalām* may contain some grains of truth. An ambivalent attitude may indicate that Jewish thinkers, both *mutakallimūn* and others, could choose and pick their ideas, from *kalām* as from Aristotelian philosophy, in a considered way. Such a considered choice has no place in Maimonides' caricature of the *kalām*: for him, the Jewish *mutakallim* is an automaton who imitates Muslim *kalām*, where logic becomes a tool for the politician to manipulate the ignorant masses, as it had been for the Christians *mutakallimūn* before him.

The sharp dichotomy that Maimonides attempts to draw between *kalām* and philosophy is important for him not only in order to have a neat picture of who is a *mutakallim*; just as important is the fact that it serves him also in his attempt to present a purist ideal of the philosopher. Maimonides' disciple, Joseph Ibn Shimʿon, was an aspiring phi-

[40] *Guide* 1.71 (*Dalāla,* 122; Pines, 177).

[41] See, for example, Ibn Rushd, *Talkhīṣ al-āthār al-ʿulwiyya*, ed. Jamāl al-Dīn al-ʿAlawī. (Beirut, 1994), 103–4.

[42] See H. Ben-Shammai, "Some Genizah Fragements on the Duty of the Nations to Keep the Mosaic Law," in J. Blau and S. C. Reif, eds., *Geniza Research after Ninety Years: the Case of Judaeo-Arabic* (Cambridge, 1992), 22; I. Sabra, "The Andalusian Revolt Against Ptolemaic Astronomy: Averroes and al-Bitrūjī," in E. Mendelsohn, ed., *Transformation and Tradition in the Sciences, Essays in Honor of I. Bernard Cohen* (Cambridge, Mass., 1984), 133–53. Ibn Rushd also testifies to the absence of Muʿtazilite writings in al-Andalus; see *al-Kashf ʿan manāhij al-adilla fī ʿaqāʾid al-milla*, ed. M. ʿA, al-Jabābirī (Beirut, 2001), 118.

losopher who displayed a complex, ambivalent attitude to the *kalām*. He had arrived to study with Maimonides in Fusṭāṭ in 1182, and stayed there for about two years.[43] Previously, he had studied philosophy and the sciences but was also attracted to *kalām*. In his "Epistle Dedicatory" to the *Guide* Maimonides lists the questions that troubled his student:

> [You] asked me to make clear to you certain things pertaining to divine matters, to inform you of the intentions of the *mutakallimūn* in this respect, and to let you know whether their methods were demonstrative and, if not, to what art they belonged. As I also saw, you had already acquired some smattering of this subject from people other than myself; you were perplexed, as stupefaction had come over you.[44]

The quest for a correct appreciation of the "the intentions of the *mutakallimūn*" was at the heart of Ibn Shimʿon's perplexity, and it is thus also at the heart of *The Guide of the Perplexed*. To the extent that Maimonides oversimplifies the description of the *kalām* and its development, he does so also in order to make sure that his student falls on the right side of the divide between *kalām* and philosophy.[45]

Judging from Maimonides' unbending opposition to the *kalām*, one would have expected him to keep at arm's length from them and to shun their meetings. We know, however, that he attended debates of *mutakallimūn* in Egypt.[46] Indeed, in modern scholarship, the place of *kalām* in Maimonides' intellectual profile remains debated. Leo Strauss had dubbed him "an enlightened *mutakallim*", whereas Zev Harvey regards Maimonides' approach as fundamentally distinct from that of the *kalām*.[47] A nuanced understanding of Maimonides' self-image can explain his ambivalent place as regards Islamic theology. In his own self-perception, there is no doubt that Maimonides was a philosopher, a proud heir to the Aristotelian tradition as it was cultivated in al-Andalus. He was, however, also acutely aware of his role as a leader of the Jewish community, and of the

[43] On Ibn Shimʿon and his relations with Maimonides, see Stroumsa, "Introduction," *The Beginnings of the Maimonidean Controversy in the East*.

[44] *Dalāla* 1; Pines, 3–4.

[45] Maimonides' bitterness in the *Epistle on Resurrection* is largely the result of his disappointment with the fact that Ibn Shimʿon remained, in the end, a *mutakallim*; see chap. 6, below.

[46] See Rosenthal, "Maimonides and a Discussion of Muslim Speculative Theology."

[47] L. Strauss, *Persecution and the Art of Writing* (Glencoe, Il., 1952), 40–41; W. Z. Harvey, "Why Maimonides Was not a Mutakallim," in Kraemer, *Perspectives on Maimonides*, 105–14; see also L. E. Goodman, *Jewish and Islamic Philosophy: Crosspollinations in the Classic Age* (Edinburgh, 1999), 89.

need to accommodate its specific needs. This awareness accounts for much of the theological content of his work. In particular, one should note the kind of writings he engaged in. His most philosophical book, the *Guide*, is very different from typical philosophical compositions of his time. It is, by its author's own claim, centered on exegesis of the Hebrew Bible. The *Guide* may not be unique in its genre (Ibn Rushd's *Kashf al-adilla*, although written for a different audience, is in many ways similar, and was probably a source of inspiration for Maimonides).[48] But whereas Ibn Rushd dedicated most of his literary energy to typically philosophical writings, and the *Kashf* is marginal to his main philosophical activity, Maimonides developed this model to make it his magnum opus. The *Guide* is thus by nature theological in the sense that it is dedicated to the effort to harmonize philosophy with Scripture. The fact that Maimonides chose to expand in this genre should not obliterate his more philosophical concerns, nor lead us to identify his theological concern as *kalām*. Maimonides was not a *mutakallim*, not because he did not engage in theological speculation, but because he vehemently opposed the content of the particular theological system called *kalām*. He was a philosopher, but not because of a lack of theological concern in his thought (like other medieval philosophers, this was not the case). He was a philosopher because he saw himself as such.

Heresies, Jewish and Muslim

The assumption that Maimonides was versed in Muslim theological literature can assist us in understanding curious or vague statements in his works. As is quite often the case, the most striking example appears when it is least expected.[49] It is thus in Maimonides' attempts to define the boundaries of the Jewish community that we find resounding proofs of the extent to which he interiorized the concerns of Muslim theologians.

In his *Commentary on the Mishnah* (known as *Kitāb al-Sirāj*) Maimonides comments on the *Mishnah* in *Ḥullin* 1.2, which discusses the persons authorized to perform ritual slaughter. Summarizing the Talmudic discussion, Maimonides lists those people whose slaughter is not valid, and says:

[48] See S. Stroumsa, "The Literary Corpus of Maimonides and Averroes," *Maimonidean Studies* 5 (2008): 193–210.

[49] Another example is Judah Halevi's use of Shiʿite terminology and concepts as building blocks for his theory of Jewish chosenness and particularism (*ṣafwa*, translated to Hebrew as *segula*); see Pines, "Shiʿite Terms and Conceptions in Judah Halevi's Kuzari."

> "And he may not be a *min*." In the language of the Sages, *minim* are Jewish heretics [*zanādiqat Yisra'el*], whereas the heretics of other nations are specifically identified as such by the use of the construct-state, and called: "the *minim* of the nations" [***miney goyyim***]. These [that is, the *minim*], are the people whose foolishness dulls their intellects, and whose lust have darkened their souls. Therefore they vilify the law [*sharī'a*] and the prophets, of blessed memory, and deny the prophets concerning matters about which they have no knowledge [*yukadhdhibūna al-anbiyā' bimā lā 'ilma lahum bihi*], and they abandon the commandments [*sharā'i'*] in contempt."[50]

One should first of all note that for Maimonides, heresy (*zandaqa* in Arabic, or *minut* in Mishnaic Hebrew) is a universal phenomenon: it can effect Judaism as well as other prophetic religions. His definition of this heresy, couched in Qur'ānic language, is such that it could easily be adopted by a Muslim.[51] A similar trait is apparent in Maimonides' definition of the *min* in his "Epistle on Forced Conversion", where he says: "The *minim* poke fun at the [revealed] religions (*datot*) and they say: 'He who adheres to them is a fool, he who studies them is mad,' and they utterly deny prophecy."[52] This *Epistle* is extant only in a medieval Hebrew translation, but the Hebrew translation, with its clear allusion to Hosea 9:7 ("the prophet is a fool, the man of spirit is mad") catches well the claim of this statement: the *minim* deny prophecy, and they mock at all religions (*datot*).

Also noteworthy in the paragraph of the *Commentary on the Mishnah* quoted above is Maimonides' highly individualizing understanding of the term *min*. As used in this passage, this is clearly a tag that certain individuals earn by their particular character traits or behavior. It does not apply to a whole group or sect, and, more specifically, it does not apply to the Karaites.

Karaite Judaism, which emerged as a distinct subgroup in the middle of the ninth century, distinguished itself from Rabbanite Judaism in its rejection of Rabbinic authority and in its denial of the monopoly of the Talmudic interpretation of the Bible. The formidable ideological challenge it presented to Rabbanite Judaism in the tenth century is evident in the writings of Saadia Gaon. Animosity and rivalry to the Karaites are also apparent in the writings of Maimonides' predecessors in al-Andalus,

[50] *Commentary on the Mishnah*, *Qodashim*, 175

[51] The word *sharī'a* was commonly used by Jews to denote the Torah, but note the expression ". . . matters about which they have no knowledge"; see, for example, Qur'ān, 6 [*al-an'ām*]: 144; 22 [*al-ḥajj*]: 71; 24 [*al-nūr*]:15; 40 [*ghāfir*]: 42.

[52] *Epistles*, 37–38; Cf. A. Halkin and A. Hartman, "The Epistle on Martyrdom," *Crisis and Leadership* (Philadelphia and New York, 1985), 20 who translate "religion."

Abraham Ibn Daud and Judah Halevi.[53] Rabbanite authors sometimes use the term *min* to denote the Karaites. For instance, an autographed letter by Judah Halevi explains his initiative to write the *Kuzari* as a response to a "*min* from the land of the Christians (*aḥad muntaqilī al-minut bi-bilād al-rūm*), a statement understood by most scholars as a reference to a Karaite from Christian Spain.[54] In the *Kuzari* itself Halevi calls the Karaites *khawārij* (dissenters) whereas the term *minim* is used to denote Talmudic sects, such as the Sadducees. This later usage is by nature more ambiguous, as one could argue that Halevi associates the emergence of the Karaite heresy with earlier Talmudic sects.[55]

The heated ideological debate, however, was not always paralleled by an equal social animosity. As Marina Rustow has shown, during the first half of the twelfth century Karaites and Rabbanites in Fustat "not only married one another; Karaites also frequented the Rabbinical courts, and the scribes who ran them uncomplainingly wrote documents in conformity with their specifications."[56] In many ways, this was also the situation in Maimonides' Cairo, where the two communities lived side by side quite peacefully. Muslim sources describe Maimonides as "Head of the Jews" (*ra'īs al-yahūd*), an administrative position that, since the end of the eleventh century, united all the Jewish communities in Egypt and Syria. Although we have no explicit evidence of that, it is likely that in his capacity as *ra'īs al-yahūd* Maimonides represented also the Karaites toward the Muslim authorities.[57] The disagreement, however, remained,

[53] See G. D. Cohen, *The Book of Tradition (Sefer ha-Qabbalah) by Abraham ibn Daud* (Philadelphia, 1967), xlvi; Judah Ha-Levi, *Kitāb al-radd wa'l-dalīl fi'l dīn al-dhalīl (al-Kitāb al-Khazarī)*, ed. D. H. Baneth and H. Ben-Shammai (Jerusalem, 1977), 2:22–63, 112–137 (English translation in H. Hirschfeld, *The Kuzari*, 2nd ed., New York, 1964); J. D. Lasker, "Judah Halevi and Karaism", in J. Neusner et al., eds., *From Ancient Israel to Modern Judaism: Intellect in Quest of Understanding. Essays in Honor of Marvin Fox*, (Atlanta, 1989), 3:11–123; idem, "Karaism in Twelfth-Century Spain," *Jewish Thought and Philosophy* 1 (1992): 179–95; and see H. Ben-Shammai, "Between Ananites and Karaites: Observations on Early Medieval Jewish Sectarianism," *Studies in Muslim-Jewish Relations* 1 (1993): 19–29.

[54] See, for instance D. H. Baneth, "Some Remarks on the Autographs of Yehudah Hallevi and the Genesis of the *Kuzari*," *Tarbiz* 26 (1956–57): 297–303 [Hebrew]; S. D. Goitein, "The Biography of Rabbi Judah Ha-Levi in Light of the Cairo Geniza Documents," PAAJR 28 (1959): 41–56; M. Gil and E. Fleischer, *Yehuda ha-Levi and His Circle—55 Geniza Documents* (Jerusalem, 2001) 324–26 [Hebrew]; but see Y. T. Langermann, "Science and the *Kuzari*," *Science in Context* 10 (1997): 501, who questions this identification.

[55] See Lasker, "Judah Halevi and Karaism," 112n4.

[56] M. Rustow, *Rabbanite-Karaite Relations in Fatimid Egypt and Syria: a Study Based on Documents from the Cairo Geniza* (Ph.D. Diss. Columbia University, 2004), 390, 397.

[57] See IQ, 392; Ben-Sasson, "Maimonides in Egypt," 15 ff.; M. R. Cohen, *Jewish Self-Government in Medieval Egypt: The Origins of the Office of the Head of the Jews, ca. 1065–1126* (Princeton, 1980), 35; J. Levinger, "Was Maimonides 'Rais al-Yahud' in

with its inbuilt "perplexing contradiction—harmonious daily life, ideological wars."[58] It has been suggested that Maimonides himself may have been partly responsible for widening the social rift between the two communities; that by denying the validity of Karaite divorce he effectively discouraged marriage with Karaites.[59] The actual impact of Maimonides' rulings on the historical development of the schism can be appraised only after a careful reevaluation of this development, which should take into account the vast amount of new information provided by recent studies of the Geniza as well by the Firkovich collections. In the present context, however, I wish to focus only on the place of the Karaites in Maimonides' heresiography. Although Maimonides was clearly irked by the Karaite challenge to Rabbinic authority, he walked a fine line in this respect. As his terminology, elaborate discussions, and in particular his occasional self-contradiction show, he recoiled from pushing for a final schism with the Karaites.[60]

The terminology he chooses is highly indicative here. An edict signed by Maimonides and other Rabbanite dignitaries attempts to counterbalance the apparently widespread influence of Karaite practices regarding women's ritual purity, and the edict identifies the Karaites' practice as that of the *minim*.[61] In his "Epistle to Yemen" Maimonides warns his Yemenite correspondents of the possible infiltration into their midst of "one of the *minim*" who deny the oral law—again, an obvious reference to the Karaite position—and points out that "according to our system (*madhhab*) one can spill the blood of these *minim* with impunity."[62] At the

Egypt?" in: I. Twersky, ed., *Studies in Maimonides* (Cambridge, Mass., 1990), 83–93; Rustow, *Rabbanite-Karaite Relations in Fatimid Egypt,* 388, 395–96; cf. H. Davidson, "Maimonides' Putative Position as Official Head of the Egyptian Jewish Community," in N. Lamm, ed., *Hazon Nahum* (New York, 1998), 115–28. I wish to thank Menahem Ben-Sasson for discussing this point with me.

[58]Rustow, *Rabbanite-Karaite Relations in Fatimid Egypt,* 400. On the combination of daily coexistence and doctrinal tension, see also see H. Soloveitchik, "*Mishneh Torah*: Polemic and Art," in Jay Harris, ed., *Maimonides after 800 Years* (Cambridge, Mass., 2007), 327–43, esp. 332.

[59]See Rustow, *Rabbanite-Karaite Relations in Fatimid Egypt,* 37-38; *Responsa*, 628–29; *Epistles*, 612–13; see also S. Assaf, "On the History of the Karaites in the East," *Zion* 1 (1935–36): 211 [Hebrew], who notes a deterioration of relations after Maimonides, but does not suggest a causal connection. S. W. Baron, *Social and Religious History of the Jews*, vol. 5 (New York, 1957), 28 and 266, points to the difficulty posed regarding intermarriage by Maimonides' view of Karaite divorce, a difficulty of which Maimonides must have been aware. Contrary to Rustow's reading, however, neither Assaf nor Baron "laid responsibility for the schism at Maimonides's doorstep"; see, also, note 60, below.

[60]Maimonides' complex but, on the whole, tolerant policy towards the Karaites is noted by Baron, *Social and Religious History of the Jews*, 5:281.

[61]See Davidson, *Moses Maimonides*, 48; *Responsa*, 434–44, 588–89; *Epistles*, 177, 412.

[62]*Epistles,* 98, 141–42.

same time, Maimonides insisted on treating the Karaites as an integral part of the Jewish community. His rule of thumb was that they should be considered as part of the community regarding all the laws that they, like the Rabbanites, accept as binding. He thus decrees, for example, that they cannot be counted when assembling the required ten men for prayer (*minyan*), since they reject this concept.[63] For the same reason he rules that it is incumbent upon Rabbanites to perform ritual circumcision for Karaite boys even on the Sabbath, the implication being that this is not considered to be desecration of the Sabbath, but on the contrary, a performance of a commandment. Nor does Maimonides leave this understanding implicit; he specifically expresses the hope that such Karaite infants will grow up to join the Rabbanite fold.[64]

Maimonides notes that his contemporaries identify the *minim* with the Sadducees and the Boethusians. Although he has theoretical qualms about the appropriateness of this identification, he concludes that the founders of these sects, like "real" *minim*, deserve the death penalty, because they introduce the notion of denying tradition (*takdhīb al-naql*). By stressing this characteristic of the *minim*, Maimonides highlights their similarity to the Karaites, and he seems to insinuate that the founders of Karaism, too, should have been executed as heretics.[65] And yet he takes pain to distinguish these historical founders from contemporary Karaites. These contemporary Karaites he regards as "captivated infants" who cannot be taken to account for their errors.[66] Moreover, and of particular importance for our present context, Maimonides explicitly says that "*these* Karaites are *not* the ones designated by the Sages as *minim*."[67]

In discussing the Talmudic chapters regarding heresy, Maimonides is not satisfied with their analysis as bygone history, and he tries to bring out their contemporary relevance. Let us go back to the passage in the *Commentary on the Mishnah*, where Maimonides defines the *minim:*

> These are the people whose foolishness dulls their intellects, and whose lusts have darkened their souls; therefore they vilify the law and the prophets, of blessed memory, and deny the prophets concerning matters about which they have no knowledge, and they abandon the commandments in contempt. They are of the faction of

[63] *Epistles*, 611.

[64] *Responsa*, 729–32; and see Baron, *Social and Religious History of the Jews*, 5:281.

[65] *Commentary on the Mishnah*, *Ḥullin* 1.2, *Qodashim*, 175–76; "Epistle to Yemen," *Epistles*, 98, 141–42; *Responsa*, 497; and see Baron, *Social and Religious History of the Jews*, 5:280; Davidson, *Moses Maimonides*, 491.

[66] *Commentary on the Mishnah*, *Ḥullin* 1.2.

[67] See *Responsa*, 499; *Epistles*, 609 (emphasis added). Maimonides' insistence may well indicate that the differentiation was not evident to everyone.

> Jesus the Nazarene, Doeg, Aḥitophel, Geḥazi, and Elisha-*Aḥer*, and those who follow their ways—may the name of the wicked rot. It is possible to know that a person belongs to this faction when one sees that he contemptuously shakes off any of the commandments, without deriving any benefit from this act.[68]

The individuals included in Maimonides' list of heretics are indeed those we would expect to see in such a list: Jesus and Elisha Ben Abuya, along with three of the four biblical figures whom the *Mishnah* (in *Sanhedrin* 11.2) lists as "commoners" (*hedyotot*, as opposed to kings) who have no share in the World to Come: namely, The Edomite Doeg (1 Sam. 21:8–22:23), Aḥitophel (2 Sam. 16:14–17:14–23) and Gehazi (2 Kings 5:20–27). These figures are mentioned in the Talmudic discussion in *Ḥagigah* (in connection with Elisha Ben Abuya's preoccupation with Greek music and heretical books) as having been remarkably learned.[69] Of these five, the most elaborate picture is given in the Talmud to the first-century Elisha. Prior to his apostasy, this arch-heretic was considered to be one of the great sages of his day. But after his apostasy he became anathema to his former colleagues. His sin was considered to be so great that, according to a Talmudic saying, a divine decree singled him out as the only person for whom no repentance remains possible. His sobriquet *aḥer* (lit. "other") came to indicate his complete alienation from Judaism.[70] Talmudic literature recounts various stories concerning the reasons and the nature of Elisha's apostasy. He is said to have been appalled by the presence of unjustified and inexplicable suffering in this world; he is described as having been attracted to Greek learning; he is claimed to have reached the conclusion that "there are two powers in heaven." Perhaps the most ancient anecdote about his apostasy associates it with his unsuccessful mystical experience, a failed attempt "to enter *pardes*." Spiteful contempt for the commandments—contempt that, according to this passage, characterizes a "heretic"—fits the Elisha of the Talmud. Also fitting to this image is Maimonides' insistence in his *Commentary on the Mishnah* in *Sanhedrin*, on the fact that the three commoners, like Elisha, were renowned for their great erudition (*ʿiẓm darajatihim fiʾl-ʿilm*).[71] But some fundamental elements in the image of Elisha in the Talmud, such as his confrontation with Metatron and the matter of "two powers in heaven," or the concern with theodicy (for example, Elisha's exclamation, "Is this Torah and is this its reward?"), are completely absent in the image of the

[68] *Commentary on the Mishnah*, *Ḥullin* 1.2, *Qodashim*, 175.
[69] *Commentary on the Mishnah*, *Sanhedrin* 10, "Introduction," in *Neziqin*, 217.
[70] On the meaning of this sobriquet, see G. G. Stroumsa, "Aḥer: A Gnostic," in B. Layton, ed., *The Rediscovery of Gnosticism*, (Leiden, 1981), 2:808–18.
[71] *Commentary on the Mishnah*, *Sanhedrin* 10, "Introduction," in *Neziqin*, 217.

Maimonidean Elisha. Also striking is the absence of the Talmudic formulation of the nature of Elisha's sin: "*Aḥer* cut down the saplings (*qiẓeẓ ba-neṭiʿot*)."[72] Still more striking than the missing Talmudic characteristics are those elements that have no evident source in the Jewish traditions regarding Elisha. The arrogant denial of the prophets, which Maimonides presents as the most characteristic trait of *minim* like Elisha, is an element not to be found in the Talmud or in any other Jewish sources, and which Maimonides adds of his own accord.

An indication of Maimonides' source for this added element can be found in the Qurʾānic formula he employs, as well as in his choice to translate the Mishnaic term *minim* as *zanādiqa* (sing. *zindīq*). Indeed, Maimonides casts the Jewish *min* in the image of the Muslim archetypal *zindīq*, the arrogant freethinker who relies on his erudition and intellectual acumen, who denies the prophets and vilifies them as charlatans.

This image is further strengthened if we add to the paragraph from the commentary on *Ḥullin* other passages where Maimonides refers to Elisha: the commentary on the specific passage of the *Mishnah* (in *Ḥagigah* 2.1) that deals with Elisha's failed mystical experience,[73] as well as his image in *Guide* 1.32. Elisha is portrayed there as a person of great erudition and learning, the origin of whose sin is his desire to know that which lies beyond human knowledge. This combination of desire and learning causes him to speak with "presumptuous assertion with regard to the Deity," not to have regard for His honor, and "to declare the falsity of that which has not been proven false." These last two accusations are couched in the specific formulations that Maimonides employs in numerous places for his discussion of the question of the eternity of the world. Although he says that the nature of the world as created in time cannot be proven, neither can its eternity be proven; and therefore, Maimonides argues, the "regard for the Lord's Honor" demands that we hold back and refrain from making hasty assertions.[74] This brazen hastiness (*tahāfut*) is a not only an error, a fault of character and a wrong approach to science: it is a sin against "the honor of the Creator." The term *tahāfut*, made famous by Ghazālī, undoubtedly reflects the influence of the latter's criticism of the Aristotelian philosophers in his *Tahāfut al-falāsifa*.[75] By using these

[72] BT *Ḥagigah* 14b–15a. On the sin of Elisha in the Jewish tradition, see Y. Liebes, *Elisha's Sin: The Four Who Entered* Pardes *and the Nature of Talmudic Mysticism* (Jerusalem, 1990), 29–51 [Hebrew], and bibliography there.

[73] *Commentary on the Mishnah*, *Moʿed*, 378

[74] See *Guide* 2.30 (*Dalāla*, 247–48; Pines, 353); *Guide* 2.15 (*Dalāla*, 203; Pines, 292): *Guide* 2.22 (*Dalāla*, 223:28–224:5; Pines, 320); *Guide* 2.29 (*Dalāla*, 243–44; Pines, 346).

[75] The standard translation of the book's title as "Incoherence of the Philosophers" is now commonly accepted; see, for example, M. E. Marmura's translation of al-Ghazālī, *The Incoherence of the Philosophers* (Provo, Utah, 2000). This translation, however, does not

particular formulations to describe Elisha, Maimonides insinuates that Elisha decided in favor of the belief in the eternity of the world. In other words, Maimonides paints Elisha as an Aristotelian philosopher.[76] This suggestion is further corroborated when we find Maimonides saying in his "Epistle on Astrology," "It is the root of the Torah that the deity alone is primordial and that He has created the whole out of nothing; whoever does not acknowledge it rejects a principle of faith and he has cut down the saplings (*kafar ba-ʿiqar ve-qiẓeẓ ba-neṭiʿot*)."[77] The Aristotelian belief in the eternity of the world is described here with the Talmudic formula specific to Elisha's sin: that he cut down the saplings.[78]

Maimonides' Elisha, as he emerges from both the *Guide* and the *Commentary on the Mishnah*, is thus a person who contemptuously and wantonly denigrates the commandments. He does not believe in the prophets, he toys with sensitive philosophical ideas concerning the creation of the world, and he hastily jumps into unproven conclusions, disregarding the respect due to the Lord's honor, and at the same time revealing the limits of his own knowledge. Some of the main characteristics of the Talmudic Elisha are missing in this portrait, and they seem to be replaced by other features. The new features of Maimonides' Elisha are wholly absent from the Jewish literature concerning Elisha-*Aḥer*. All these features appear, however, in the figure of the Muslim archetype of the *zindīq*, Ibn al-Rāwāndī.

Abū al-Ḥusain Aḥmad b. Isḥaq al-Rāwandī lived in Iraq in the second half of the ninth century.[79] At the beginning of his career, Ibn al-Rāwāndī was an ordinary *mutakallim*, and was even a respected figure among the

reflect the gravity of the accusation leveled against them, and the moral and religious aspects of their hubris. See also F. Griffel, *Apostasie und Toleranz im Islam: Die Entwicklung zu al-Ġazālī's Urteil gegen die Philosophie und die Reaktionen der Philosophen* (Leiden, 2000), who opts for a translation that indicates the book's purpose ("Die Wiederlegung der Philosophen," for example, 268); and M. Asín Palacios, "Le sens du mot '*tahāfot*' dans les œuvres d'el-Ghazalī et d'Averroës," *Revue Africaine* 261–62 (1906) (reprinted in idem, *Obras Escogidas* [1946], 185–203); and see note 94, and chap. 5, below, *apud* note 40.

[76] See *Guide* 1.32 (*Dalāla*, 46–47; Pines, 68–70); and see S. Stroumsa, "Elisha Ben Abuya and Muslim Heretics in Maimonides' Writings," *Maimonidean Studies* 3 (1995): 173–93.

[77] *Epistles*, 483; Lerner's translation ("Maimonides, Letter on Astrology", in R. Lerner, and M. Mahdi, eds., *Medieval Political Philosophy: A Sourcebook* [Ithaca, 1963], 231) "is guilty of radical unbelief and is guilty of heresy," obliterates the resonance of the Talmudic formula as well as the typically Maimonidean insistence on articles of faith.

[78] See note 72, above.

[79] For a summary of the biographical sources concerning Ibn al-Rāwāndī, see H. S. Nyberg, in the introduction to his edition of *Kitāb al-intisār* by al-Ḥayyāṭ (Cairo, 1925); ʿAbd al-Amir al-Aʿsam, *Ta'rīkh Ibn al-Riwandī al-mulḥid* (=*History of Ibn ar-Riwandi the Heretic* [Beirut, 1975]); S. Stroumsa, *Freethinkers of Medieval Islam: Ibn al-Rāwandī, Abū Bakr al-Rāzī, and Their Impact on Islamic Thought* (Leiden, 1999), 37–46.

mu'tazila of Baghdad. Because of reasons that are not entirely clear, however (the Muslim sources speak of some blow to his pride), he then turned his back upon his Mu'tazilite colleagues and began to direct verbal barbs against them. He rapidly became known as the archetype of the heretic in Islam, despite the fact that there is no agreement (either in the Muslim sources or, in their wake, in the modem studies) concerning the exact nature of his heresy.

Notwithstanding the haziness of his historical image and of the uncertainty regarding the true nature of his heresy, one can reconstruct a rather clear, consistent picture of what one might call "the polemical image of Ibn al-Rāwāndī," that is, the image he assumes in the polemical literature. He is designated as a *zindīq* even by those who do not specifically intend to accuse him of Manicheanism. He is connected to the *Dahrīya* who assert the eternity of the world, and it is related that one of his books, the *Kitāb al-Tāj*, was devoted to a presentation of the proofs for the eternity of the universe.[80] He is described as an educated man, led by his erudition, which caused him to miscalculate the limitations of his own wisdom (in this connection, some sources apply to him the cliché used by orthodox intellectuals to discount heretical intellectuals: that his erudition outstripped his intelligence [*kāna 'ilmuhu akthar min 'aqlihi*]).[81]

Ibn al-Rāwāndī, however, is primarily known for two other characteristics: one concerning his character, the other concerning his ideas. In terms of character, he is described as a haughty individual who, with a sharp tongue and arrogance, enjoyed satirizing and mocking his rivals and all that was holy to them. In terms of the contents of his words, Ibn al-Rāwāndī became a byword for one who denied prophecy.

The features that mark Ibn al-Rāwāndī as a *zindīq*—that is, denial of the prophets and attachment to the *Dahrīya,* who believe in the eternity of the world—are the same ones we find emphasized in the Maimonidean Elisha, and which are not expressed anywhere in the previous Jewish tradition. Hence, we may legitimately ask the question whether Maimonides' portrayal of Elisha ben Abuyah was influenced by the figure of Ibn al-Rāwāndī.

[80] See Nyberg, "Introduction," 26 (based on *Maḥāsin Khorāsān* of Abū al-Qāsim al-Balkhī). The *Dahriya* and the Aristotelian aspects of the figure of Ibn al-Rāwāndī are discussed at length by H. S. Nyberg in his article, "Amr ibn 'Ubayd et Ibn al-Rawandi, deux réprouvés," in R. Brunschvig and G. E. Von Grunebaum, eds., *Classicisme et déclin culturel dans l'histoire de l'Islam* (Paris, 1977), 125–39.

[81] For example, he is described in this fashion by the poet Abū'l-'ālā' al-Ma'arrī (who was himself accused of heresy). See *Risālat al-Ghufrān* (Beirut, 1980), 232. On the expression in general, see F. Rosenthal, *Aḥmad ibn at-Ṭayyib al-Saraḥsī* (New Haven, 1943), 33.

This question may be divided into two parts. We must first ask whether Maimonides may have read the numerous writings of Ibn al-Rāwāndī. While such a possibility cannot be ruled out entirely, it seems to me rather unlikely. The Muslims mercilessly persecuted Ibn al-Rāwāndī while he was alive, and did not give him rest even after his death. His books were in effect banned, and there is reason to suspect that already during the eleventh century even Muslims found it difficult to find any manuscripts of his books.[82]

This being so, is it conceivable that Maimonides did not know at all about Ibn al-Rāwāndī? This, too, is highly unlikely. True, Maimonides does not mention Ibn al-Rāwāndī by name, nor does his name appear in the extant writings of the Muslim philosophers whom he was accustomed to read, such as Fārābī, Ibn Bājja, and Ibn Rushd.[83] In the works of Muslim theologians, however, the image of Ibn al-Rāwāndī, the debate with him, and quotations from his works are very common, whether in their polemical writings or in *kalām* writings. Ibn al-Rāwāndī's words are occasionally quoted when he expresses his opinion concerning some inoffensive issue, but he is primarily mentioned as one who argues against prophecy. Although the Muslim theological and heresiographical literature contains a plethora of heretics, Ibn al-Rāwāndī occupies a central place in this literature as the arch-heretic, one who is a heretic out of spite—a role parallel to that occupied by Elisha ben Abuyah among Jewish heretics. As mentioned above, Maimonides met with Muslim theologians on various occasions, and even participated with them in discussions of *kalām*.[84] If we accept the assumption of Pines, mentioned at the beginning of this chapter, that Maimonides was familiar with the writings of Muslim theologians, and not only with those of Muslim philosophers, we must assume that Maimonides encountered the image of Ibn al-Rāwāndī in one way or another. And if Maimonides encountered any mention at all of Ibn al-Rāwāndī, be it only one sentence, we may reasonably assume that this sentence described him as a *zindīq*, a Dahrite, and as one who denied the prophets. If this is the case, it seems quite possible that this image influenced Maimonides when he shaped the image of the Jewish *zindīq*, Elisha ben Abuyah.

Maimonides offers a very free adaptation of Ibn al-Rāwāndī to his own purposes. He breaks down the image into its components, drawing from it those elements that constitute the stereotype of the *zindīq*, the

[82] See Stroumsa, *Freethinkers of Medieval Islam*, 207–8.

[83] On the repercussion of Ibn al-Rāwāndī and of his freethinking on Islamic philosophy, see ibid., 188–92.

[84] See note 46, above; P. Fenton, "A Meeting with Maimonides," *BSOAS* 45 (1982): 1n1.

Dahrite, or the "denier of prophecy." Maimonides does not see any need to relate to Ibn al-Rāwāndī himself or to mention him anywhere by name. All of the elements characteristic of Ibn al-Rāwāndī appear in Maimonides' writings under the name of Elisha-*Aḥer*.

The dynamics that lead Maimonides in this "creative reading" are complex, and its subtlety deserves to be traced with care. We would be wrong to summarize it in a simplified way, and to state, for instance, that Maimonides identifies the *minim* of the Talmud with Muslim freethinkers rather than with Karaite Jews, since his identification of the term *min* seems to change according to the context.

Maimonides moves between various registers: past and present, Hebrew and Arabic. When reading the Hebrew and Aramaic texts, he thinks first of all about traditions regarding sectarians from the Second Temple period. He is cognizant of the views (expressed by both Karaites and Rabbanites) that present these sectarians as the precursors of Karaism. He is also aware of the fact that Karaites can sometimes be called *minim*, and may himself use this appellation when it is meant to exhort his own Rabbanite congregation.

When he translates *minim* into Arabic, and speaks of *zanādiqa*, the Arabic appellation conjures up a whole new set of associations, with their own characteristics. The archetypal Muslim *zanādiqa* are, for him, the freethinkers of the Muslim past, and their image triggers the appropriate orthodox reaction: they are anathema, they deserve the death penalty, spilling their blood is licit. In this context, Maimonides records such executions in the contemporary Maghreb.[85] The literary images of the past, both Jewish and Muslim, are clearly very vivid in his mind.

When, however, he returns, with this set of Jewish-Muslim images of the heretic to think about its implications regarding the Karaite next door, the juxtaposition of his own reality with the literary legacy reveals a "cognitive dissonance." The half-mythical ostracized *min/zindīq* fits badly into the relatively irenic social coexistence of Karaites and Rabbanites, and at this point, Maimonides breaks sharply: one should not be carried away with the literary images. The contemporary Karaites are to be treated as erring Jews, not as dangerous enemies. When it comes to the actual life of the contemporary Jewish community, Maimonides' final

[85] *Wa-qad inʿamala min hādha* ***halacha le-maʿase*** *fī ashkhāṣ kathīrīn fī bilād al-maghrib kullihā*; *Commentary on the Mishnah*, *Ḥullin* 1.2, *Qodashim*, 176; and see note 65, above. Since the paragraph discusses the application of capital punishment in "the days of Exile," this sentence is usually understood in this context, too; see Baron, *Social and Religious History of the Jews*, 5:280. No such executions of budding heresiarchs by Jewish courts in the West are known to us. One should note, however, that Maimonides becomes uncharacteristically vague in this sentence, and his wording may refer to Jewish courts as well as to what he has seen in Muslim courts in Almohad North Africa.

verdict is down-to-earth and unambiguous: "*These* Karaites are *not* the ones designated by the Sages as *minim*."[86]

Elisha ben Abuya is not the only case in which Maimonides taps into Muslim heresiography in order to deal with problems in his own, Jewish world. In his introduction to *Pereq Ḥeleq* Maimonides enumerates three classes of people in relation to the interpretation of the words of the Sages in the *midrash*: 1) Those who understand them literally, and accept them: women and the uneducated as well as the *darshanim* who cater to them—and these are numerous.[87] 2) Those who read them literally and reject them, and these are also a large group. 3) The small number of people who understand that the words of the Sages contain hidden wisdom, concealed in riddles and parables. What characterizes the second group (those who understand the words of the Sages in a literal manner, and reject them) is their contempt and scorn for the words of the Rabbis and their excessive arrogance. Maimonides says of this group:

> They repeatedly mock the sayings of the Sages; they claim to be more intelligent and brighter than the Sages, and that the Sages, peace upon them, were simpletons who suffered from inferior understanding, that they were ignorant of the entirety of Being, and understood nothing whatever. Most of those who have stumbled into this error are those who claim [to know] medicine and those who rave about the decree of the stars. They claim to be cultivated men, physicians and philosophers. How remote they are from true humanity in the eyes of real philosophers.[88]

One might ask: who are these people, who claim to be physicians, who deal with astrological delusions and claim to engage in philosophy, and who scorn the words of the Sages and the Talmudic *midrashim*? Offhand, one would seek here Jewish doctors, and more than one, as Maimonides speaks here of a group that "are also numerous."

In his letter to Ibn Tibbon, Maimonides refers critically to Isaac Israeli, who is "only a physician" (and not a real philosopher). But Isaac Israeli is far from meeting the specifications given here by Maimonides, and it is

[86] See note 67, above.

[87] On this category, see chap. 4, below, *apud* notes 161–62.

[88] *Commentary on the Mishnah, Sanhedrin* 10, "Introduction," in *Neziqin,* 201–2. Cf. the translation of A. J. Wolf, in I. Twersky, ed., *A Maimonides Reader* (New York and Philadelphia, 1972), 408. A similar discrepancy between self-perception and true intellectual level is mentioned by Maimonides regarding the Sabians, who claim to be philosophers, but are in fact "more remote from philosophy than any other [men]." See *Guide* 3.29 (*Dalāla,* 376:5-6; Pines, 516), and see chap. 4 and chap. 5 note 82, below.

generally difficult to know where Maimonides would find a group of Jewish physicians to fit this description.[89]

On the other hand, another individual, mentioned in that same letter to Ibn Tibbon as "only a physician," is very suitable to this description. He is the tenth-century Abū Bakr al-Rāzī, who was indeed renowned as a physician, but was also a philosopher. Like Ibn al-Rāwāndī, Rāzī was noted for his claim that prophecy is opposed to Divine wisdom, and for the contemptuous remarks he made against the prophets. Like Ibn al-Rāwāndī, Rāzī became an archetype of the heretic, but his reputation was more widespread in philosophic circles. Of course, Rāzī did not write about the *midrashic* exegeses of the Talmudic Sages, but we do know of contemptuous remarks that he directed against religious sages in general (and probably Muslims in particular), whom he calls "the bearded goats."[90] It seems that, in his portrayal of those who hold the words of the Sages in contempt while understanding them literally, Maimonides incorporated the image of Rāzī, as a stereotype of one who mocks the tradition with the arrogance of the man of science and philosophy. It is not that Maimonides had any reason to think that Rāzī's words or his approach had any hold among the community of Jewish physicians. Rather, as Maimonides was engaging in typologies, and attempting to portray clear-cut types in relation to their understanding of the words of the Sages, he tried to build the image of one who has contempt for the words of the Sages in the sharpest and most extreme way possible. The image of the physician-heretic Rāzī served him as a model for this purpose.

In putting forward this suggestion, it is worth mentioning here the fact that, unlike Ibn al-Rāwāndī, who is not mentioned by Maimonides, Rāzī is singled out by Maimonides for severe and explicit criticism. In the second part of the *Guide*, Maimonides attacks at length the "ravings" (*hadhāyānāt*) of Rāzī.[91] In chapter 12 of this book, he quotes the remarks of

[89]The Spanish Muslim theologian Ibn Ḥazm (d. 1064) mentions two Jewish physicians who upheld the "Equivalence of Proofs" (see *K. al-Fiṣal fi'l-milal wa'l-niḥal* V, 119), but no contempt toward the Sages is discernable in their words. As suggested by J. van Ess ("Disputationpraxis in der islamischen Theologie," *Revue des Etudes Islamiques* 44 [1976], 47), the Jewish interlocutors of Ibn Ḥazm probably reverted to this argument as a convenient defense in an uneasy polemical situation. They thus cannot be taken to be authentic representatives of a skeptical trend within Spanish Judaism, as suggested by M. Fierro, "Ibn Ḥazm et le Zindīq juif," *Revue du Monde Musulman et de la Mediterrannée* 63–64 (1992): 81–89.

[90]See P. Kraus, "Raziana," *Orientalia* n.s. 4 (1935): 300–304; 5 (1936): 35–56, 358–78; Stroumsa, *Freethinkers of Medieval Islam*, chap. 3. The question whether Rāzī was indeed a freethinker or only portrayed as such is marginal to our discussion here; as far as Maimonides is concerned, Rāzī's heresy is an undisputed fact.

[91]On this term and its meaning, see chap. 5.

Rāzī in the latter's *al-Ilāhiyāt.* According to Maimonides, Rāzī argues there that "there is more evil than good in what exists."[92] Maimonides goes on to discuss the words of the Aristotelian philosophers who, noting the injustice in the division of good and evil in the world, challenge the notion of Divine providence (*Guide* 3.16). Then, in chapter 19, while still within the broad context of the question of providence and God's knowledge of individuals, Maimonides cites Psalm 94:8–9, "Consider, ye brutish among the people; and ye fools, when will you understand? He that planted the ear, shall He not hear? He that formed the eye, shall He not see?" He then says:

> I shall now explain to you the meaning of this argument after I have mentioned to you the way in which those who assault the prophets' discourse misunderstand this discourse. Several years ago some distinguished individuals of our religious community, who were physicians, told me that they wondered at this dictum of David. They said: According to his way of reasoning, it would follow necessarily that the Creator of the mouth eats and the Creator of the lung shouts and the same would hold for all the other members.[93]

The question cited here by Maimonides challenges the logic of this verse, on the assumption that the argument made in the verse is that whoever makes any sort of vessel himself acts in accordance with the qualities of that vessel. Maimonides replies by explaining that the logic of the verse is in fact different: he who makes any vessel must certainly understand its way of functioning. At first glance, this passage does not present any difficulty. The question as such is a plausible exegetical one. Maimonides' answer to the question, intended to show the providence and wisdom inherent in creation, is related to the subject of the chapter. Since the issue at hand is the wisdom revealed in the creation of the organs of the human body, one can understand why physicians would be particularly interested in this.

Nevertheless, the reader is left with a certain feeling of unease. The question itself is a logical one, and has nothing to do with medicine. One can understand why the one *answering* it might be a physician, who constantly encounters the complexity of the human body; but his interlocutor

[92] *Guide* 3.12 (*Dalāla*, 318; Pines, 441). One should note that these unambiguous remarks of Maimonides against Rāzī are not without difficulty. There are passages that have been preserved from a book of Rāzī's bearing a similar name (*Kitāb al-ʿilm al-ilāhī*), and from other works of Rāzī. The statement attributed to him by Maimonides does not appear there in this precise form. See Abū Bakr al-Rāzī, *Rasāʾil Falsafiyya,* ed. P. Kraus (Cairo, 1939) 165–90; M. Mohaghegh, *Filsuf-i-Rayy* (Tehran, 1974), 273–76.

[93] *Guide* 3.19 (*Dalāla*, 346; Pines, 478); my translation here differs slightly from that of Pines; see note 94, below.

could be any person. One cannot understand Maimonides' emphasis on the fact that those referred to are "some distinguished individuals of our religious community, who were physicians," in the plural, as if this were a typical question of physicians. Even less clear is why Maimonides formulates this exegetical question in the words: "I have mentioned to you the way in which those who assault the prophets' discourse misunderstand this discourse." It follows from this that those selfsame "distinguished individuals of our religious community, who were physicians," who ask a question stemming from their misunderstanding of the verse in Psalms, are defined as those who "assault the prophets' discourse"—surely a severe accusation.[94]

The accusation placed in the mouth of the physicians is not specifically a medical one, and its wording has a provocative ring, pointing out the absurd and ridiculous in the verse.[95] We thus have reason to suspect that here, too, Maimonides has mixed into the framework of the discussion elements that do not properly pertain to it in the historical sense. Because of the proximity of this discussion to that concerning the philosopher who "assault the prophets' discourse," Abū-Bakr al-Rāzī, it is possible that these elements were borrowed from the Muslim struggle against this philosopher.

As this chapter has shown, Maimonides had a thorough knowledge of the theological trends in the Islamic world. His familiarity with Muslim *kalām* and with Christian theology permitted him to analyze Jewish *kalām* and its development. His knowledge of the polemical scene within Muslim theology allowed him to weave it into his own thought and to use it in his attempts to address Jewish heresies, both past and present. The literary baggage that contained this theology and these polemics was based mostly on material developed in the Islamic East before Maimonides' time. The next chapter is dedicated to a brand of Muslim thought that seems to have had the most powerful influence upon Maimonides' thought, and which emerged in the Islamic West during his own lifetime.

[94] Pines's translation (478), "Those who are overhasty in their interpretation of the prophets' discourse," evidently comes from the assumption that he indeed speaks of "distinguished individuals of our religious community," and moderates the translation accordingly. But the word "overhasty" does not reflect the belligerence of the expression *mutahāfitīn*; and see note 76, above.

[95] Cf. the manner in which Maimonides presents a legitimate, nonprovocative exegetical question in *Guide* 3.32 (*Dalāla*, 385:13–15; Pines, 526–27).

Chapter Three

An Almohad "Fundamentalist"?

As a young adult, between the years 1148 and 1165, Maimonides lived under Almohad rule. The immense impact of these formative years on his thought has been almost totally overlooked by modern scholarship.[1] This chapter will investigate the permeation of his thought, both halachic and philosophical, by Almohad doctrine.

Almohads

In 1148, Cordoba, Maimonides' birthplace, was conquered by the *Muwaḥḥidūn* (known in Latin as the Alomohads), a Berber dynasty that had by then established its rule in North Africa. The founder of the movement, Muḥammad ibn Tūmart (1078 [or 1081]–1130) and his successor and the actual founder of the dynasty, ʿAbd al-Muʾmin (d. 1165), gained political and military power and ousted the previous Berber dynasty, that of the *Murābiṭūn* (known in Latin as the Almoravids). Revivalist movements aiming to restore Islam to its pristine purity, and to replace a previous (already corrupt) such movement, are a recurrent phenomenon in Islam in general and in North Africa in particular. Sociologists, from Ibn Khaldūn (d. 1406) to Ernest Gellner (d. 2006), view the emergence of such movements as a periodic cycle related to the mutual relations between nomad desert-dwellers and settled societies.[2] The Almohad movement, however, was not merely yet another revivalist wave emerging from the rough and remote regions to restore old mores and values in the

[1]The possibility that Maimonides is indebted to the Almohads was already raised by I. Heinemann, "Maimuni und die arabischen Einheitslehrer," *Monatschrift für Geschichte und Wissenschaft des Judentums* 79 (1935): 102–48, esp. 147 ff. The specific influences suggested by Heinemann, however, are improbable. Also improbable is the suggestion that Maimonides was influenced by the Almohad aversion to poetry; see D. Urvoy, *Pensers d'al-Andalus. La vie intellectuelle à Séville et Cordoue au temps des empires berbères [fin XIe siècle–début XIIIe siècle]* (Toulouse, 1990), 119. Maimonides was opposed to vocal and musical entertainment, but he does not seem to have objected to poetry, and in fact had written some himself; see Y. Yahalom, "'Sayeth Tuviyyah ben Ẓidkiyyah': The *Maqama* of Joseph ben Simeon in Honor of Maimonides," *Tarbiẓ* 66 (1997): 543–77, esp. 552, 558–60 [Hebrew]; but see note 39, below.

[2]Cf. E. Gellner, "Flux and Reflux in the Faith of Men," *Muslim Society* (Cambridge, 1981), 1–85, esp. 46 (quoting Friedrich Engels).

fattened and corrupt cities. Ibn Tūmart presented himself as the Mahdī: his leadership retained aspects of millenarian messianism, and his movement was truly revolutionary in all domains.[3]

The revolutionary zeal that informed Almohad law is manifest, first of all, in Almohad theology. They identified themselves as *muwaḥḥidūn* ("those who proclaim the (true) unity of God") as opposed to the *murābiṭūn* ("those who hold the hermitage-outpost [*ribāṭ*]"), whom they labelled "*mujassima*," ("those who profess a corporeal understanding of God"). In the Almohads' view, true monotheistic belief does not allow for anthropomorphic understandings of God. By presenting the Almoravids as anthropormophists, the Almohads thus portrayed them as unbelievers, polytheists against whom one can and should wage war.[4]

The rejection of anthropomorphism was not, however, a mere strategy, conceived in order to legitimize the declaration of *jihād* on fellow Muslims. The abstract, incorporeal conception of God was a cornerstone of the Almohad doctrine of divine unity (*tawḥīd*). This doctrine was incorporated into short catechisms (known as the *murshida* and the *ʿaqīda*), the recitation of which was imposed on all Muslims, elite and common people alike. A close-knit elite (the *ṭalaba*) served as the cadre for the Almohad higher administration.[5] This elite was instructed in the higher level of theology, based on an adaptation of the theology of Abū Ḥāmid al-Ghazālī, that is to say, on Ashʿarite *kalām*.[6] Unlike the Almoravids, the Almohad regime was relatively tolerant toward philosophy (although it was not itself committed to philosophy).[7]

Among the successive Muslim dynasties that ruled the Maghreb and al-Andalus, the Almohads stand out in their attempt to break away from the established legal tradition. The importance of legal issues in

[3] On the Almohad dynasty, which ruled between 1121–1275, see I. Goldziher, "Introduction," in D. Luciani, ed., *Le Livre de Mohammed Ibn Toumert, Mahdi des Almohades* (Algiers, 1903); A. Huici Miranda, *Historia Politica del Imperio Almohade* (Tetouan, 1956–57); H. Kennedy, *Muslim Spain and Portugal: A Political History of al-Andalus* (Edinburgh, 1996), 196–272; M. Fierro, "La religión," *El retroceso territorial de al-Andalus. Almorávides y almohades, Siglo XI al XIII. Historia de España fundada por R. Menéndez Pidal y dirigida por J. M. Jover, coord. por M. J. Viguera* (Madrid, 1997), 8:2, 435–546; P. Cressier et al., eds., *Los Almohades: Problemas y Perspectivas* (Madrid, 2005.); M. Shatzmiller, "*al-Muwaḥḥidūn*," *EI* 7:801–7; idem, *Messianism and Puritanical Reform: Mahdīs of the Muslim West* (Leiden, 2006), 174–92.

[4] See D. Serrano, "Por qué llamaron los almohades antropomorfistas a los almorávides?" in Cressier et al., *Los Almohades*, 815–52.

[5] See E. Fricaud, "Les *Ṭalaba* dans la société almohade. (Le temps d'Averroës)," *Al-Qanṭara* 18 (1997): 331–88; idem, "La place des *ṭalaba* dans la société almohade mu'minide," in Cressier et al., *Los Almohades*, 525–45; T. Nagel, *Im Offenkundigen das Verborgene, Die Heilszusage des sunnitischen Islams* (Göttingen, 2002), 145.

[6] Nagel, *Im Offenkundigen das Verborgene*, 120, 143

[7] See below, *apud* note 24.

Almohad thought in general and in the thought of the *faqīh* Ibn Tūmart in particular has been highlighted by several modern scholars.[8] In particular, the Mālikī school of law, which had ruled in al-Andalus for centuries (and to which the Almohads remained in many ways attached), is usually characterized (in a somewhat stereotypical, but not altogether incorrect way) as conservative. It developed the study of casuistics (*furūʿ*), paying relatively little attention to the other "sciences of the Qurʾān," such as exegesis and theology (uṣūl al-dīn). Time-honored practices, which demanded precise listing of the transmitters for each tradition, bore a voluminous bio-bibliographical literature. The fact that Islam recognizes the legitimacy of several schools of law rendered the record of their various opinions and disagreements an integral part of Mālikī legal scholarship. Ibn Tūmart and his followers sought to reform this legal system.[9] Ibn Tūmart began spreading his doctrine among the Berbers by "composing for them scholarly tracts [in their own language] . . . on the basic religious doctrines."[10] As a basic doctrine of religion (*aṣl*) Ibn Tūmart defined whatever is based solely on the revealed tradition: *Qurʾān,* the prophetic *sunna* as recorded in the canonical compilations, and the agreement of scholars (*ijmā*). Instead of the Mālikī reliance on precedents, the Almohads returned to the sources (*uṣūl*) of jurisdiction (*Qurʾān* and *sunna*). Only rarely do we find Ibn Tūmart referring to a secondary source of law. Claiming that Truth is one and not multiple, he rejected the legitimacy of legal controversy (*ikhtilāf*) and admitted no plurality of schools. Unlike the extensive multivolume compositions typical of Māliki law, Ibn Tūmart and his followers summarized their legal opinions in small compendia (which together constitute what we now know as "The Book of Ibn Tūmart").[11] These compendia do not list the chains of transmitters, nor do they record the disagreements of scholars. Instead, they endeavor to offer a succinct summary of

[8] See Nagel, *Im Offenkundigne das Verborgene,* 35–44; M. Fierro, "Proto-Mālikis, Mālikis and Reformed Mālikis in al-Andalus," in P. Bearman, R. Peters and F. E. Vogel, eds., *The Islamic School of Law: Evolution, Devolution, and Progress* (Cambridge, Mass., 2005), 57–76.

[9] On the Almohad revolutionary attitude, especially in the domain of Islamic law, see T. Nagel, "La destrucción de la šarīʿa por Muhḥammad b. Tūmart," *Al-Qanṭara* 18 (1997): 295–304; W. Montgomery-Watt, "Philosophy and Theology under the Almohads," *Actas del Primer Congreso de Estudios Arabes e Islámicos*, Córdoba 1962 (Madrid, 1964), 101–7; L. E. Goodman, "Maimonides' Philosophy of Law," *Jewish Law Annual* 1 (1978): 84; Fierro, "The Legal Policies of the Almohad Caliphs," 227–28; idem, "Proto-Mālikīs, Mālikīs and Reformed Mālikīs in al-Andalus," 57–76 and note 116.

[10] ʿAbd al-Wāḥid al-Marrākushī, *al-Muʿjib fī talkhīṣ akhbār al-Maghrīb*, ed. R. Dozy (Leiden, 1881), 275, 270.

[11] Goldziher, in Luciani, *Le Livre de Mohammed Ibn Toumert;* Kennedy, *Muslim Spain and Portugal*, 198.

the relevant rulings, sometimes accompanied by a theological explanation of the law's meaning.

Much of the Almohad legal system remains unclear to us, mainly because of the process of extensive "de-almohadization" that presumably took place after the fall of the dynasty.[12] The radical, revolutionary character of their interpretation of the law (that is to say, the fact that they introduced drastically new practices, and were not satisfied with cleansing and reinstating the traditional ones) is nevertheless well documented.[13]

A striking example of the Almohads' legal innovation is their treatment of religious minorities. Muslim law, according to all its schools, grants the "people of the book" (primarily Jews and Christians) a status of protected minority (*ahl al-dhimma*), which allows them, with certain preconditions, to practice their religion.[14] Yet the Almohads abolished this protected status, and forced Jews and Christians to convert to Islam. Although several explanations were offered for this legal idiosyncrasy it remains, on the whole, unaccounted for.[15] The peculiarity of this ruling is such that several scholars, from various angles, have expressed skeptical views in this regard.[16] The accumulated evidence of the diverse sources, however, leaves no doubt that the rule was indeed applied in all Almohad lands, and in particular in al-Andalus itself.

[12] On the "de-almohadization," see Fricaud, "Les *Ṭalaba* dans la société almohade," 331–32. The almohadization process must not, however, serve to corroborate hypotheses that cannot be substantiated otherwise. See further Stroumsa, "Philosophes almohades? Averroès, Maïmonide et l'idéologie almohade," in Cressier et al., *Los Almohades,* note 10.

[13] As amply demonstrated by Fierro (note 9, above).

[14] On the status of the minorities in Islam, see chap. 1, note 27, above.

[15] See, for example, D. Corcos, "On the Attitude of the Almohad Rulers towards the Jews," *Studies in the History of the Jews in Morocco* (Jerusalem, 1976), 136–60 [Hebrew]; J. F. P. Hopkins, *Medieval Muslim Government in Barbary until the Sixth Century of the Hijra* (London, 1958), 61; J.-P. Molénat, "Sur le rôle des almohades dans la fin du christianisme local au Maghreb et en al-Andalus," *Al-Qanṭara* 18 (1997): 389–41; Fierro, "The Legal Policies of the Almohad Caliphs," 227–28; N. Roth, *Jews, Visigoths and Muslims in Medieval Spain: Cooperation and Conflict* (Leiden, 1994), 113 ff.; A. A. Akasoy, *Philosophie und Mystik in der späten Almohadenzeit: die Sizilanischen Fragen des Ibn Sabʿīn* (Leiden and Boston, 2006), 75–76; Idris, "Les tributaires en occident musulman," 182, #58. The most plausible explanation to date suggests that the Almohads applied to the lands under their power the ruling that in Islamic law pertains only to the Ḥijāz, where no non-Muslims are allowed, thus trying to imitate its sanctity; See Fierro, "Spiritual Alienation and Political Activism: the *Ghurabā'* in al-Andalus during the Sixth–Twelfth Century," *Arabica* 47 (2000): 231; idem, "Revolución y tradición: algunos aspectos del mundo del saber en al-Andalus durante las épocas almorávide y almohade," in M. L. Ávila and M. Fierro, eds., *Biografías almohades*, (Madrid-Granada, 2000), 2:133–34.

[16] See, for instance, Davidson, *Moses Maimonides,* 9–28; M. García-Arenal, "Rapports entre les groupes dans la peninsula ibérique. La conversion des juifs à l'Islam (XIIe–XIIIe)," *RMMM* 63–64 (1992): 91–101.

The persecution of minorities, however, was not uniformly enforced in all Almohad territories and at all times. Whereas in the Iberian peninsula the conversion policy remained strictly enforced throughout Almohad rule, it seems to have relaxed at times in North Africa.[17] While some sources recount that the choice given to certain communities was that of conversion or death, others indicate that the possibility of going into hasty exile, abandoning all property, was also available. Even in this last case, however, the hardship involved was such that many people who owned property opted to feign conversion.[18] The Christian communities of North Africa did not survive these persecutions, and gradually withered, but the Jewish communities managed to weather the storm.[19] Some idea about the way in which they survived can be gained from the description given by the historian al-Marrākushī, who says that during the rule of the Caliph Abū Yūsuf Yaʿqūb al-Manṣūr (r. 1181–1198) the state of *dhimma* was denied to both Jews and Christians, but the authorities suspected the sincerity of the Jewish converts:[20] "Jews in our midst behave outwardly as Muslims: they pray in the mosques, they teach their sons the Qur'ān,

[17]Thus, following the agreements signed in 1186, Pisan merchants were allowed into North African harbors, but only in an emergency were they permitted to take refuge in the harbors of al-Andalus, and then only in Almeria. See D. Abulafia, "Mediterraneans," in Harris, *Rethinking the Mediterranean*, 69, 114 (quoting M. Amari, *I diplomi arabi del R. Archivio Fiorentino* [Florence, 1863], 20); O. R. Constable, *Trade and Traders in Muslim Spain: the Commercial Realignment of the Iberian Peninsula, 900–1500* (Cambridge and New York, 1994), 79.

[18]As the case of Maimonides' student Joseph Ibn Shimʿon clearly indicates. On the identity of this Joseph, to be distinguished from Ibn ʿAqnīn, see Stroumsa, *The Silencing Epistle*, 13–15. Ibn al-Qifṭī was a close friend of Maimonides' student (*pace* Lewis, "Jews and Judaism in Arabic Sources", 178, who relies on Munk; and Bos, *Maimonides on Asthma*, xxix, who quotes Lewis). According to him, "when the Jews and Christians in those countries were forced to choose between embracing Islam or exile, he concealed his religious belief. Then, when the opportunity to travel presented itself, he contrived to leave and go to Egypt, and managed to take his money with him." See IQ, 392. The casual way in which this information is given adds a ring of truth to it. Ibn al-Qifṭī does not elaborate on the hardships of going hastily into exile without any source of livelihood, but Joseph's choice to stay as a false convert clearly did not appear to him as reflecting a "crass motive," but rather as a self-explanatory move for survival. Ibn al-Qifṭī's longer and more explicit remarks on the economic aspect of Maimonides' decision to feign conversion (IQ, 318) must be read in this light, too; cf. Lewis, "Jews and Judaism in Arabic Sources", 173; Davidson, *Moses Maimonides,* 27. On the possible hardships that determine a similar decision in a later period, cf. also Harvey, *Muslims in Spain: 1500–1614*, 48.

[19]On the Christian communities, and on possible explanations for the different resilience of the two religious communities, see Burman, *Religious Polemic*, 191; M. Talbi, "Le christianisme maghrébin de la conquête musulmane à sa disparition: une tentative d'explication," in *Conversion and Continuity: Indigenous Christian Communities in Islamic Lands, Eighth to Eighteenth Centuries*, M. Gervers and R. J. Bikhazi, eds. (Toronto, 1990), 330–31.

[20]It is noteworthy that the Christians are not included in this suspicion.

they behave like our coreligionists and adhere to our tradition; but God alone knows what they hide in their hearts and what they do in their houses."[21]

The persecution of religious minorities contributed to the depiction of the Almohads in modern scholarship as benighted fanatics,[22] what can be described as "fundamentalists" in the pejorative sense sometimes attached to this word today. More recent scholarship revokes this description, underlining the intellectual openness of the Almohads toward the study of philosophy.[23] As I have argued elsewhere, this last depiction is also greatly exaggerated.[24] The goal of the present study, however, is not to evaluate the Almohads, but rather to examine the impact of their thought on Maimonides. In this context, and before approaching the thought of Maimonides himself, it is worth noting a central trait of Almohad revolutionary thought: the primary place of *uṣūl*, a term denoting both the authoritative primary sources of law and the fundamental doctrines of belief. In this sense, one is tempted to see them as "fundamentalists" in the original sense of the word, as coined to describe some trends in late nineteenth-century Christian thought: namely, a militant movement that formulates the foundational doctrines of religion, and regards them as the sole binding "testimony of truth."[25] Unlike modern-day fundamentalists, however, the Almohads did not advocate a literalist interpretation of the Scriptures. This point is worth stressing: several sources indicate that the Ẓāhirī Andalusi scholar Ibn Ḥazm (d. 1026) was respected by the Almohads, and that they were influenced by his literalist thought. In particular, the second Almohad ruler, Abū Yaʿqūb Yūsuf, seems to have had some sympathy with the *Ẓāhirī* school.[26] The Almohads' strict rejection of anthropomorphism, however, precludes seeing them as literalists or scripturalists. We may thus use the term "fundamentalists"—in its original sense—in order to highlight the paramount importance of *uṣūl*

[21] Marrākushī, *Muʿjib*, 435; and see Roth, *Jews, Visigoths and Muslims*, 118; and see note 36, below.

[22] See, for instance, Goldziher, "Introduction," in Luciani, *Le Livre de Mohammed Ibn Toumert*, 1: "Le mouvement almohade qui, en peu de temps, devait répandre la terreur à travers le monde maghrébin," or: "l'ardeur dogmatique d'un pauvre berbère fanatique."

[23] See, for instance, Fierro, "The Legal Policies of the Almohad Caliphs," 239; Fricaud, "Les *Ṭalaba* dans la société almohade"; G. F. Hourani, "Averroes: The Decisive Treatise, Determining what the Connection is between Religion and Philosophy," in Lerner and Mahdi, eds., *Medieval Political Philosophy*, 164; Geoffroy, "L'almohadisme théologique d'Averroès," 9–47.

[24] See Stroumsa, "Philosophes almohades?" 1139–44.

[25] See, for instance, M. Marsden, "Evangelical and Fundamental Christianity," in *The Encyclopedia of Religion*, ed. M. Eliade (New York and London, 1987), 5:190–97, esp. 193, and bibliography there.

[26] See below, *apud* note 115.

in the Almohad system, provided it be understood that the parallelism is not complete.

Maimonides and the Almohads

Maimonides spent almost twenty years of his life—between 1148 and 1165—under the Almohads, and he retained contacts with Jews living under this regime after he had moved out of its reach, to Egypt. According to Muslim sources, Maimonides' family underwent forced conversion, like the rest of the Jewish community.[27] Jewish sources, which attest to the forced conversion of the Jewish communities and lament it, refrain from openly discussing the forced conversion of individuals. This results in a paradoxical situation, where, according to Jewish sources, the Maghrebi community as a whole suffered greatly from *shemad*, or forced conversion, while hardly anyone among its members seems to have converted, even if only outwardly. It would be mistaken, however, to interpret the silence regarding individuals as indicating anything except the decision of the Jewish sources to keep silent. The general feeling must have been that in mass conversion under duress, individuals had no free choice. Conversion under such conditions should not, therefore, be held against a person, and should not be recorded as a blemish on him or on his family. Even in the course of debates and bitter polemics, a decorous hush was preserved regarding this painful part of an ex-convert's biography. Bringing it up must have been considered a dirty campaign that, if used, might boomerang. It is thus no wonder that Jewish sources pass in silence the forced conversion of Maimonides and his family. By the same token, we would be wrong to conclude from this silence that Maimonides did not have to feign conversion to Islam.[28] Indeed, the only exemptions from conversion were grudgingly granted to itinerant Italian merchants, who were allowed entrance to the North African harbors. None of our sources records any other exceptions to the forced conversions, and there is no reason to believe that Maimonides' family alone would have been granted the abolished status of *dhimma*.

The less strict supervision of the converts in North Africa may explain the choice of Maimūn's family to move from al-Andalus to Fez, close

[27] See IQ, 317–19; IAU, 582; M. A. Friedman, *Maimonides, The Yemenite Messiah and Apostasy* (Jerusalem, 2002), 31–37 [Hebrew]; A. Mazor, "Maimonides' Conversion to Islam: New Evidence," *Pe'amim* 110 (2007): 5–8 [Hebrew].

[28] Cf. Davidson (note 16, above).

to the Almohad capital.[29] Even in these more relaxed circumstances, however, young converts were expected to study the Qurʾān.[30] While bright young men were usually expected to join the Almohad cadre of *ṭalaba*, this was probably not the case for Maimonides, in view of the above-mentioned suspicions regarding the sincerity of the conversion of the Jews. With his insatiable intellectual curiosity, however, Maimonides must have decided to make the best of his predicament, and to study whatever his situation as a putative Muslim brought his way. Indeed, Ibn Abī Uṣaybiʿa specifically reports that after his "conversion" Maimonides "memorized the Qurʾān and became engaged in [the study of] Islamic law."[31]

Maimonides never mentions the Almohads by name, but there are quite a few instances where he alludes to their regime and to their persecution of the Jews.[32] He thus compares a forced conversion that occurred in the Yemen to "what the Canaanites (*al-kenaʿani*) have done in the lands of the Maghreb,"[33] and to "the opponent (*al-mukhālif*)" whose appearance in the Maghreb thwarted Messianic hopes.[34] He may even be alluding to his own experience when he quotes, in his "Epistle on Forced Conversion," the verse from Jer. 2:25: "Let our disgrace cover us; for we have sinned against the Lord our God, we and our fathers."[35] Maimo-

[29] As suggested by H. Z. (J. W.) Hirschberg, *A History of the Jews in North Africa* (Leiden, 1979), vol. 1, *From Antiquity to the Sixteenth Century*, 136; Roth, *Jews, Visigoths and Muslims*, 119.

[30] See Marrākushī's evidence (note 21, above).

[31] IAU, 582: "*ḥafiẓa al-qurʾān wa-ʿshtaghala biʾl-fiqh*." Ibn Abī Uṣaybiʿa's source for this was probably Maimonides' only son, who was his colleague at the Nāṣirī hospital; see Lewis, "Jews and Judaism in Arabic Sources," 176. Ibn al-Qifṭī, who must have gotten his information directly from Maimonides' student Joseph, gives similar information in a more nuanced way: "*wa-lammā aẓhara shiʿār al-islām, iltazama bi-juzʾiyyātihi min al-qirāʾa waʾl-ṣalā*." (IQ, 317–19). This indicates Ibn al-Qifṭī's awareness that Maimonides "professed the Muslim credo only outwardly (*aẓhara shiʿār al-islām*), although he behaved as a Muslim and practiced the particular rules of Islam (*iltazama bi-juzʾiyyātihi*) such as reciting [the Qurʾān] and prayer." For a similar use of *juzʾiyyāt* (in the sense of the particulars of the commandments) by Maimonides himself, see *Guide* 3.26 (*Dalāla*, 371:10; Pines, 510).

[32] See the "Epistle on Forced Conversion" (*Iggeret ha-shemad*), *Epistles*, 30 ff. Davidson (*Moses Maimonides*, 509) concludes that "there are very strong . . . grounds for rejecting the authenticity of Maimonides' authorship of the *Epistle*." This conclusion is probably related to Davidson's initial reluctance to accept that Maimonides himself had to feign conversion.

[33] "Epistle to Yemen," *Epistles*, 83. The term "Canaanite" is probably Maimonides' way of alluding to the Berber origin of the Almohads.

[34] "Epistle to Yemen," *Epistles*. 104. In one of the Arabic manuscripts the word *al-mukhālif* is replaced by the hybrid "*al-mored,*" perhaps a veiled allusion to Ibn Tūmart, as suggested by Sheilat, *Epistles,* 150 and note 6.

[35] *Epistles*, 43; Halkin and Hartmann, *Crisis and Leadership*, 22. An explicit reference to his family "having escaped from the forced conversion" (*nitzalnu min ha-shemad*) appears

nides seems to corroborate al-Marrākushī's claim that the Almohads were aware of the insincerity of the Jewish conversion, since he says that "they [the Muslims] know that in no way do we believe in him [the prophet Muhammad]; we only deceive the ruler."[36] In his overview of the intellectual "State of the Nation," he alludes to the Almohad persecution and to its negative effect on the level of learning among the Jews in the Islamic West.[37] This persecution is probably the reason for Maimonides' harsh words about Islam, and his claim that "no other religion was as cruel to us as this religion."[38] Notwithstanding his lasting rancor, however, the acquaintance with the regime under which he lived for more than twenty years, and whose religion he was forced to feign, must have left its mark on his thought. Furthermore, with his alert mind, it is not likely that he could have remained ignorant of the content of their revolution. The existence of such marks must therefore, I submit, be our working hypothesis. In the remainder of this chapter I will try to demonstrate that, if we bear this hypothesis in mind, we can indeed recognize Almohad influence in many of Maimonides' innovations, both on the large scale as also in the details.

Legal Aspects

One can probably identify the echo of Almohad practices in individual rulings of Maimonides. To cite just one example: when Maimonides rules against the enjoyment of musical entertainment, he carefully buttresses the ruling with citations from the Jewish sources. And yet it is hard to read his fierce objection to the use of musical instruments in weddings without being reminded of Ibn Tūmart's display of puritanical zeal in the streets of Almoravid Tlemcen.[39] The following pages will, however, focus on issues of legal methodology.

---

in an autobiographical note attached to the commentary on tractate *Rosh ha-Shana* in ms. Paris BN, héb. 336; see *Epistles*, 224–25; Cohen, Carmiel, "The Correct Meaning of an Autobiographical Note Attributed to Maimondes," *Tarbiz* 76 (2006–2007): 283–87 [Hebrew]

[36] *Epistles*, 41, 43; *Crisis and Leadership*, 20, 30; and see note 21, above.

[37] See chap. 1, note 77, above.

[38] "Epistle to Yemen," *Epistles*, 109, 160. This aspect of Maimonides' attitude to Islam—namely, the polemical tone of a member of a persecuted minority is discussed in B. Lewis, "Maimonides and the Muslims," *Midstream* 25, no.9 (1979): 16–22.

[39] *Epistles*, 426–27; Baydhaq, *Ta'rīkh al-muwaḥḥidīn*, in E. Lévi-Provencal, ed., *Documents inédits d'histoire almohade* (Paris, 1928), 60 (French translation, 95). On Ibn Tūmart's assiduous application of "forbidding wrong," see M. Cook, *Commanding Right and Forbidding Wrong in Islamic Thought* (Cambridge, 2000), 458–59; M. García-Arenal, "La

Maimonides major halachic work, the *Mishneh Torah*, was sharply criticized as soon as it was published. People contested some of its rulings, and criticized Maimonides for neglecting to clarify his position on the resurrection of the dead. The sharpest criticism, however, was leveled against Maimonides' method: his failure to mention his sources for each *halacha*, they said, would result in "having the names of the *Tannaim* and *Amoraim* fall into oblivion"; and his omission of the disagreements between the Sages would make it licit "to neglect the study of the Talmud."[40] Maimonides himself, while vehemently rejecting such criticism, admitted to introducing stark innovations. He repeatedly emphasized the pioneering character of this composition "in which none in our nation had preceded me."

> There were before me Gaonim and great men who composed tracts, in Hebrew or Arabic, to determine the rulings in specific matters. But as for establishing the rulings regarding *all* the Talmud and *all* the laws of the Torah—no one has done this before me, since the days of our Holy Rabbi [i.e. Rabbi Judah "the Prince"] and his holy companions.[41]

In response to his detractors, Maimonides specifically denies the accusation that he intended to demote the study of the Talmud,[42] and offered several explanations for composing the *Code* in this form. He says that he meant the *Code* to serve only as a digest for those who cannot fathom the Talmudic discussion;[43] he also says that he omitted the names of individual scholars in order to stress the universal agreement on final rulings, so as to counterbalance Karaite claims that it is the fruit of individual whims.[44] He even mentions his wish to prepare an *aide-mémoire* for his old age.[45] There can be no doubt, however, that these were only excuses (and some of them, rather feeble excuses at that). As Maimonides himself forcefully and repeatedly declares, the composition of the *Code* was a calculated decision on his part to assemble disparate rulings and to present them in a finite form "succinctly and clearly, so that all the Oral

práctica del precepto *de al-amr bi-l-maʿrūf wa-l-nahy ʿan al-munkar en la hagiografía magrhebí*," *Al-Qanṭara* 13 (1992): 156; idem, *Messianism and Puritanical Reform*, 176.

[40] "Epistle to Rabbi Phinehas the Judge," *Epistles*, 439. On Rabbi Phinehas ben Meshullam, the judge of Alexandria, and on this epistle, see I. Twersky, *Introduction to the Code of Maimonides* (*Mishneh Torah*) (New Haven and London, 1980), 30–37.

[41] "Epistle to Rabbi Phinehas," 439–40 (emphasis added).

[42] Ibid., 439; Twersky, *Introduction to the Code*, 37.

[43] "Epistle to Rabbi Phinehas," *Epistles*, 439.

[44] Ibid., *Epistles*, 4. On the anti-Karaite polemical element in the *Mishneh Torah*, see Soloveitchik, "*Mishneh Torah*: Polemic and Art," 329–32.

[45] "Letter to Joseph Ibn Shimʿon," *Epistles*, 293, 330–31; and see Twersky, *Introduction to the Code*, 42.

Law will be easily accessible to all."[46] The terms in which Maimonides chooses to present his decision to compose this book are indicative of the importance he granted it and of his own sense of prophetic mission: "For I—by God—*I have been very zealous to the Lord, the God* of Israel, as I saw a nation devoid of a [legal] compendium (*dīwān*), devoid of correct, well-organized opinions (*arāʾ*)."[47] In his correspondence with his disciple Joseph Ibn Shimʿon, Maimonides repeatedly emphasized the value of studying the *Code*. He presented this book as destined to correct something that, as a result of the Talmudic method of study, went sorely wrong in the course of the previous generations:

> I urge you not to neglect the study of this book until you apprehend all of it. Make it your own book; teach it everywhere to disseminate its usefulness. For the purpose intended in composing the Talmud was lost and has vanished. The purpose of the erudite [today] is to waste time in Talmudic discussions, as if the purpose and intention was solely to exercise polemical skills. This, however, was not the first intention:[48] discussions and polemics occurred only accidentally. . . . Therefore I was moved to [recall] the first purpose, to facilitate the task of remembering it, and furthermore: to make it known, for it had been lost among all the polemical words.[49]

Maimonides' declared aim in this book was to replace the written Oral Law, that is to say, the *Mishnah* and theTalmud (while reaffirming their authority), and to make it possible to dispense with the later legal literature, a body of texts that had accumulated over the ages. Maimonides' explicit declaration refers only to Talmudic and post-Talmudic literature. In fact, however, as the name "*Mishneh Torah*" (lit., "re-iteration of the Torah," but also "second to the Torah") reveals, and as the introduction to the book openly states, Maimonides intended this book to make the whole body of written Oral Law redundant, "so that a person may first read the written Torah, then read this book and know through it the

[46] "Introduction to the *Code*," *Mishneh Torah*, 3.

[47] "Epistle to Joseph Ibn Shimʿon," *Epistles*, 293, 330–31 (note the allusion to I Kings 19:10, 14, where the prophet Elijah recounts his solitary, uncompromising war against idolatry and bemoans his ensuing isolation). A similar sense of mission is reflected in Maimonides' "Introduction to the *Code*": "Therefore I braced myself . . . and relied on the Holy, may He be blessed."

[48] *Al-qaṣd al-awwal*; On first intention, in Maimonides' thought, see chap. 4, note 58, below.

[49] "Epistle to Joseph Ibn Shimʿon," 256–59. A similar evaluation of Talmudic learning as necessary but insufficient is expressed in *Guide* 1.51 (*Dalāla*, 455; Pines, 619); See chap. 6, below.

whole oral Torah, requiring no book between them."[50] In the introduction to his *Book of Precepts*, Maimonides spelled out his methodology in the *Mishneh Torah*:

> I saw fit to prepare also a composition that includes all the laws and precepts of the Torah . . . and to proceed as I am wont to do, namely: to avoid mentioning disagreements (*ikhtilāfāt*) and positions that were rejected, and to list only finite rulings . . . And I also opt for omitting the justifications and arguments in support of each ruling, and the names of transmitters.[51]

Maimonides also declares his intention to go back to the primary sources of legislation (*uṣūl*) and to avoid casuistics (*furūʿ*) as much as possible, and he gives precedence to rulings that rely on earlier sources (*de'orayta*) over those presented as relying on later interpretation (*de-rabbanan*).[52] He uses the term *uṣūl* also to denote the guiding principles of legislation,[53] and when speaking of the *Mishneh Torah*, he says: "We also mentioned in it all the religious and legal principles (*uṣūl*), intending all those who are called "Disciples of the Sages," or "Sages," or "Gaonim," or however you wish to call them, to establish their derivative legal ruling (*furūʿ*) on legal principles (*uṣūl fiqhiyya*)."[54] Maimonides' scathing criticism of contemporary Talmudic scholarship, and his analysis of the state of Jewish learning, provides the inner Jewish background for his realization of the need to break new ground in legal scholarship. The explanation for the particular path he chose, however, must be sought outside of the Jewish

[50] See also Maimonides' *Book of Commandments*; *Sefer ha-Mitzvot*, 2–3; *Maimonides: The Commandments*, trans. C. Chavel (London, 1967).

[51] *Sefer ha-Mitzvot*, 1–2.

[52] See, for instance, *Sefer ha-Mitzvot*, 1–29. On Maimonides' "obsessive" preoccupation with the relative rank of legal sources, see G. J. Blidstein, "Where Do We Stand in the Study of Maimonidean Halakhah?," in I. Twersky, ed., *Studies in Maimonides* (Cambridge, Mass., 1990), 13; M. Halbertal, "*Sefer Ha-Mizvot* of Maimonides—His Architecture of *Halakha* and Theory of Interpretation," *Tarbiz* 59 (1990), 462–68 [Hebrew]; J. S. Levinger, *Maimonides as Philosopher and Codifier* (Jerusalem, 1989), 56–66 [Hebrew].

[53] See *Sefer ha-Mitzvot*, 23–24, where the fourteen guiding principles of the division of commandments are called *uṣūl*.

[54] *Treatise on Resurrection*, 4; *Epistles*, 320–21, 342–43; and see I. Twersky, "The Mishneh Torah of Maimonides," *Proceedings of the Israel Academy of Sciences and Humanities* 5 (1976): 265–95. On the meaning of *fiqh* in Maimonides' writings, see M. Schwarz, "*Al-fiqh*, a Term Borrowed from Islam Used by Maimonides for a Jewish Concept in his *Sefer ha-Mitzwoth* and in *The Guide of the Perplexed*," in Y. Tzvi Langermann and J. Stern, eds., *Adaptations and Innovations: Studies on the Interaction between Jewish and Islamic Thought and Literature from the Early Middle Ages to the Late Twentieth Century, Dedicated to Professor Joel L. Kraemer* (Paris-Louvain-Dudley, 2007), 349–53.

tradition.[55] This is indicated by Maimonides himself: although he evokes the precedent of Rabbi Judah the Prince, the redactor of the *Mishnah*, he is, as mentioned above, proudly conscious of his own innovation. The example of Judah the Prince serves to legitimize the daring move to innovate, but it does not provide the model for the specific character of the innovation.

Maimonides' claim for innovation is accepted by modern scholarship, which also discusses possible models of inspiration for his move. Lenn Goodman has observed that "there is something artificial (that is to say, not authentically Jewish) in Maimonides' way of action" and in particular, in his legal syllogism, which Goodman sees in Aristotelian terms.[56] Isadore Twersky, in his masterful study of the *Mishneh Torah*, explained Maimonides' decision to compose such a book mainly as motivated by his awareness that there was a lacuna to be filled. Twersky, however, offered no suggestion as to Maimonides' source of inspiration.[57] Twersky noted the possibility of an Islamic influence, since "books of law were used in the Islamic world," but he dismissed this possibility as marginal, arguing that "the main motive . . . derives from independent legal-literary requirements."[58] A similar reluctance to seriously examine Islamic influence can be detected in the analysis offered by Gerald Blidstein. Blidstein takes for granted the impact of Muslim society on Maimonides' thought, but treats it as "a delicate issue," first and foremost due to what he regards as our limited knowledge of the extent of Maimonides' involvement in the wider Muslim culture. Blidstein therefore insists (no doubt correctly) on the fact that Maimonides continued the Gaonic legal tradition, and more precisely the North African Andalusian Gaonic tradition.[59]

Quite contrary to this cautious scholarly stand, however, we do know the extent of Maimonides' involvement in the wider Islamic culture. We know that, as far as science and learning are concerned, he was deeply immersed in this culture, and did his best to remain abreast of the developments that occurred in it. The reluctance to adcknowledge his familiarity with Muslim law is therefore puzzling, particularly since there is no evidence for such reluctance on Maimonides' part.

Indeed, other leading contemporary scholars accept the assumption that Muslim law, as part of Islamic culture, was also part of Maimonides'

[55] Although earlier Gaonic legal compendia may have helped Maimonides to justify his move, they do not provide a model for his ambitious comprehensive composition. Cf. Davidson, *Moses Maimonides,* 201–2.

[56] Goodman, "Maimonides' Philosophy of Law," 91.

[57] Twersky, *Introduction to the Code of Maimonides*, 3; idem, "The Mishneh Torah of Maimonides," 265–95.

[58] Twersky, "The Mishneh Torah of Maimonides," 289.

[59] Blidstein, "Where Do We Stand in the Study of Maimonidean Halakhah?" 28.

world. Joel Kraemer has forcefully argued for a substantial influence of Muslim law (*fiqh*) on Maimonides. Kraemer's claim is based on the examination of a wide body of Muslim legal texts, from the East and West of the Islamic world.[60] A similar argument has been made by Gideon Libson, who has noted parallels to Maimonides' legal terminology and rulings in the writings of all Muslim legal schools: Shafiʿites in particular, but also Ḥanafites, and even Mālikites.[61]

Blidstein is undoubtedly right in arguing that Gaonic literature in general and the North-African Gaonic tradition in particular formed the basis for Maimonides' legal thought. To the extent that this Gaonic tradition, in Judaeo-Arabic as well as in Hebrew, was influenced by contemporary Muslim thought, dating from the formative period of Islamic law, this, too, fed into Maimonides's thought, and one should not be surprised to detect in his writings parallels and similarities to it. These early contacts in the formative period do not, however, exclude the possibility, indeed the probability, of continuous influences, resulting from the contacts of Jews with their contemporary Muslim neighbors. We must therefore keep our ears cocked for echoes of Maimonides' immediate Muslim environment in his legal rulings.

One particularly telling example of such an echo, which has hitherto remained unnoticed, can be seen in Maimonides' decree in a case of matrimonial discord. A man complained that his wife, having raised a very large family, refused to sleep with him, an accusation that the wife denied. Maimonides ruled that reliable persons (*qawm mawthūqūn*), who can deduce from the couple's behavior what the situation really is, should move in with the couple. These persons would then be able to determine whether the wife is guilty of neglecting her marital obligations, in which case she could be divorced without her *mu'akhkhar*.[62] This ruling, which has no precedence in Jewish law, seems to reflect a peculiar interpretation of Māliki law, which was typically practiced in al-Andalus.[63] According to this practice, couples with marital problems were either sent to the house of a trustworthy person (*dār amīn*), or the *amīn* was lodged

[60] J. Kraemer, "The Influence of Islamic Law on Maimonides: The Case of the Five Qualifications," *Teʿudah* 10 (1996): 225–44 [Hebrew].

[61] G. Libson, "Interaction between Islamic Law and Jewish Law during the Middle Ages," in E. I. Cuomo, ed., *Law in Multicultural Societies: Proceedings of the International Association of Law Libraries (Jerusalem, July 21–26, 1985)* (Jerusalem, 1989), 96, 98.

[62] *Responsa*, 40–41. On the *mu'akhkhar*—the late installation of the wedding gift—see chap. 4, note 142, below.

[63] See M. Fierro, "Ill-Treated Women Seeking Divorce: The Qur'ānic Two Arbiters and Judicial Practice Among the Malikis in al-Andalus and North Africa," in M. Kh. Masud, R. Peters, and D. Powers, eds., *Dispensing Justice in Islam: Qadis and their Judgement* (Leiden and Boston, 2006), 323–47, esp. 331–35.

in the couple's house. The *amīn*'s role was to determine the source of estrangement, attempt to reconcile the spouses, and, in case of divorce, determine whether or not the divorce should include monetary penalty to the wife. This judicial practice, which was also known in Almoravid Cordoba, is probably the source for Maimonides' ingenious ruling.

The Arabic terminology employed by Maimonides in the passages quoted above, however, highlights the affinity of his legal method with another contemporary source, the legal thought of the Almohads. It appears that in his decision to compose a relatively short compendium of law, as well as in the principles that guided him in this composition (namely, going back to the *uṣūl*, presenting a final ruling, and dispensing with the scaffoldings that traditionally accompanied it), Maimonides was closely following the Almohad example. It should not come as a surprise that, when deciding to revolutionize Jewish legal compositions, Maimonides borrowed the model used by his persecutors. In this, as in other things, he was true to his dictum: to look for the truth, *whoever* may have said it.[64]

It is interesting to compare Maimonides' legal work with that of his contemporary, the Muslim philosopher and jurist, Abū'l-Walīd Ibn Rushd, known in the Latin West as Averroes. Although Maimonides and Averroes probably never met, the similarities in their biographies and intellectual careers justify their consideration as kindred spirits, who, in some ways, lived parallel lives.[65] Indeed, statements that associate Maimonides with Averroes are quite common in contemporary scholarship.[66] Such statements stem, first of all, from the philosophical heritage of the European Middle Ages. Jewish medieval thinkers regarded these two authors as the two main philosophic authorities and grouped them together, and Christian thinkers such as Meister Eckhart or Albert the Great quoted and debated both Averroes's *Commentaries* and Maimonides' *Guide*.[67] Besides the medieval philosophical tradition, however, modern

[64] See, chap. 1, above, *apud* note 42.

[65] See also chap. 5, below, *apud* note 23.

[66] See, for instance, Joseph. A. Bujis, ed., "Introduction," in *Maimonides: A Collection of Critical Essays* (Notre Dame, 1988), 2; and, in the same volume, A. Hymann, "Interpreting Maimonides," 20; Menocal, *The Ornament of the World*, 208. The temptation to connect these two luminaries is reflected in fiction as well as in scholarship; see, for instance, the imaginary (Hebrew) correspondence between them in I. Gorlizki, *The Latent Secret—Maimonides and his Friend Ibn Rushd* (Tel-Aviv, 2002) [Hebrew]; French translation: *Maïmonide-Ibn Rushd, Une correspondance rêvée* (Paris, 2004).

[67] See, for instance, C. Rigo, "Zur Rezeption des Moses Maimonides im Werk des Albertus Magnus," in W. Senner et al., ed., *Albertus Magnus zum Gedenken nach 800 Jahren: Neue Zugänge, Aspekte und Perspektiven* (Berlin, 2001), 29–66; and, in the same volume, E.-H. Wéber, "Un thème de la philosophie arabe interpreté par Albert le Grand," 79–90; A. Bertolacci, "The Reception of Avicenna's 'Philosophia Prima' in Albert the Great's

attempts to associate the two thinkers also reflect the fact that there are indeed some striking biographical similarities between them: two philosophers, both Andalusians and both of them physicians, both deeply immersed in reflection upon their respective religions and involved in the practice of their law. There are also remarkable similarities in their legal method: like Maimonides' *Mishneh Torah*, Averroes' *Bidāyat al-mujtahid* ignores the fine points of the legal discussions, attempts to transcend the traditional division into legal schools, and disregards the large body of accumulated casuistic literature.[68] Unlike Maimonides, however, Averroes does not offer a substitute for the dethroned corpus. Instead, he lays out the principles of how to get directly to the texts and do the legal work (*ijtihād*). In this approach Averroes follows, on the one hand, Ibn Tūmart's rejection of the *furū*ʿ; at the same time, he also contradicts Ibn Tūmart, by using *ijtihād* and by referring to *ikhtilāf*.[69] Like Averroes, Maimonides assumes in the *Mishneh Torah* the responsibility of making a personal decision (*ijtihād*), a daring act that was not received favorably by his peers. In their original legal works, both Averroes and Maimonides adopt the Almohad approach, which regarded the preoccupation with casuistry as both wasteful and false, and which required a return to the primary sources of the law. In their respective legal writings, both authors are thus, in different ways, Almohads. Maimonides, however, seems to be more receptive of Almohad thinking than Averroes.

The affinity of Maimonides' legal thinking with that of the Almohads is not restricted to terminology and method; it is also evident in their respective definition of the parameters of jurisdiction. For Maimonides as for the Almohads, religious indoctrination was a legitimate concern of the jurist. Maimonides therefore included in the *Code* thirteen principles (*qawāʿid*) of faith, the belief in which is a precondition for belonging to

---

Commentary on the 'Metaphysics': The Case of the Doctrine of Unity," 67–78; and see Y. Schwartz, "Meister Eckharts Schriftauslegung als maiminodisches Projekt," in G. Hasselhoff and O. Fraisse, *Moses Maimonides (1138–2004): His Religious, Scientific and Philosophical Wirkungsgeschichte in Different Cultural Contexts* (Würzburg, 2004), 173–208. On Maimonides' reception in the Latin West, see also G. Dahan, "Maïmonide dans les controverses universitaires du XIIIe siècle," *Maïmonide: philosophe et savant*, 367–93, esp. 369; W. Kluxen, "Maïmonide et l'orientation philosophique de ses lecteurs latins," *Maïmonide: philosophe et savant* 395–409; G. K. Hasselhoff, *Dicit Rabbi Moyses: Studien zum Bild von Moses Maimonides im lateinischen Western vom 13. bis zum 15. Jahrhundert* (Würzburg, 2004); Kraemer, "Moses Maimonides: An Intellectual Portrait," 14–15.

68 See Ibn Rushd, *Bidāyat al-mujtahid wa-nihāyat al-muqtaṣid* (Cairo, n.d); Ibn Rushd, *The Distinguished Jurist's Primer—Bidāyat al-Mujtahid wa Nihāyat al-Muqtaṣid*, trans. Imran Ahsan Khan Nyazee (Reading, 2000).

69 See Fierro, "The Legal Policies of the Almohad Caliphs," esp. 244.

the Jewish people.[70] Furthermore, he chose to begin his *Code of Law* with a chapter of theological, philosophical, and even scientific catechism, the *Book of Knowledge*.[71] In some ways, this decision is probably related to the structure of theological (*kalām*) works, which begin with epistemology. But unlike most of these epistemological chapters, the *Book of Knowledge* is about content: what we know (and not just how we know it), what we must believe in. A parallel structure can be found in Ghazālī's *Iḥyā' 'ulūm al-dīn*. As noted above, Maimonides was obviously familiar with Ghazālī's works, although he never quotes him by name.[72] More specifically, Steven Harvey has shown the close similarity between Ghazālī's *Book of Knowledge* and Maimonides' own book bearing the same title, and it is indeed quite possible that Maimonides was familiar with this particular part of Ghazālī's magnum opus.[73] One should note, however, the essential difference in the overall structure into which the two Books of Knowledge are integrated. Although the *Iḥyā'* contains matters of religious law, it is not a legal codex, as the *Mishneh Torah* is.

An oft-repeated anecdote stages a meeting between Ibn Tūmart and Ghazālī, and depicts the former as a disciple of the latter.[74] Although this tradition is probably spurious, Ibn Tūmart was deeply influenced by Ghazālī, and Ghazālī's influence on the Almohads was considerable.[75] Like Ghazālī, Ibn Tūmart, too, opens his book with a *Book of Knowledge*.[76] Unlike the *Iḥyā'*, the *Book of Ibn Tūmart* includes manuals for everyday law, and can thus be said to offer a closer parallel to the *Mishneh*

[70] *Commentary on the Mishnah, Neziqin*, Tractate *Sanhedrin*, "Introduction," in *Pereq Ḥeleq*, 211.

[71] See the translation of H. M. Russell and Rabbi J. Weinberg, *The Book of Knowledge from the Mishneh Torah of Maimonides* (New York, 1983).

[72] See chap. 2, note 6, above.

[73] S. Harvey, "Alghazali and Maimonides and their Books of Knowledge," in J. M. Harris, ed., *Be'erot Yitzhak: Studies in Memory of Isadore Twersky* (Cambridge, Mass., 2005), 99–117. See also F. Rosenthal, *Knowledge Triumphant: The Concept of Knowledge in Medieval Islam*. (Leiden, 1970), 96.

[74] See M. Fletcher, "Ibn Tūmart's teachers: The Relationship with al-Ghazālī," *Al-Qanṭara* 18 (1997): 305–30; F. Griffel, "Ibn Tūmart's Rational Proof for God's Existence and Unity, and His Connection to the Niẓāmiyya *Madrasa* in Baghdad," in Cressier et al., eds., *Los Almohades*, esp. 753–56.

[75] See Goldziher, "Introduction," in Luciani, *Le Livre de Mohammed Ibn Toumert*, 2ff.; M. al-Manūnī, "*Iḥyā' 'ulūm al-dīn fi manẓūr al-gharb al-islāmī ayyām al-murābiṭin wa'l-muwaḥḥidin*," in *Abū Ḥāmid al-Gazālī, Dirāsāt fi fikrihi wa-'aṣrihi wa-ta'thīrihi* (Rabat, 1988), 125–37.

[76] Another possible model for Ibn Tūmart's "Book of Knowledge" could have been Ibn Ḥazm's *Al-Muḥallā fī'l-āthār*, which begins with a dogmatical exposition, titled *Kitāb al-tawḥīd*.

Torah. In other words, it seems plausible that in this case Ghazālī's influence reached Maimonides through the Almohad prism.

Like Ibn Tūmart and Ghazālī, Maimonides defines "belief" as knowledge. According to him "there is no belief except after a representation; belief is the affirmation that what has been represented is outside the mind just as it has been represented in the mind."[77] Belief is defined here as identical to correct knowledge, both conceptual ("representation" or *taṣawwur*) and affirmative (*taṣdīq*). One should also note that Maimonides opens his *Book of Knowledge* with *Laws of the Foundations of the Torah*. The Foundations are the scientific and theological basics, necessary for laying the ground for correct belief. Maimonides' Hebrew title, *Yesodei ha-Torah* (which is a Hebrew neologism), most probably renders the Arabic *uṣūl al-dīn*. His decision to incorporate these foundations, as an opening chapter, in his *Code of Law* obviously reflects the Almohad conception of faith as definable by jurisdiction and subject to juristic ruling.

Theology

The most obvious case of influence of Almohad indoctrination can be seen in Maimonides' evaluation of anthropomorphism as incompatible with monotheism. Among Muslims, the Almohads were not unique in their objection to anthropomorphism, but, as mentioned above, they made this objection into their distinctive hallmark, by declaring it an article of faith that separates the believer from the heretic. Similarly, Maimonides was not the first Jewish thinker to reject anthropomorphism, but none of his predecessors had defined this so clearly as an article of faith, incumbent on all levels of society. In *The Guide of the Perplexed* Maimonides says:

> The negation of the doctrine of the corporeality of God and the denial of His having a likeness to created things and of His being subject to affections are matters that ought to be made clear and ex-

[77] *Guide*, 1.50 (*Dalāla*, 75; Pines, 110): *Lā i'tiqād illā ba'da taṣawwur, li-anna al-i'tiqād huwa al-taṣdīq bi-mā taṣawwara annahu khārij al-dhihn 'alā mā taṣawwara fī'l-dhihn.*; cf. *Al-kalām 'alā al-'ibāda*, in Luciani, *Le Livre de Mohammed Ibn Toumert*, 221; Abū Ḥāmid al-Ghazāli, *Iḥyā' 'ulūm al-dīn* (Beirut, 1994), *Kitāb qawā'd al-'aqā'id*, 150–54, esp. 154: "*al-īmān 'ibāra 'an al-taṣdīq*." Notwithstanding Maimonides' definition of belief, however, he also distinguishes between belief (*i'tiqād*)—the opposite of which is heresy *(kufr)*—and knowledge (*'ilm*) supported by a demonstrated proof (*burhān*), the opposite of which is ignorance (*juhl*). See *Guide*, 1.36 (*Dalāla*, 56:15–16; Pines, 83); and *Guide*, 1.35 (*Dalāla*, 57:23; Pines, 85): "I do not consider as an infidel one who cannot demonstrate that the corporeality of God should be negated. But I do consider as an infidel one who does not believe in its negation." See also chap. 6, below, *apud* note 103.

plained to everyone according to his capacity, and ought to be inculcated in virtue of traditional authority upon children, women, stupid ones, and those of defective natural disposition, just as they adopt the notion that God is one.[78]

Maimonides, just like the Almohads, identified true monotheism with a noncorporeal perception of God. Although he states unambiguously that this understanding should be instructed to all, regardless of their intellectual capacity, one could argue that the *Guide* is a philosophical book, accessible only to the elite. Maimonides, however, also included this opinion among the thirteen principles, the belief in which are preconditions for belonging to the Jewish people. Here, too, the Almohad catechism, the *ʿaqīda*, must have served as an important model for Maimonides.[79]

It is interesting to observe the development of Maimonides' position in this respect, and to follow its hardening. In his *Commentary on the Mishnah* he mentions the special rank of Moses' prophecy, and dwells briefly on God's saying [Num. 12:8]: "With him I speak mouth to mouth." This verse, says Maimonides, calls for an explanation, but the explanation requires a lengthy discussion of subtle matters, which he promises to offer elsewhere, in a separate work (which he never wrote). His list of "subtle matters" includes the angels and the soul, as well as the forms that the prophets attribute to God and to His angels. In an early version of this text Maimonides said that the issue to be discussed "includes also the measurement of [the divine] stature and its meaning" (*wa-yandariju fī dhālika* ***shiʿur qoma*** *wa-maʿnāhu*). This statement, which does not appear in Maimonides' later recension of the same text, is usually understood as alluding to the book called *Shiʿur Qoma*—a mystical, exegetical elaboration on the anthropomorphic descriptions of God. It is further assumed that the allusion discloses his belief at that stage of his life that this book was an authentic composition by the Sages, or a later composition of some value, a belief that he later abandoned.[80]

One should first note that Maimonides does not mention the book at all, but only the imagery referring to the divine measurement. Nevertheless, he probably associated the Hebrew words *shiʿur qoma* with the book, as he knew his readers would. There is, however, nothing in his

[78] *Guide*, 1.35 (*Dalāla*, 54–55; Pines, 81).

[79] As suggested already by Heinemann, "Maimuni und die arabischen Einheitslehrer," and S. Pines, "A Lecture on *The Guide of the Perplexed*," *Iyyun* 47 (1998): 116 [Hebrew].

[80] See J. Qafiḥ note to the *Commentary on the Mishnah*, "Introduction," in *Pereq Heleq*, note 42 on 213; and see, for instance, S. Lieberman, Appendix D [Hebrew] to G. Scholem, *Jewish Gnosticism, Merkabah Mysticism and Talmudic Tradition* (New York, 1965), 124; Shelat, *Epistles*, 578 and note 3; Twersky, *Introduction to the Code*, 54 and note 84, and note 39 on 369.

words to suggest that he accepted the book as an authentic, authoritative work, or that he condoned the book's anthropomorphism. Quite on the contrary, he promises to devote a book to explain the Bible's imagery as precisely that: imagery. The suggestion that he saw any value in a book that developed, on the basis of biblical verses, an anthropomorphic perception of God is no more likely than to say that he accepted, at any stage of his life, a literal understanding of the verse mentioning God's mouth.[81]

Nevertheless, Maimonides obviously did change his mind: not in the attitude to the book, but in the policy toward discussing it. As a general rule, Maimonides tries to avoid criticizing the Sages, lest such criticism be interpreted as challenging Rabbinic authority. Therefore, although he is far from espousing the book's content, he also does not criticize it openly.[82] One may assume that, when first composing the *Mishneh Torah*, he intended to tread gently, and to prepare the ground for a later discussion of *shiʿur qoma*. As he never wrote the planned books on *midrash* and on prophetic language, this promised discussion never materialized. At some point later, however, a question addressed to him highlighted the popularity of the book, as well as its reputation as dealing with "formidable issues, pertaining to physics or to theology." At this point Maimonides saw the danger of this book, whose topic he identified as specifically anthropomorphic, as more pressing. He may also have realized that his soft-spoken, vague words could have been misinterpreted. He therefore implicitly refers to this previous position, and explains it, saying:

> I have never thought that this is a composition of the Sages . . . ; God forbid that this would be one of their compositions! This [book] is nothing but a composition of one of the Christian preachers (*aḥad **ha-darshanīn** al-rūm*). The bottom line is that it is a great virtue to destroy this book and to wipe out its memory. [For it is written:] "And make no mention of the name of other gods" [Ex. 23:13]—and whoever has a bodily stature is undoubtedly an other god."[83]

And indeed, Maimonides followed his own ruling, removing any reference to the book from his *Commentary of the Mishnah*.[84]

[81] Num. 12:8 is explained in the *Mishneh Torah*, the Foundations of the Law (*Yesodei ha-Torah*), 7:6

[82] See chap. 4, below.

[83] *Responsa*, 200–201; *Epistles*, 578.

[84] See Shelat, *Epistles*, 578n3.

Exegesis and Political Theory

The extent to which Maimonides internalized the Almohad doctrine can be best appreciated if we compare him to his contemporary Averroes. It is usually assumed that Maimonides was not influenced by Averroes' *Faṣl al-Maqāl* (*Decisive Treatise*).[85] Both Shlomo Pines and Alfred Ivry discuss, and discard, the possibility that Maimonides had read Averroes's independent writings—that is to say, the philosophical works other than the *Commentaries*—before writing the *Guide*.[86] Pines argues that "no clear evidence" can be adduced for such a possibility. Contrary to this view, there are enough indications that Maimonides did read Averroes's theological works, both the *Decisive Treatise* and the *Exposition of the Traditions of Proofs Regarding Muslim Beliefs* (*al-Kashf ʿan manāhij al-adilla*).[87] In fact, the *Guide* can in some ways be seen as a reaction and answer to Averroes.[88] A striking example of this reaction can be seen in *Guide* 2.25, where Maimonides incorporates in his discussion a Qur'ānic verse employed by Averroes.[89] This is not the only occasion where the two thinkers discuss similar concerns in very similar terms, but whereas other cases may be explained in different way, the remarkable presence of this particular Qur'ānic verse in the *Guide* would seem to clinch the case for Maimonides' direct familiarity with the *Faṣl al-Maqāl*. The same chapter of the *Guide* (2.25) also reflects Maimonides' basic hermeneutical disagreement with Averroes. As Averroes argues throughout the *Kashf*, the intention of the lawgiver was to spread, as widely as possible, the best beliefs to be accepted by all and sundry. This means that the lawgiver must have looked for the lowest common denominator that everyone can understand. This common denominator, says Averroes, is, more often

[85] See Ibn Rushd, *Faṣl al-maqāl wa-taqrīr mā bayna al-sharīʿa wa'l-ḥikma min al-ittiṣāl*, ed. A. Nader (Beirut, 1973); Averroes, *The Book of the Decisive Treatise Determining the Connection between the Law and Wisdom; &, Epistle dedicatory*, ed. and trans. C. E. Butterworth (Provo, Utah, 2001); and see A. de Libera "Introduction," in Averroès, *Discours décisif*, trans. M. Geoffroy (Paris, 1996), 76.

[86] See Ivry, "Maimonides' Relation to the Teachings of Averroes," 62; Pines, "Translator's Introduction," cviii.

[87] See *al-Kashf ʿan manāhij al-adilla fī ʿaqāʾid al-milla*, ed. M. ʿA. al-Jābirī (Beirut, 1998).

[88] Ivry ("Maimonides' Relation to the Teachings of Averroes," 71) points out the differences between their respective opinions and audiences. He underlines Maimonides' frequent recourse to an allegorical reading of biblical verses, as opposed to Averroes's reluctance to use allegorical Qurʾānic interpretation. This precise difference seems to me to be part of Maimonides' response to Averroes.

[89] The use of this verse (Q. 59 [*al-ḥashar*]:2) was identified and analyzed by Zev Harvey; see W. Z. Harvey, "Averroes and Maimonides on the Duty of Philosophical Contemplation (*iʿtibār*)," *Tarbiẓ* 58 (1989): 75–83 [Hebrew]; and see Stroumsa, "The Literary Corpus," 234–37.

than not, the exoteric teaching, which reflects the lowest level of understanding. Averroes frequently uses the expression "the intention of the Lawgiver."[90] Therefore, when Maimonides says in *Guide* 2.25 that the interpretation of anthropomorphic verses in the Bible does not contradict the text, but is in fact "the intention of the text" (*qaṣd al-naṣṣ*) he may well be responding to Averroes' line of argument in the *Kashf,* according to which the literal, anthropomorphic level of understanding of Qurʾānic verses is "the intention of the Law."[91]

In other cases, the dialogue nearly slips into an argument. One example may suffice: in summing up his position regarding the need to interpret the sacred text, Averroes identifies several categories of texts that are in fact parables. The fourth and last category includes texts that are difficult to perceive as being parables. Once this fact is disclosed, however, the intention of the parables is almost evident.[92] Such a disclosure is exactly what Maimonides promises to do in the *Guide*: In some matters, Maimonides says, "it will suffice you to gather from my remarks that a given story is a parable (*mathal*) . . . for once you know it is a parable, it will become clear to you what it is a parable of."[93] Such a decision would clearly have been frowned upon by Averroes. Averroes expresses the fear that the disclosure of the parabolic nature of the text may engender "strange beliefs, far from the exoteric teaching of the law; these teachings may become widespread, and the multitudes may disclaim them."[94] It is thus as a response to Averroes's concerns that one can read Maimonides' defiant conclusion of his "Instruction" (*waṣiyya*) to the reader of the *Guide*:

> To sum up: I am the man who, when the concern pressed him and his way was straitened and he could find no other device by which to teach a demonstrated truth other than by giving satisfaction to a single virtuous man while displeasing ten thousand ignoramuses—I

[90] *Maqṣad al-shāriʿ* or *mā qaṣada al-sharʿ*. See, for instance, *Kashf*, 99–100.

[91] Zev Harvey has noted that the expression "*qaṣd al-naṣṣ*," which appears in *Guide* 2.25 (*Dalāla*, 328), does not appear in the *Faṣl*; See W. Z. Harvey, "On Maimonides' Allegorical Readings of Scripture," in J. Whitman, ed., *Interpretation and Allegory: Antiquity to the Modern Period* (Leiden-Boston-Köln, 2000), 182. In the *Kashf*, however, as noted above (note 90), a similar expression does appear. This strengthens Harvey's suggestion that Maimonides was influenced by Averroes in his formulation of *Guide* 2.25. The influence, however, reflects Maimonides' acquaintance with the whole of Averroes's theological complex, and not only with the *Faṣl*.

[92] See *Kashf*, 207–8. The *mithāl*, translated here as "parable," need not necessarily have all the literary features of the genre of parables. Its main characteristic in this context is that it cannot be understood literally, and that its true understanding calls for *ta'wīl*.

[93] "Introduction," in *Guide* (*Dalāla*, 9:22-25; Pines, 14).

[94] *Kashf*, 208.

am he who prefers to address that single man by himself, and I do not heed the blame of those many creatures.[95]

The difference between the *Kashf* and the *Guide* is partly due to the different audiences for which they are intended (as well as to the different place of these books in the literary corpus of the two authors). Maimonides directs his work to people with some philosophical training, whereas the *Kashf* is directed to a larger public. The closing paragraph of Averroes' *Decisive Treatise* bows to the Almohad ruler and flatters him;[96] and, in what appears to be a second recension of the *Kashf*, he wriggles in an obvious effort to placate the Almohads.[97] The Almohads, however, were no philosophers, and were not considered as such by Averroes.[98] As far as the philosopher Averroes was concerned, the Almohad elite was also a nonphilosophical public. Maimonides, on the other hand, wrote for people with philosophical aspirations and with some philosophical training, people like his own student whom he treated as "one out of thousands" and who could be trusted with philosophical chapter headings.

The disagreement between Averroes and Maimonides is not only sociological and theological (that is, who should be taught and how much), but also hermeneutical (that is, what is the meaning of the exoteric level of the text, the *ẓāhir*). Maimonides distinguishes the *ẓāhir* from the *bāṭin*, the inner, esoteric, and true meaning of the text. Nevertheless, as his introduction to the *Guide* shows, he is convinced that already the *ẓāhir* of the text allows for various interpretations, and the correct interpretation is never the physical, material, or anthropomorphic one. Like Saadia before him (and perhaps in his wake),[99] Maimonides includes in the term *ẓāhir* contextual and theological considerations. Maimonides' understanding of the term allows him to say that everyone should be taught the noncorporeality of God, without claiming that everyone should be taught the hidden meaning (*bāṭin*) of the text.

[95] *Dalāla*, 11; Pines, 16.

[96] See Averroès, *Discours décisif*, 170; D. Urvoy, *Averroès. Les ambitions d'un intellectuel musulman* (Paris, 1998), 59.

[97] M. Geoffroy, "Ibn Rušd et la théologie almohadiste: une version inconnue du *Kitāb al-kašf ʿan manāhiğ al-adilla* dans deux manuscrits d'Istanbul,"*Medioevo* 26 (2001): 346–50; idem, "A propos de l'almohadisme d'Averroès: l'anthropomorphisme (*tağsīm*) dans la seconde version du *Kitāb al-kašf ʿan manāhiğ al-adilla*," in Cressier et al., *Los Almohades*, 853–94; Stroumsa, "Philosophes almohades?," 1148–49.

[98] See Ivry, "The Utilization of Allegory in Islamic Philosophy," *Interpretation and Allegory*, 153–80, and note 171; see also Averroes's *Commentary on Plato's Republic*, ed. E. I. J. Rosenthal (Cambridge, 1966), 82 (trans. 211).

[99] I owe this observation to Zeev Elkin. For Saadia's contextual understanding, see, for instance, *Kitāb al-amānāt wa'l-iʿtiqādāt*, ed. Y. Qafiḥ (Jerusalem, 1970), 7: 223–24.

Averroes, on the other hand, does not use the term *bāṭin* in this context (an omission that looks like a conscious choice to avoid this term). He juxtaposes the *ẓāhir* with the *muʿawwal* ("interpreted"), and it seems that he understands *ẓāhir* as it has been understood by Dāwūd *al-Ẓāhirī* and by Ibn Ḥazm—that is to say, as the primary lexical meaning of each word on its own.[100] Without a contextual meaning, the *ẓāhir* of a verse can hardly be reconciled with its philosophical meaning. The dichotomy between the two levels thus makes the exposition of the multitudes to the esoteric meaning even riskier, and one can see why Averroes was adamant against such an exposition.

Unlike Maimonides' *Guide*, Averroes's *Kashf* does not intend to disclose the philosophical secrets, because, as noted by Pines, Averroes's position on such disclosure differs from that of Maimonides.[101] Pines approached both authors in the context of Almohad theology, a theology that imposed on the multitudes a nonanthropomorphic understanding of the Scriptures. While Averroes regarded this development as both unrealistic and imprudent, Maimonides adopted it.

Indeed, it is noteworthy that, although Maimonides was probably influenced by Averroes, their positions on some issues are diametrically opposed. They agree on the legitimacy of *ta'wīl*, and on its philosophical necessity; but they disagree on the necessity to divulge it. Averroes speaks resolutely against divulging the details of the *ta'wīl*, and he is even opposed to declaring the very principle of God's incorporeality.[102] Maimonides, on the other hand, adopted the Almohad position and imposed on the multitudes—simpletons, children, and women—a catechism that declared God's incorporeality, just as it declared His unity.[103]

By shaping a compact and authoritative *Code of Law*, and by including indoctrination in the *Code*, Maimonides was playing the role assigned to the ruler according to the Platonic philosophical tradition: the role of the lawgiver who builds a virtuous city, the one who guides his flock toward true beliefs. The idea that the philosopher must play this role was, of course, part of the Hellenic legacy. Maimonides' definition of the exact parameters of this role, however, reflects, as I hope to have shown, a strong Almohad influence.

Moreover, it is not only Maimonides' overall perception of the role of the ruler that is modeled according to Almohad thought. Several of its implementations may also reflect this influence. As mentioned above, Ibn

[100] For Averroes's definition of *ta'wīl*, see *Faṣl*, 119.

[101] Pines, "A Lecture on the *Guide of the Perplexed*," 117–18.

[102] See *Kashf*, 138–41, and see his diplomatic retraction in the second recension; see also note 97, above.

[103] *Guide*, 1.35 (*Dalāla*, 54–55; Pines, 79–81).

Tūmart presented himself as the Mahdī, and his leadership retained aspects of millenarian messianism. Maimonides' depiction of the Messianic era is therefore a case in point.

By way of comparison, one should recall that Maimonides was criticized for his interpretation of the World to Come, and was accused of denying the resurrection of the dead, and of trying to interpret it away. In this context, Maimonides protested that the storm against him rose despite his outspoken declaration of his belief in the resurrection.[104] In what concerns the Messianic era, however, Maimonides explicitly says that the text of the Scriptures must not be taken literally, but should rather be read as a parable, and he even hints at what it is a parable of. As we have seen above, in the introduction to the *Guide of the Perplexed* Maimonides emphasizes his careful, measured usage of this procedure, which he presents as equivalent to divulging the secrets of the Torah. And yet, regarding the Days of the Messiah, Maimonides adopts this procedure, and he does so clearly and outspokenly, in the *Guide of the Perplexed*, as well as in the last chapters of *Mishneh Torah*: "What is said in the book of Isaiah [Is.11:6]: "The wolf will dwell with the lamb, and the leopard will lie down with the young goat" . . . and all similar sayings regarding the Messiah . . . —[all] these are parables. And when the days of the King Messiah come, it will be made known what are they parables of."[105] In other words, contrary to Maimonides' usual methodology of revealing only chapter headings, and only to a choice audience, in what concerns the Days of the Messiah Maimonides goes out of his way to make public his demythologizing reading of the Scriptures.

One could of course argue, following Leo Strauss's interpretive method, that Maimonides adopts here an esoteric technique of "uncovering a cubit, covering two." A more plausible explanation, however, seems to be offered by reading Maimonides in his historical context. Maimonides believed that the true head of state has to teach "true beliefs."

[104]See, for example, *Treatise on Resurrection*, 10–15. On the controversy, see chap. 6, below.

[105]*Mishneh Torah, Laws of Kings (Hilkhot melakhim)*, 12:1 (208); See J. Kraemer, "On Maimonides' Messianic Posture," in I. Twersky, ed., *Studies in Medieval Jewish History and Literature* (Cambridge, Mass., and London, 1984), 2:109–42; Aviezer Ravitzky, "'As Much as is Humanely Possible'—The Messianic Era in Maimonides' Teaching," in Z. Baraz, ed., *Messianism and Eschatology* (Jerusalem, 1983), 194 and 204, and note 33. Ravitzky stresses Maimonides' claim that "all these things, no one knows how they will be until they come to be," which Ravitzky sees as "Maimonides's agnostic stance." In fact, there is very little agnosticism in Maimonides' saying. He is very clear in saying that the things described in the verse will *not* happen as they are described, and that the verse must therefore be taken out of its literal sense.

He clearly was an elitist,[106] but he also believed that some fundamentals (*uṣūl*) ought to be taught to people belonging to all levels of society. As mentioned above, Maimonides adopted the Almohad position in imposing the rejection of anthropomorphism as an article of faith. Apparently, he viewed the demythologizing interpretation of scriptures regarding the Messiah as belonging, to some extent, to the same category.

Maimonides' approach to this question may be reflected in yet another aspect of his description of the Messiah. In general, Maimonides sees the duties of the righteous king—any king, not just the Messiah—as "to proclaim the true religion, to fill the world with justice, to break the arm of evil and to fight the wars of the Lord; for the first purpose of appointing a king is to do justice and fight wars."[107] In describing the role of the king as spreading justice, Maimonides' Hebrew here ("*le-mal'ot ha-olam tzedeq*") is strikingly reminiscent of the Arabic formula for describing the role of the *Mahdī* ("*an yamla'a al-arḍ ʿadlan ka-mā muli'at jūran*"). This formula is prevalent in both Shiite and Sunni texts, and was also used to describe the *Mahdī* Ibn Tūmart.[108] The role of the king, however, is not just to spread justice and proclaim the true religions, but to do so by sword. This royal image becomes even more pronounced in the description of the ultimate king, the Messiah. As noted by Joel Kraemer, Maimonides' depiction of the Messiah is characterized by an overwhelming insistence on his military role.[109] One suspects that the frequent military campaigns of the Almohads, in which they were accompanied by a magnificent copy of the Qur'ān and advancing under the banner of the *Mahdī*, offered Maimonides a Messianic model that went well with his reading of the *Laws of Kings,* both in Deuteronomy and in the Talmud.

The presence of this model imposes on us a slight modification of our somewhat bookish image of Maimonides as a political philosopher. As "the disciple of al-Fārābī," Maimonides "took the Alfarabian theory of the relationship between philosophy, religion, jurisprudence and theology and applied it in a thoroughgoing manner to a particular religion, Judaism."[110] Both the Platonic and the Jewish models, however, remained

[106] Twersky, *Introduction to the Code of Maimonides*, 469–71, speaks of Maimonides' "overt acknowledgement of elitism."

[107] *Mishneh Torah*, *Laws of Kings*, 4:10.

[108] See, for example, a variation of it in a panegyric poem on Ibn Tūmart; Luciani, *Le livre de Mohammed Ibn Toumert,* 11.

[109] Kraemer, "On Maimonides' Messianic Posture," 130–31 ("a warrior-Messiah, an armed prophet").

[110] See Berman, "Maimonides the Disciple of al-Fārābī."

for him abstract constructs. The Almohads, on the other hand, offered a living model: a political regime that, despite the fact that it persecuted Maimonides' own people, presented some traits with which Maimonides could identify.[111]

As in the domain of law, so also in hermeneutic and political theory Maimonides seems more receptive of Almohad thinking than Averroes. The status of Maimonides within his own community was strikingly different from that of the Muslim philosophers of his generation within their society. While the latter had no communal authority unless it was bestowed upon them by a Muslim ruler, Maimonides was (besides his role as a physician at the Ayyūbid court) the leader of the Jewish community. As the spiritual leader of a minority group, Maimonides could feel, perhaps more than a Muslim philosopher marginalized in the court, that he was able to shape the minds of his flock. The position of the leader of a minority group allowed him, paradoxically, more freedom to adopt Almohad ideology than that left to his Muslim counterpart.[112] For Maimonides, the Almohad revolution could serve as a source of inspiration, precisely because (unlike for an Ibn Rushd, for example) his applications of Almohad ideas were not monitored and could not be manipulated by Almohad rulers. As a member of a religious (and ethnic) minority, Maimonides was barred from any real participation in government. His distance from the center of Almohad ideology may explain why Maimonides was, perhaps, less irked by it than Averroes might have been.[113] In other words, perhaps paradoxically, it may have been precisely Maimonides' marginal social position that permitted him to espouse Almohad ideas. He watched Almohad practices just as he read Arabic political philosophy, and both of these sources served him as building blocks for constructing his own ideology, integrating both models into his reading of the Jewish texts. He could thus construct a model image of kingship and sovereignty, which he could uphold as the true image of the Jewish polity.

[111] The phenomenon of thorough acculturation and adaptation, which results in an imitation of the persecutor by the persecuted, is well known. See, for instance, I. Y. Yuval, *Two Nations in Your Womb: Perceptions of Jews and Christians* (Tel Aviv, 2000), 30–31, 36 [Hebrew]; I wish to thank Yoram Bilu and Israel Yuval for discussion of this phenomenon with me.

[112] See Stroumsa, "The Literary Corpus"; idem, "Philosopher-King or Philosopher-Courtier? Theory and Reality in the *Falāsifa*'s Place in Islamic Society," in C. De la Puente, ed., *Identidades Marginales* (Madrid, 2003), 453–58; and see chap. 6, below.

[113] At the time of writing the *Guide*, Maimonides was also physically distant from the center of Almohad power, but this was not the case when he began writing the *Mishneh Torah*.

Philosophy and Astronomy

An anecdote recounted by the historian ʿAbd al-Wāḥid al-Marrākushī depicts the second Almohad ruler Abū Yaʿqūb Yūsuf as genuinely interested in scientific and philosophical speculation and as well versed in its intricacies. The anecdote presents the ruler as capable of engaging a timid Averroes in conversation about Aristotelian physics, a conversation at the end of which Averroes was commissioned to write commentaries on the whole Aristotelian corpus.[114] This anecdote is probably as fictitious as it is appealing to the imagination, as I have argued elsewhere. Although this particular Almohad ruler seems to have been relatively more inclined to science and speculation than other Almohads, the attempt to depict him as a philosopher-king is much exaggerated.[115] This being said, it is nonetheless true that philosophy and science flourished under the Almohads. The twelfth century (in the middle of which al-Andalus came under Almohad rule) is the most important period (some say, the only significant period) of Andalusian philosophy.[116] One should therefore not exclude the possibility that the Almohad way of thinking may have left its marks on both scientific and philosophical thought in al-Andalus.

Such Almohad influence was suggested by Sabra regarding what he dubbed "the Andalusian revolt against Ptolemaic astronomy."[117] As is well known, the astronomical models suggested by Ptolemy offer explanations for otherwise unresolved observations, but these models contradict Aristotelian physics. Arab astronomers in general accepted a self-contradictory position, following Ptolemaic astronomy while continuing to uphold Aristotelian physics. Several Andalusian thinkers, however, like Bitrūjī, saw this contradictory position as untenable, and rejected the Ptolemaic models and solutions. As noted by Sabra, this "revolt" coincides with the rise of the Almohads in North Africa, and is concentrated in the Almohad realm of influence. Sabra therefore suggested seeing this astronomical trend as another expression of "Almohad literalism." As mentioned above, however, notwithstanding the sympathies of Abū Yaʿqūb Yūsuf, the second Almohad ruler, with the *Ẓāhirī* school, the

[114] See Marrākushī, *Muʿjib*, 174–75; and see, for instance, F. Griffel, *Apostasie und Toleranz im Islam*, 421.

[115] See Stroumsa "Philosophes almohades?," 1139–44.

[116] See S. Pines, art. "Philosophy," in P. M. Holt et al., eds., *The Cambridge History of Islam* (Cambridge, 1970), 2B: 814–15.

[117] A. I. Sabra, "The Andalusian Revolt against Ptolemaic Astronomy: Averroes and al-Bitrūji," in E. Mendelsohn, ed., *Transformation and Tradition in the Sciences: Essays in Honor of Bernard Cohen* (Cambridge, 1984), 133–53; J. Kraemer, "Maimonides and the Spanish Aristotelian Tradition," 50–54.

Almohads were no literalists.[118] To the extent that the "revolt" reflects Almohad tendencies, it may rather be explained as another example of the Almohad attitude to foundational texts. Within the corpus of authoritative texts, the Almohads established a hierarchy, where some texts enjoyed a clear supremacy over others. In the realm of religion, this place was obviously reserved for the Qur'ān and the *ḥadīth*; and in the realm of science, it was kept to Aristotle. This, at least, seems to be the situation regarding Maimonides.[119]

In several of his writings Maimonides expresses (with varying degrees of determination) skeptical views regarding Ptolemaic astronomy. Although he is well aware of the shortcomings of Aristotelian physics, he strives to preserve the integrity of Aristotelian science.[120] In order to navigate around this difficulty, Maimonides resorts to the convenient position of agnosticism—as he does with regard to other sensitive issues, such as the creation of the world in time, or divine attributes. The formulation Maimonides chooses in order to express his agnostic position is strikingly similar to the one used by Ibn Tūmart: Human intellect, he says, has a limit at which it stops.[121] It is unclear whether Maimonides' agnosticism in astronomy reflected his views of an inherently limited human knowledge, or whether he regarded it as a temporary state, and believed that at some point in the future human beings would be able to understand the movement of the spheres.[122] Be that as it may, the agnostic

[118] See above, *apud* note 26.

[119] On Averroes's position on this issue, see Stroumsa, "Philosophes almohades?," 1146; and see also T. Langerman, "Another Andalusian Revolt? Ibn Rushd's Critique of Al-Kindi's Pharmacological Computus," in J. P. Hogendijk and A. I. Sabra, ed., *The Enterprise of Science in Islam—New Perspectives* (Cambridge, Mass., and London, 2003), 363: "Ibn Rushd stands out for his resolute commitment to Aristotle—not to Aristotelianism [. . .] but rather to a purified, strict reading of Aristotle's own writings." The issue of Almohad attitude to Aristotelianism and to Aristotelian science deserves a separate study.

[120] See *Guide* 2.24; T. Langermann, "Maimonides and the Sciences," in D. H. Frank and O. Leaman, eds., *The Cambridge Companion to Jewish Philosophy* (Cambridge, 2003), 166–67; idem, "The 'True Perplexity': *The Guide of the Perplexed*, Part II, Chapter 24," in Kraemer, *Perspectives on Maimonides*, 159–74; J. L. Kraemer, "Maimonides on Aristotle and Scientific Method," in E. L. Ormsby, ed., *Moses Maimonides and His Time* (Washington, D.C., 1989), 76–84.

[121] See, for instance, *Guide*, 1.31 (*Dalāla*, 44:13 and 45: 17; Pines, 65) (*li'l-ʿaql al-insānī ḥadd bi-lā shakk yaqifu ʿindahu*); cf. Luciani, *Le Livre de Mohammed Ibn Toumert*, 233 (*li'l-ʿuqūl ḥadd taqifu ʿindahu*); M. Massé, "La profession de foi (*ʿaqīda*) et les guides spirituels (*morchida*) du Mahdi Ibn Toumart," *Mémorial Henri Basset* (Paris, 1928), 110.

[122] On this much debated question, see Pines, "Translator's Introduction," lxiii, cxi; Langerman, "The 'True Perplexity,'" 165–66; S. Pines, "The Limitations of Human Knowledge according to Al-Fārābī, Ibn Bājja, and Maimonides," in I. Twersky, ed., *Studies in Medieval Jewish History and Literature* (Cambridge, Mass., 1979), 82–109; J. Kraemer, "How (Not) to Read the *Guide of the Perplexed*," *JSAI* 32 (2006): 350–409.

position allows him to continue using Ptolemaic astronomy without claiming it to be the truth. He can thus point to the limitations of Aristotle's knowledge, which reach only below the sphere of the moon, and at the same time, insist on presenting Aristotle's knowledge as the utmost human achievement.[123]

Maimonides' admiration of Aristotle is indeed consistent. In his letter to Samuel Ibn Tibbon Maimonides evaluates Aristotle's knowledge as "the utmost that a human being can achieve, unless this human being receives the divine flow of emanation, so that he attains the rank of prophecy."[124] Advising his translator about his readings, Maimonides continues to say that "Aristotle's books, and only them, are the roots and principles for all other scientific compositions." Although the relevant passage of this letter is extant only in Hebrew, the original Arabic terminology of *uṣūl* is echoed in the Hebrew words "roots and principles" (*shorashim ve-ʿiqqarim*). It is also quite clear that these words are not mere rhetorical hyperbole, admiringly attached to the name of Aristotle. As we have seen in various instances above, wherever Maimonides employs the term *uṣūl* he intends it in the precise technical meaning that this term had in his milieu, and there is no reason to assume that the case here is different. In categorizing Aristotle's books as "roots," Maimonides makes a methodological statement, establishing the relative rank of Aristotle in the philosophical and scientific curriculum. The Aristotelian corpus receives the status of a primary, foundational text, equivalent to the status of scriptures in legal thought. Aristotle is established as scientific and philosophical *aṣl*: as such, his teaching overrules any other authority in this category (regardless of its utility), including that of Ptolemy.

Conclusion

Tilman Nagel, who pointed out certain similarities of Maimonides' metaphysics to that of Ibn Tūmart, cautiously stated that "it remains unclear whether Maimonides was familiar with Ibn Tūmart's writings."[125] The accumulated evidence of the previous pages indicates, I believe, that despite the absence of any explicit quotation, we must assume such familiarity.

[123] See, for instance, *Guide*, 2.9–11. Although written in Egypt, these chapters reflect the scientific education acquired by Maimonides in his youth in Andalus; see chap. 1, *apud* note 49, above. This does not exclude the possibility that Maimonides was also influenced by a similar critique of Aristotle, pronounced by the Egyptian astronomer Ibn al-Haytham.

[124] *Epistles*, 553.

[125] *Im Offenkundigen das Verborgene*, 116.

As mentioned above, the Almohads were depicted in earlier modern scholarship as what are popularly called today "fundamentalists." To the extent that the Almohads' propensity for "fundamentals" allows us to use, tongue in cheek, this outdated term of opprobrium in its contemporary sense, we can also see Maimonides as a "fundamentalist." Like the Almohads, and under the direct influence of their powerful model, Maimonides looked for *uṣūl* in several senses: authoritative primary sources (as opposed to secondary sources); laws in their broader formulations (as opposed to the "branches" dealing with particular cases); and fundamental beliefs. Already David ben Judah Leon could call Maimonides "*shorshi*," a Hebrew word that, as suggested by Moritz Steinschneider, translates the Arabic *uṣūlī*.[126] By giving the "fundamentals" pride of place in his thought, Maimonides closely followed the Almohad paradigm. His astounding ability to cast the Almohad revolution in Jewish terms allowed him to incorporate this paradigm seamlessly in his works. Through these works, the creative originality of the Almohads fed into Jewish medieval thought.

[126]See M. Steinscheider, *Jewish Literature* (London, 1857), 310, quoted in J. Faur, *Studies in Maimonides' Mishneh Torah: The Book of Knowledge* (Jerusalem, 1978), 9n41 [Hebrew]. I owe this reference to Joseph David. As noted by Faur, Maimonides himself uses the term *uṣūlī* only to denote the *mutakallimūn*, and probably not in a laudatory sense.

Chapter Four

La Longue Durée:

Maimonides as a Phenomenologist of Religion

Through his studies of what he considered to be ancient pagan texts Maimonides believed to have cracked the code of biblical commandments. He identified these ancient texts with the culture of the Sabians. This chapter will analyze Maimonides' insight, which he himself describes as his great scientific discovery. It will also study Maimonides' ensuing analysis of contemporary religions: Islam and Christianity, as well as contemporary Judaism.

Sabians

The Sabians (*al-ṣāba*, *al-ṣābi'a*, or *al-ṣābi'ūn*) appear in Arabic literature as an ancient nation that lived in the Near East from antiquity up to the Abbasid period. This nation is never mentioned in the writings of historians and thinkers in antiquity, and it makes its first appearance in Arabic, Islamic literature.[1] Despite this surprising fact, most scholars accept at its face value the testimony of Arab writings, and invest considerable effort in the attempt to identify the Sabians. The sudden appearance of this nation is not the only difficulty involved in identifying it. Sabians are mentioned already in the Qur'ān,[2] but most scholars believe that the Sabians of the Qur'ān are not identical with the Sabians who appear in heresiographical Arabic literature.[3] The descriptions of this latter group are beset with contradictions. They are usually referred to as the "Sabians of Harrān," but their alleged descendants are encountered primarily in Baghdad. In some writings, the Sabians are described as a people who

[1] See F. C. de Blois, "The 'Sabians' (*Ṣābi'ūn*) in Pre-Islamic Arabia," *Acta Orientalia* (1995): 41n8; Stroumsa, "Sabéens de Harran et Sabéens de Maïmonide." I wish to thank Jessica Bonn for her help in translating this article.

[2] Qur'ān 2 [*al-Baqara*]: 26; 5 [*al-Mā'ida*]: 69; 22 [*al-Ḥajj*]:17. See also J. D. McAuliffe, "Exegetical Identification of the Ṣābi'ūn, *Muslim World* 72 (1982): 95–106.

[3] Regarding the Sabians of the Qur'ān, see de Blois, "Ṣābī," *EI*, 8: 672–75, esp. 672; idem, "Sabians"; G. Strohmaier, "Die Ḥarrānischen Sabier bei Ibn an-Nadīm und al-Bīrūnī," in *Ibn al-Nadīm und die mittelalterliche arabische Literatur: Beiträge zum 1. Johann Wilhelm Fück Kolloquium (Halle, 1987)* (Wiesbaden, 1996), 55–56.

practice pagan worship, conducting ceremonies universally considered to be cruel and repulsive.[4] The individuals to whose name the epithet *al-ṣābī* is attached, however, are usually noted for their cultural refinement and high level of education, and are involved in the translation and composition of philosophical, astronomical, and mathematical writings. Abraham, the first *ḥanīf*, is said to have opposed Sabian religion,[5] but in some writings the Sabian religion is actually identified as *ḥanīffīyya*.[6]

The earliest descriptions of the Sabians preserved in Arabic literature—at varying levels of detail—date from the tenth century.[7] This leaves a gap of approximately four centuries in the textual continuity of descriptions of the pagan worship in Ḥarrān. Given the lack of early sources, scholars are forced to rely on testimonies written between the tenth and the thirteenth centuries, and to assume that these late testimonies are likely to reflect lost earlier sources. In this particular case, however, such an assumption adds to the existing confusion, since the later works contain muddled and sometimes contradictory descriptions.[8] The detailed Sabian calendar that Ibn al-Nadīm presents does not correspond to the one preserved by Bīrūnī,[9] and the philosophical conceptions (namely, pre-Socratic atomism) that Abū Bakr al-Rāzī may have attributed to the Sabians differ from those attributed to them by Masʿūdī or Ibn al-Nadīm. Arab heresiographers seem to have been aware of the contradictions in

[4] See *Ghāyat al-ḥakīm*, ed. H. Ritter (Leipzig and Berlin, 1933), 225, 228; *"Picatrix": Das Ziel des Weisen von Pseudo-Majrīṭī*, trans. H. Ritter and M. Plessner (London, 1962), 237, 240; Ibn al-Nadīm, *al-Fihrist*, ed. G. Flügel (Leipzig, 1872), 231; C.S.F. Burnett, "Arabic, Greek and Latin Works on Astrological Magic Attributed to Aristotle," in Jill Kraye et al., eds., *Pseudo-Aristotle in the Middle Ages: The* Theology *and Other Texts* (London, 1986), 87. For a summary of sources and theories regarding the Sabians, see T. M. Greene, *The City of the Moon God: Religious Traditions of Harran* (Leiden, 1992).

[5] See, for example, Shahrastānī, who describes at length a debate between a Ḥanīf and a Ṣābī; *Kitāb al-milal wa'l-niḥal, Book of Religious and Philosophical Sects,* ed. W. Cureton (Leipzig, 1923), 126–41, 147–49. On the concept "Ḥanīf," see Qur'ān 3 [*āl-ʿImrān*]: 6; 16 [*al-Naḥl*]: 122. See also W. Montgomery Watt, "Ḥanīf," *EI*, 3: 165–66.

[6] As, for example, in the writings of Ibn Ḥazm and Bīrūnī—see H. Corbin, "Rituel sabéen et exégèse ismaélienne du rituel," *Eranos Jahrbuch* 19 (1950): 181–246.

[7] The Sabians are mentioned by the ninth-century Jewish philosopher al-Muqammas, but the chapters preserved from his book do not contain detailed descriptions of them. See S. Stroumsa, ed. and trans., *Dāwūd ibn Marwān al-Muqammiṣ's ʿIshrūn Maqāla* (Leiden, 1989), 107 and note 30, and 130 and note 12. From the descriptions of the ninth-century philosopher Sarākhsī only excerpts have been preserved, quoted by the tenth-century Ibn al-Nadīm; See *Fihrist,* 373 ff. The composition of Thābit Ibn Qurra (835–901) regarding the Sabian religion did not survive at all.

[8] Greene, *The City of the Moon God*, 144, states that "Muslim material on Harran is wildly contradictory."

[9] Ibn al-Nadīm, al-*Fihrist*, 318–27; Abū Rayḥān al-Bīrūnī, *al-Āṭār al-bāqiya ʿan al-Qurūn al-Khāliya*, ed. C. E.Sachau (Leipzig, 1878), 331–81; Greene, *The City of the Moon God*, 142–52.

the information they had received, and attempted to resolve them by distinguishing between several kinds of Sabians. Masʿūdī, for example, suggests in one of his books a sociocultural stratification of the Sabians, distinguishing between the pagan Sabian masses, on the one hand, and the philosophically oriented elite, on the other.[10] In another treatise, however, Masʿūdī suggests different distinctions, including a distinction between the Greco-Byzantine, Egyptian, Chinese, and Zoroastrian Sabians.[11] Another taxonomy can be found in the work of Shahrastānī, who distinguishes between the "original Ṣābi'a," in whose description there is an evident Hermetic element, and other Sabians, whose description mainly emphasizes their idolatrous practices revolving around the worship of the planets.[12] In yet another common division, a distinction is made between the Sabians living in Ḥarrān and the splinter group that settled in Baghdad.[13]

The Sabian religion is sometimes described as polytheistic, characterized by a large number of divinities and spirits whose worship follows the seasons of the year and is dictated by an agrarian calendar. On other occasions, however, it is described as an essentially monotheistic religion in which the celestial bodies are worshipped in order to safeguard the absolute transcendence and incorporeal nature of God. The sacrifices offered by the Sabians are sometimes described simply as pagan rites aimed at placating the gods, at other times as theurgical practices, employed by philosophers who believe in an eternal world governed by the planets. Even the magic attributed to the Sabians is presented in some of our sources as the scientific pursuit of alchemy.

The archaeological findings at Ḥarrān and in its surroundings reveal little regarding the period following the Muslim conquest. As for the preceding period, they do confirm the existence of a pagan culture in

[10] Masʿūdī, *Murūj al-dhahab*, ed. C. Barbier de Meynard (Paris, 1865), 4, 64.

[11] *Al-Tanbīh wa-al-ishrāf*, ed. ʿAbdallāh Ismāʿīl al-Ṣāfī (Cairo, n.d.), 4, 18, 101, 138–39. As noted by Corbin ("Rituel sabéen", 182), the name "China" sometimes refers to the borders of the inhabited world. Hämeen-Anttila's suggestion (that by "Egyptian Sabians" Masʿūdī actually means Harranians, as their esoteric learning was seen as the continuation of the Alexandrian school, deported to Harran in 717 by the caliph ʿUmar II), presupposes a real community of Sabians in Harran; cf. J. Hämeen-Anttila's *The Last Pagans of Iraq: Ibn Waḥshiyya and His Nabatean Agriculture* (Leiden, 2006), 49n131.

[12] Shahrastānī, *al-milal wa'l-niḥal,* 202–3. It is likely that the expression "*al-Ṣāba al-ūlā*" appearing in Shahrastānī's work is inspired by the Qur'ānic expression (33 [*al-Aḥzāb*]: 33) "*al-jāhiliyya al-ūlā*." On Maimonides' identification of the Sabians with the *jāhiliyya*, see *apud* notes 49–50, below.

[13] See Strohmaier, "Die Ḥarrānischen Sabier," for a summary and refutation of this common description.

Ḥarrān, but are far from reflecting the colorful descriptions in the Arab sources.[14]

The plethora of difficulties and contradictions was bound to arouse a degree of caution and even skepticism regarding the information provided by our sources. Indeed, most of those scholars who have carefully considered this issue since the mid-twentieth century comment on the collective or paradigmatic nature of the Sabians in the Muslim sources. Yet many among the same scholars also attempt to harmonize the contradictory texts in a manner that would allow us to point to the Sabians, and in particular to those Sabians who lived in Ḥarrān, as a people endowed with a more or less clear identity, a nation possessing its own religion, or at least as a family of religions.[15] It has thus been suggested that the Sabians of the Qur'ān should be identified as Mandeans,[16] a Gnostic group,[17] or as adherents of a Hermetic religion.[18] For de Blois, who identifies the Sabians of the Qur'ān with the Manicheans, the Sabians of Ḥarrān are "a community following an old Semitic polytheistic religion, but with a strongly Hellenized elite, one of the last outposts of late antique paganism."[19]

[14]For a summary of the textual and archaeological findings, see Greene, *The City of the Moon God*, 65–72; H. Drijvers, "The Persistence of Pagan Cults and Practices in Christian Syria," in N. Garsoïan et al., eds., *East of Byzantium: Syria and Armenia in the Formative Period; Dumbarton Oaks Symposium, 1980* (Washington, D.C., 1987), 35.

[15]Pines, for example, cautiously maintains that the name "Ṣabian" "came to be applied to a Syriac-speaking pagan community which survived in Ḥarrān and practiced a cult which is reported to have been impregnated with philosophical elements." And yet, he also adds that "Ṣābi'a" "became a blanket designation for pagan religion"—s.v. "philosophy," in *The Cambridge History of Islam*, 786–87. Drijvers ("The Persistence of Pagan Cults," 34) views Sabians as "a paradigm of later Syrian intellectual paganism rather than an isolated phenomenon." Despite this, he subsequently seems to relate to them as an isolated phenomenon, since, referring to Bardaisān's observation of the syncretism of pagan rites and philosophical ideas, he states that these "should be compared with the Sabians in nearby Ḥarrān who did the same" (ibid., 38). See also F. Rosenthal, "The Prophecies of Bābā the Ḥarrānian," in W. B. Henning and E. Yarshater, eds., *A Locust's Leg: Studies in honour of S. H. Taqizadeh* (London, 1962), 232.

[16]D. Chwolsohn, *Die Ssabier und der Ssabismus,* 2 vols (St. Petersburg, 1856).

[17]See, for example, J. Pedersen, "The Ṣābians," in T.W. Arnold and R. A. Nicholson, eds., *A Volume of Oriental Studies Presented to Edward G. Browne on His Birthday,* (Cambridge, 1922), 383–91; J. Hjärpe, *Analyse critique des traditions arabes sur les sabéens ḥarraniens* (Uppsala, 1972); A. Funkenstein, *Perceptions of Jewish History* (Berkeley, 1993), 144. The association with the Gnostics is also mentioned by Rosenthal, "The Prophecies of Bābā the Ḥarrānian," 232.

[18]See A. E. Afifi, "The Influence of Hermetic Literature on Muslim Thought," *BSOAS* 13 (1951): 840, 855, esp. 842; J. Assmann, *Moses the Egyptian: The Memory of Egypt in Western Monotheism* (Cambridge, Mass., 1997), 58.

[19]De Blois, "Ṣābi," 672. See also Strohmaier, "Die Ḥarrānischen Sabier," 51, 53.

De Blois's suggestion reflects a theory proposed some dozen years ago by Michel Tardieu. According to this leading scholar of Gnosticism, the Sabians of the Qur'ān were the adherents of a specific Gnostic sect,[20] while the Sabians of Ḥarrān were indeed an ancient people, adherents of a pagan religion. According to his suggestion, the Neoplatonist philosophers who were exiled from Athens by Justinian in 529 and took refuge in Persia passed through Ḥarrān on their way back. The Sabian inhabitants of Ḥarrān invited them to become their leaders, and they accepted the offer.[21] This arrangement—the fulfillment of the Platonic vision of the philosopher-king—remained in effect until the tenth century. According to Tardieu, "Pagan Harran could have been a place of refuge for the Greek philosophers who were exiled from Athens, and thus became a Greek- and Aramaic-friendly environment that could serve as a starting point for the philosophical school which later gave rise to Ṯābit Ibn Qurra."[22] Tardieu's suggestion has the merit of highlighting the existence of theurgic trends among pagan Neoplatonist philosophers, and the possibility that these trends were also manifested in pagan Ḥarrān. This line of thinking could prove helpful, provided that one does not attempt—as Tardieu did—to use our hazy data in order to paint too precise a picture.[23] Tardieu's claim relies mainly on Arabic sources, which he presents with impressive erudition and persuasiveness. At the same time, a careful examination reveals the entire theory to rely on a few lines written by Mas'ūdī,[24] or rather, on Tardieu's reading of these lines. Mas'ūdī is certainly an important source, but his reliability, consistency, and precision

[20] According to Tardieu, they should be identified with the *stratiotikoi* mentioned by Epiphanius. Despite the change in identification of the Sabians, Tardieu in effect continues in the direction already proposed by Edward Pococke, who sought the origin of the name "Ṣabian" in the Hebrew: "*tzeva ha-shamaayim*"(heavenly host); see E. Pococke, *Specimen historiae Arabum* (Oxford, 1649), 141–43, quoted in M. Tardieu, "Ṣābiens coraniques et Ṣābiens de Ḥarrān," *Journal Asiatique* 274 (1986): 41.

[21] Tardieu, "Ṣābiens."

[22] M. Tardieu, *Les paysage reliques: routes et haltes syriennes d'Isidore à Simplicius* (Louvain and Paris, 1990), 161. Hämeen-Anttila, who does not cite Tardieu, offers a similar description of a two-tiered Sabian society (that is, a society composed of learned philosopher pagans and of commoners), and he seems to leave open the possibility that this arrangement held true not just in Ḥarran, but also in rural Mesopotamia; see *The Last Pagans of Iraq*, 52.

[23] A clear and balanced way of connecting these data was proposed, for example, by Frank Peters, who examined the sources of the Arab Platonic tradition. See F. E. Peters, "The Origins of Islamic Platonism: The School Traditions," in P. Morewedge, ed., *Islamic Philosophical Theology* (Albany, 1979), 14–45. See also N. P. Joose, "An Example of Medieval Arabic Pseudo-Hermetism: The Tale of Salāmān and Absāl," *Journal of Semitic Studies* 38 (1993): 289–90.

[24] If Mas'ūdī's claim that he visited Ḥarrān in 943 is accepted, he would be the only eyewitness to have visited Ḥarrān during this period.

are sometimes dubious.[25] In particular, one cannot ignore the fact that Masʿūdī lived four centuries after the events on which his entire theory is based. Moreover, Tardieu's interpretation of Masʿūdī's assertions in these lines is not supported by any other text. For example, it is difficult to understand the basis for his suggestion to identify the Sabian hall of meeting (*majmaʿ*) as a Platonist academy.[26]

Tardieu's theory was accepted by a number of leading scholars,[27] and rejected outright by others.[28] While it is difficult to refute a theory that lacks proof, Dimitri Gutas has decisively proven that the designation *Ḥarrānī* is also used in the sense of "pagan," and therefore, when sources associate the Sabians with the area of Ḥarrān, the name should be understood as a general term, and not as denoting a particular religion or people.[29] Joep Lameer refuted Tardieu's theory from another angle, showing that "we do not possess any positive evidence for the existence of a philosophical 'academy' of any kind in Antioch or Ḥarrān in the eighth and ninth centuries."[30]

[25] No one, for example, proposes to accept Masʿūdī's fantastic descriptions regarding the Sabian palaces on the Chinese border as historical evidence—see Masʿūdī, *Murūj al-dhahab,* 4:169 ff.; Corbin, "Rituel sabéen", 181–84.

[26] Tardieu, "Ṣābiens," 17–18. The usual term to denote an encounter of intellectuals for discussion, as well as the place where such encounters took place, is *majlis*. Masʿūdī himself uses this latter term when discussing the instruction of the Aristotelian tradition, in a passage quoted by Tardieu, "Ṣābiens," 20–21.

[27] See, for example, G. W. Bowersock, *Hellenism in Later Antiquity* (Ann Arbor, 1990), 36; J. Teixidor, *Bardesane d'Edesse, la première philosophie syriaque* (Paris, 1992), 127 and note 4; J. Jolivet "Esquisse d'un Aristote arabe," in A. Sinaceur, ed., *Penser avec Aristotle* (Toulouse, 1991), 179–85, esp. *apud* note 18; J. Parens, *Metaphysics as Rhetoric: Alfarabi's Summary of Plato's "Laws"* (Albany, 1995), xxx–xxxi, and 151n4; J. Stern, "The Fall and Rise of Myth in Ritual: Maimonides versus Nahmanides on the *Ḥuqqim*, Astrology and the War Against Idolatry," *Journal of Jewish Thought and Philosophy* 6 (1997): 189.

[28] See, for example, C. Luna's review of R. Thiel, *Simplikios und das Ende der neuplatonischen Schule in Athen* (Stuttgart, 1999), in *Mnemosyne* 54 (2001): 482–504; A. Becker, *Fear of God and the Beginning of Wisdom: The School of Nisibis and Christian Scholastic Culture in Late Antique Mesopotamia* (Philadelphia, 2006), 129, and note 25; K. van Bladel, *The Arabic Hermes* (forthcoming), chap. 3 ("Hermes and the Ṣābians of Ḥarrān"); I am indebted to Kevin van Bladel for allowing me to consult his book before publication. See also C. D'Ancona Costa, "Commenting on Aristotle: From Late Antiquity to the Arab Aristotelianism," in W. Geerlings and C. Schulze, *Der Kommentar in Antike und Mittelalter: Beiträge zu seiner Erforschung* (Leiden, Boston, and Köln, 2002), 228–29; and see below.

[29] D. Gutas, "Plato's *Symposion* in the Arabic Tradition," *Oriens* 31 (1988): 44n34.

[30] J. Lameer, "From Alexandria to Baghdad: Reflection on the Genesis of a Problematical Tradition," in G. Endress and R. Kruk, eds., *The Ancient Tradition in Christian and Islamic Hellenism: Studies on the Transmission of Greek Philosophy and Sciences, Dedicated to H.J. Drossart Lutlofs on his Ninetieth Birthday* (Leiden, 1997), 181–91, esp. 189. Lameer (ibid., 186) rightly states that "we do not know a single scholar's name to be associated with an academy at Ḥarrān in the period under consideration and neither do we

In analyzing the Arabic sources regarding the Sabians, one must take into account the development of the local religions over the centuries, a development that enabled the emergence of a syncretistic synthesis of ancient traditions, like the synthesis of philosophies and religions in the Roman Empire in Late Antiquity. It is also necessary to consider the development of traditions within Arabic literature that, alongside the use of reliable traditions, also left room for creative imagination. Tamara Greene collected the Sabian traditions and analyzed them in great detail, and her balanced evaluation might be used here as a kind of summary:

> Muslim interest in pre-Islamic paganism may be broadly characterized as antiquarian and perhaps a-historical. . . . [T]he interpretation of the esoteric doctrines of Hermeticism is in large measure shaped by ideological concerns of Muslim reporters, the sources of which may have little to do with the actual beliefs and practices of the Harranians.[31]

As Greene demonstrates, there are various competing elements in the descriptions of the Sabians in Muslim literature. Any attempt to reconcile and harmonize *all* the fragments of information in our possession, to unite them into an overarching picture in which the Sabians would be presented as a single people with a single religion, and to set this rigid rendering in a Muslim context, is doomed to fail. In all likelihood, any such harmonizing attempt would include, alongside correct historical insights, a substantial mythical basis. In this context, one might speak of "the modern Sabian myth," one based on uncritical reading of medieval sources, sources that themselves reflect a mythical conception of the Sabians.

In the effort to collect all possible information about Sabians, proponents of the various theories also look to Maimonides and his discussions of the Sabians.[32] Daniel Chwolsohn, for example, embarked on his seminal study of the Sabians after reading *Guide of the Perplexed*. Ulti-

---

know the title of a single book to have been written at that place." Despite their critical approach toward the existence of an academy in Ḥarrān, however, Gutas and Lameer accept the existence of a Ḥarrānic identity and a Sabian religion as a matter of course. See Gutas, "Plato's *Symposion* in the Arabic Tradition," 45; Lameer, "From Alexandria to Baghdad," 190.

[31] Greene, *The City of the Moon God*, 163.

[32] See, for example, Tardieu, "Ṣābiens," 12. While Tardieu rejects Maimonides' testimony, he substantiates the rejection in the same way that he argues for a rejection of the testimony of the Muslim heresiographers, and not because he views him as another type of witness. Tardieu associates Maimonides with authors such as ʻAbd al-Jabbār, Ibn Ḥazm, Shahrastānī, and Dimashqī, regarding whom he states: "None of these authors has visited Ḥarrān or the region. Their information is derived from the Ḥarranians' adversaries, whether Christians or Muslims, who project scholastic exercises onto contemporary reality. Consequently, all their information should be dismissed."

mately, however, Maimonides' writings are unhelpful for identifying the Sabians, since for Maimonides, the Sabians were not a specific people.[33] For him, they are a *milla*, a term that he employs to denote a broad phenomenon and that does not relate to a distinct religious group.[34] According to Maimonides, in the days of the patriarch Abraham "this was a religious community that extended over the whole earth";[35] and since this was later than the generation of the Tower of Babel, one must conclude that this *milla* comprised different peoples, belonging to various races and speaking a multitude of languages. According to Maimonides, the last of the Sabians can be found to this day "in the extremities of the earth, as for instance the infidels among the Turks in the extreme North and the Hindus in the extreme South."[36] For Maimonides, therefore, "Sabians" is a collective name, and his numerous references to the Sabians show that in his opinion this appellation is applicable to the pagans among whom Abraham grew up, the Egyptians who enslaved the Israelites, and even the Zoroastrians of his own days,[37] simple folks as well as those with philosophic pretensions.[38] If we take into account all the types of people whom Maimonides considers to be Sabians, it becomes clear that he was aware of the fact that such a universal *milla* never existed in the same sense that specific nations or religions, such as the Egyptians or the Christians, exist. The efforts he invests in presenting the Sabians as an international community are anchored precisely in the fact that he does not treat them as a historically identifiable people.[39]

[33] Chwolsohn has already pointed out that Maimonides' writings contribute nothing to our efforts to identify the true historical Sabians (as opposed to Shahrastānī, for example, whom Chwolsohn views as a useful historical source for this purpose). See Chwolsohn, *Die Ssabier*, 1:689–90.

[34] As noted by Pines, Maimonides does not use the term "Ṣāba" in the sense of *Hellenes*, that is, "adherents of the paganism prevalent in the Roman Empire in the first centuries of the Christian era;" see "Translator's Introduction," cxxiv. He does, however, use it in the general sense of "idolaters"—see Chwolsohn, *Die Ssabier*, 1:692, 696. Maimonides' use of the word "*milla*" is not monolithic. At times the word denotes particular religions (e.g. *Guide* 1.71; *Dalāla*, 121:9, 123:4–6), whereas on other occasions it bears a collective, phenomenological meaning (e.g. *Guide* 3.51; *Dalāla*, 459:28). His use of the latter meaning is definitely influenced by Fārābī. See note 44, below.

[35] *Guide* 3.29 (*Dalāla*, 375:24; Pines, 515).

[36] Ibid.

[37] *Guide* 3.29 (*Dalāla*, 375:21–22; Pines, 515), 3.37 (*Dalāla*, 395:29–396:1; Pines, 540–41), 3.47 (*Dalāla*, 436:28–29; Pines, 595). In his "Letter on Astrology" (*Epistles*, 481), Maimonides excludes the Greeks from the discussion. This exclusion strengthens the impression that this worldwide community is defined, in his opinion, by their level of development and metaphysical conceptualization, rather than by ethnic or religious identity.

[38] *Guide* 3.29 (*Dalāla*, 375:24; Pines, 515).

[39] See Assmann, *Moses the Egyptian*, 58; Pines, "Translator's Introduction," cxxiii.

In order to reach such a phenomenological view, Maimonides undoubtedly perused sources different from those used by contemporary scholars in their search for the Sabians. All the modern theories rely on a number of works that describe the Sabian rites, temples, and customs. In all likelihood, Maimonides was familiar with these or similar works. His description of Sabian rites and beliefs, however, includes also many elements that do not appear in these works, and indeed he quotes other sources in this context.

In order to better understand Maimonides' writings on the Sabians we must briefly survey Maimonides' view of the development of religions. According to Maimonides, the religious development of humanity must be seen in the context of what might be termed "the realistic Divine economy." In His efforts to educate human beings God acts (as He does in any other realm) according to the laws of nature, using these laws to guide humans and to press them forward, rather than imposing His omnipotence and forcing them to change.[40] Humankind naturally tends to adhere to acquired habits, and abandons them only with great difficulty.[41] God takes this natural tendency into account, and rather than forcing a sudden change onto humankind, He encourages them to advance by stages (*bi-tadrīj*), to abandon earlier, "primitive" habits and replace them with incrementally higher levels of worship that reflect an increasingly pure metaphysical understanding. Such a tactic of accommodation, which Maimonides calls *talaṭṭuf*, ("shrewdness in the service of loving kindness") is reflected, for example, in the fact that God prepares mother's milk for infants to nourish them until they gradually become accustomed to the heavy food of adults.[42] In this way Maimonides interprets God's decision to lead the Israelite exodus from Egypt along the more difficult

[40] *Guide* 3.32 (*Dalāla*, 386:25–387:4; Pines, 529).

[41] See *Guide* 1.31 (*Dalāla*, 45:3–16; Pines, 670; Bos, Maimonides, *On Asthma,* 110. Habit as a cause of human behavior also appears, in a similar context, in the writings of Ibn Rushd; see *Faṣl al-maqāl*, 45–46; Averroes, *The Book of the Decisive Treatise*, 19. This may indicate, as I have suggested elsewhere, that the two thinkers have used a common source, perhaps a commentary on Aristotle or on Alexander of Aphrodisias; see note 56, below. If so, the emphasis on the power of habit is not Maimonides' original addition to the discussion, as Pines had assumed ("The Limitations of Human," appendix, 100–104, esp. 104); see S. Stroumsa, "Habitudes religieuses et liberté intellectuelle dans la pensée arabe médiévale," in M. Abitbol et R. Assaraf, eds., *Monothéisme et tolérance: Actes du Colloque du Centre international de recherche sur les Juifs du Maroc, 1–4 Octobre, 1996* (Paris 1997), 57–66. It is, however, more likely that the similarity is yet another indication of Maimonides' direct familiarity with *Faṣl al-maqāl*, and that Averroes himself was Maimonides' source for this idea.

[42] *Guide* 3.32 (*Dalāla*, 384:6–10, 20–25; Pines, 525–26); see also *Guide* 1.33 (*Dalāla*, 384:7–10; Pines, 525).

route rather than taking the shortest way: "God did not lead them by way of the land of the Philistines, *ki* it was nearer" (Ex. 13:17). The Hebrew particle *ki* (because) is usually understood in this context as "although" (*ki* in the sense of *af ki*). Maimonides, however, understands it in its usual meaning, "because." God did not lead them through the land of the Philistines precisely because it was shorter. The short path would not have allowed this nation of recently freed slaves sufficient time to become accustomed to the responsibility required of free, sovereign citizens.[43] For the same reason, God gave the Israelites, accustomed to idolatry, laws that would gradually guide them toward the pure philosophic truth.

In Maimonides' understanding, idolatry is the first and primitive stage of religion in human history. Although it may take on different shapes in different religions, at its base are foundations shared by all. Ethically speaking, idolatry is characterized by licentiousness and the pursuit of the gratification of pleasures in general and of sexual pleasures in particular. When discussing idolatry from this standpoint, Maimonides refers to it as *jāhiliyya*. Maimonides uses this term, derived from Muslim historiography, as a generic term to express the ethical aspect of the initial stage of development in every religion.[44] From a theological standpoint,

[43] *Guide* 3.32 (*Dalāla*, 385:20–25; Pines, 527); "Treatise on Resurrection" (*Epistles*, 355). See also Berman, "Maimonides the Disciple of al-Fārābī," 165–68. See also R. Brague, "La ruse divine (*talaṭṭuf*); quelques textes nouveaux," in T. Langermann and J. Stern, eds., *Adaptations and Innovations: Studies on the Interaction between Jewish and Islamic Thought and Literature from the Early Middle Ages to the Late Twentieth Century, Dedicated to Professor Joel L. Kraemer* (Paris 2007), 17–26.

[44] *Jumhūr al-jāhiliyya*; *Guide* 2.32 (*Dalāla*, 253:17; Pines, 160, translates: "the multitudes among the Pagans"). S. Munk (Maïmonide, *Le Guide des égarés: traité de théologie et de philosophie par Moïse ben Maimoun dit Maïmonide*, [Paris 1881], 3:260n2) rightly points out that in using this term, Maimonides "is referring to . . . the condition of nations who had never benefited from divine revelation, namely the age of paganism." In contrast to Munk's assertion, however, Maimonides did not use this term "in conformity with the practice of the Arab writers," since the latter employ it, as a rule, solely to denote the pre-Islamic period. This consistent terminology of the Arab writers led Hourani to view Maimonides' use of this term as a veiled reference to Islam. See G. F. Hourani, "Maimonides and Islam," in W. N. Brinner and S. D. Ricks, eds., *Studies in Islamic and Judaic Traditions* (Atlanta, 1986), 153–165, esp. 156, on *Guide* 2.32. See also *Guide* 3.33 (*Dalāla,* 389:12) and *Guide* 3.35 (*Dalāla*, 393:29–394:1), where Munk (Maïmonide, *Le Guide des égarés*, 3:273) translates the word *jāhiliyya* as "the ignorant" (and cf. Pines, 532 and 537, respectively). In contrast, in *Guide* 3.39 (*Dalāla*, 406:21–24; Pines, 554), the word *jāhiliyya* apparently does denote the pre-Islamic period and its ideals of unconditional generosity and hospitality. It is likely that when Maimonides juxtaposes "*al-milal al-jāhiliyya*" with "*milla fāḍila*" he is influenced by Fārābī's taxonomy; See Kraemer, "On Maimonides' Messianic Posture," 109–10, and note 2. Idolatry as an early stage of human religion appears also in *Mishneh Torah*, Laws of Idolatry, 1–2, where Maimonides sketches a gradual deterioration

the beliefs of idolatry are false, even when they contain a grain of truth. For example, some idolaters believe in prophesy, but their conception of prophesy is simplistic and misguided.[45] All idolaters believe in the existence of God, but they worship idols as symbols of the entities that mediate between humans and the Divine. Echoing the Greek philosophical tradition regarding the role of idols, Maimonides writes that "no human being of the past has ever imagined on any day, and no human being of the future will ever imagine, that the form that he fashions either from cast metal or from stone and wood has created and governs the heavens and the earth."[46] Maimonides further adds that all idolaters believe in the eternal existence of the world.[47]

The Israelites were accustomed to the rites and beliefs of the idolaters in whose midst they lived, and God knew that they would be incapable of abandoning them abruptly. He therefore granted them commandments that serve as intermediary steps toward the truth, preparing the way for purer forms of worship. The sacrifice of animals to the true, one God is an intermediary step between sacrifices made to the idols and worship through prayer or philosophical study alone. The anthropomorphic verses of the Torah are also an intermediate step between idol worship and a pure, abstract understanding of God. In other cases, God uses a different method to educate humans by commanding them to do the opposite of that to which they have been accustomed.[48] In the first method, God makes concessions, as it were, to the habits of the past, while in the second, He insists that humans overcome their habits. Both methods are based on the same conception, according to which educators must take into account the human inborn tendency to remain attached to habits and past traditions, and to base an educational approach on an intimate knowledge of these habits.

Maimonides uses the principle of "divine accommodation" as the basis for his explanation of those biblical commandments that have no obvious purpose. The centrality of this issue for him is reflected clearly in the fact that he devotes to it some twenty chapters of *Guide of the Perplexed*, in addition to many references and discussions in his other

---

from "soft" idolatry in the times of Enosh to the more offensive versions in later pre-Abrahamic times. As a prooftext for the earlier stage, Maimonides mentions Jer. 10.8 ("But they are brutish and foolish"). He thus seems to offer "foolishness" (*ksilut*, derived from the "*yskhalu*" in the verse) as the Hebrew equivalent of *jāhiliyya*.

[45] *Guide* 2.32 (*Dalāla*, 253:17; Pines, 360). See also *Guide* 1.63 (*Dalāla*, 105:22–106: 6; Pines, 153–54).

[46] *Guide* 1.36 (*Dalāla*, 56:19–57:7; Pines, 83).

[47] *Guide* 3.29 (*Dalāla*, 375:26; Pines, 515), 3:41 (*Dalāla*, 414:5; Pines, 565).

[48] Assmann proposes calling this method "normative inversion." See *Moses the Egyptian*, 57–59.

writings as well.[49] His main interest is in the development of Judaism, but it seems that he used this same basic principle to understand the development of Islam in relation to the practices of the *jāhiliyya*, and the religious development of the human race in general.[50] In all of his discussions of these matters, he refers to idolaters as "Sabians." He first describes their beliefs, according to which the spirits (*ruḥānīyāt*), related to the planets, govern the world and all earthly phenomena. He touches briefly on Sabian historiography (which from a certain angle may be viewed as a reversal of biblical history, similar to the historiography found in Gnostic writings),[51] and subsequently describes their practices and theurgic rites.

Maimonides viewed himself as close to the Maghrebi-Andalusian intellectual tradition in general and to its philosophical tradition in particular.[52] It is therefore no wonder that even regarding the principles of religious theory that he developed, the influence that he admits explicitly is that of the philosophers who belong to this tradition. In summarizing the philosophical ideas of the ancient Sabians, he recalls their belief that God is the spirit of the sphere, and invokes in this context the *Commentary* on Aristotle's *Physics* written by Ibn Bājja.[53]

[49] See *Guide* 3.29–50; The "Treatise on Resurrection" (*Epistles,* 355); "Letter on Astrology" (*Epistles,* 481); "Letter to Joseph Ibn Jābir (*Epistles,* 408–9); introduction to *Pereq Heleq* (*Commentary on the Mishnah*, Tractate *Nezikin,* 203–4); *Mishneh Torah, Laws of Idolatry (Hilkhot Avodah Zarah)* 1:3. See also Twersky, *Introduction to the Code,* 292 and note 81.

[50] See further below.

[51] On this "reversal," see G. G. Stroumsa, *Another Seed: Studies in Gnostic Mythology* (Leiden, 1984), esp. 170. Maimonides takes a particular interest in the stories about Adam and the Garden of Eden, and points out the danger of the Sabian myths (*khurāfāt*); see *Guide* 3.29 (*Dalāla,* 375:27–376:5 [Pines, 515–16], 379:27–380:7 [Pines, 520]); cf. H. M. Y. Gevaryahu, "Paganism According to Maimonides," in A. Weiser and B.-Z. Lourie, eds., *Tzvi Karl Memorial Volume* (Jerusalem, 1960), 354, 357. The place of Adam, Seth, and Noah in Maimonides' synopsis of the Sabian myths faithfully reflects the content of *al-Filāḥa al-Nabaṭiyya*, a work that reflects late renderings of Gnostic and Manichean sources. Therefore, this tradition contains nothing that can clarify the question of the "*ibrāhimiyya*" or the "*Barāhima*"; cf. B. Abrahamov, "The Barāhima's Enigma: A Search for New Solution," *Die welt des Orients* 18 (1987): 72–91, and particularly 84–91.

[52] See chap. 1, note 24, above; and see also *Guide* 1.71 (*Dalāla,* 122:9–13; Pines, 177). On the question of the existence of an Andalusian philosophical school, see L. I. Conrad, "The World of Ibn Ṭufayl," in L. I. Conrad, ed., *The World of Ibn Ṭufayl: Interdisciplinary Perspectives on Ḥayy ibn Yaqẓān* (Leiden, 1996), 12–13.

[53] See *Guide* 3.29 (*Dalāla,* 375:18–26; Pines, 515); "Treatise on Resurrection" (*Epistles,* 335); Pines, "Translator's Introduction," cvii. Ibn Bājja's *Commentary* on the *Physics* is extant in two versions; see *Sharḥ al-Samāʿ al-ṭabīʿī li-arisṭuṭālis*, ed. Mājid Fakhrī (Beirut, 1974); *Shurūḥāt al-Samāʿ al-ṭabīʿī li-bni Bājja*, ed. Amīn Zīyādah (Beirut, 1978); Maimonides is probably referring to the eighth chapter of the commentary, whose topic is the

According to Maimonides' description, at the basis of Sabian theurgy is the belief in the *ruḥāniyyāt* associated with the various planets and governing the diverse objects of the world. This belief is often mentioned in Arabic literature, which sometimes (but not always) associates it with the Sabians and with Hermetic literature.[54] This belief was clearly known to contemporary Jews and Muslims as related to astrological and magical theories.

The description of the Sabians as believing in the eternity of the world appears already in the oldest extant theological *summa* in Arabic, *Twenty Chapters,* written in the first half of the ninth century by Dāwūd al-Muqammaṣ. Muqammaṣ, a Jew who was educated by Christians in Nisibis, identifies the Sabians with *aṣḥāb al-hayūlā*, and associates them with the Manicheans.[55] The appearance of this association in the writings of al-Muqammaṣ indicates that already in the ninth century such a description of the Sabians existed among the Oriental Christians. These Christians are therefore a likely source from which Jewish and Muslim heresiographers could draw their information regarding the Sabians.

As Pines has shown, the origin of Maimonides' concept of *talaṭṭuf* is probably Alexander of Aphrodisias' *On the Principles of the All*, a work that Maimonides mentions explicitly in a different context. Theoretically, his direct sources for this concept could also be some commentaries on either Aristotle or Alexander.[56]

In addition to the philosophical sources that he mentions explicitly, Maimonides had recourse to other sources that he leaves unmentioned, although some of them seem to have had a profound impact on

---

moving principle of the eternal motion of rotation, but I was unable to find the opinion to which Maimonides refers in either of the published texts.

[54] For example, Shahrastānī, *Kitāb al-milal wa'l-niḥal,* 203–6. Shahrastānī actually identifies the Sabians as "*asḥāb al-rūḥāniyyāt*"; and cf., for example, Judah Halevi (*al-Kitāb al-Khazarī*), 20. See also S. Pines, "On the Term *Ruḥaniyyot* and its Origin and on Judah Halevi's Doctrine," *Tarbiz* 57 (1988): 511–40. On the Arabic Hermetic literature, see van Bladel, *The Arabic Hermes.*

[55] See Stroumsa, *Dāwūd ibn Marwān al-Muqammiṣ's Twenty Chapters*, 107 and note 30, 130 and note 12. On the association of the Sabians with this belief, see also Sayed Nomanul Haq, *Names, Natures and Things: The Alchemist Jābir b. Hayyān and His* Kitāb al-aḥjār (Book of Stones) (Dordecht and Boston, 1994), 156 (=Arabic 38:14), 246.

[56] Pines, "Translator's Introduction," lxii–lxxiv; "*Maqālat al-Iskandar al-afrūdīsī fi al-qawl fi mabādi' al-kull,*" ʿAbd al-Raḥmān Badawī, *Arisṭū ʿinda'l-ʿArab* (Cairo, 1947), 253–77, esp. 265 ff; Ch. Genequand, *Alexander of Aphrodisias on the Cosmos* (Leiden, Boston, and Köln, 2001), 16, 168; *Guide* 2.3; and see note 41, above. Maurice Kriegel has pointed to Galen as a possible source for Maimonides' concept of *talaṭṭuf*. See M. Kriegel, "Messianisme juif, dissidence chrétienne et réformes: les usages d'une thèse de Maïmonide," *Pardès* 24 (1998): 197–98 and note 5.

his thought. For example, Maimonides distinguishes between "the first (Divine) intention," which is the elimination of idolatry, and "the second intention," which is the ethical improvement of individuals and the just governance of society.[57] This distinction, a cornerstone in his understanding of the role of religion, appears in the writings of the Aristotelian philosophers (including Alexander of Aphrodisias's above-mentioned *On the Principles of the All*), where it has a somewhat different meaning.[58] It does, however, occupy a central place in the "The Epistles of the Pure Brethren," where it is used in similar political contexts.[59] Maimonides was familiar with these epistles, to which he refers in a derogatory manner in his letter to Samuel Ibn Tibbon.[60] His criticism of their approach in itself does not, however, preclude their influence on him. His unacknowledged usage of their understanding of a two-tiered Divine intention may well reflect this ambivalent attitude.[61]

In the historiographic and heresiographic literature of Maimonides' time the Sabians have a considerable presence, and it is likely that Maimonides read this literature and that it had a significant impact on his views. It was commonplace to associate the Sabians with the biblical Abraham, an association that emphasizes the role of Ḥarrān and that presents the Harranian Sabian religion as paradigmatic idolatry.[62] Works that may have reached Maimonides also indicate an association of the Sabians with the Nabateans.[63] Already Masʿūdī identifies the Sabians/

[57] See *Guide* 3.27 (*Dalāla*, 371–73; Pines, 510–12), 3.29 (*Dalāla*, 377:11; Pines, 517), 3.32 (*Dalāla*, 385:17, 27; 386:11, 17, 21; Pines, 527–28).

[58] The formula is common in the philosophers' discussion of divine providence; see, for example, *Discourse of Alexander of Aphrodisias on the Governance (tadbīrāt) of the Sphere*, 53.1–59.3; See Genequand, *Alexander of Aphrodisias on the Cosmos*, 45, 66. The terms *al-qaṣd al-awwal /al-qaṣd al-thānī,* which appear in Abū Bishr Mattā's Arabic translation in the sense of "primarily/secondarily," have no equivalent in the Greek original of that text. I am indebted to Fritz Zimmerman for bringing this text to my attention and for discussing it with me.

[59] *Rasāʾil ikhwān al-ṣafāʾ wa-khillān al-wafāʾ* (Beirut, n.d.), 3:476–78 (*al-Risāla al-ūlā min al-ʿulūm al-nāmūsīya*).

[60] See Stroumsa, "A Note on Maimonides' Attitude to Joseph ibn Ṣadiq," 33–38.

[61] On the Neoplatonic Ismāʿīlī influence on Maimonides, see A.L. Ivry, "Ismāʿīlī Theology and Maimonides' Philosophy," in D. Frank, ed., *The Jews of Medieval Islam: Community, Society and Identity* (Leiden, 1995), 271–99; idem, "Neoplatonic Currents in Maimonides' Thought," 115–40; and see chap. 1, note 35, above. An unacknowledged use of Ismāʿīlī sources was a common practice in Judeo-Arabic literature. See Stroumsa, "Citation Traditions," 170–72.

[62] See Gen. 11:31, 12:4; and see, for example, Ibn al-Nadīm, *Fihrist*, 373.

[63] For example, *Ghāyat al-Ḥakīm*, attributed to the philosopher Majrīṭī; see, M. Fierro, "Bāṭinism in al-Andalus: Maslāma b. Qāsim al Qurṭubī (d.353/964), Author of the *Rutbat al-Ḥakīm* and the *Ghāyat al-Ḥakīm (Picatrix)*," *Studia Islamica* 84 (1996): 7–112. As noted by D. Chwolsohn ("Über die Überreste der altbabylonischen Literatur in arabischen

Nabateans with the Egyptians,[64] an identification recorded also by Shahrastānī.[65] The Sabians are also mentioned, already before Maimonides, in the context of explaining the commandments of the Torah. As Pines has shown, this explanation, which appears in the writings of the tenth-century Qaraite Qirqisānī, is a development of the Church Fathers' concept of "divine accommodation," and it may have reached Qirqisānī and Maimonides—directly or indirectly—from Christian sources. It is perhaps not superfluous to recall that Qirqisānī relies heavily on Muqammaṣ, in both his polemics and exegesis. Muqammaṣ may thus have been a transmission link of this particular idea to Jewish thought.[66] The notion that the behavior of the Israelites must be explained in the context of their times is also propounded by Judah Halevi.[67] Judah Halevi mentions *al-Filāḥā al-nabaṭiyya* but he does not associate it with the Sabians, and, although he presents the contemporaneous, idolatrous culture as attenuating circumstances for the sins of the Israelites, he makes no attempt to explain the historical context for the commandments.[68] By contrast, Abraham Ibn Ezra, in his commentary on Ex. 2:10, mentions an agricultural book translated from the Egyptian (!) into Arabic.[69] Maimonides was influenced by Ibn Ezra in general, and in particular by his views regarding the historical context of the Exodus,[70] and it is possible that this

Übersetzung," *Mémoires des savants étrangers*, [St. Petersburg, 1850], 8:17), the Arab use of "Nabatean" denoted all peoples of the Ancient Near East, including the Canaanites.

[64] See note 11, above.

[65] Shahrastānī, *Kitāb al-milal wa'l-niḥal*, 139. According to Shahrastānī, Pharaoh was a Sabian until he deviated from their religion (apparently a pun on a common etymology of the word *ṣābi'a*; see ibid., 125).

[66] See Pines, "Some Traits of Christian Theological Writing in Relation to Muslim Kalām and to Jewish Thought," *Proceedings of the Israel Academy of Sciences and Humanities* 5 (1976): 104–25, (reprinted in *The Collected Works of Shlomo Pines,* 3, *Studies in the History of Arabic Philosophy*, ed. S. Stroumsa, [Jerusalem 1996], 79–99); Qirqisānī, *Kitāb al-anwār wa'l-marāqib,* ed. L. Nemoy (New Haven, 1940–45), 43–44, and 214, 326, 587–88, 676; A. Funkenstein, "Gesetz und Geschichte: Zur historisierenden Hermeneutik bei Maimonides und Thomas von Aquin," *Viator* 1 (1970): 147–78. Assmann, *Moses the Egyptian,* 53; S. D. Benin, "The 'Cunning of God' and Divine Accommodation," *Journal of the History of Ideas* 45 (1984): 181–85; for the broader context of the concept of accommodation since Late Antiquity, see S. D. Benin, *The Footprints of God: Divine Accommodation in Jewish and Christian Thought* (Albany, 1993).

[67] See *Rabbi Yehuda Halevi, The Kuzari: In Defense of the Despised Faith,* trans. N. Daniel Korobkin (Northvale, N.J., and Jerusalem, 1998), 38–42, 99–100.

[68] See *al-Kitāb al-Khazarī*, 17; and see note 86, below.

[69] As Steinschneider has suggested, Ibn Ezra relied apparently on an erroneous reading of the Arabic, which replaced the Nabatean agriculture with Coptic; see Chwolsohn, "Über die Überreste de altbabylonischen Literatur," 12.

[70] See S. Pines, "Ibn Khaldūn and Maimonides, a Comparison between Two Texts," *Studia Islamica* 32 (1979): 265–74, esp. 270. See also I. Twersky, "Did R. Abraham Ibn Ezra Influence Maimonides?" in I. Twersky and J.M. Harris, eds., *Rabbi Abraham Ibn Ezra: Studies in the Writings of a Twelfth-Century Jewish Polymath* (Cambridge, Mass. 1993), 21–48.

error played a role in Maimonides' identification of the Egyptians with the Sabians and with *al-Filāḥā al-nabaṭiyya*.

Maimonides repeatedly declares that he has read "[the Sabians'] books, translated into Arabic, which are in our hands today."[71] These books represent, in his opinion, only a small fraction of the Sabian literature, most of which was never translated into Arabic or is no longer extant. In *Guide of the Perplexed*, he notes in detail the books he has read, promising the reader that "I shall mention to you the books from which all that I know about the doctrines and opinions of the Sabians will become clear to you."[72] Maimonides' reading list includes books most of which are known to us, at least in the sense that they are also mentioned by other authors. The most important among them are *al-Filāḥā al-nabaṭiyya*[73] and the *Book of Ṭumṭum*,[74] but he also mentions the *Book of Istimākhis*,[75] two books of Isḥāq al-Ṣabī,[76] a book of charms attributed to Hermes, and a book of talismans attributed to Aristotle, as well as "The Book of the Degrees of the Sphere,"[77] and a book known as "*Kitāb al-Sarab*."[78] These are works on astrology, magic, and theurgy, whose origin is Indian,[79] Hermetic, or pseudo-Aristotelian literature. They were apparently known

---

[71] *Guide* 3.29 (*Dalāla*, 374:26, 380:16; Pines, 514, 521); see also "Epistle on Astrology," *Epistles*, 281.

[72] *Guide* 3.29 (*Dalāla*, 378:11–12; Pines, 518). See also *Guide* 3.37 (*Dalāla*, 395:28, 397:3–4, 399:8; Pines, 540, 542, 544).

[73] Some scholars maintain that the composition of this book indeed goes back to the pre-Islamic period. See, for instance, F. Sezgin, *GAS*, 4:307, 318–29; T. Fahd, "Retour à Ibn Waḥshiyya," *Arabica* 16 (1969): 83–88; Peters, "Hermes and Harran" (reprinted by Savage Smith), 64. Others claim that the book was written after the rise of Islam. See, for example, A. von Gutschmid, "Die nabatäische Landwirtschaft und ihre Geshwister," *ZDMG* 15 (1861): 1–110; Th. Nödecke, "Noch Einiges über die 'nabatäische Landwirtschaft'," *ZMDG* 29 (1875): 445–55; M. Ullmann, *Natur-und Geheimwissenschaften im Islam* (Leiden, 1972), 441–42. According to Hämeen-Anttila (*The Last Pagans of Iraq*, 24) the original text was written in Syriac, "just before the Islamic conquest or at the beginning of the Islamic period. Even a very late date, more or less coinciding with the beginning of the translation movement . . . cannot be ruled out." It should, however, be noted that Maimonides was confident of the book's ancient origin, and the thorny question regarding its actual origins is thus peripheral to our topic.

[74] See A. Hauber, "Ṭomṭom (Ṭimṭim)=Dandamis=Dindymus," *ZDMG* 63 (1909): 457–72; Ullmann, *Natur-und Geheimwissenschaften im Islam*, 299–300, 381.

[75] See Ullmann, *Natur-und Geheimwissenschaften im Islam*, 374; Burnett, "Arabic, Greek and Latin Works on Astrological Magic," 85–86.

[76] For more on Isḥāq al-Ṣabī, see C. Brockelmann, *Geschichte der arabische Literatur*, 1: 399.

[77] *Kitāb Daraj al-falak;* see Ullmann, *Natur-und Geheimwissenschaften im Islam*, 329 ff.

[78] On these books, see Chwolsohn, *Die Ssabier*, 1: 697–716; Munk, *Le Guide des égarés*, 2: 239–42; Ullmann, *Natur-und Geheimwissenschaften im Islam*, 329–30; Burnett, "Arabic, Greek and Latin Works on Astrological Magic," 87.

[79] Or at least influenced by Indian literature; see D. Pingree, "Indian Planetary Images and the Tradition of Astral Magic," *Journal of the Warburg and Courtauld Institute* 52 (1989): 1–13, esp. 9.

in Maimonides' environment, in al-Andalus as well as in North Africa.[80] A similar list appears in the *Ghāyat al-ḥakīm*, as well as in "*The Epistles of the Pure Brethren*."[81]

Among the books mentioned in this context by Maimonides, *al-Filāḥā al-nabaṭiyya* is the best known, and the only one that survived in its entirety. This fact brought scholarly attention to focus on this work and contributed to creating the impression that Maimonides attempts to identify the Nabateans (a specific and identifiable nation) with the Sabians. While Maimonides does describe this book as "the most important book about this subject,[82] he also emphasizes that he has reviewed all the books on the subject, or at least all material translated into Arabic. He repeatedly cites the books he read and their influence on the development of his thought. As noted by Pines,[83] it appears that Maimonides believed that his written sources on the Nabateans were reliable historical accounts. At the same time, it is also obvious that he read this work as a phenomenological document, and not as a detailed description of any particular nation. We may say, with Steinschneider, that Maimonides identifies as Sabian anything related to astrology.[84] For Maimonides, the boundaries of the Sabian *milla* were not determined by ethnic, geographically defined identity, but rather by the astrological literature.[85]

It is thus relatively easy to identify the sources from which Maimonides could have drawn the various components of his theory; the theory itself, however, as a consolidated entirety, cannot be found in these sources.

To the best of my knowledge, none of the Arab heresiographical or philosophical sources available to Maimonides had attempted to draw an inventory of Sabian literature, with the *al-Filāḥā al-nabaṭiyya* as its

[80] On Hermetic literature preserved in the Cairo Genizah, see A. Eliyahu, "Genizah Fragments from the Hermetic Literature," *Ginzei Kedem* 1 (2005): 9–29 [Hebrew]. As suggested by Gregor Schwarb, the presence of these texts in Egyptian Christian-Arabic literature after Maimonides suggests that they were also available for Maimonides in Egypt (and not just a literary bag he carried with him from al-Andalus); see G. Schwarb, "Die Rezeption Maimonides' in der christlich-arabischen Literatur," *Judaica* 63 (2007): 24–38.

[81] See *Ghāyat al-Ḥakim*, 83 (*Picatrix*, 80), 179 (190), 339 (309), and 19, 190, 198, 242 (*Picatrix*, 187, 200, 201, 253); see also *Rasā'il Ikhwān al-Safā'*, 4: 295.

[82] *Guide* 3.29 (*Dalāla*, 378:18; Pines, 518). On Maimonides' use of this book, see, P. Fenton, "Une source arabe du *Guide* de Maïmonide: L'agriculture nabatéenne d'Ibn Waḥshiyya," in Lévy and Rashed, eds., *Maïmonide philosophe et savant*, 303–33.

[83] Pines, "Translator's Introduction," cxxiii.

[84] See Steinschneider, "Zur pseudepigraphischen Literatur, insbesondere der geheimen Wissenschaften des Mittelalters aus hebräischen und arabischen Quellen," *Wissenschaftlische Blätter aus der Veitel Heine Ephraim'schen Lehranstalt (Beth Ha-Midrasch) in Berlin* (Berlin, 1862), 3: 3.

[85] Cf. Stern, "The Fall and Rise of Myth in Ritual," 190, 224.

cornerstone.[86] Furthermore, as far as I know, in none of these sources—naturally not the Muslim, but also not the Jewish or Christian sources—can we find a methodical analysis of the commandments and verses of the Torah that associates them with rites described in the literature that Maimonides classifies as "Sabian." Maimonides is not content with a vague reference to the Sabians, or even a general explanation of the commandments. He offers a highly detailed analysis of the sources, and presents a meticulous comparison of the Torah, on the one hand, and the literature described as "Sabian," on the other. Maimonides' originality lies in his idea to systematically compare these two groups of texts, an idea that represents a revolutionary breakthrough in medieval reflection on religion.

Paradoxically, the very scientific precision that brought Maimonides to identify his sources explicitly has also obscured his originality, creating the impression that, if indeed he used all the sources he cites, then everything he wrote must derive from them. Precisely because of his meticulous recording of what he learned from others, however, one must be attentive to his repeated declarations regarding his own discoveries, the ones he did not find in any other book. Maimonides repeatedly emphasizes that he did his own research on the Sabians.[87] In the "Letter on Astrology," for example, he states, "I also have read in all matters concerning all of idolatry, so that it seems to me there does not remain in the world a composition on this subject, having been translated into Arabic from other languages, but that I have read it and have understood its subject matter and have plumbed the depth of its thought," and he hastens to add, "From those books it became clear to me what the reason is for all those commandments that everyone comes to think of as having no reasons at all other than the decree of Scriptures." In his detailed analysis of the reasons for the commandments he painstakingly adds footnotes.[88]

[86] *Ghāyat al-ḥakīm* discusses *al-Filāḥā al-nabaṭiyya* in proximity to its mention of the Sabians, but does not identify them explicitly with each other. Judah Halevi regards the *Filāḥā* as an Indian work, and describes the Indians as "a wayward people" (*umma sā'iba*); see *al-Kitāb al-Khazarī* 16–17 (Korobkin, 21).

[87] *Epistles*, 481; "Letter on Astrology," in Lerner and Mahdi, *Medieval Political Philosophy*, 227–36, on 229 (my emphasis). See also S. Sela, "Queries on Astrology Sent from Southern France to Maimonides; Critical Edition of the Hebrew Text, Translation and Commentary," *Alef* 4 (2004): 89–190.

[88] Regarding the verse, "A woman must not put on man's apparel, nor shall a man wear woman's clothing" (Deut 22:5), he says: "*tajiduhu fī kitāb ṭumṭum*" (*Guide* 3.37; *Dalāla*, 399:9; Pines, 544). In his explanations of the prohibition of agricultural grafts he explains that "*ḍhakarū bi-bayān fī tilka al-filāḥā* (*Guide* 3.37; *Dalāla*, 402:14; Pines, 549)." The prohibition on eating blood arises, he claims, from the prevalence of the consumption of meat at that time as part of idolatrous practices, "*ka-mā bāna fī ṭumṭum.*" (*Guide* 3.41; *Dalāla*, 411:13–15; Pines, 561); and the prohibition to sacrifice "leaven or honey" (Lev. 2:11) arises from the pagan custom of sacrificing sweets," *ka-mā huwa mashhūr fī'l-kutub allātī ḍhakartu laka* (*Guide* 3.46; *Dalāla*, 427:18; Pines, 582).

Maimonides' originality, the fact that he presents the fruits of his own scholarship rather than reiterates the ideas of his predecessors, is also readily apparent in the way he constructs and substantiates his claims, while openly admitting the limitations of his scholarship.[89] At the same time, he is clearly aware of the radical innovation that he is making, and of the strong resistance that his ideas are likely to meet.[90]

Maimonides' repeated insistence on his innovation is not empty vainglory. As far as I can tell, Maimonides was indeed the first author to offer an explicit and detailed analysis of pagan influence on the development of monotheistic religions. Maimonides' originality should be viewed in the context of the Jewish, Rabbinic tradition, on the one hand, and of the contemporary Arabic culture, on the other. This deserves to be emphasized not only in order to give Maimonides the honor he is due, but also because the explanation for Maimonides' discovery lies in his relationship to both cultures. Maimonides is positioned at a cultural crossroads that, because of his own openness to the possibilities it offered, proved particularly fecund. His broad education in Arabic culture gave him access to philosophical and heresiographical literature, through which he learned of the Sabians: not the historical Sabians sought by modern scholarship, but rather the confused myth of the Sabians as a collective name that includes different peoples, as they were known in the twelfth century. The encounter with these Sabians led Maimonides to believe that he had discovered the essence and foundation of idolatry. The combination of his broad Arabic education with his tremendous erudition in the Jewish sources, and his interest in understanding the commandments of the Torah, enabled him to make a major breakthrough. It is this combination that allowed him to identify in the Sabian writings—so he believed—the idolatry for which the commandments of the Torah are meant to serve as an antidote. This identification, and its detailed analysis, is Maimonides' original discovery; it was not made by anyone before him, and, if we consider the special admixture of fields of knowledge and areas of

---

[89]When Maimonides is unable to provide an explanation for a commandment, he states this outright. For example, regarding the commandment of libations as part of some sacrifices, he says: "As for the offering of wine, I am up to now perplexed with regard to it: How could He have commanded to offer it, since the ***idolaters*** offered it? No reason for this has occurred to me" (*Guide* 3.46; *Dalāla*, 434:12–14; Pines, 591). To his explanation for the prohibition of eating meat cooked with milk, he adds: "According to me, this is the most probable view regarding the reason for this prohibition; but I have not seen this set down in any of the books of the Sabians that I have read" (*Guide*, 3.48; *Dalāla*, 440:1–7; Pines, 599). See also Gevaryahu, "Paganism According to Maimonides," 358.

[90]See *Guide* 3.32 (*Dalāla*, 385:13–17; Pines, 527): "I know that on thinking about this at first your soul will necessarily have a feeling of repugnance toward this notion and will feel aggrieved because of it."

interest that this discovery requires, one might say that no one prior to him could have made it.

The method of taking data acquired from a "secular" culture and using them for understanding the religious tradition is typical of Maimonides. Lawrence Berman has demonstrated that "[Maimonides] took the Alfarabian theory of the relationship between philosophy, religion, jurisprudence and theology and applied it in a thorough manner to a particular religion, Judaism."[91] Berman further adds that "Maimonides did what no one else did explicitly in medieval Middle Eastern culture." In Maimonides' study of the Sabians, he uses the same method, with similarly revolutionary results. In identifying the magical or "agricultural" literature attributed to the Nabateans and to others with Sabian culture, Maimonides believed that he had discovered the textual basis for the study of paganism in antiquity. The insights he developed on this basis suggest a line of thought similar to the one pursued by modern biblical scholarship in its quest for the origins of Israelite religion, and its attempts to understand it in the context of the polytheism in which it germinated. One might say that in this way Maimonides developed the first systematic Jewish attempt to carry out a comparative study of the history of religion, an attempt to understand the laws of the Torah within their cultural context.

Maimonides' innovation has not been acknowledged by modern scholars, who read the *Guide* within the confines of their specific areas of expertise. For scholars of Arabic culture, in pursuit of the Sabian nation, Maimonides is only a late source who reflects the confusion found in earlier sources. Chwolsohn has already asserted that Maimonides' Sabians are useless in the attempt to identify the historical Sabians, and he dismisses him saying, "[Maimonides'] statements must therefore be viewed as nothing but stories about the pagans and paganism, recounted by an uncritical Jewish-Arab sage of the Middle Ages."[92] Steinschneider, who disagreed with Chwolsohn in other matters, shared his opinion regarding Maimonides' uncritical scholarly approach.[93] A similar judgment was issued by Baron,[94] as well as by Tardieu.[95]

[91] Berman, "Maimonides the Disciple of al-Fārābī," 155; See also Kraemer, "On Maimonides' Messianic Posture," 100–109.

[92] Chwolsohn, *Die Ssabier*, 1: 716.

[93] Steinschneider, "*Zur pesuepigraphischen Literatur,*" 4–5.

[94] S. Baron, "The Historical Outlook of Maimonides," *PAAJR* 6 (1935): 5–113 (Reprinted in S. W. Baron, *History and Jewish Historians* [Philadelphia, 1964], 109–63, and esp. 115). A similar reservation is also implied by Halbertal and Margalit, who do not mention the topic of the Sabians in their book on idolatry. The summary of their analysis of Maimonides' position begins with the words, "whatever historical validity Maimonides' description may have had, . . ."; see M. Halbertal and A. Margalit, *Idolatry* (Cambridge, Mass., 1992), 44.

[95] See note 32, above.

Scholars of Judaism, on the other hand, who seek to understand Maimonides in the context of Jewish thought, accept the position of the "Arabists," according to which Maimonides' interest in the Sabians is no more than a natural continuation of what can be found in the Muslim heresiographical literature. Therefore, even when they pay lip service to Maimonides' originality, it appears from their writing that if he made any innovation at all, it was marginal and insignificant. Isadore Twersky, who dedicated a bulky monograph to Maimonides' legal compendium and to his legal philosophy, devoted just a few words to the Sabians (who occupy several dozen pages in Maimonides' writing). Twersky makes a passing reference to Maimonides' innovation, describing it as "quite novel, and highly controversial in the opinion of most of Maimonides' successors."[96] "Quite novel" seems to me a rather pale epithet to describe Maimonides' discovery, in particular since Twersky does not dwell on the topic.

Similarly, Halbertal and Margalit discuss at length Maimonides' views on idolatry. Maimonides' phenomenological efforts, however, and the painstaking cultural study of which he was so proud are not discussed in their book at all, and his innovative insight is reduced to a "change . . . in the direction of internalization."[97] Josef Stern recognizes Maimonides' originality within the Jewish tradition, describing him as "the first figure within the rabbinic tradition . . . to explicitly acknowledge the formative role of pagan myth on the rituals and commandments of the Mosaic Law."[98] Limiting the evaluation to the Rabbinic tradition, however, obfuscates Maimonides' sources, on the one hand, and does not do justice to his independence from them, on the other. As argued here, an explicit and developed analysis of the role of pagan myth in shaping monotheistic religions in general and the specific commandments of the Torah in particular is not found prior to Maimonides, in either Jewish or non-Jewish sources.

The historian Heinrich Graetz evaluated Maimonides' explanations as "superficial."[99] Amos Funkenstein, who quotes Graetz in his study on the topic of "divine accommodation" is milder: he provides an overview of Maimonides' ideas and admits that "it is still possible that the argument of Maimonides is new and reliable in its method rather than in the

[96] Twersky, *Introduction to the Code of Maimonides,* 389 and note 81. In the footnote, Twersky writes: "I have prepared a separate monograph on Maimonides as a historian of religion." Unfortunately, such a monograph was never published.

[97] Halbertal and Margalit, *Idolatry*, 109.

[98] Stern, "The Fall and Rise of Myth in Ritual": 187–88; see also Gevaryahu, "Paganism According to Maimonides," 353, 357.

[99] H. Graetz, *Die Konstruktion der jüdischen Geschichte* (Berlin, 1936), 84–86.

actual validity of his historical reconstruction." With regard to the Sabians, however, Funkenstein seems to share Graetz's view, according to which Maimonides tried his hand at historic and anthropological research, and failed.[100]

Indeed, if we assume that Maimonides believed in the historical existence of a universal polytheistic religion, and that he based his writings on prior heresiographers, the lukewarm scholarly evaluation of his achievement is understandable. One can also understand Funkenstein's puzzlement about the fact that Maimonides writes about the Sabians "with the genuine enthusiasm of a discovery."[101] It is, however, precisely Maimonides' enthusiasm that should alert us to his true discovery. Both the Sabians and the concept of "divine accommodation" were well known in his day.[102] Taken separately, neither of these two topics would have aroused in Maimonides the enthusiasm that is so obviously reflected in his writing. The combination of the two together, however, allowed Maimonides the flash of discovery. Maimonides is very conscious of the phenomenological nature of his discovery. His original contribution does not lie in the identification of a nation or a religion in the ordinary sense, and historical identification is not what he aspires to do. As Twersky noted, this discovery was rejected by most of Maimonides' Jewish successors.[103] One would have to wait until the seventeenth century, when the Christian Hebraists (who were also the first Orientalists), such as John Spencer and Edward Pocock, rediscovered Maimonides and his Sabians, and turned them into the basis for the modern study of religions in the Ancient Near East.[104]

[100] A. Funkenstein, *Theology and the Scientific Imagination: From the Middle Ages to the Seventeenth Century* (Princeton, 1986), 233–35.

[101] Ibid.

[102] See note 66, above. An interesting example of the broad dissemination of this concept can be found in the writings of the tenth-century Shiite scholar Muḥammad al-Nuʿmānī. In his commentary on Qur'ān 2 [*al-Baqara*]: 106, Nuʿmānī evokes the gradual divine pedagogy in order to explain the concept of abrogation of previous revelations (*naskh*). Nuʿmānī does not employ the term *talaṭṭuf*, but he explains that God, in his tender compassion, did not force the Arabs to abandon abruptly the practices of the *jāhiliyya*; See M. M. Bar-Asher, *Exegesis in Early Imami Shiism* (Jerusalem and Leiden, 1999), 68–70.

[103] See note 96, above. The thirteenth-century Jewish scholar Saʿd Ibn Manṣūr Ibn Kammūna, who used Maimonides' writings faithfully, is an exception; see *Tanqīḥ al-abḥāth li-'l-milal al-thalāth*, ed. M. Perlmann (Berkeley and Los Angeles, 1967), 37. Regarding the response of Maimonides' successors, see also F. Dreyfus, "La condescendance divine (*synkatabasis*) comme principe herméneutique de l'ancien testament dans la tradition juive et dans la tradition chrétienne," *Supplements to Vetus Testamentum* 36, 101–2.

[104] See Benin, "The 'Cunning of God,'" 179–80, 190–91: and see G. G. Stroumsa, *A New Science: The Discovery of Religion in the Age of Reason* (Cambridge, Mass., forthcoming.)

Maimonides as an Historian of Religion

The seventeenth-century Hebraists whose approach to the study of religion was inspired by "Rabbi Moyses" were conditioned by the religious and cultural concerns of their time. It would be incorrect, however, to say that they imposed their ideas on the Maimonidean text. Maimonides' keen interest in religion as a human phenomenon is indeed well attested. As mentioned above, he was greatly influenced by Fārābī's studies of the political and educational role of religion in society, but he carried Fārābī's theory further and investigated its specific implementation in concrete religions.[105] His main interest was his own religion, and he dedicated his analytical energy mostly to the study of the development of Judaism. Nevertheless, he also used the same basic principles to understand the development of Islam.

As noted by Hourani, medieval Jewish thinkers perceived the emergence of Islam as a turning-point in history, since from that point Jews came under Arab rule.[106] In seeking to understand such historical turning-points, and in particular to fathom the reasons for their own submission to other nations, Jewish thinkers usually focused on the relations between God and the Jewish people, and their explanations were formulated in terms of punishment and exile, repentance and redemption. Nevertheless, the third side of the triangle, the nations who serve as God's punishing rod, could not be ignored. Jewish historiography was required to provide explanations for the choice of particular nations to rule over the Jews and for the vicissitudes in their power, and the need to find such explanations became more urgent whenever their dominion was felt as more oppressive. From the general presupposition that God governs history in the best and wisest way, it followed that there must be a reason for the rise of one religious community and for the fall of another, and, in the particular case at hand, there must be a reason for the disintegration of formidable kingdoms and bastions of culture like Christian Byzantium and Sassanian Iran and their conquest by a nation of uncouth nomads.

Few medieval Jewish thinkers engaged in systematic historiography.[107] The study of history, when not part of the *historia sacra*, was often per-

105 See above, *apud* note 91.

106 Hourani, "Maimonides and Islam," 158. On the different shades of Jewish attitudes to Islam, see P. B. Fenton, "Jewish Attitudes to Islam: Israel Heeds Ishmael," *Jerusalem Quarterly* 29 (1983): 84–102.

107 See Y. Heinemann, "Judah Halevi's Historical Perception," *Zion* 9 (1949): 147–77 [Hebrew]. The Midrashic and eschatological literatures tend to give more weight to historical events, and the ones who were composed close to the rise of Islam refer to the Islamic

ceived as a waste of time.[108] In *Guide of the Perplexed*, Maimonides refers dismissively to the perusal of history books (*ta'rīkh min al-tawarīkh*).[109] The same dismissive attitude is expressed in his *Commentary on the Mishnah*, where he describes the "Books of Ben Sirah" as

> ravings (*hadhayān*) concerning the meaning of physiognomy, in which there is neither science nor profit, but sheer wasting of time in idleness, like these books which are found among the Arabs: books of annals (*tawarīkh*), biographies of kings (*siyar al-mulūk*) or genealogies (*ansāb al-ʿArab*), or books on songs (*kutub al-aghānī*), and other books in which there is neither science nor profit to the body, only waste of time.[110]

Despite his poor opinion of this literature, Maimonides' detailed list of literary genres, invoking their precise technical terms in Arabic, demonstrates his close familiarity with it and probably also with specific famous works. This is no surprise: Maimonides, as we have seen above, made a point of reading the books of "ravings" before dismissing them. The purpose for which they were written, however—presenting a historical narrative that glorified the Arabs and Islam, and transmitting their legacy—did not interest him. He used them, as he used Sabian literature, to study human nature.

Because of their general lack of interest in Islamic historiography, medieval Jewish thinkers refer to Islam in their writings mostly in a polemical context, and their discussions of Islam (and of Christianity) remain, more often than not, polemical or apologetic. This is also true for Maimonides, in most of whose explicit and implicit references to Islam and Christianity the polemical tone prevails.[111] Occasionally, however, one can detect in the writings of Jewish thinkers an attempt to place Islam within a historiographical, etiological framework. In these attempts, one can distinguish two main approaches, both of which can be found in Maimonides' writings: a linear approach and a comparative one.

The linear approach (the more prevalent one) arranges human religious experience on a consecutive timeline, whose climax lies in the future, in the days of the Messiah. History is seen as centered on the Jewish nation and on its destiny, while the discussion of other religions is

---

conquest, often favorably. See, for instance, P. Crone and M. Cook, *Hagarism: The Making of the Islamic World* (Cambridge, 1977), 109–10 and note 2.

[108] See Heinemann, "Judah Halevi's Historical Perception," 170.

[109] *Guide* 1.2 (*Dalala*, 16:11; Pines, 24).

[110] *Commentary on the Mishnah*, *Neziqin*, tractate *Sanhedrin*, 210.

[111] See, for instance, chap. 3, note 38, above; also *Guide* 1.50 (*Dalāla*, 75:7–11; Pines, 111); *Guide* 1.71 (*Dalāla*, 123: 4–10; Pines, 178).

meant to assign them a role in the redemption of Israel. Typical examples of this approach can be found in the writings of Saadia Gaon, Abraham ibn Ezra, and Judah Halevi.[112] In Maimonides' works this approach is manifest in his attempt to fit Islam and Christianity into his historiography. In *Guide of the Perplexed* he alludes, without specifically mentioning Islam or Christianity, to these religions' contribution to raising the religious level of humanity. Comparing the contemporaneous situation to that of the days of the Patriarchs, who lived in a Sabian environment, Maimonides says: "If the belief in the existence of the deity were not generally accepted at present to such an extent in the religious communities, our days in these times would be even darker than that epoch."[113] This enigmatic statement does not reveal much about Maimonides' view regarding the direction of religious development in the world. In his *Mishneh Torah*, however, he speaks more clearly, saying:

> As far as the Jewish nation is concerned, [these two religions] only pave the way for the Messiah, to prepare the whole world to worship God in unison, as it is said [Zeph. 3:9]: "For then will I turn to the people a pure language, that they may all call upon the name of the Lord, to serve Him with one consent."
>
> These notions have spread to distant isles, among many peoples, uncircumcised of heart. They discuss these matters and the commandments of the Torah. Some [that is, the Muslims] say: Those commandments were true, but they were abrogated in our times, and were not meant to be binding for generations to come. Others [that is, the Christians] say: Those matters have esoteric meanings; they were not meant to be taken literally, but the Messiah has already come and revealed their meaning.
>
> When the true King-Messiah will appear, when he succeeds and is exalted and glorious, they will all repent immediately. They will then realize that they have inherited naught, and that their prophets and ancestors led them astray.[114]

[112] See S. Stroumsa, "Islam in the Historical Consciousness of Jewish Thinkers of the Arab Middle Ages," in N. Ilan, ed., *The Intertwined Worlds of Islam: Essays in Memory of Hava Lazarus-Yafeh* (Jerusalem, 2002), 447–48.

[113] *Guide* 3.29 (*Dalala*, 379:13–14; Pines, 519). The concluding hint at the dark potential of his own times is crowned with the remark: "However, their darkness is of a different kind."

[114] *Mishneh Torah, Laws of Kings* 11:4 (facsimile of the Rome edition; Jerusalem, 1956). On the polemical themes of abrogation (*naskh*) and corruption (*taḥrīf*), see, for example, H. Lazarus-Yafeh, *Intertwined Worlds: Medieval Islam and Bible Criticism* (Princeton, 1992), 19–49.

This paragraph was censored in Christian lands, and does not appear in most editions.[115] It points to what Maimonides sees as the typical errors of Islam and Christianity. The Muslims claim that the Torah was abrogated by subsequent revelations, and is thus obsolete. They also claim, as Maimonides mentions elsewhere, that the original text of the Torah was corrupted by the Jews, and that the biblical text in their possession is mostly man-made. Because of this Muslim position, which leaves no scriptural common ground for discussion, Maimonides forbids teaching the Torah to Muslims.[116] The Christians, on the other hand, accept the text of the Torah as authentic, but they argue for a radical reinterpretation.[117] Christian hermeneutics is also presented by Maimonides as Christianity's error in his "Epistles on Resurrection." In his *Guide of the Perplexed*, Maimonides adds two other errors of these religions: the Christian doctrine of Trinity, and the question, much debated in Islam, of God's Created Speech.[118]

It is thus obvious that Maimonides was well aware of the doctrinal rifts that separate Judaism from Islam and Christinaity, and he did not take these differences lightly. And yet, in the passage from the *Mishneh Torah* quoted above, he insists on the long-term positive role that Islam and Christianity play. Despite their respective errors, they represent an advancement compared to previous beliefs of their nations, and a stepping-stone on the way to correct beliefs. In this presentation Maimonides adopts (and adapts), consciously or unconsciously, the linear approach of his Jewish predecessors, and in particular Judah Halevi.[119]

In other places, however, another approach emerges where, rather than a linear historical development that leads from one religion to the other, there seems to be a universal, inherent, and continuing process of development within all religions. This approach can be best seen in the *Letter to Obadia the Proselyte*, where Maimonides discusses the permissibility of wine produced by Muslims. The key to the legal decision here lies in the question whether or not Islam is to be considered a monotheistic religion; and the answer to this question lies in the evaluation of Muslim

[115] See Ben-Sasson, "The Singularity of the Jewish Nation as seen in the Twelfth-Century," 145–218 [Hebrew]; Twersky, *Introduction to the Mishneh Torah*, 452; E. Schlossberg, "Maimonides' Attitude to Islam."

[116] See *Responsa*, 285.

[117] *Epistles*, 319, 339.

[118] See *Guide* 1.71 (*Dalala*, 123:4–6; Pines, 178).

[119] As suggested by Twersky, *Introduction to the Mishneh Torah*, 453. On Maimonides' attitude to Islam and Christianity, see also D. J. Lasker, "Tradition and Innovation in Maimonides' Attitude towards Other Religions," in J. M. Harris, ed., *Maimonides after 800 Years: Essays on Maimonides and His Influence* (Cambridge, Mass., 2007), 167–82.

rituals (particularly the ones related to the pilgrimage), which, as Obadia's teacher seems to have pointed out, originate in pagan rituals. Maimonides, on the other hand, stresses the monotheistic nature of Islam, and consequently allows the use of Muslim wine.[120]

The legal status of Muslim wine, and its linking to the rituals of the *ḥajj*, had been discussed before Maimonides by the Gaonim, who have suggested that despite their origin, these rituals as performed in a monotheistic context do not constitute idolatrous practices. Although the Gaonic *responsa* focused on the specific legal question, its implications for the issue of whether or not of Islam is truly monotheistic must have been evident to the Gaonic authorities. In this sense, Maimonides' response to Obadia toes the line of previous Rabbinic tradition. Its examination in the wider framework of Maimonides' perception of religion, however, highlights his innovation.

As we have seen in the previous chapter, Maimonides developed a perception of Mosaic religion as an expression of God's pedagogic ruse. Rather than abruptly severing a nation from its past, God gave it a law that is accommodated to the idolatrous ways of life to which it was accustomed. In the *Guide of the Perplexed* Maimonides elaborates on this theory, and lays out in detail its manifestation in the precepts of the Torah. His discussion revolves around the Israelites and their pagan background, but it evidently reflects a broader anthropological understanding. The fact that Maimonides' discussion is replete with Hebrew and Aramaic quotations camouflages, as it were, the relativistic and phenomenological aspect of his claims, as if even when he provides a comparative explanation, he is really interested only in Judaism. Such a configuration of Maimonides' concerns would be, I believe, a gross misinterpretation. The *Letter to Obadia* shows that the phenomenological insight was foremost in Maimonides' thought, and that he saw it as universal and overarching, and thus applicable also to other religions.

Maimonides' *Letter to Obadia* is formulated in terms that suit its legal and personal character. If, however, we were to translate it into the language of the *Guide*, we could probably construct the following argument: "The Arabs ("Ishmaelites") lived in a pagan, 'Sabian' environment. Instead of commanding them to abandon their ways abruptly, God in his grace guided them to consecrate their old rituals to the worship of the one God. Thus, although the Muslim religion comprises rituals that

[120]This *responsum* confirms the well-known fact that, despite the unambiguous Muslim prohibition on drinking wine, its production and use were common in Muslim lands. The letter does not specify the kind of permissible usage, but another *responsum* clarifies Maimonides' permission as relating to commerce; the actual drinking of this wine is to be avoided, and is condoned only in social situations where its avoidance can be perceived as an offensive insult; see *Epistles*, 427.

can indeed be traced back to idolatrous ceremonies, these rituals have lost their pagan sting and can now be considered an integral part of a truly monotheistic religion." In Maimonides' own words, this argument is summed up succinctly: "Even though the origin of these practices was in idolatry, no person today throws those stones, or prostrates himself in that place [Mekka], or does any of these things intending to worship idols, neither in his mouth nor in his heart. Rather, their heart's [intention] is devoted to worship the Lord."[121] Without mentioning the Sabians or the concept of *talaṭṭuf,* Maimonides thus presents Islam, in comparison to that which preceded it, as a step in the gradual educational process, in a similar manner to his portrayal of Judaism. He claims that the pre-Islamic pagan rites were sublimated by Islam into monotheistic rituals, which to this day serve to condemn the memory of the pagan gods.[122]

The Letter to Obadia thus highlights the thoroughly phenomenological character of Maimonides' perception of religion. For him, "Sabians" was the generic name for a universal ailment—idolatry; *jāhiliyya* was the generic name for the environment that bred this ailment as well as for its symptoms—ignorance, licentiousness, and barbarism; and the divine remedy—accommodation—was fitted to all the manifestations of this ailment, in Judaism as well as in Islam.

"A Wise and Understanding People?": The Religion of the People

The Sabians and *jāhiliyya* provide, as we have seen above, a phenomenological framework for Maimonides' historical analysis of the development of religions. It would be incorrect, however, to classify these concepts as denoting solely, or even primarily, relics of the ancient past. Sabianism as well as *jāhiliyya* are perceived as sociological phenomena that transcend history. Maimonides sees potential Sabians lurking in every nation, at all times. Their ideas cater to the lower ranks of the social structure: the multitudes, the ignorant, and those who can be characterized

[121] "*Libbam massur la-shammayyim* (literally: to Heaven); *Responsa*, 726–27. In the "Epistle on Forced Conversion" Maimonides mentions the claim that "the Ishmaelites worship idols in Mekka and elsewhere," and dismisses it out of hand; see *Epistles*, 42.

[122] See Maimonides, *Responsa*, 726–27; *Epistles,* 427. See also, *Mishneh Torah*, Laws of Kings (*hilkhot melakhim*), 11:4 (Jerusalem and Bnei-Brak, 1999), 12: 289. This section was censored in the common versions; Funkenstein, *Theology and the Scientific Imagination*, 234; H. Lazarus-Yafeh, "The Religious Problematics of Islamic Pilgrimage: Islamicization of Ancient Rites of Worship," *Proceedings of the Israeli Academy of Sciences*, 5 (1972–76), 222–43, and esp. 242–43.

as intrinsically *jāhilī*: simpletons, children, women. The role of religious commandments is therefore to identify these Sabian ideas and to curb them.

The religion of the simple people is present in all Maimonides's writings, and he obviously evaluates his own religiosity as superior to it. Maimonides neatly sums up his feelings in this respect when he says:

> What I try to do—I and all the people of the elite who seek to attain perfection (*ahl al-taḥṣīl min al-khawāṣṣ*)—is quite different from what the masses attempt to do. For what the masses of religious people (*ʿawāmm al-sharāʾiʿ*) love most of all, and what they, in their foolishness, find most pleasurable, is to present religion and the intellect as diametrically opposed.[123]

At the same time, he regards this simple religiosity as something that must be treated with care, as it is essential to the preservation of a functioning community. Navigating between his own ideals and the reality of everyday life, he accommodates his reactions to the situation at hand. The way he handles this complex reality is reflected in his *responsa* and letters.

Maimonides usually treats the simple men who turn to him with paternal condescension, extending to them a welcoming, encouraging hand. In particular, he responds warmly and patiently to the humble and unassuming men who strive to acquire knowledge. Thus, for instance, Obadia the Proselyte, asking him about the wine produced by Muslims, mentions a previous discussion he has had with his own teacher on the same topic, in which the teacher insulted him, calling him "stupid" (**ksil**). Maimonides goes out of his way to take the sting out of Obadia's humiliation and to reassure him. He recalls the merits of the convert, "A man who left his father, birthplace, and the prosperous kingdom of his people . . . and entered under the wings of the divine presence," elaborating this point at length and concluding: "God forbid that you should be called stupid (***ksil***)! the Lord did not call you, 'stupid,' but on the contrary: 'intelligent' (***maskil***): that is to say, understanding and clever, going on the right path and a disciple to Abraham our father."[124] When Joseph ibn Jābir, a manifestly studious but unaccomplished merchant, introduces himself as an ignoramus (*ʿ**am ha-ʾaretz***), Maimonides rebukes him gently: "First of all . . . you should know that you are not an *ʿ**am ha-ʾaretz***; no, you are our student whom we love—you, and anyone engaged in the

[123] *Essay on Resurrection*, *Epistles*, 330 [Hebrew, 360]; and see below, *apud* note 161. On Maimonides' attitude to popular religion, see also K. Seeskin, *Searching for a Distant God: The Legacy of Maimonides* (New York and Oxford, 2000), 142–54.
[124] *Epistles*, 240–41; and see chap. 6, below, *apud* note 110.

quest of learning,[125] and it does not matter if this person understands only one verse, or only one commandment."[126] The warmth that transpires in these two correspondences may well reflect a trait of character; this was, at least, Maimonides' self-perception, and it was a trait of character that he tried to cultivate. We thus find him describing himself to his student, saying: "You know well how humbly I behave towards everyone, and that I put myself on a par with everyone, no matter how small he may be."[127] At the same time, the gentle, encouraging approach also stems from Maimonides' understanding of his role as an educator and a leader, who must prod and encourage his followers, but should never assign for them an unattainable goal. A particularly telling example of Maimonides' pragmatic approach can be seen in the following question, which was addressed to him regarding a Jew who uses Torah codices (*maṣāḥif*) to cast lots (*'alā sabīl al-qur'a*). A similar practice, known as *istikhāra*, is prevalent in the Muslim world, then as today: the Qur'ān is opened at random, and the verses in the open page are taken to indicate divine advice or even instructions regarding pending decisions.[128] It is no wonder that Jews used to do the same with the Torah. The interesting angle to this case is the fact that the person discussed in the question, a functionary of the synagogue (*shli'aḥ tsibbur*; that is, the one who leads the congregation in prayer) was also asked to cast lots for non-Jewish neighbors. This, too, is a known phenomenon, that the "other" is considered to possess some magical powers.[129] The petitioners who present the question were clearly uneasy regarding the practice in general, to the point of contemplating the possibility of removing the person from office. On the other hand, they were also aware of the fact that his services to non-Jews could prove profitable to the community. From their opaque reference to this profit it does not seem to suggest a monetary gain but rather some help in the contacts with the non-Jewish environment.

Before we examine Maimonides' answers, it is worth recalling his general view regarding divinations. Maimonides presents the science of astronomy as the hallmark of a civilized nation. It is in the context of his discussion of astronomy in the *Guide* that he recalls that "our nation is a nation that is full of knowledge and is perfect (*milla 'ālima kāmila*), as He, may He be exalted, has made it clear through the intermediary of the

[125] Or "quest for learning the Talmud."

[126] *Epistles*, 404, 408; see also chap. 1, note 73, above, and chap. 6, note 94, below.

[127] *Epistles*, 296. This side of Maimonides' personality is also reflected in the warm hospitality he extended to an envoy of one of the communities, who came to him accompanied by his small son; see Fenton, "A Meeting with Maimonides."

[128] See T. Fahd, "*Istikhāra*", *EI*, 4: 259–60.

[129] See, for example, Shaul Tchernichovsky's "Baer'le is Ill," *Poems* (Tel Aviv, 1959), 233–45 [Hebrew].

Master who made us perfect, saying: 'Surely, this great nation is a wise and understanding people.' "[130]

Following the Sages, he also presents the study of astronomy and the scientific calculation of astronomical cycles as the Jewish people's "wisdom and understanding in the sight of the [gentile] people."[131] Juxtaposed to this true science is the worthless, unscientific preoccupation with astrology, "the assertions of the stupid astrologers."[132] Divination, alchemy, magic, and the so-called sciences of the occult in general embody for him stupidity and superstition. On the one hand, he presents the preoccupation with astrology as the sin that brought exile upon the Jewish people and for which the prophets "called them 'fools and dolts' [Jer. 4:21], and truly fools they were." On the other hand, he blames the exile among ignorant nations (*al-milal al-jāhiliyya*) for the loss of science among Jews, "so that, because of our sins, we have become ignorant (*ʿudnā jāhiliyya*), as we have been threatened: 'And the wisdom of their wise men shall perish, and understanding of their prudent men shall be hid.' "[133]

Astrology in particular is, for Maimonides, the root and essence of idolatry, and his usual reaction to any manifestation of it is immediate repudiation.[134]

It is therefore somewhat surprising to read Maimonides' response regarding the practice of foretelling the future by opening the Torah. He answers curtly, navigating deftly between all the problems involved:

"He should be warned not to perform this for non-Jews, for it is disrespectful [*zilzul*; that is, toward the Torah]; but he should not be removed from office, nor should he be punished."[135]

Although Maimonides himself has no use for divinations and does not believe in them, whatever form they may take, he refrains from pronouncing here a global prohibition of this practice. His reticence is striking, particularly when compared to his unequivocal proscription of such practices in the *Mishneh Torah*.[136] Here, however, he says only that the person should be warned not to offer this service to non-Jews, and he specifically instructs the petitioners to refrain from taking any sanctions against him. This tight-lipped *responsum* is a clear case of accommodation. It reflects Maimonides' awareness that, following the model of divine peda-

[130] *Guide* 2.11 (*Dalāla*, 192:19–20; cf. Pines, 276); see also note 166, below.

[131] *Epistles*, 482 (Lerner, "Letter on Astrology," 230); and see Deut. 4:6; BT, *Shabbat*, 75a; and see note 166, below.

[132] *Epistles*, 482 (Lerner, "Letter on Astrology," 230).

[133] *Guide* 2.11 (*Dalāla*, 192:22–23; cf. Pines, 276).

[134] See, for instance, *Epistles*, 480 (Lerner, "Letter on Astrology," 229).

[135] *Epistles*, 631.

[136] *Hilkhot Avoda Zara*, 11:5; and see Shelat's note, *Epistles*, 631.

gogy, the leader of the community must not impose on his flock more than they can handle, and must take the context into account before issuing his dicta.

In general, Maimonides regards most members of society not only as incurably obtuse, "like domestic animals," but also potentially dangerous "like beasts of prey."[137] Human society, however, is not made of one cloth, and every group therein requires a different approach. Maimonides' gentle and humble attitude is thus not all-encompassing, and some people receive a much harsher treatment. Two groups deserve to be mentioned in particular: women and preachers.

Women, who are half of any given "nation," play a major role in fashioning the common religiosity, and in Maimonides' view it is a deplorable one. Their decisions, like their very *imaginaire,* is dictated by matter. They are "prone to anger, being easily affected and having weak souls."[138] This, combined with their limited intellectual capacity, renders them prone to superstitions, and as such, also active perpetrators of "Sabian" abominations. Thus for example, he explains the idolaters' practice of "passing children through the fire" as follows:

> The worshippers of the fire spread abroad the opinion in those times that the children of everyone who would not "make his son or his daughter to pass through the fire" [Deut. 18:10] would die. And there is no doubt that because of this absurd belief everybody hastened to perform this action. . . . This was more particularly so because care for little children is generally entrusted to women, and it is well known how quickly they are affected, and speaking generally, how feeble are their intellects.[139]

In this attitude, Maimonides is not only the child of his time, but also heir to an ancient and solid misogynous tradition in both philosophy and medicine. By way of an example one may mention "the philosophical stories" composed by Ibn Sina and Ibn Ṭufayl, in which women, perceived as a hindrance to the philosopher's quest, are either violently eliminated or are magically wished away from the process of procreation.[140]

[137] See *Guide* 2.36 (*Dalāla*, 262; Pines, 371–72).

[138] *Guide* 3.48 (*Dalāla*, 441:5–6; Pines, 600).

[139] *Guide* 3.37 (*Dalāla*, 400:10–15; Pines, 546).

[140] See F. Malti-Douglas, *Woman's Body, Woman's Word: Gender and Discourse in Arabo-Islamic Writing* (Princeton, 1992), 67–84 ("Flight from the Female Body: Ibn Tufayl's Male Utopia"); idem, "Ḥayy Ibn Yaqẓān as Male Utopia," in L. I. Conrad, *The World of Ibn Ṭufayl: Interdisciplinary Perspectives on Ḥayy Ibn Yaqẓān* (Leiden, 1996), 52–68. See also A. Melamed, "Maimonides on Women: Formless Matter or Potential Prophets?" in A. L. Ivry et al., eds. *Perspectives on Jewish Thought and Mysticism* (Amsterdam, 1998), 99–134, esp. 100; M. Kellner, "Philosophical Misogyny in Medieval Jewish Philosophy—Gersonides

It is nevertheless noteworthy that Maimonides' usually independent mind does not exert itself in this matter, where he adopts a rather conservative view, even for his times. By comparison, his contemporary Averroes deplores the loss of material gain to society, which, confining women to procreative and domestic roles, forces them to vegetate at home.[141] Averroes's words are not independent statements; they are offered as a commentary on Plato's *Republic* and elaborate Plato's ideas. It is nevertheless remarkable that Averroes allows himself to toy with novel ideas regarding the place of women in the workforce, and to make penetrating, critical observations regarding his own society. No such ideas are contemplated by Maimonides.

Maimonides' conservative position is manifest not only in his philosophical ruminations but also in his stringent legal rulings. A poignant example can be seen in a case in which a neglectful, idle husband forbids his wife from teaching in order to earn the family's daily bread, and threatens to take a second wife if she continues to do so. Members of the community appeal to Maimonides in support of the wife. They expound in great length the misery in which the wife lives, her resourcefulness, her dignified behavior despite abject poverty, and the husband's consistent neglect to provide for his family. They also seem to suggest, in the question itself, that Jewish law supports her case, since the husband is in disdain of his obligations in the marriage contract: "He does not provide her with food, drink or clothing, and does not do anything which the Torah commands." Maimonides, however, upholds the husband's right to prevent his wife from working. As a ruse to regain her liberty, he suggests that she should provoke a divorce by becoming "a rebellious wife," and thus forfeit her right for her *mu'akhkhar*.[142] Maimonides acts here strictly within the law; but despite his use of the word "ruse," there seems to be little effort on his part to find a helpful interpretation of the law. The difference between his position and that of the supplicants (in all likelihood men like him, and apparently with some learning) is also striking. His

v. Maimonides," in Aviezer Ravitzky, ed., *Joseph Baruch Sermoneta Memorial Volume* (*Jerusalem Studies in Jewish Thought* 14; Jerusalem, 1998), 113–28 [Hebrew], esp. 121.

[141] See Averroes' *Commentary on Plato's Republic*, 54; see also R. Lerner, *Averroes on Plato's Republic* (Ithaca and London, 1974), 59. Averroes' commentary, preserved only in a medieval Hebrew translation (and Latin translations made from the Hebrew), was retranslated into Arabic by A. Shaḥlān; see Ibn Rushd, *al-Ḍarūrī fī'l-siyāsa—mukhtaṣar kitāb al-siyāsa li-Aflāṭūn* (Beirut, 1998), 144; see also M. ʿA. al-Jabābirī's analysis of this passage, ibid., 61–63.

[142] *Responsa*, 49–53. For another version of the same case (probably an earlier version, recounted from the husband's point of view), see *Responsa*, 71–73. The *mu'akhkhar*—the late installation of the wedding gift—was part of the wedding contract (*ketubah*). In case of divorce or of the husband's death, this money served women for alimony or as life insurance; see Goitein, *Mediterranean Society* (1967), 1: 369; (1978), 3: 250, 267.

curt ruling includes neither censoring of the husband's conduct, nor any expression of empathy for the plight of the woman. Maimonides' habitual broadmindedness and daring legal thinking disappear here, giving way to rigid legalism.

Maimonides' profound suspicion of women reflects not only the philosophical and medical traditions, but also his own ascetic inclinations. He repeatedly expresses the view that the sexual impulse is a disgrace to us, "for we have it in so far as we are animals like the other beasts, and nothing that belongs to the notion of humanity pertains to it."[143] He firmly opposes anything that might awaken this bestial desire. He thus bans public performances of music, with or without singing, particularly if they are accompanied with drinking, and if the singer is a woman,

> for it has been patently proven that the divine intention regarding our nation was that we shall be holy, and that every act or saying of us will be in perfection or one that leads to perfection; we were not meant to awaken the faculties that prevent all good, nor to abandon ourselves in merriment and frivolity.[144]

Maimonides associates women with these base, bestial faculties, and therefore even their hardships and anxieties, which are apt to trigger harmful superstitious behavior, do not earn his compassion. He thus notices the special role that women play in witchcraft in the Sabian literature.[145] He then finds in the Scriptures a confirmation that witchcraft is indeed notoriously the domain of women, and he reads the Scriptures as a warning against the natural tendency to be lenient toward the delicately nurtured:

> And inasmuch as in all these practices the condition is posed that for the greater part they should be performed by women, it says [Ex. 22:17]: "Thou shalt not suffer a sorceress to live." And as people naturally feel pity when women are to be killed, it also states specifically with regard to idolatry [Deut. 17:2]: "man or woman" and again reiterates [Deut. 17:5]: "Even the man or the woman. . . ." The reason for this is to be found in the fact that naturally women often inspire pity.[146]

Maimonides' passion for eradicating idolatry is of course not limited to women; but whereas manifest idolaters were hard to come by in his

[143] See, for example, *Guide* 2.36 (*Dalāla*, 262:9–14; Pines, 371).

[144] *Responsa*, 400.

[145] *Guide* 3.37 (*Dalāla*, 396:28; Pines, 541). See also D. Schwartz, *Astral Magic in Medieval Jewish Thought* (Ramat Gan, 1999), 92, 95 [Hebrew].

[146] *Guide* 3.37 (*Dalāla*, 397:10–15; Pines, 542).

time, women were readily available. They therefore become emblematic of the shallow, superstitious multitudes, and of their crafty, rebellious instincts.

Maimonides does make room for exceptions, all of them dictated by the Scriptures' reference to feminine wisdom, but he usually uses the scriptural context to give this wisdom a restricted interpretation. Thus, when the Bible mentions the men and women who are "wise-hearted," Maimonides explains that it refers to their skill in an acquired art; and when the Bible mentions "a wise woman" Maimonides explains it as meaning "that she had an aptitude for stratagems and ruses (*dhāt talaṭṭuf wa-'ḥtiyāl*)."[147] The Bible refers to Moses' sister Miriam as a prophetess, and the Sages say that she, like Moses and Aharon, "also died by a kiss." Maimonides therefore counts her, like her two brothers, among those who achieved human perfection and died in the pleasure of apprehending the truth. But he notes the fact that "with regard to her, it is not said 'by the mouth of the Lord'; because she was a woman, the use of the figurative expression was not suitable with regard to her."[148] Furthermore, unlike Moses, who is presented by Maimonides as the model for all who seek perfection, Miriam is not presented as a possible model to either man or woman. For Maimonides, sociologically speaking, all women belong to the crass multitudes, and are thus automatically classified together with ignoramuses, simpletons, and children.[149]

Among the many shades of popular religiosity, the one propagated by preachers receives Maimonides' special attention. Although this kind of religiosity may appear more refined, Maimonides' attitude toward it is at the very least ambivalent. The ambivalence stems first of all from the material that serves preachers in practicing their art: *midrash aggada*, mythical or legendary texts that abound in Rabbinic literature. On the one hand, Maimonides insists on the obligation to treat the Sages of the Talmud with deference, and to assume that they did not speak lightly or out of ignorance. He lashes out at those who, taking the Sages literally, denigrate them.[150] He also scorns the pious multitudes who, taking the

[147] *Guide* 3.54, on Ex. 38:25 and on 2 Sam. 14:2 (*Dalāla*, 466:18–19, 23; Pines, 632).

[148] *Guide* 3.51 (*Dalāla*, 462:26–463:3; Pines, 627–28). On the metaphor of "death by a kiss," see chap. 6, below, *apud* note 32.

[149] See, for instance, chap. 3 note 78, above, and see also *Epistles*, 320, 326 [Hebrew 341, 345]; for an extensive list of such stereotypic combinations, see Melamed, "Maimonides on Women," 119–22. On Maimonides' attitude to women, see further W. Z. Harvey, "The Obligation of Talmud on Women According to Maimonides," *Tradition* 19 (1981): 122–30.

[150] See chap. 2, above, *apud* note 88.

Sages' words literally, unquestioningly accept these fantastic tales. When it suits him, Maimonides plunges into elaborate interpretations showing that these mythical sayings are in fact parables that conceal profound truths, and that they, just like the parables of the Bible, must not be taken at their face value.[151]

Unlike the Bible, however, where Maimonides is committed to interpret every single difficulty and render it acceptable to reason, in the case of the Sages' sayings Maimonides retains the option to bail out. The Sages, sage as they were, were human beings and thus fallible. Furthermore, they were not prophets, whose words are sanctioned by revelation. The option to reject what the Sages say remains therefore open and this is the option chosen at times by Maimonides.

In a Hebrew *responsum* to Rabbi Phinehas, regarding the denizens of Noah's ark (*yotz'ei teva*), he thus says:

> All these things are legends (*divrei haggada*), and in what pertains to legends one should not attempt a rational examination. . . . [152] Each person contemplates the [scriptural] verse according to that which he sees in the verse. [Such ruminations] do not contain [anything sanctioned] by tradition, nor commands and prohibitions, nor any legal matter, and therefore there is no room there for rational examination. Now you may say, as many do: "What, do you call things written in the Talmud 'legends?'" [I say]: Yes I do! The content of these things, and whatever belongs to this category, defines them as legends, regardless of where they are written, whether it is in the Talmud, or in homiletics writings, or in books of legends.[153]

This terse text reveals Maimonides' complex attitude to authoritative texts that record what he regards as sheer nonsense. In his attempts to isolate such records and to strip them of their sanctity, he treads carefully, so as not to jeopardize the authority of the text as a whole.

Some precedents for this careful approach are to be found in the writings of earlier Jewish thinkers. Saadya Gaon, for example, presents at the end of his discussion of the resurrection a series of questions regarding the *realia* of resurrection: Will those resurrected require food and drink? Will they rise dressed or naked? Will they get married? Will each person find his erstwhile wife, or does death annul matrimonial ties? In his response, Saadya paraphrases the Talmudic response to the question

[151] See, for instance, *Guide* 2.26.

[152] Literally: "one does not ask" (*ein maqshin*), meaning, it is not fitting to present the kind of questions that one asks when trying to reconcile a text with reason.

[153] *Epistles*, 461.

whether those raised from the dead require ablutions, and says: "Since our Master Moses will also be present among those resurrected, we are dispensed with wrecking our brains on these issues."[154] Such a humorous response allows for a rebuttal of excessively literal thinking, albeit without outright mockery. Maimonides is obviously familiar with these discussions, as well as with Saadya's *Amānāt*. When he mentions the same kind of questions, he also avoids a direct mockery of those who ask them, and instead points to the marginality of these questions in comparison to the truly important issue: the World to Come.[155]

Maimonides' basic methodological principle is that a text making a claim for truth can never contradict reason. In the case of the Scriptures, therefore, a problematic verse must be interpreted in a way that will make it acceptable, and present it "in a form that reason will abide," as Onkqelos has done in his Aramaic translation of the Hebrew Bible.[156] If, however, the difficult text is a Talmudic saying, such an interpretative effort is not obligatory, and the saying may simply be ignored: "It is not proper to abandon matters of reason that have already been verified by proofs, . . . and depend on the words of a single one of the Sages from whom possibly the matter was hidden. . . . A man should never cast his reason behind him, for the eyes are set in front, not in back."[157] In this rationalizing effort, Maimonides repeatedly distinguishes the content from the wrappings. Many accept without question anything that was committed to writing in books, or pronounced by the Sages, but Maimonides encourages his readers to question both. He constantly struggles to strip the written books from the halo that they have acquired. Speaking against astrology, he dismisses some oft-quoted Talmudic sayings that seem to support it, and says:

> The "great sickness and the grievous evil" [Eccles. 5:12, 15] consist of this: that all the things that man finds written in books, he presumes to be true, particularly if the books are old. And since many individuals have busied themselves with those books and have engaged in discussions concerning them, the rash fellow's mind at once leaps to the conclusion that these are words of wisdom.[158]

Maimonides had already stressed the same point some twenty two years earlier, also in the context of refuting astrology, in the *Epistle to Yemen*: "A liar who tells lies with his mouth will not be hindered from telling lies

[154] See *Kitāb al-amānāt wa'l-iʿtiqādāt*, 231; and cf. BT, *Nidda* 70b.
[155] See "Essay on Resurrection," *Epistles*, 321 [Hebrew 343].
[156] "Epistle on Astrology," *Epistles*, 488 (Lerner, 235)
[157] Ibid.
[158] Ibid., 480 (Lerner, 229).

with his pen. But the ignorant simpletons are those for whom the fact that something is written proves its truth."[159] The misleading wrappings include, in addition to the authority of the texts, people invested with authority who propagate such texts. Maimonides pronounces himself repeatedly in ways that show his indifference to the title of the speakers, "those who are called 'Disciples of the Sages,' or 'Sages,' or 'Gaonim,' or whatever you wish to call them."[160] This jibe is clearly an aside to his rival, the Gaon Samuel ben ʿEli, for whose intellect Maimonides had little respect. In a private correspondence with his student regarding the debate with the Gaon, Maimonides expresses his opinion of such people even more clearly.

> When I composed [the *Mishneh Torah*], I was well aware that the book would surely fall into the hands of the ill-intentioned and the jealous, who would disparage its good qualities and endeavor to expose it as superfluous or as wanting; of the brainless ignoramus, who would not be able to appreciate its achievements and will think it of little value; of the deluded, misled beginner, who would not recognize the source of certain things or whose mind would not be able to grasp my insights; and of the obtuse reactionary (*al-jāmid al-fadm*) claiming to be a man of religion, and who would attack the principle of beliefs the book contains—and such are most people.[161]

As we have seen above, heresy, whether called *zandaqa* or *minut*, is for Maimonides a generic phenomenon. The same holds true regarding the pious masses, whose opposition to reason Maimonides describes in generic terms, as common to *ʿawāmm al-sharāʾiʿ*, the masses in (all) religions.[162] Maimonides' phenomenological approach encompasses also the preachers, whose activity transcends ethnic and religious barriers. In his attitude to the *darshanim*, Maimonides joins the chorus of both orthodox and rationally inclined Muslims who identify the preachers (*wuʿʿāẓ*) and those who tell edifying stories (*quṣṣāṣ*) as ignorant and superstitious. "The long and respected line of anti-*qaṣaṣ* sentiments," to quote Merlin Schwartz, triggered a parallel long and respected line of Muslims who strove to define the right kind and right amount of admonitions. The ongoing debate touched the heart of Muslim religious practice. The

[159] *Epistles*, 103. The *Epistle to Yemen* is mentioned by Maimonides in his *Epistle on Astrology*, *Epistles*, 489; see also the *Epistle on Forced Conversion,* where he says: "We know that anyone who composes a book, regardless of whether what he says is true or false, will surely become famous among men." *Epistles*, 43.
[160] *Treatise on Resurrection*, 4; *Epistles*, 320–21, 342–43; and see Twersky, "The *Mishneh Torah* of Maimonides," 265–95.
[161] *Epistles*, 293.
[162] See above, *apud* note 44.

evidence that the preachers' activity is not restricted to the Jewish community was thus readily available to Maimonides.[163] We thus find him denigrating the book called *Shiʿur Qoma*, saying that it is "nothing but a composition of one of the Christian preachers (*aḥad ha-darshanīn al-rūm*)."[164] The implication of this hybrid term is that the Byzantine Christians (called here *rūm*) must also have a category of people who fulfill the function of the Jewish *darshanim*. Whatever name the *rūm* might give them, everyone knows what kind of discourse one can expect them to deliver.

One of the main functions of the *darshan* is, for Maimonides, to comfort and encourage simple people in distress. His typical audience would be bereaved women who gather at the mourners' house.[165] In his observation of this phenomenon, Maimonides' disdain for women colors also the attitude to the *darshan*. In spite of his scorn, however, Maimonides seems to accept this form of discourse as a fact of life, and does not attempt to eradicate such homilies. The point where he does react sharply is when the *darshanim* overstep their turf and presume to be something else.

In his introduction to *Pereq Heleq* Maimonides describes the approach of simple people to the *midrashim* regarding the afterlife. These simple folks accept the most fantastic *midrashim* at face value, and, although Maimonides regrets their poor understanding, he refrains from trying to change them. He specifically warns the reader who belongs to this credulous crowd from continuing to read Maimonides' analysis, since the things Maimonides is about to expound are bound to be too much for him, just as fine food would be indigestible for a person used to heavier fare.[166] Maimonides does try, however, to curtail the additional support that this poor thinking receives through homilies, and he says:

> Resorting to the technique of *midrash*, this category of people interpret what the Sages say literally, and extract from them things that, if the [gentile] nations would have heard, they would have said: "Surely, this small nation is a stupid and vile people."[167] This is frequently done by preachers, who explain to people what they themselves do not understand. If they do not understand, would that they

[163] See, for example, Pedrsen, "The Criticism of The Islamic Preacher," *Die Welt des Islams* 2 (1953): 215–31; M. L. Schwartz, *Ibn al-Jawzī's Kitāb al-Quṣṣāṣ wa'l-Mudhakkirīn* (Beirut, 1969), 46–60, esp. 55–60.

[164] *Responsa*, 200–201; *Epistles*, 578; and see chap. 3, above, *apud* note 80.

[165] See, for instance, *Essay on Resurrection*, *Epistles*, 322, 325 [Hebrew 345, 351].

[166] Introduction to *Pereq Heleq*, *Commentary on the Mishna*, *Neziqin*, 200–201, 203; and see above, *apud* note 42.

[167] The Hebrew words, inserted in the Judaeo-Arabic text, are obviously a parody on Deut. 4:6; cf. above, *apud* note 131.

> kept their mouth shut! "Would that you kept silent, it would be counted as wisdom on your part" [Job. 13:5]. Or else, they could have said: "We do not know what the Sages intended here, nor how it is to be interpreted." But no, they claim to understand it, and they roll up their sleeves, trying to explain to people what they themselves understood rather than what the Sages said, holding forth in front of the multitudes about the homilies found in Tractate *Berachot* and Tractate *Ḥeleq* and elsewhere, presenting them according to their literal meaning, word for word.

These impassioned lines, written relatively early in Maimonides' life, are striking, particularly since they are presented as a general observation. It is therefore not surprising to find Maimonides speaking on the same subject, and with the same tone, years later in a more personal context. During the controversy over the resurrection of the dead, he refers to the Gaon of Baghdad, "he or [even] those who are better than him," as people who know nothing. In Maimonides' view, the Gaon is "like any *darshan*, babbling like the others."[168] He calls the Gaon's literary style "this poor man's rhetoric" and expresses regret that the Gaon did not limit himself to the preachers' bread and butter of Talmudic *midrashim*, rather than presume to discuss the soul and the opinions of the philosophers—"although even people who are better than him indulge in ravings (*hadhayān*) and he undoubtedly transmitted the ravings of someone else."[169]

This brief exposition of Maimonides' references to the expressions of popular religiosity allows us a glimpse into the kind of religiosity that surrounded Maimonides, that of his own community. Maimonides' aspirations for perfection, his sophisticated reading of the Jewish sources, and his attempts to harmonize them with science and philosophy, and in particular his profound loneliness, all these can be better appreciated when set against the backdrop of the opinions that were prevalent among his own people.

The exposition also allows us to see the broad palate of Maimonides' reactions to his intellectual environment. When he tries to "save the appearance" of a *midrashic* text, and, recalling the wisdom of the Sages, to interpret it allegorically, Maimonides' approach can be compared to that of Ghazālī in his *Fayṣal al-tafriqa*.[170] In such places, where he shows commitment to the Rabbinic text despite its problematic content, Maimonides behaves as a traditional *mutakallim*.

[168] *Epistles*, 297.
[169] *Epistles*, 298.
[170] See Abū Ḥāmid al-Ghazālī, *Fayṣal al-tafriqa bayna al-islām wa'l-zandaqa*, ed. Sulaymān Dunyā (Cairo, 1961), esp. 184.

On the other hand, when he exhorts his simple readers to remain within the limits of their understanding and not to seek further, he seems closer to Averroes's position in *Faṣl al-maqāl*, a book written as a response to Ghazālī's *Fayṣal al-tafriqa*.[171] If Maimonides knew Averroes's *Faṣl al-maqāl*, as I believe he did, it is also very likely that he was familiar with Ghazālī's *Fayṣal al-tafriqa*. Along with the works of previous Jewish thinkers, these and similar works by contemporary Muslims served Maimonides as a reservoir of precedents for his treatment of the *midrashim* as well as of the people who believe in them. Adapting his response to the particular cases he had to confront, he tapped into this reservoir, making the necessary adjustments to the particularity of the Jewish community. One should also note, however, that no Muslim thinker could simply reject traditions that had been accepted as recording the Prophet's saying. Early muʿtazilite *kalām*, which very reluctantly accepted traditions in general and irrational traditions in particular, could do so only by denying the authenticity of these traditions. When Maimonides rejects out of hand some of the recognized Talmudic *midrashim* as idle fantasy, he is thus going further against religious literary tradition than any of the Muslim thinkers did.[172]

[171] The relation between the two books is evident in their titles as well as in their contents; see Stroumsa, "Philosophes almohades?" 1147–48.

[172] This does not include, of course, the freethinkers like Abū Bakr al-Rāzī, who seems to have remained a Muslim only nominally. On Maimonides' "politics of public teaching," see R. Lerner, *Maimonides' Empire of the Light: Popular Enlightenment in an Age of Belief* (Chicago and London, 2000).

Chapter Five

A Critical Mind: Maimonides as Scientist

Medicine and Science

In modern consciousness Maimonides the physician is probably as famous as Maimonides the philosopher. A search on the web, in either Hebrew or English, is likely to bring up first of all half a dozen hospitals and medical centers named after him. Of all the sciences, medicine was indeed the one in which Maimonides was most intimately involved. He was also interested in astronomy and in mathematics; he mentions his meeting with the son of the astronomer Ibn al-Aflaḥ,[1] and from the context it seems that the texts he read with a student of the philosopher Ibn Bājja were also related to astronomy.[2] Because of his view of the close relations betweem physics and metaphysics, astronomy can be seen, as noted by Tzvi Langermann, as "arguably the most important science for Maimonides."[3] He insists on the scientific value of astronomy, and recalls the Talmudic saying according to which it is the calculation of astronomical cycles that is intended in Deuteronomy 4:6, which refers to "your wisdom and understanding in the eyes of the nations."[4] Later in life, already in Egypt, he even tried his hand at correcting works on astronomy and mathematics, but only in medicine did he become a real practitioner.[5]

[1] See chap. 1, notes 28 and 49, above, and see note 2, below. For a general overview, see the articles collected in H. Levine and R. S. Cohen, eds., *Maimonides and the Sciences* (Dordrecht, Boston, and London, 2000).

[2] Maimonides refers to the opinions of Ibn al-Aflaḥ and Ibn Bājja regarding the respective positions of Venus and Mercury; see *Guide* 2.9 (*Dalāla,* 187; Pines, 269). He also mentions a rumor he has heard, that Ibn Bājja had invented an astronomical system in which no epicycles exist, a rumor that was not confirmed by Ibn Bājja's students; see *Guide* 2.24 (*Dalāla,* 226:3–5; Pines, 323). A third reference to Ibn Bājja, which cites his commentary on Aristotle's *Physics*, also relates to the heavenly spheres: see *Guide* 3.29 (*Dalāla,* 375:23–26; Pines, 515); and see chap. 4, note 53, above.

[3] Langermann, "Maimonides and the sciences," 159.

[4] BT *Shabbat* 75a; *Letter on Astrology*, *Epistles*, 482 (Lerner, 230); and see below, *apud* note 80.

[5] Ibn al-Qifṭī mentions that Maimonides (perhaps responding to Joseph ibn Shimʿon's request) worked on Ibn al-Aflaḥ's *Kitāb al-istikmāl fī'l-hay'a* and on Ibn Hūd's *Kitāb al-istikmāl fī ʿilm al-riyāḍa*. According to him, the original manuscripts of both books were

In his youth in al-Andalus he studied "the ancient sciences," that is to say: philosophy and the sciences that were translated into Arabic, mostly from Greek,[6] and this is also what he taught in the still Fāṭimid Egypt.[7] Ibn al-Qifṭī notes in particular that he mastered mathematics (*aḥkama al-riyāḍiyyāt*), and that he "got a grip on some things pertaining to logic" (*shadda ashyā' min al-manṭiqiyyāt*). This peculiar formulation may mean that Maimonides acquired the knowledge of some parts of logic. If so, Ibn al-Qifṭī would be using *shadda* as a synonym of *aḥkama*.[8] This, however, is an unusual way to convey this idea.[9] With a slight correction (*shadā*) this sentence could be understood as saying that he learnt only a smattering of logic,[10] but incomplete mastering of logic is, however, at odds with Maimonides' firm belief that a solid training in logic, as in mathematics, belongs to the elementary stage of philosophical education.[11] For him "no orderly instruction or learning can be sound save by the art of logic," and logic thus serves as a precondition and an instrument for the acquisition of the sciences.[12] It seems more likely that Ibn al-Qifṭī is referring here to Maimonides' *Treatise on Logic*.[13] The

defective, and Maimonides corrected them (*ḥaqqaqa, aṣlaḥa, hadhdhaba*); see IQ, 319, as well as IQ, 392:22. See also T. Langermann, "The Mathematical Writings of Maimonides," *JQR* 75 (1984): 57–65; T. Lévy, "Maïmonide et les sciences mathématiques," in Lévy and Rashed, eds., *Maïmonide: philosophe et savant,* 219–52; R. Rashed, "Philosophie et mathématique selon Maïmonide. Le modèle andalou de rencontre philosophique," in ibid., 253–73; G. Freudenthal, "Maimonides' Philosophy of Sceince," in Seeskin, *The Cambridge Companion to Maimonides*, 134–66; M. A. Friedman, "Did Maimonides Teach Medicine? Sources and Assumptions" (forthcoming), 361–76.

[6] Maimonides' abovementioned studies of astronomy are probably subsumed under this category, too. On Maimonides' rabbinic and scientific education, see Davidson, *Moses Maimonides*, 75–121.

[7] See IQ, 393:11–12.

[8] See E. W. Lane, *Arabic-English Lexicon* (London, 1893 [reprinted 1984]), 3:1517.

[9] The peculiarity of the expression may account for its replacement by a simpler, more familiar term (*akhadha*) in another edition of the text (*Dār al-Mutanabbī* [Cairo, n.d.], 209). The edition does not specify the manuscripts on which it is based.

[10] Such a formulation appears, for example, in Ibn al-Qifṭī's entry on Maimonides' student Joseph Ibn Shim'on: see IQ, 392. It also appears in the biography of Ghazālī, where al-Subkī reports (on the authority of Fārisī), that in his childhood in Ṭūs Ghazālī acquired a smattering of knowledge (*shadā ṭarfan*) in *Fiqh*, which he later perfected. See Subkī, *Ṭabaqāt al-shāfi'iyya al-kubrā* (Cairo, 1968), 6:204. I am indebted for this reference to the anonymous reader.

[11] See, for example, *Guide*, "Epistle Dedicatory" (*Dalāla,* 1; Pines, 3); *Guide* 3.51 (*Dalāla,* 455:29; Pines, 619).

[12] See J. L. Kraemer, "Maimonides on the Philosophic Sciences in his *Treatise on the Art of Logic*," in *Perspectives on Maimonide*, 89; A. Hasnawi, "Réflexions sur la terminologie logique de Maïmonide et son contexte farabien: Le *Guide des perplexes* et le *Traité de logique*," in Lévy and Rashed, eds., *Maïmonide: philosophe et savant*, 78.

[13] The verb *shadda* is attested in the meaning of "binding a book"; 1: On the *Treatise on Art of Logic*, see I. Efros, "Maimonides' Treatise on Logic," *PAAJR* 8 (1938); idem, "Mai-

introduction to the *Treatise* presents its composition as having been suggested by "an eminent man, one of those engaged in the sciences of religious law and of those possessing both clarity of style and eloquence in the Arabic language."[14] This eminent man—who may or may not have been a Muslim—"had asked a man who was studying the art of logic" to explain to him the meaning of some oft-repeated logical terms.[15] The tortuous formulation does not support the generally accepted interpretation, that this *Treatise* was commissioned from its author. In formulaic introductions to commissioned works the opening words would normally be: "*You* have asked *me*. . . ." The treatise has been shown to depend closely on Fārābī (who is also the only philosopher cited in it), and in particular on Fārābī's *Introductory Treatise on Logic*.[16] Rather than a commissioned work, it seems more likely that Maimonides was summarizing (and adapting) a work by another person, perhaps Fārābī. He also did not make any attempt to present it as an original work: he introduced it as the summary that it was, describing the circumstances of the original text's composition.

More than a century ago, Julius Derenburg, followed by Moritz Steinschneider, suggested that this *Treatise* was a youthful work, composed by Maimonides in Spain.[17] This suggestion, widely adopted by scholars, has been dismissed by Davidson as "asserted without a shred of evidence." Davidson, for whom the *Treatise on Logic* is spurious, regards the idea that Maimonides could have written such a treatise when he was still in his teens as utterly fanciful. In particular, he rejects the notion that "a Muslim of rank would select a teenage Jewish Talmudic student" and would commission him to write an introduction on logic, as the product of a "singularly unfettered imagination."[18]

---

monides' Arabic Treatise on Logic," *PAAJR* 34 (1966), Hebrew section 9–62; M. Türker, "*Al-maqāla fī ṣināʿat al-manṭiq* de Mūsā Ibn Maymūn," *Review of the Institute of Islamic Studies* 3 (1959–1960): 55–60, 87–110.

[14] Cf. Kraemer, "Maimonides on the Philosophic Sciences," 77; see Efros, "Maimonides' Treatise on Logic," 5 (Hebrew section); cf. Efros's translation in ibid., 34.

[15] Cf. Kraemer, "Maimonides on the Philosophic Sciences," 78; see Efros, "Maimonides' Treatise on Logic," 5 (Hebrew section); Davidson, *Moses Maimonides*, 318–19.

[16] See. Kraemer, "Maimonides on the Philosophic Sciences," 81; D. M. Dunlop, "Al-Fārābī's Introductory *Risāla* on Logic," *Islamic Quarterly* 4 (1957): 224–35; Hasnawi, "Réflexions sur la terminologie logique de Maïmonide et son contexte farabien," 39–78.

[17] J. Derenburg, review of Beer, *Leben und Wirken des Rabbi Moses ben Maimon, Wissentschaftliche Zeitschrift für jüdische Theologie* 1 (1835): 424 (cited by Davidson); M. Steinschneider, *Die hebräischen Übersetzungen des Mittelalters und die Juden als Dolmetscher* (Berlin, 1893; reprinted Graz, 1956), 434.

[18] H. A. Davidson, "The Authenticity of Works Attributed to Maimonides," in E. Fleischer et al., eds., *Me'ah She'arim: Studies in Medieval Jewish Spiritual Life in Memory of Isadore Twersky* (Jerusalem, 2001), 118–25; idem, *Moses Maimonides*, 318.

Davidson's claim that this treatise was misattributed to Maimonides met (as Davidson predicted) with scholarly resistance, based mostly on internal evidence and on the manuscript evidence.[19] The information provided by Ibn al-Qifṭī was not brought to bear in this context, but if the suggestion made here is accepted, Ibn al-Qifṭī may be our only contemporary source to mention Maimonides' authorship of an early work on logic.

There can be no doubt, of course, that the study of the Talmud was Maimonides' bread and butter (or, as Maimonides would put it, bread and meat). But Davidson's narrow definition of Maimonides as "a Talmudic student" predetermines his image of what Maimonides could or could not have written. It also creates a misconceived, compartmentalized view of medieval thought and scholarship. Contrary to Davidson's view, it was not unusual for a particularly bright teenager to be consulted by people of rank, in theoretical as well as in practical matters;[20] and, in what pertains to philosophy or science, Muslims did not think twice of commissioning works from non-Muslims. Furthermore, if the suggestion offered above is accepted, this treatise was not commissioned from Maimonides, but rather prepared as a digest of a work commissioned from another person. Such a digest would be, by all accounts, suitable for the work of a young, albeit advanced student.

Ibn al-Qifṭī, whose text was not available to Derenburg and Steinschneider, seems to corroborate the hunch of these two remarkable scholars, that the *Treatise on Logic* was a youthful work of Maimonides. As an introductory work, the treatise was not meant to be either innovative or comprehensive, but rather a compilation of elementary concepts. In some of the manuscripts of its Hebrew translation, its title is preserved as *A Treatise on Some Logical Terms* (*qetsat millot ha-higayyon*).[21] Ibn al-Qifṭī's terse reference seems to reflect this version of the title, saying that Maimonides composed or compiled [a work] on some elements of logic (*shadda ashyā' min al-manṭiqiyyāt*).

In addition to mathematics and logic, Maimonides also studied medicine. Two leading historians of medicine were in the position to have first-hand information about him: Ibn al-Qifṭī (d. 1248) was a very close friend of Maimonides' disciple, Joseph Ibn Shim'on; and Ibn Abī Uṣaybi'a (d. 1270) was a colleague of Abraham, Maimonides's only son, at the Nāṣirī hospital

[19] See Davidson, *Moses Maimonides*, 313. On the manuscript evidence, which on the whole does not support Davidson's claim, see Hasnawi, "Réflexions sur la terminologie logique de Maïmonide et son contexte farabien," 69–78.

[20] Avicenna practiced medicine when he was barely sixteen; see D. Gutas, *Avicenna and the Aristotelian Tradition: Introduction to Reading Avicenna's Philosophical Works* (Leiden, 1988), 27.

[21] Steinschneider, *Die hebräischen Übersetzungen des Mittelalters,* 434 and notes there.

in Cairo.[22] And yet, neither of these two tells us much about Maimonides' training. The claim made by Leo Africanus (alias Yuḥanna al-Asad) that Maimonides' teachers in medicine were his great Andalusian contemporaries, Ibn Zuhr and Ibn Rushd, has been refuted.[23] Unlike the medical training in the East, which was done either privately or in the framework of established hospitals, al-Andalus had no hospitals at the time, and medical training often remained within the family.[24] What we know of Maimonides' medical education comes mostly from his own writings, where he also recounts anecdotes relating to cases he had seen while accompanying other doctors in the Maghreb.[25] The purpose of the following pages is not to summarize these bits of information, which have been published before; nor do I presume to venture into the history of medicine. Medicine and science will be examined here only insofar as they help us draw a rounder, more accurate intellectual profile of Maimonides. Following the method adopted throughout the present book, medicine will serve here to demonstrate how a contextual reading of all the different pieces of information can offer a deeper understanding of each of them.

In his entry on Maimonides (Mūsā Ibn Maymūn al-Isrāʾīlī), Ibn Abī Uṣaybiʿa records a panegyric poem composed by the Muslim scholar Ibn Sanāʾ al-Mulk, in which the latter praises Maimonides' medical skill, describing him in hyperboles as superior to Galen, and as the physician who could cure the heavenly bodies from their chronic ailments.[26] The relevant entry in Ibn al-Qifṭī's work, on the other hand, is generally understood as offering a rather poor opinion of Maimonides' medical acumen. As Gerrit Bos (following others before him) translates this text, Ibn al-Qifṭī states that Maimonides "was not daring" in his practice,[27] and that he "used to work with other physicians and would not rely on his opinion

[22] See Lewis, "Jews and Judaism in Arabic Sources," 176; and see chap. 3, notes 18, 31, above.

[23] Meyerhof, "The Medical Works of Maimonides," 266n1; S. Munk, "Notice sur Joseph ben Iehoudah," *Journal Asiatique* 14 (1842): 31–32; Bos, *Maimonides on Asthma,* xxv; and see N. Z. Davis, *Trickster Travels: A Sixteenth-Century Muslim Between Worlds* (New York, 2006), 85–86, and note 91 on 309.

[24] On hospitals and hospital training in the Orient, see, for instance, IAU, 414–15 (about Rāzī); about al-Andalus, see IAU, 517–30 (regarding the Ibn Zuhr family); M. Marín, *Mujeres en al-Andalus* (Madrid, 2000), 296–97 (regarding the women of this family); and see D. M. Dunlop and G. S. Colin, "Bīmāristān," *EI,* 1: 1222–25.

[25] See Davidson, *Moses Maimonides,* 28, 80, 85–86; and see Y. T. Langermann, "L'œuvre médical de Maïmonide: Un aperçu general," in Lévy and Rashed, eds., *Maimonide: philosophe et savant,* 275–302, esp. 281–82; G. Bos, "Maimonides' Medical Works and Their Contribution to His Medical Biography," *Maimonidean Studies* 5 (2008): 244–45.

[26] IAU, 582; Rosenthal, "Maimonides and a Discussion of Muslim Speculative Theology," 110.

[27] *Wa-lam yakun lahu jassāra fīʾl-ʿamal*; IQ, 317.

alone, because he [felt that he] lacked collaboration[28] [with others]. He had no skill either (in treating [the sick] or prescribing a regimen [for the healthy]."[29] We should first of all note that in the presentation quoted above, Ibn al-Qifṭī's information appears as one continuous evaluation. This presentation, however, is grossly misleading. Ibn al-Qifṭī's entry is arranged in chronological order, beginning with Maimonides' youth and education in al-Andalus. Just as he discusses Maimonides' education in mathematics and his youthful composition in logic, he recounts his early achievements in medicine. He thus reports: "He studied medicine there [that is, in al-Andalus], and knew its theory well, but did not acquire confidence in practice."[30] This description is not meant to sum up Ibn al-Qifṭī's evaluation of the physician Maimonides, but rather to report on his accomplishments before he left al-Andalus. After reporting on this initial stage, Ibn al-Qifṭī discusses the Almohad persecution and its effect on Maimonides' family until Maimonides finally settled in Egypt, which is where he eventually began to work as a physician. From Maimonides' own writings it appears that a significant part of his clinical training was indeed done after he left al-Andalus, in the years spent in North Africa (which are not mentioned by Ibn al-Qifṭī).

The other part of Ibn al-Qifṭī's supposedly negative evaluation is equally problematic. While the first sentence is quite clear ("he used to work with other physicians"), the reading of the last part of the text is uncertain, and even in the proposed reading the syntax remains rather awkward. The text is thus translated *ad sensum*. For such a translation to be valid, however, one has to assume that we can be certain regarding the gist of the text, and that it is indeed intended to present a negative evaluation of Maimonides' expertise. In the present case, such a presupposition is unwarranted, relying as it does only on the very text it seeks to clarify.

Furthermore, although physicians, like philosophers, could sharply criticize one another, in this particular case the text does not fit the characters. Ibn al-Qifṭī's main source on Maimonides must have been Maimonides' student Joseph Ibn Shimʿon, Ibn al-Qifṭī's intimate friend, of whose medical expertise Ibn al-Qifṭī had a very high opinion;[31] and Joseph (himself a renowned physician who ministered to high officials of the Ẓāhirī court

[28] The reading is unclear: *rifqan, waqafan*, or *wifqan;* the Cairo edition (on 210) reads *rafīqan.*

[29] IQ, 318; Bos, *Maimonides on Asthma*, xxviii.

[30] IQ, 317:17: *wa-qara'a al-ṭibb hunāk fa-ajādahu ʿilman, wa-lam yakun lahu jassāra fī'l-ʿamal.*

[31] According to Ibn al-Qifṭī, Joseph "had studied medicine in his city of origin [i.e., Ceuta], and excelled in it"; see IQ, 318.

in Aleppo) had a total and unwavering admiration for his teacher Maimonides. The criticism is so much out of character here that Bernard Lewis regarded it as an additional proof that this Joseph could not possibly be Maimonides' student.[32]

The reading that understands Ibn al-Qifṭī's evaluation of Maimonides the physician as negative underlines two items that can serve as criteria for judging a physician: daring and collaboration with other physicians. In the prevalent reading of this text, daring would be a good quality in a physician, while dependency on collaboration with other physicians would typify a hesitant, unskilled physician.[33]

These two items are discussed by Maimonides himself, and a comparison with his view on their relative merit is revealing. In his treatise *On Asthma* Maimonides presents his observations regarding the working methods of physicians in the different countries where he practiced medicine. According to him, the Egyptians always prefer simple drugs to combined drugs, and they "recoil from [applying] it [=the stronger drug] because of their lack of experience with strong treatments." His note that they lack experience may sound derogatory, but then he adds that "for this reason, nothing of their usual treatment produces any harm; in general, their method succeeds more often than it fails."[34]

Maimonides also mentions the Egyptian collaborative method, saying that he has "regularly seen in the land of Egypt that only rarely would a single physician be entrusted with the treatment of a patient from the beginning to the end of his disease." He points out the possible shortcomings of this system, but concludes:

> if the physicians gather together [for treating a patient], as in the case of kings and rulers, and debate and argue until they have come to a decision about what should be done, it is most appropriate and best. For then the patient benefits from the sum of their correct judgments. . . . If there are some physicians gathered together and they remind and assist each other in reaching their goal together they will achieve the perfection for which they strive.[35]

[32] Lewis, who believed that Maimonides' student was called Joseph Ibn ʿAqnīn, states: "It is hard to believe that Ibn ʿAqnīn would criticize in this fashion the master he admired." See Lewis, "Jews and Judaism in Arab Sources," 178; and chap. 3, note 18, above.

[33] See Bos, *Maimonides on Asthma,* xxviii; and Lewis, "Jews and Judaism," 172–73, 178.

[34] Bos, *Maimonides on Asthma*, 107. On Maimonides' advocacy of minimal medical intervention, see Langermann, "L'œuvre médicale de Maïmonide," 285–86.

[35] See the text and translation in Bos, *Maimonides on Asthma,* 108–9; and cf. Langermann, "L'œuvre médicale de Maïmonide," 291–92; Bos, "Maimonides' Medical Works," 245.

Despite the shortcomings of the Egyptian system, Maimonides favors the collaborative method, according to which a physician does not presume to have absolute knowledge, and does not act without consulting colleagues. In this context, Maimonides' concluding advice to his patient is revealing: "I have told you all this merely as a warning to beware of the physicians and not to surrender yourself hastily to whomever you find. Rather, be satisfied with a good regimen. . . . For the errors of the physicians are much more frequent than their correct [prescriptions]."[36] He buttresses this warning by a quotation from Aristotle's *De sensu et sensato*: "Most people die as a result of medical treatment." And adds: "I think that Aristotle should be trusted in this assessment."[37]

Lest these harsh words sound like a devastating criticism of the professional level of his fellow physicians, Maimonides hastens to add that this description is intrinsically true for medicine in general; it is therefore valid for all physicians, however conscientious and skilled they may be, and Maimonides himself is no exception to the rule:

> Having heard my words, do not assume that I am the one into whose hands you should deliver your soul and body for treatment. May God be my witness that I know for certain about myself that I, too, am among those who are deficient in this art, [who] stand in awe of it, and who find it difficult to achieve its goal. . . . Again, may God be my witness that I do not state this out of modesty, nor in the customary manner of the virtuous,[38] who say about themselves that their knowledge is deficient even when it is perfect and that their deeds fall short even when they are very diligent. But I state the truth of the matter as it is.[39]

For Maimonides, the physician is inherently ignorant of his profession, feeling his way in the dark. This, says Maimonides, is a simple fact, and recognizing it does not merit to be praised as virtuous modesty. The physician's rule of thumb should be that the less he interferes, the safer it is for the patient. The prowess of a wise, skilled, and daring physician can often yield disastrous results. Such independent prowess reflects, therefore, rather than laudable daring, presumptuous foolhardiness.

As we have seen above, Ibn al-Qifṭī's statement that Maimonides lacked confidence in his practice had a restricted meaning. It marked a stage in his studies, which, being curtailed by the Almohad persecution, left him

[36] Bos, *Maimonides on Asthma*, 91.

[37] Ibid.

[38] *Fuḍalā'*. Bos translates: "erudite." See D. H. Frank, "Humility as a Virtue: A Maimonidean Critique of Aristotle's Ethics," in E. L. Ormsby, ed., *Moses Maimonides and His Time* (Washington, D.C., 1989), 89–99.

[39] Bos, *Maimonides on Asthma*, 95.

accomplished in theory but not yet confident in practice. The closer examination that allows us to correct the prevalent mistake in the interpretation of this passage, however, offers an insight into Maimonides's medical method. In all likelihood, a statement that would describe Maimonides as lacking in daring would not have offended him. He would probably have read it as a faithful description of his approach to the practice of medicine. In Maimonides' view, daring for the physician can be tantamount to playing with his patient's life; it is the kind of conceited overconfidence that in metaphysical contexts he calls *tahāfut*.[40]

The reading of Ibn al-Qifṭī as offering a poor evaluation of Maimonides' medical daring led to a negative *ad sensum* rendering of his other statement, regarding Maimonides' skill. If, however, we assume the tenor of Ibn al-Qifṭī's entry on Maimonides to be factual rather than derogatory, then the translation of this second passage, too, must be corrected accordingly. Maimonides believed that the collaboration of several physicians, who can discuss the case and agree on a treatment, is in the best interest of the patient. Ibn al-Qifṭī probably refers to this practice, and the gist of the problematic sentence in his text must be: "He used to work with other physicians. He would not rely on his opinion alone, but rather on jointly achieved [opinion][41] achieved by agreement (*wafqan*), both in treatment and when assigning a regimen." Maimonides' minimalist, cautious approach in the practice of medicine is closely tied to his view of the nature of this profession. There can be no doubt that he took his profession very seriously, and sought to master its secrets as much as he could. In his correspondence, he describes his extreme fatigue after a long day at the palace or in the hospital. He also describes his tenacity in perfecting his knowledge in this domain, reading medical literature into the night, despite his exhaustion, "for you know how long this art is and how difficult it is for the punctual and conscientious [doctor] who does not want to say anything without first knowing its proof."[42] For Maimonides, who follows here Fārābī, medicine is an art (*ṣināʿa*), and his words here allude to Hippocrates' first *Aphorism*. In his commentary on this aphorism Maimonides states that, because of the complexity of the medical art, its study is more time-consuming than the study of other arts. He then says: "Abū Naṣr al-Fārābī has mentioned that the parts, the knowledge of which constitutes the art of medicine, are seven in number."[43]

[40] See chap. 2, above, *apud* note 75.

[41] An examination of the manuscripts may offer a correct reading of the text, or a proper emendation. Perhaps *lakinna mushārakatan*?

[42] *Epistles*, 313.

[43] See M. Plessner, "Al-Farabi's Introduction to the Study of Medicine," in S. M. Stern et al., eds., *Islamic Philosophy and the Classical Tradition: Essays Presented by His Friends and*

Maimonides's source for his taxonomy of medicine may well have been Fārābī's Encyclopedia of the sciences (*Iḥṣā' al-ʿulūm*), which Maimonides may have read in a fuller recension than the one known to us.[44] Whatever his source may have been, however, the division of medicine into regulated parts is in line with the technical image of medicine. In his *Epistle on Medicine* Fārābī refers to medicine as "a practical art" (*ṣināʿa fāʿila*)[45] rather than as a "science" (*ʿilm or maʿrifa*).

For Fārābī, each science has its practical and theoretical branches, but only the theoretical can be properly called "science." In Fārābī's definition, "A multitude of separate things becomes an art[46] or is included in an art when it is summarized in rules that are imprinted in the person's mind in a specific order; for example, orthography, medicine, agriculture, construction, and other arts, (regardless of) whether they are practical or theoretical."[47] Relying again on Fārābī, Maimonides emphasizes the experimental (and therefore uncertain) character of the art of medicine. Unlike true science, where, given correct premises and correct reasoning, one can attain certain knowledge, in the art of medicine a correct treatment does not guarantee the expected result.

> Abū Naṣr al-Fārābī has mentioned [in this connection] that, in the art of medicine, in seamanship, and in agriculture, the outcome does not necessarily depend upon the efforts invested. For the physician may do whatever is necessary in the best possible way, without any error committed either by him or by the patient, yet he may not attain the cure which is the ultimate goal. The reason for this is clear, for the active factor in us is not medicine alone, but medicine and nature.[48]

Medicine, however, is not only different from hard science, but also from other arts:

> For the art of medicine is not like the craft of carpentry or weaving, which can be learnt through observation and can be mastered through

---

Pupils to Richard Walzer on his Seventieth Birthday (Oxford, 1972), 310:4–5. For the medieval Hebrew translation of this text, see S. Muntner, *Maimonides' Medical Writings* (Jerusalem, 1961), 3:8–10.

44 As suggested by M. Steinschneider, *Al-Farabi, des arabischen Philosophen Leben und Schriften* (Mémoires de l'Académie Impériale des Sciences de Saint-Pétersbourg, VIIe série, t. 13, 4; 1869), 248b–249a; idem, *Die hebräischen Übersetzungen des Mittelalters,* 293; and see S. Stroumsa, "Al-Fārābī and Maimonides on Medicine as a Science," *Arabic Sciences and Philosophy* 3 (1993): 235–49.

45 Plessner, "Al-Farabi's Introduction to the Study of Medicine," 312.

46 Lit.: arts, *ṣanāʾīʿ*.

47 Al-Fārābī, *Iḥṣā' al-ʿulūm,* ed. ʿUthmān Amīn (Cairo, 1939), 45; and see also 106:1.

48 Bos, *Maimonides on Asthma,* 84.

> repetition, because the practice of this art [of medicine] is subordinate to [theoretical] speculation and reflection (*naẓar wa-taʾammul*). . . . Knowledge is the root (*aṣl*) and practice is the branch (*farʿuhu*), and there is no branch without the root.[49]

This view of medicine is reflected in the way Maimonides practiced it. As Ibn al-Qifṭī's report testifies, Maimonides had perfected his knowledge of "the root"—the theoretical part of medicine—before moving on to "the branch," the actual practice. He himself was trained by accompanying other doctors and by observing them in their practice, and he appreciates the hands-on learning.[50] At the same time, he sharply criticizes physicians who rely on experience (*tajriba*) alone. While medicine is not a pure science, the physician cannot forgo the use of scientific methods, and Maimonides insists on the need to find the medical "proof" and to use analytical reasoning (*qiyās*) in the study of medical etiology.[51]

The physician most admired by Maimonides' was Galen,[52] and he also relied on the medical opinions of Hippocrates and of Abū Bakr al-Rāzī. In his general, theoretical observations regarding the art of medicine, however, he often quotes Fārābī. This would not be surprising in philosophy, where Maimonides' admiration for Fārābī is amply attested.[53] In the realm of medicine, however, these extensive quotations deserve to be noted. Like other Islamic philosophers, Fārābī had studied medicine, but as far as we know he had never practiced it.[54] Maimonides' choice to rely on him rather than on the great physicians is, therefore, puzzling. The solution of this puzzle lies in the tension between Maimonides' deep involvement in the practice of medicine, on the one hand, and the place he grants it among human intellectual quests, on the other

In chapter 15 of the second part of the *Guide* Maimonides quotes Fārābī as having held Galen in "extreme contempt," because of the latter's agnostic position concerning the question of whether the world is created or eternal.[55] Georges Vajda, who was able to identify Fārābī's original

[49] Ibid., 97.

[50] Note, for example, the difference between the way he reports on procedures that he himself has seen tested (*jarrabahu ḥudhdhāq al-aṭibbāʾ bi'l-maghrib wa-raʾaynāhu ʿiyānan*; Bos, *Maimonides on Asthma*, 76); and the ones he had learnt only by received instruction (*akhadhnāhā talqīnan*; ibid., 78; compare Bos's translation there).

[51] See Langermann, "L'œuvre médicale de Maïmonide," 292–93.

[52] See *Medical Aphorisms* (*Pirqei Moshe*), ed. Muntner, 25, #59; Davidson, *Moses Maimonides*, 85–86; Bos, *Medical Aphorisms*, xxiv–xxv.

[53] See chap. 2, notes 16–19, above; chap. 4, note 91, above.

[54] See IAU, 603.

[55] "*Istakhaffa bi-Jālīnūs kull al-istikhfāf*": *Dalāla,* 203; Pines, 292. In the twenty-fifth chapter of his *Medical Aphorisms* Maimonides discusses at length Galen's agnostic position

text in his commentary on Aristotle's *Topics* (104. b. 5–18), was puzzled by the fact that in Fārābī's words no outspoken contempt is noticeable. Fārābī speaks there only of the wrong assertions of "Galen the physician" (*Jālīnūs al-ṭabīb*).[56] Vajda considered this wording to be very mild, but for Maimonides, Fārābī's statement was, apparently, far from being neutral. As already mentioned, Maimonides uses the phrase "only a physician" to denigrate the philosophical qualities of both Muḥammad b. Zakariyyāʾ al-Rāzī and of Isaac Israeli.[57] Coming from the successful physician that he was, his already famous formula of denigration, "only a physician," could seem a bit surprising. It is easily understood, however, if we consider the relative subordinate rank of medicine as a human intellectual endeavor. Unlike Galen, who believed that "every physician must be a philosopher" and composed a treatise with this title, Maimonides followed Fārābī's view, that every philosopher must be a physician, but not every physician is a philosopher. It seems that for Maimonides the description—in a philosophical context—of Galen as "the physician" was in itself enough to conclude that Fārābī had no respect whatsoever for Galen as a philosopher.

This suggestion is strengthened by a paragraph in the *Kitāb al-amad ʿalā al-abad* of the Khurasanian philosopher Abū al-Ḥasan al-ʿĀmirī (d. 992), who says:

> Now Galen, in his time, having composed many works, aspired to be described as wise—that is, to be called "the Sage"[58] instead of "the Physician." But people made fun of him and said, "Go back to your ointments and laxatives, and to treating sores and fevers. . . . For he who testifies against himself that he is in doubt whether the world is without temporal beginning or created in time, and whether the Hereafter is real or not, and whether the soul is a substance or an accident, occupies too humble a rank to be called a Sage."[59]

Like Fārābī and Maimonides, ʿĀmirī criticizes Galen's agnosticism concerning the creation of the world; like Fārābī, he mentions Galen's being a

---

concerning the creation of the world; see J. Schacht and M. Meyerhof, "Maimonides against Galen, on Philosophy and Cosmogony," *Bulletin of the Faculty of Arts of the University of Egypt* 5 (1937): 53–88; Maimonides, *Letters*, appendix 2, 148–67, esp. 162–63; Bos, *Medical Aphorisms*, xxv.

[56] See G. Vajda, "A propos d'une citation non identifiée d'al-Fārābī dans le *Guide des égarés*," *Journal Asiatique* 253 (1965): 43–50; see also Rafīq al-ʿAjam, ed., *al-Manṭiq ʿinda al-Fārābī*, vol. 3: *Kitāb al-jadal* (Beirut, 1986), 82.

[57] Marx, "Texts by and about Maimonides," 379–80.

[58] Or "the philosopher" (*an yunqal ʿan laqab al-ṭabib ilā laqab al-ḥakīm*).

[59] See Rowson, *A Muslim Philosopher on the Soul and Its Fate*, 74–75.

physician, and like Maimonides, he speaks of ridiculing Galen for his views. But in ʿĀmirī's text the ridicule is explicitly connected to the statement that the appropriate appellation for Galen is "the physician," despite his aspirations to be considered a philosopher. It is interesting to note that for ʿĀmirī, as for Maimonides, the modern-day example of a physician who is unduly considered a philosopher is Abū Bakr al-Rāzī, about whom ʿĀmirī says: "The extraordinary thing about the people of our time is that, when they see a man has read Euclid's book and mastered the principles of logic, they describe him as a Sage. . . . Thus they ascribe wisdom to Muḥammad b. Zakariyyāʾ al-Rāzī: because of his proficiency in medicine, in spite of his various ravings (*hadhayān*)"[60] ʿĀmirī's work circulated widely, and was used extensively by Muslim writers, even when they did not cite their source.[61] We cannot be sure that Maimonides read ʿAmirī's work, but it stands to reason that a similar account, in which Galen the physician is ridiculed, reached Maimonides. It may even have been the case that such an account figured in the version of Fārābī's words as read by Maimonides. Even if Fārābī had only said "Galen the physician," however, Maimonides could have felt himself to be on solid ground when interpreting this appellation to be strongly pejorative.

We can thus complete our picture of the image that Maimonides had of medicine. Technically speaking, medicine is a science, but its limits are well defined: the physician who oversteps these limits will gain only scorn. Maimonides' reliance on Fārābī in the evaluation and description of medicine thus reflects his ambivalence toward the profession he himself practiced and studied late into the night.

Maimonides' reflections on medicine highlight his continuous monitoring of human intellectual activities. On the one hand, he avidly strives for the acquisition of knowledge and understanding, pushing himself to exhaustion in the desire to learn more. On the other hand, he restrains the craving for unattainable knowledge and warns against false pretense that comes with it. He repeatedly admonishes the student of metaphysics not to be like Elisha ben Abuya, rushing forward as if there were no limitations on human intellect, but to hold back.[62] And he repeatedly admonishes the physician to tread carefully, consult others and refrain from

[60] See below, *apud* note 89. Rāzī was painfully aware of this kind of criticism; see his *Kitab al-sīra al-falsafiyya,* in *Rasāʾil falsafiyya,* ed. P. Kraus (reprinted Beirut, 1982), 109:15–16.

[61] For ʿĀmirī's sources for this specific passage and for his quotation by others, see Rowson's commentary, *A Muslim Philosopher on the Soul and Its Fate*, 216, and also the introduction, 29.

[62] See chap. 2, notes 73–74, above; and see Langermann, "Maimonides and the Sciences," 167.

hasty interference. As he himself points out, the restraint is not in itself a mark of modesty or humility. Rather, it is a cautious calculation that measures each intellectual step and tests the ground: Is the foot holding firm, or is this a treacherous quagmire? Is this an apodictic science, where we know the facts and the way to deduce from them certain knowledge, or is this a chimera leading us into perdition?

As part of this continuous examination, Maimonides tags each intellectual enterprise, marking it as right or wrong and how much so. The following section deals with one of his most distinctive tags: Ravings.

"Ravings": Maimonides' Concept of Pseudo-Science

In several of his writings Maimonides uses the word "ravings" (*hadhayān*) to discredit certain theories and intellectual endeavors. This word (which we have already encountered a few times in the present book)[63] appears in contexts as different as the reasons for the particulars of the law, on the one hand, and the discussion of the movements of celestial bodies on the other.

The frequent recurrence of this word was noticed by Jerome Gellman, who attempted to examine its meaning in Maimonides' thought.[64] Gellman observes that Maimonides uses this word whenever he "rejects views he does not approve of in what seems to be an especially cavalier, unphilosophical manner," and that "his rejection of them seems little more than mere name calling."[65] But, Gellman argues, precisely because of its nonphilosophical, nontechnical quality, this word may help us "uncover something of Maimonides' true mind."[66] After examining four examples of Maimonides' use of the word, Gellman suggests that the word indicates a metaphysical misconception, mostly such as contradicts Galen's dictum concerning the relations between matter and the individual. As Gellman himself admits, the word occurs more than four times in Maimonides' writings, and some of these other occurrences do not seem to fit this interpretation.

In what follows I shall argue that, rather than being an "innocent" word that betrays his innermost views, for Maimonides *hadhayān* is almost a technical term. I shall survey Maimonides' use of the term, analyze it in

[63] See chap. 2, note 91, above; chap. 4, above, *apud* notes 110 and 169; chap. 5, note 60, above.

[64] J. I. Gellman, "Maimonides' 'Ravings,'" *Review of Metaphysics* 45 (1991): 309–28.

[65] Ibid., 311.

[66] Ibid., 310, 312.

its historical context, and argue that it always designates pseudo-science and the philosophy that is based on it.

Perhaps the most important context in which Maimonides develops the concept of *hadhayān* is his discussion of the Sabians.[67] Although Maimonides provides some chronological and geographical landmarks for the identification of the Sabians, these actually indicate that he does not identify the Sabians as a specific nation with an identifiable religion of its own. Rather, Maimonides uses the name *ṣāba* as a generic name for all idolatrous religions, past and present.[68] In the *Guide of the Perplexed* (3.29–49), Maimonides summarizes the theoretical contours of what he calls "the nation of *al-ṣāba*." A common feature of the religion of this "nation" is the belief in spirits that control the material world and whose actions can be influenced by human behavior.[69] This belief results in the development of a complex theurgical system, in which astrology, magic, alchemy, and knowledge of the occult are treated as noble sciences, both scientifically and religiously.[70] Maimonides mentions several books from which he claims to have learnt about the Sabian religion. These books contain the supposedly scientific information required for the theurgical practices, as well as historical and mythological tales and accounts.

For Maimonides, everything in the Sabian system contradicts his idea of balanced, scientific thought: their historical writings and their myths are ridiculous nonsense; their science is a sham. They claim to deal with philosophical matters, such as the eternity of the world; but, he says, they "tell most ridiculous lies that show a great deficiency of intellect and . . . they are more remote from philosophy than any other man and are extremely ignorant."[71] When Maimonides speaks specifically about their myths, he calls them *khurāfāt*.[72] This word was regularly used by the philosophers as a technical term, to denote myths in the Platonic sense; but

[67] According to Gellman, Maimonides repeats this word in this context no fewer than seven times. Gellman, who deals with this cluster only in the last note of his article, admits that it does not fit his thesis (ibid., 328, note 23).

[68] See chap. 4, above.

[69] See also Pines, "On the Concept of 'Spirits.'"

[70] On astral magic, see Schwartz, *Astral Magic in Medieval Jewish Thought,* 11–21. On Sabian astral magic and its role in Maimonides' thought, see Schwartz, ibid., 92–110; and see R. Leicht, *Astrologumena Judaica: Untersuchungen zur Geschichte der astrlogischen Literatur der Juden* (Tübingen, 2006), esp. 295 ff.

[71] *Guide* 3:26 (*Dalāla,* 376:5–6; Pines, 516).

[72] *Guide* 3:26 (*Dalāla,* 379:9; Pines, 519 [where the word is translated as "fables"]); see also *Dalāla*, 380:7; Pines, 520.

it was also used contemptuously, to designate senseless mythologies.[73] Ibn Ṭufayl reports that Fārābī, in his lost *Commentary on the Nicomachean Ethics*, called belief in the afterlife "ravings and old-wives' tales" (*hadhayān wa-khurāfāt ʿajāʾiz*).[74] Fārābī may have intended to speak of myths in the Platonic sense, but readers like Ibn Ṭufayl could not help noticing a scornful tone. In the Arabic philosophic tradition inherited by Maimonides, the two terms *khurāfa* and *hadhayān* are closely linked. It is thus not surprising to find them appearing together in Maimonides' discussion of the Sabians. When the Sabian myth involves cultic and magical practices that are intended to influence the spirits and control the natural elements of the sublunar world, Maimonides brands the whole discourse as *khurāfāt wa-hadhayānāt*[75] or "*hadhayānāt* and stupidities which tarnish the intellect."[76] In his parlance, "ravings" or "myths and ravings" indicate both the mythology itself and its cultic, applied aspect, theurgy based on the interpretation of esoteric texts and on the supposedly scientific view of the world. He states categorically that these "fables of the Sabians and . . . ravings of the Chasdeans and Chaldeans . . . are devoid of all science that is truly science."[77]

Maimonides' lengthy discussion of the Sabians and their literature prepares the ground for his explanation of those commandments that do not have an obvious rational explanation. In his *Epistle on Astrology* he reiterates his interest in these kinds of commandments, as well as the importance of pagan literature for understanding them. In this work Maimonides also sets clear criteria for accepting something as true. One should believe only in what is sanctioned by rational evidence, by the evidence of the senses, or by that of prophetic traditions. A person who believes anything else fits the dictum that "the fool would believe anything."[78] Maimonides mentions that thousands of books have been composed dealing with futile ideas and stupidities that people have imagined to be science, and that the books on astrology are prominent among them. He also says that the ancient Persians and Greeks, who were trained in the sciences, had nothing to do with astrology. Only the Chaldeans, Egyptians,

[73] See, for instance, Abū Bishr Mattā's commentary on Aristotle's *Metaphysics*, as quoted in Pseudo-Majritī's *Ghāyat al-ḥakīm*, 283.

[74] *Risālat Ḥayy ibn Yaqẓān*, ed. Fārūq Saʿd (Beirut, 1980), 112.

[75] *Guide* 3:26 (*Dalāla*, 380:7; Pines, 520); *Guide* 3:37 (*Dalāla*, 396:27; Pines, 542).

[76] *Commentary on the Mishnah, Qodashim, Ḥullin*, 173 ("*al-hadhayānāt wa'l-sukhuf al-muwassikha al-ʿaql*").

[77] "*ʿArīyīn ʿan kull ʿilm huwa ʿilm bi'l-ḥaqīqa*"; *Guide* 3:26 (*Dalāla*, 380:7; Pines, 520). It is noteworthy that both *khurāfāt* and *hadhayānāt* are used in a derogatory sense by Maimonides' main source for the Sabian theurgy; see *al-Filaḥa al-nabaṭiyya* (*L'agriculture nabatéene*), ed. T. Fahd (Damascus, 1993), 1: 155:2–4.

[78] *Epistles*, 479.

Babylonians, and Canaanites (the same nations grouped in the *Guide* under the name "Sabians") occupied themselves with this fraud (*ṭaʿut*), which they called "science."[79] He then proceeds to distinguish this pseudo-science from astronomy, "that science of the stars which is scientifically certain" (*ḥokhmah vaddaʾit*, lit.: "certain [or: apodictically proven] science"). To this true science, extolled in Deuteronomy 4:6 as "your wisdom and understanding in the eyes of the nations," Maimonides opposes astrology, which, he says, is intended by the prophet when he warns [Is. 29:14] that "the wisdom of their wise men shall perish and the understanding of their prudent men shall be hid."[80]

The *Epistle on Astrology* is, in many ways, a postscript to the Sabian chapters of the *Guide*. If we read them together, the notion of *hadhayān* becomes clear: it is the pseudo-science that is not based on the evidence of the senses or on rational argument, the nonconsequential discourse that presumes to be science.[81]

In the *Epistle on Astrology*, astrologers are called "*ḥozim ba-kokhavim*" (lit.: "those who observe the stars")[82] and astrology is described as "empty nonsense" (*hevel va-riq*), "stupidity" (*ṭipshut*), and "sheer lies" (*sheqer ve-kazav*). The impact of the whole diatribe is such that one would expect to see, instead of the factual *ḥozim*, another biblical word, *hozim* (daydreamers or hallucinating). It thus does not come as a surprise that we find the Arabic equivalent of *hozim* in Maimonides' attack on astrology in another, earlier work.

In his introduction to the tenth chapter of the Mishnah in tractate *Sanhedrin* (known as *Pereq Ḥeleq*), Maimonides criticizes a category of scholars who, taking the *midrashim* literally, ridicule them. These scholars presume to be wiser and more intelligent than the Sages and say that the latter were ignorant of the nature of the universe. According to Maimonides, "Most prone to fall into this belief are those who have pretense to practice medicine, and those who rave about the decrees of the stars. They claim to be cultivated men, physicians and philosophers. How remote they are from true humanity in the eyes of real philosophers!"[83]

[79] Cf. Maimonides, *Epistles*, 479–81. The astrologers' claims that a person's character is decreed at birth are also described as *hadhayānāt* in the "Eight Chapters"; see *Commentary on the Mishnah, Neziqin*, 396.

[80] *Epistles*, 101; and see note 4, above.

[81] See also the *Epistle to Yemen*, where Maimonides dismisses the astrologers' claim to predict the future as "things that have no base in reality (*umūr lā ḥaqīqa la-hā*), and which are governed by chance (*ittifāq*)"; see Maimonides, *Epistles*, 103; see also Schwartz, *Astral Magic*, 105.

[82] In reference to Isa. 47:13 (cf. Lerner's translation, 228).

[83] *Commentary on the Mishnah, Seder Neziqin*, on *Sanhedrin* 10, Introduction, 202: "*wa-akthar mā yaqaʿu fī hādha al-iʿtiqād muddaʿīyī al-ṭibb waʾl-hādhiʾiyīn bi-qaḍāyā*

Astrologers, the *ḥozim ba-kokavim*, are called here *al-hādhi'iyyīn bi-qaḍāyā al-nujūm*. Their science is mere raving; Maimonides insists on the disparity between their philosophical pretenses and their actual intellectual level, just as he did in the *Guide* concerning the Sabians.[84] In this paragraph, Maimonides adds two other characteristics that describe the scholars who fall into this category: they are often physicians (or claim to be) and they scoff at the wisdom of the Sages. As we have seen above, the combination of these characteristics recalls Maimonides' criticism of the tenth-century freethinking philosopher and physician Abū Bakr al-Rāzī.[85] Indeed, Rāzī seems to have played an important role in the development of the term *hadhayān* in Maimonides' vocabulary.

In *Guide* 3:12 Maimonides says: "Rāzī has written a famous book, which he entitled *Divine Things*. He [has] filled it with the enormity of his ravings (*hadhayānāt*) and his ignorant notions. Among them there is a notion that he has thought up, namely, that there is more evil than good in what exists."[86] Gellman's interpretation of Maimonides' concept of "ravings" is anchored in this passage. As Gellman understands it, the notion of the predominance of evil in the world constitutes, for Maimonides, the core of Rāzī's "ravings." Gellman thus proceeds to analyze the concept of "ravings" in light of Maimonides' subsequent refutation of Rāzī's notion of the predominance of evil in this world. Maimonides, however, sees the predominance of evil as only one of the "ignorant notions" found in Rāzī's book. Maimonides applies the term "ravings" not just to this particular notion, but to the entire content of Rāzī's *Divine Things*. Furthermore, it seems that, for him, the "ravings" and the "ignorant notions" are two distinguishable categories of fallacies in Rāzī's book.

Maimonides again refers to Rāzī's book in his letter to Samuel Ibn Tibbon. In this letter, Maimonides dismisses Rāzī's book on metaphysics as worthless, "because Rāzī was only a physician"; that is, his pretense to be a philosopher was unwarranted. Although here Maimonides does not use the word "ravings" to describe Rāzī's book, this description seems to hang like a shadow over the whole paragraph. Immediately preceding

---

al-nujūm, li-annahum bi-za'mihim ḥudhdhāq ḥukamā' falāsifa, wa-mā ab'adahum min al-insāniyya 'inda al-falāsifa 'alā al-ḥaqīqa."

[84] See chap. 2, note 88, above.

[85] See chap. 2, above (*apud* note 80 ff.). It is interesting to note that Maimonides' translator and first commentator, Samuel Ibn Tibbon, regarded the Sabians as people who took the biblical stories literally and did not realize their parabolic nature; see his remarks on *Guide* 3:29, quoted in C. F. Fraenkel, *From Maimonides to Samuel ibn Tibbon: The Transformation of Dalalat al-Ha'irin into the Moreh ha-Nevukhim* (Jerusalem, 2007), 142–43 [Hebrew].

[86] *Guide* 3:12 (*Dalāla*, 318; Pines, 441).

Rāzī in the list are two Aristotelian pseudepigrapha, the *Book of the Apple* and the *Book of the Golden House*, which Maimonides describes as "ravings (*hazayot*), empty words, and nonsense." Immediately following Rāzī on the list are two works by the Jewish Neoplatonist Isaac Israeli, the *Book of Definitions* and the *Book of Elements*. These are given the same description, with an added explanation that puts Israeli in the same category as Rāzī: "[These books] are all ravings (*hazayot*), empty words and nonsense, because Isaac Israeli was only a physician." Thus Rāzī appears bracketed between two entries that describe authors who, like him, are guilty of false pretenses. Their literary productions deserve the title "ravings" because of their false pretenses, but one suspects that they also receive the title, as it were, by contamination, because of their proximity (and similarity) to Rāzī.[87]

A comparison with other medieval Arabic texts indicates that the application of the term *hadhayān* to Rāzī's book on metaphysics and to his thought reflects a standard practice among Muslim writers. Particularly close to Maimonides in this respect is the tenth-century philosopher ʿĀmirī, who wonders at the fact that people are willing to describe Rāzī as a philosopher "because of his proficiency in medicine—this, in spite of his various ravings (*ṣunūf hadhayānātihi*) about the five eternal principles and about the corrupt spirits."[88] ʿĀmirī alludes here to two central elements in Rāzī's metaphysics: his creation myth, which was based on the interaction between the five eternal principles, and his antiprophetic teaching, which regarded the prophets as inspired by the souls of evil men who had become demons.[89] These notions were developed in Rāzī's book on metaphysics (*K. al-ʿilm al-ilāhī*, which is apparently identical with the book mentioned by Maimonides as *Ilāhiyāt*). The comparison with ʿĀmirī's text suggests that Maimonides may be using the term *hadhayān* to denote specifically the mythical part of Rāzī's philosophy.

This conjecture is supported by the evidence of Abū Rayḥān al-Bīrūnī, who says that, while reading Rāzī's book on metaphysics, he came across the names of Mani's books, especially the *Book of Secrets*, on which Rāzī draws. This reference intrigued Bīrūnī for more than forty years, until a caravan leader (*barīd*) arriving from Hamadhān came to him in Khwārism and offered him a load of Manichean books, among them the coveted *Book of Secrets*. Bīrūnī says that upon receiving this book and consulting it, "the joy that engulfed me was like the joy of a thirsty person beholding a mirage, and my grief thereafter was similar to his disappointment as he

[87]See *Epistles*, 552.
[88]Rowson, *A Muslim Philosopher on the Soul and its Fate*, 74–75; and see above, *apud* note 60.
[89]Ibid., 203, 214–17.

approaches it. Then I proceeded to summarize the sheer ravings and the pure obscenities[90] which this book contains, so that anyone inflicted with my disease would be quickly healed from it, as I was."[91] For al-Bīrūnī, then, *hadhayān* describes the kind of mythological tales that are contained in the Manichean *Book of Secrets* and its mirage-like temptation for the seekers of truth. He also associates it, like Maimonides, with Rāzī in general and with his book on metaphysics in particular.

The same evaluation of Rāzī's thought is expressed, in identical terms, by Marzūqī (d. 1030), who lists four groups of people who believe in some pre-eternal entity in addition to the Creator, and says: "The fourth group is the one in which the physician (*mutaṭabbib*) Muḥammad b. Zakariyyā' is foremost; for he added the rational soul to the aforementioned Eternals, and thus their number reached five, according to his ravings (*hadhayān*)."[92] Marzūqī considers Rāzī's ideas to be so revolting that he describes them as myths (*khurāfāt*) that the hand cannot write, the tongue cannot express, and the heart cannot imagine.[93]

Another Muslim writer, Ibn Ḥazm, offers the same evaluation of Rāzī's thought in different words belonging to the same semantic field. He calls Rāzī's theory of metempsychosis "trickeries and myths which are not based on any proof' (*da'āwīn wa-khurāfāt bi-lā dalīl*).[94] Ibn Ḥazm's reasoning may be reflected in the words of Ibn al-Jawzī, who often relies on the former. In his criticism of the other foremost Muslim freethinker, Ibn al-Rāwandī, Ibn al-Jawzī says, "I have consulted [his] *Book of the Emerald* (*Kitāb al-zumurrud*) and I have found such senseless ravings there that do not [even] have the pretense of a logical argument."[95] For Ibn al-Jawzī as for Ibn Ḥazm, the absence of any proof or of the pretense of a logical

[90] "*Al-hadhayān al-bakht wa'l-hujr al-maḥḍ.*"

[91] *Risālat al-Bīrunī fī fihrist kutub Muḥammad b. Zakariyā' al-Rāzī. Epitre de Bīrunī contenant le répertoire des ouvrages de Muḥammad b. Zakarīyā ar-Rāzī*, ed. Paul Kraus (Paris, 1936), 3–4.

[92] *Kitāb al-Azmina wa'l-Amkina* (Hyderabad-Deccan, AH 1332 [1914]), 1:144; quoted by Kraus in Rāzī, *Rasā'il falsafiyya*, 197:1–5.

[93] Rāzī himself had used similar derogatory terms to describe the Muslim traditions. According to him, the Muslims "were deluded by the beards of the goats, who sit in ranks in their councils, straining their throats in recounting lies, senseless myths (*al-akādhib wa'l-khurāfāt*) and 'so-and-so told us in the name of so-and so.'" See Abū Ḥātim al-Rāzī, *A'lam al-nubuwwa* (*The Peaks of Prophecy*), ed. Ṣalāḥ al-Sāwy (Tehran, 1977), 32; Stroumsa, *Freethinkers*, chap. 3, *apud* note 72.

[94] Ibn Ḥazm, *Al-Fiṣal fī'l-milal wa'l-ahwā' wa'l-niḥal*, ed. Muḥammad Ibrāhim Naṣr and 'Abd al-Raḥmān 'Umayra (Beirut, 1995), 75; quoted by Kraus in Rāzī, *Rasā'il falsafiyya*, 174.

[95] "*Al-hadhayān al-bārid alladhī lā yata'allaqu bi-shubha*"; see *al-Muntaẓam fī ta'rīkh al-mulūk wa'l-umam*, ed. Muḥammad 'Abd al-Qādir 'Aṭā and Muṣṭafā 'Abd al-Qādir 'Aṭā (Beirut, 1992), 13: 110:8.

argument qualifies a person's argument as "ravings," particularly when one can point to a mythical discourse of the kind presented by Rāzī.

It is thus clear that Maimonides is following his Muslim predecessors when he brands Rāzī's book on metaphysics as *hadhayān*. Maimonides, however, employs this word beyond the particular context of the polemics with Rāzī, as we have already seen in his writings on the Sabians.

The technical use of the word *hadhayān* is indeed attested in Arabic philosophical literature prior to Maimonides.[96] This word is sometimes used (along with several of its cognates) to translate the Greek *adoleskhein*. For example, according to Aristotle, one of the sophists' methods of refutation is "to reduce the opponent in the discussion to babbling (that is, to constrain him to repeat himself a number of times)."[97] This is rendered by Yaḥyā b. ʿAdī as *an yahdhiya wa-yahmiza*;[98] in the corresponding section of Avicenna's *Kitāb al-shifāʾ* we find the words *hadhayān wa-takrīr*.[99] Avicenna also uses the word to denote a seemingly logical statement that is in fact tautological or senseless: he describes such a statement as *hadhayān min al-kalām*.[100]

Maimonides obviously draws on this philosophical usage and may even have been familiar with Avicenna's use of *hadhayān*. Maimonides, however, uses the term as a sweeping condemnation, a tag that he affixes to certain kinds of literature. The appearance of this tag is an indication that the book or books so labeled contain lengthy incoherent babbling (*hadhayān ṭawīl*), like the talk of a person afflicted with madness or hallucinations.[101] More specifically, this tag indicates books produced by some schools and revealing a rather superstitious frame of mind. A poorly written book on Aristotelian philosophy is not likely to earn this epithet. It seems that a process of narrowing down of its semantic field led to the

[96] I am indebted to Robert Wisnowski for drawing my attention to this use of the term *hadhayān* in Arabic Aristotelian literature and for kindly furnishing the examples that follow.
[97] Aristotle, *Sophistical Refutations* 165^{b}15, trans. W.A. Pickard-Cambridge, in Jonathan Barnes, ed., *Complete Works of Aristotle* (Princeton, 1984), 1:279.
[98] *Kitāb al-sūfisṭiqā*, in *Manṭiq Arisṭū*, ed. ʿAbd al-Raḥmān Badawī (Cairo, 1948), 3:750; translating the same passage, Ibn Zurʿa uses the words *hadhr wa-hitār* (see Badawī, *Manṭiq Arisṭū*, 3:751)
[99] Ibn Sīnā, *Kitāb al-shifāʾ*, *La logique: la sophistique (al-Safasṭa)*, ed. A. F. al-Ahwānī (Cairo, 1958), *al-manṭiq* (7); 1.1, 7:5.
[100] Ibn Sīnā, *Kitāb al-shifāʾ*, *Ilāhiyāt*, ed. G. Qanawātī et al. (Cairo, 1960), 1.5 (33:16–18); see also Avicenna, *De Anima*, ed. F. Rahman (London, 1959), 8–9, where the muʿtazilite arguments on whether the non-existent (*maʿdūm*) is a thing (*shayʾ*) is described by Avicenna as *mā hadhaw bi-hi min aqāwilihim*.
[101] The medical term *hadhayān* is, of course, attested also in Maimonides' medical writings. See, for example, *Commentary on the Aphorisms of Hippocrates* 143, [Hebrew]: "Hippocrates calls the confusion of the weak mind *hadhayān*."

association of *hadhayān* with non-Aristotelian systems of thought and to its use as a pointer to such systems.

I have found no clear instances of a similar use of the term in the writings of Maimonides' predecessors. Avicenna's *Epistle Against Astrology* is a case in point.[102] He presents the epistle as an innovative work that he decided to write because "no one had written anything of the sort, that is to say, a refutation of astrology."[103] For Avicenna, astrology is one of the pseudo-sciences, among which he counts divination of all sorts and alchemy of the kind that he explicitly associates with the names of Jābir b. Ḥayyān and Abū Bakr al-Rāzī.[104] He regards these "sciences" as undeserving of refutation, because their futility should be obvious to anyone with a modicum of intelligence and scientific education (*man lahu adnā maʿrifa biʾl-ʿulūm*). As Avicenna repeatedly states, what characterizes such a pseudo-science is the fact that it is not based on any evidence. He says:

> The proponents of astrology composed many books about it, but there is no evidence to prove what they wrote, and no logical argument testifies to its soundness. . . . Neither their books nor the books which serve as their sources contain any proof (*ḥujja*) whatsoever for their claim. Rather, this is a senseless saying (*qawl khurāf*) which they invented out of their own heads, and they adopted it blindly, without any logical argument (*min ghayr burhān wa-lā qiyās*).[105]

Avicenna repeats this evaluation: "All the things on which they rely and which they state have no sound basis, nor does this have any proof or evidence. Rather, it is a senseless[106] statement. One should know that everything they say about the decree of the stars resembles what women say about divination by casting lots."[107] Avicenna insists on the difference between this kind of book and truly scientific books like Ptolemy's *Almagest*, which is based on experimental observation and geometrical proofs.[108]

According to Avicenna, the inclination of human beings to astrology is to be explained chiefly by their natural laziness and desire to achieve things without toil. People may wish to see distant places, but they are loath to undertake the difficult journey that this would require. Therefore, he says,

[102] Ibn Sīnā, *Risāla fī ibṭāl aḥkām al-nujūm, Rasāʾil Ibn Sīnā*, ed. Hilmi Ziya Ülken (Istanbul, 1953), ii, 49–67; Y. Michot, *Avicenne, Réfutation de l'astrologie* (Beirut, 2006).
[103] Ibid., 50.
[104] Ibid., 50:16 and 51:15.
[105] Ibid., 52:8–20.
[106] Reading *khurāf* instead of *jurāf*.
[107] Ibid., 61:20–23.
[108] Ibid., 60.

"they invented the notion that it can be done by flying rather than walking, and they imagined a flying human being, or else they believed in its existence."[109]

Fantastic combinations of things that exist separately in this world are, for the philosophers, the specific role of the faculty of the imagination. It is this faculty that is responsible for dreams and hallucinations; a favorite example of its operation is the idea of a flying heavy body, be it a ship, an animal, or a human being.[110] Thus Avicenna describes astrology as "ravings" without actually calling it so.

Compositions such as Avicenna's *Epistle against Astrology* could have influenced Maimonides' concept of "ravings." We cannot be certain that the technical use of *hadhayān* was Maimonides' own development.[111] What we can say with certainty is that in Maimonides' usage of this word became a shibboleth, marking all pseudo-science and sham philosophical rigmarole as distinct from the true science, based on rigorous reasoning.

Several other instances in which Maimonides employs this term may help us understand the meaning it carried for him. The first instance appears in the context of Maimonides' discussion of the reasons for the commandments:

> The generalities of the commandments necessarily have a cause. . . . But no cause will ever be found for the fact that one particular sacrifice consists in a lamb and another in a ram. . . . Accordingly, in my opinion, whoever occupies himself with finding causes for any of these particulars is stricken with a prolonged madness (*yahdhī hadhayānan ṭawīlan*)[112] in the course of which he does not put an end to incongruity, but rather increases the number of incongruities.[113]

Maimonides' criticism seems to be addressed to those whose zeal for a rationalistic interpretation of the commandments goes too far. But the

[109] Ibid., 51.

[110] See, for instance, Maimonides, "Eight Chapters," *Commentary on the Mishnah, Neziqin*, 375. For another example of Avicenna's fascination with imaginative combinations of the human body, see S. Pines, "La conception de la conscience de soi chez Avicenne et chez Abū'l Barakāt al-Baghdādī," *Archives d'histoire doctrinale et littéraire du Moyen Age* 21 (1954): 25 (reprinted in Pines, *Collected Works*, Vol. 1, *Studies in Abūl-Barakāt al-Baghdādī, Physics and Metaphysics* [Jerusalem and Leiden, 1979], 185).

[111] The word *hadhayān* is not found in al-Jurjānī's *Kitāb al-taʿrīfāt*, ed. G. Flügel (Leipzig, 1845) or in al-Tahānawī's *Dictionary of Technical Terms* (*Kashshāf iṣṭilāḥāt al-funūn* [Cairo, 1963]).

[112] Pines's translation here emphasizes the fact that the *hadhayān* in this case does not consist of a single occurrence of raving and babbling, but rather has become a chronic infirmity of these people. See below, *apud* note 125.

[113] *Guide* 3:26 (*Dalāla*, 370, esp. lines 17–18; and cf. Pines' translation, 508–9).

larger context remains that of the interpretation of the commandments against the background of the ancient pagan religions. Therefore, although the Sabians are not directly criticized in this paragraph, Maimonides' preoccupation with them is the key to its understanding. The attempt to find intrinsic meaning in the details of every commandment reflects the same mindset that lies behind the Sabian theurgical practices. A person who thinks that, where the sacrifice of a ram is prescribed, a lamb could not serve the same purpose, is applying the logic of the pagan magical cults to the biblical commandments. His way of thinking remains that of the Sabians and consequently merits the designation "ravings."

Another error that Maimonides criticizes in his introduction to the *Guide* is related to the misconceived attempt to interpret the details of commandments. Maimonides explains that some of the prophetic parables intend to convey a single general idea. Hence, although they are presented as an elaborate story, only this general idea should be sought. It would be wrong to search for the meaning of each detail in such fables, because

> doing so would lead you . . . into assuming an obligation to interpret things not susceptible of interpretation and that have not been inserted with a view of interpretation. The assumption of such an obligation would result in extravagant fantasies (*hadhayān*) such as are entertained and written about in our time by most of the sects of the world, since each of these sects desires to find certain significations for words whose author in no wise had in mind the significations wished by them.[114]

Here the obsessive attempt of religious scholars to find meaning in technical details is labeled by Maimonides as *hadhayān*.[115]

This paragraph is not connected with Sabian theurgy, but it hints at the *Sitz im Leben* for Maimonides' strong reaction to this obsession. He expressly tells us that this foolish obsession is rampant among contemporaneous "sects" (*firaq*). Another passage of the *Guide* helps us identify at least some of these sects.

[114] *Guide*, Introduction (*Dalāla*, 9:15–21; Pines, 14).

[115] Maimonides' scorn for those who try to understand the details of complicated systems is expressed also in *Guide* 2:24. Concerning the impossibility of knowing the exact physics of the celestial movements, he writes: "And to fatigue the minds with notions that cannot be grasped by them and for the grasp of which they have no instrument, is a defect in one's inborn disposition or some sort of delusion (*ḍarb min al waswās*)." See *Dalāla*, 228:26–27; Pines, 327. *Waswās*, like *khurāfa*, thus seems to belong at times to the same semantic field as *hadhayān*.

In *Guide* 2:25, Maimonides sets down the reasons for his denial of the eternity of the world and his refusal to interpret the verses that contradict this belief allegorically. He says that Aristotle's position, according to which

> no nature changes at all, and . . . the customary course of events cannot be modified with regard to anything, destroys the Law in principle, necessarily gives the lie to every miracle, unless, indeed, one interprets the miracles figuratively also, as was done by the Islamic internalists (*ahl al-bāṭin min al-islām*); this, however, would result in some sort of crazy imaginings (*ḍarb min al-hadhayān*).[116]

Pines' translation here attempts to convey the gap that exists between this interpretation of the miracles and the truth: *hadhayān* is the "imaginings" of crazy people and has no connection to the facts as they are. Indeed, for Maimonides the word *hadhayān* no longer denotes only the fact of raving or hallucinating, but also points to an ingrained intellectual deficiency of certain approaches. Allegorical interpretation of miracles can take a variety of forms, but Maimonides makes plain that the variety he finds objectionable in this context is that of *ahl al-baṭin min al-islām*, which probably denotes here the Ismaʿīliyya. In Ismāʿīlī theology, the miracles performed by the prophets are often explained as resulting from the prophets' superior knowledge of the nature of the world and its components.[117] In other words, Ismāʿīlī *ta'wīl* incorporates miracles in a general theurgical system, which claims to control and manipulate the world by scientific methods. For Maimonides, this whole system is false and accordingly deserves to be labeled as "ravings."

The systems of thought of the Sabians, of Rāzī, and of the Ismāʿīlīs all constitute for Maimonides *hadhayān* par excellence. But his use of the term is not limited to the particular fallacies of these people. He also uses

[116] *Guide* 2:25 (*Dalāla*, 229:22–26; cf. Pines, 328).

[117] See I. K. Poonawala, "Ismāʿīlī *ta'wīl* of the Qur'ān," in G. R. Hawting and A. A. Shareef, eds., *Approaches to the Qur'ān* (London and New York, 1993), 199–222. On the Ismāʿīlī interpretation of miracles, see, for example, *Al-Risāla al-jāmiʿa*, ed. J. Ṣalība (Damascus, n.d.), 2:83; see also P. E. Walker, *Early Philosophical Shiism: The Ismaili Neoplatonism of Abū Yaʿqūb al-Sijistānī* (Cambridge and New York, 1993), 60; Y. Marquet, *La philosophie des Ikhwān al-ṣafā* (Algiers, 1973), 485–91. Although the Ismāʿīlī texts discussed in these studies date from around the tenth century, Maimonides' view of Ismāʿīlī *ta'wīl* seems to agree with these early texts. See also Maimonides, *Epistle on Resurrection* (*Epistles*, 334), where he explains that the *ta'wīl* of miracles he has in mind in this chapter of the *Guide* is indeed the one that would explain the miracles as a natural phenomenon. In the same Epistle (*Epistles*, 335) he also mentions the Sabians as the nation that rejected the possibility of miracles.

the term to denigrate any form of nonscientific thinking. Two examples of this general use may suffice here.

In his *Commentary on the Mishnah, Pesaḥim* 4:10, Maimonides discusses the content of the *Book of Medicines* (*Sefer refu'ot*) that King Hezekiah had put away, and the reasons why this act was (generally) applauded. According to him, "*The Book of Medicines* was a book which decrees healing by methods that are not approved[118] by the Law, like the claims of the perpetrators of talismans that a talisman in a certain form should be done [to cure] a certain disease." Maimonides' wording here resembles the one used in his description of the theurgical practices of the Sabians in the *Guide;* "that such and such . . . should be done for so and so. . . ." The comparison with the Sabians leaves little room for doubt that Maimonides regarded such talismans as sheer nonsense.[119] One would have expected him to object to the very content of such a book, but this option does not really exist for Maimonides: the book is listed in the *Mishnah* together with hallowed relics from the distant past, such as the brazen serpent made by Moses in the desert [Num. 21:8]. The *Mishnah* thus presents the book as having been acceptable prior to Hezekiah's ban. As we have seen above, in the case of the book of *Shiʿur Qoma*, Maimonides dodges unnecessary criticism of what people believe to have been sanctioned by the Sages, lest it be interpreted as challenging their authority. Whenever possible, he looks for ways to skirt such criticism without compromising his principles.[120] He therefore says: "Its author had composed it with the intention of learning the nature of the world (*ʿalā ṭarīq al-ʿilm bi-ṭabīʿat al-wujūd*) and did not intend its content to be used. This [in itself] is permissible." In other words, the scientific endeavor undertaken by the author of the *Book of Medicines* was not in itself reprehensible, nor was the reading of the book forbidden. Both the composition of the book and its reading were then legitimate manifestations of academic curiosity, but they became harmful when the book was used for the wrong purposes.

The relevance of this passage for our discussion, however, does not lie in the explanation Maimonides suggests, but in the one he rejects. According to a widespread story, the *Book of Medicines* was composed by King Solomon. It prescribed medicines for all kinds of ailments,[121] and Hezekiah banned it because he saw that people turned to medicine rather

[118] *Mā lā tūjibu sharīʿa*; literally: "What the Law does not oblige [to do]," but in fact equivalent to the *umūr maḥẓūra* ("forbidden things") at the end of this sentence.

[119] Guguenheim's claim (*Aristote au mont Saint-Michel*, 145) that Maimonides shared the belief in astrological amulets is as baseless as it is puzzling.

[120] See chap. 3, above, *apud* note 80 ff.; and chap. 4, above, *apud* note 163.

[121] Contrary to Gellman's interpretation ("Maimonides' 'Ravings,'" 315–22), the book is not described as a "cure all" and Maimonides does not argue against such a description.

than to God. It is this latter notion—that true reliance on God precludes the use of medicine—which Maimonides calls "ravings" (*hadhayān*). He pours abuses on the disseminators of this notion, which he calls "a vile statement" (*qawl munḥatt*), adding:

> According to their confused and stupid logic (*ʿalā qiyāsihim al-mukhtall al-sakhīf*), if a hungry man grabs bread and eats it, [an act] which is sure to cure this painful suffering, does this mean that he stopped relying on God?! They should be told: "You fools (*yā majānīn*)! As I thank God for the food which He provided me, which alleviates my hunger and sustains me, in the same way I thank Him for providing a medicine which heals my illness when I use it."[122]

The "ravings" here are not an erroneous scientific method, but, on the contrary, the pious objection to scientific, empirical medicine. Maimonides is clearly outraged by the religious notion of these people, but he does not accuse them of blasphemy. He brands them as upholding "ravings," in that they propound a way of thinking that does not take into account the empirical knowledge of how things are.

The second example comes from the *Commentary on the Mishnah, Sanhedrin*, where Maimonides attempts to define the "external books" (*sefarim ha-ḥitzoniyyim*), the reading of which qualifies one as *epiqoros*. As we have seen above, among these books he lists the books of Ben Sirah, who, he says, "was a man who composed ravings (*hadhayān*) about the meaning of physiognomy (*firāsa*)."[123]

In this passage, the word "ravings" applies specifically to a written text. For Maimonides, Ben Sirah's book falls into the category of useless books that serve only to idle away one's time. To this category belong also Arabic books of poems, genealogy, and history. But the books on physiognomy are also "ravings," because they falsely claim to contain factual, scientific knowledge.

The fact that the word "ravings" carries special meaning in Maimonides' thought was first noticed by Samuel Ibn Tibbon, who found it necessary to explain it in his *Lexicon of Foreign Words*. According to Ibn Tibbon, *hazayya* (the phonetically close Hebrew translation he chose for *hadhayān*) is a verbal noun derived from "*hozim*" (as in Isa. 56:10): that is, "those who say senseless things, which have no connection to reality, like

[122] *Commentary on the Mishnah, Moʿed*, 177–78.

[123] *Commentary on the Mishnah, Sanhedrin*, 209–210; and see chap. 4, note 110, above. Maimonides probably indeed has in mind *Ecclesiasticus*, the discovery of the original Hebrew version of which in Cairo, in the late nineteenth century, initiated the modern interest in the Cairo Geniza.

those who speak incoherently in their sleep." Indeed, an important characteristic of "ravings" for Maimonides is their incoherence and lack of connection with realia. But Maimonides does not use this word to designate just any superstitious saying; he does not usually employ it when criticizing the nonscientific homilies of simple-minded *darshanim*, for instance.[124] He often adds to the term "ravings" the epithet "lengthy" (*ṭawīl*), but verbosity by itself does not constitute "ravings." In Maimonides' work, the scathing dismissal as "ravings" comes close to being a technical term reserved for superstitious, nonscientific, or pseudo-scientific discourse that presumes to offer a coherent system. Whenever he employs this word in his discussion of a theory or a person, it should serve as a pointer. Its use indicates that Maimonides regards the theory under discussion as related in some way to the esoteric non-Aristotelian philosophies of his times, and in particular to their irrational, mythical discourse and to the sciences of the occult. By describing them as "ravings" he intends to underline their false pretense to be scientific knowledge. According to him, a true science must be based on the evidence of the real world.[125] A system that ignores this evidence, whether by rejecting it completely (as in the case of those who refuse to use medicine) or by exaggerating the human ability to understand and control it (as in the claims of the astrologers) is superstition rather than science, a delusion rather than a wakeful enterprise.

[124] See chap. 2, above.

[125] See his quotation of Themistius in *Guide* 1:71 (*Dalāla*, 123:29–30; Pines, 179): "That which exists does not conform to the various opinions, but rather the correct opinions conform to that which exists."

Chapter Six

"From Moses to Moses": Maimonides' Vision of Perfection

NOTWITHSTANDING MAIMONIDES' COMPLETE IMMERSION in the cultural world of his time, the Jewish tradition and the Jewish community were at the heart of his thought and activity. As the community's leader, he aspired to reach the point at which the Jewish people would be found deserving of being described by the nations as "a wise, understanding nation" [Deut. 4:6]. At the same time, he sought to attain a personal level of understanding that he knew was suited only for a few individuals, and not for the masses. This chapter will examine the tension between Maimonides' role as a community leader, and his craving for solitary, individual salvation.

"True Felicity": The Hereafter in Maimonides' Thought

Although Maimonides' discussion of the hereafter is couched in the terms of traditional Jewish sources, his position must be understood against the backdrop of Islamic philosophy. We should therefore begin with a brief description of the hereafter of Muslim philosophers.[1]

The attitude of Muslim philosophers to the hereafter was determined by the sacred text. Both eternal punishment for the wicked and everlasting bliss for the righteous are depicted in the Qur'ān in vivid colors. Paradise is described in sensuous, corporeal terms, and the Qur'ān dwells in detail on the garden's pleasures or delights. *Ḥadīth* literature expounds on the Qur'ānic descriptions of paradise and adds to them still more colorful, more sensuous descriptions. This corporeal paradise could not be accepted by the philosophers. When the *falāsifa* speak of the hereafter, they consider it to be the culmination of human perfection. According to all *falāsifa,* the human being is composed of body and soul. Following Platonic teaching, they see the soul as including vegetal and animal souls or parts, and a rational soul. The body perishes with death, regardless of

[1] On the depiction of the hereafter in Islam and in Islamic philosophy, see further S. Stroumsa, " 'True Felicity': Paradise in the Thought of Avicenna and Maimonides," *Medieval Encounters* 4 (1998): 51–77.

a person's behavior or understanding. With the disintegration of the body, the vegetal and animal souls, which depend for their existence on the bodily organs, also perish. The rational soul or the intellect can, however, hope for a survival independent of the body.

Whereas the Qur'ānic description promises eternal bliss to all righteous believers, irrespective of their intellectual level, the philosophers tie the reward to the individual's intellectual achievements. They consider the intellect to be the real "form" of the human being, that by which it deserves to be called human. The material body is necessary for the activation of the human potential, but in itself this body is insignificant and disappears with death. Only the realization of human potentiality allows a person to survive beyond death. This realization occurs when a person reaches during his lifetime understanding of the "separate forms" or "separate intellects" that do not reside in matter. When a human being contemplates these separate intellects and apprehends them, he is united with them, and that part of him that grasped the eternal separate entities, his intellect, becomes itself eternal. The object of contemplation is in particular the Active Intellect, which governs the sublunar world. The unification or conjunction with the Active Intellect is the closest a human being can aspire to get to the realm of the divine. For the *falāsifa*, therefore, the conjunction with the Active Intellect is the foremost goal of human beings. It is the completion of human perfection, and it alone guarantees immortality and eternal reward. When speaking of the higher levels awaiting perfect souls, the *falāsifa* almost invariably speak of "felicity" (*saʿāda*, a translation of the Greek *eudaimonia*). Avicenna stands out among the *falāsifa* in his explicit insistence that souls retain their individuality even at the highest rank of immortality; but other *falāsifa*, such as Averroes, believed that at this level the souls conjoin also with each other and lose their individuality.

Among the philosophers, Avicenna is of particular importance for understanding Maimonides. Attempting to explain "the Soul's Felicity and Misery After Death," Avicenna says, "The divine philosophers desire to attain this felicity more than they desire the corporeal felicity. In fact, they seem oblivious to the latter, and they do not deem it as anything of importance compared to that felicity which is close to the First Truth."[2] Avicenna describes in detail the pleasure of the cognitive faculty when it "observes that which is absolute beauty and absolute good, when it is unified with it and is imprinted in its resemblance and arrangement, engraved in its ways and becomes part of its substance."[3] This state is comparable to

[2]Ibn Sīnā, *Risālat aḥwāl al-nafs wa-baqā'ihā wa-maʿādihā* (Cairo, 1952), 126–27; see also Abū ʿAlī b. Sīnā, *al-Najāt* (Cairo, 1321H), 477–78.

[3]*Aḥwāl al-nafs*, 130–31; *Najāt*, 480–81.

nothing we know from our worldly experience, from which it differs in both its permanence, the difficulty in achieving it, and the pleasure that accompanies it; and Avicenna tries to illustrate our difficulty in grasping and depicting this pleasure, saying:

> In this respect, we are like a eunuch, who does not crave the pleasure of sexual intercourse nor does he desire it, because he has never experienced it and does not know what it is, although both induction and widespread sayings inform him of its existence and indicate to him that sexual intercourse entails pleasure. This is our situation regarding the pleasure of whose existence we know but which we cannot conceive.[4]

This inability holds true for all human beings, but philosophers and prophets, who have perfected their rational faculty, have some notion of what awaits them, and they long for it, whereas the multitudes are totally ignorant of this possibility:

> Know that just as young boys are insensitive to the pleasures and pains proper to adults, and they poke fun at them, and find pleasure in that which in reality is not pleasing and which mature people distaste, so are the young of intellect—mundane people and those attached to the body—in the eyes of those of mature intellect, who are the ones freed from Matter.[5]

For Avicenna, the prophets inform people "through symbols and similitudes derived from things that for them are majestic and great" and "tell them about eternal bliss and misery in parables they can comprehend and conceive . . . and that there are pleasures that are great possessions."[6] But the difficulty in grasping spiritual pleasure is reflected also in the inability to convey it in words. Avicenna makes repeated attempts to give his reader an idea of spiritual bliss, often resorting to parables and similes. Thus, for example, in his attempt to convince us of the superiority of spiritual pleasures, he evokes the case of the chess player, who prefers the joy of winning to the pleasures of food and love making. In the same context he also reminds us that people will often shun physical pleasures, out of fear that such pleasures would bring them reproach and shame

[4] *Al-mabda' wa'l-ma'ād,* ed. ʿAbdallāh Nurānī (Tehran, 1 343H), 112; on this work, see Gutas, *Avicenna and the Aristotelian Tradition,* 98–99; In *Najāt*, 479, Avicenna lists the eunuch together with the blind and deaf as examples of people who cannot apprehend certain pleasures; see R. Michot, "L'eschatologie d'Avicenne selon F.D. al-Rāzī," *Revue Philosophique de Louvain* 87 (1989): 243.

[5] *Al-mabda' wa'l-ma'ād,* 114.

[6] Healing: *Metaphysics* X, trans. M. E. Marmura, in Lerner and Mahdi, *Medieval Political Philosophy*, 101.

(ḥishma).[7] Avicenna also employs metaphorical language of the kind that is usually described as mystical. Typical of Avicenna is the frequent use of the notion of love (ʿishq), which he elaborates in order to describe the soul's longing for this pleasure and the happiness that is associated with it.[8] Paradise, or "the place of (eternal) dwelling," is, according to Avicenna, the intellectual world, whereas the imaginative world, that of the senses, is the world of corruption and of the graves.[9] The body and its pleasures are thus excluded from Avicenna's paradise.

This interpretation was considered by orthodox Muslims to be simply heretical. The orthodox reaction is exemplified by Ghazālī, whose *Intentions of the Philosophers*, in which he summarized the various philosophical positions, was based on Avicenna. In his critique of philosophers' *tahāfut*,[10] al-Ghazālī says: "What . . . contradicts religion among the things they say is the denial of bodily resurrection, the denial of corporeal pleasures in paradise and bodily sufferings in hell, and the denial of the existence of paradise and hell as described in the Qurʾān."[11] Unlike their Muslim contemporaries, Jewish medieval philosophers did not have to contend with a sacred text offering plastic, corporeal descriptions of the afterlife. In fact, as both Muslim and Christian polemicists repeatedly reminded their Jewish interlocutors, the Hebrew Bible hardly discusses the soul's survival and the hereafter.[12] One could thus expect the problems that faced Jewish philosophers to be much simpler than those facing their Muslim counterparts. Already the Talmud, however, contains corporeal descriptions of the hereafter: the souls of the righteous are kept under the divine throne, the righteous sit under canopies and enjoy the splendor of the divine presence (*shekhina*).[13] Rabbinic tradition identifies paradise (*gan ʿeden*) as the abode of the righteous, as opposed to hell (*gehinnom*), the abode of the wicked,[14] but the Rabbis

---

[7] *Ishārāt, al-namaṭ al-thāmin*, in M.A.F. Mehren, *Traités mystiques d'Abou Alī al-Hosain b. Abdallah b. Sīnā ou d'Avicenne* (Leiden, 1889–99), 1.

[8] See, for instance, his *risāla fī'l-ʿishq*, in Mehren, *Traités mystiques*; see also *Ishārāt, al-namaṭ al-thāmin* (Mehren, *Traités mystiques*, 8–9). On Avicenna's vision of the hereafter, see further in Stroumsa, "True Felicity."

[9] *Fī ithbāt al-nubuwāt wa-ta'wīl rumūzihim*, in *Tisʿ rasāʾil fī'l-ḥikma wa'l-ilāhīyyāt* (Istanbul, 1298H), 82–90, on 89; trans. M. E. Marmura, "On the Proof of Prophecies and the Interpretation of the Prophets' Symbols and Metaphors," in Lerner and Mahdi, *Medieval Political Philosophy*, 112–21, on 120.

[10] See chap. 2, note 74, above.

[11] *Tahāfut al-Falāsifa*, ed. M. Bouyges (Beirut, 1927), 354.

[12] See, for example, Saʿadya, *Amānāt*, 264; Ibn Kammūna, *Tanqīḥ al-abḥāth fī'l-milal al-thalāth*, ed. M. Perlmann (Berkeley and Los Angeles, 1967), 40; Avraham ibn Dāʾūd, *Sefer Emmunah Ramma* (Frankfurt, 1852; reprinted Jerusalem, 1967), 39.

[13] BT, *Baba Batra* 75.

[14] See BT, *Ḥagiga* 15a; *Baba Batra* 15a.

often refer to the hereafter with another term, "the world to come." In later Midrashic literature, the notions of the Garden of Eden, the days of the Messiah, the world to come, and the resurrection of the dead blend together, and are all given colorful, often corporeal descriptions.[15] The association of the final reward with the resurrection of the dead contributed to the tendency among Jews to hold a physical, material image of a bodily reward in paradise. It seems that although Jewish polemicists ridiculed Muslim perceptions of the hereafter, these same perceptions had a profound impact on Jewish contemporary beliefs. Thus, despite the apparent lack of scriptural constraints, a philosopher like Maimonides had to contend with popular views that were much the same as those with which Avicenna had struggled. When Maimonides records the beliefs of those Jews who identify reward with the Garden of Eden, he attributes to them a belief in what sounds like a Qur'ānic paradise: "A place where people eat and drink without bodily toil or faintness. Houses of costly stones are there, couches of silk and rivers flowing with wine and perfumed oils."[16] The corporeal image of paradise was not restricted to the uneducated multitudes, but was also held by the elite of the Jewish community. Maimonides quotes a saying of the Sages, which, according to his understanding, denies physical pleasures in the hereafter: "In the world to come there will be no eating nor drinking, but only the righteous sitting with crowns on their heads, enjoying the splendor of the divine presence." According to him, it is evident from this saying that there is no corporeality in paradise, since there is no eating and drinking.[17] Years later, however, we still find Maimonides' toughest rival, the Gaon Samuel ben Eli, interpreting the same Talmudic saying in a very different way: the righteous sit on chairs, they have crowns, hence they must have bodies.[18]

Maimonides discusses the hereafter in both his halakhic and philosophical writings. His most detailed discussion of the Jewish tradition in this respect is found in his *Commentary on the Mishnah*, in the introduction to *Pereq Ḥeleq*. One should first note the absence of the punishment

[15] See, for example, Rabbi Joshua ben Levi's description of paradise, *Yalqut Shim'oni* on Genesis, and see E. E. Urbach, *The Sages, Their Concepts and Beliefs* (Jerusalem, 1975), 276.

[16] Introduction to *Pereq Ḥeleq*, *Commentary on the Mishnah*, *Neziqin*, 196; J. Abelson, "Maimonides on the Jewish Creed," in J. I. Dienstang, ed., *Eschatology in Maimonidean Thought: Messianism, Resurrection and the World to Come* (New York, 1979), 29; and cf., for instance, Qur'ān 45 (*Muḥammad*): 15; 83 (*al-muṭaffifīn*): 22–27.

[17] *Mishneh Torah*, *Hilkhot Teshuva* 8:2.

[18] See Y. T. Langermann, "Samuel ben Eli's Epistle on Resurrection," *Qovetz 'al Yad* 15 (2001), 78 [Hebrew]. This argument of the Gaon is quoted and refuted by Maimonides' student; see Stroumsa, *The Beginnings of the Maimonidean Controversy*, #20 and #137 and commentary on 139; and see chap. 6b, below.

of the wicked in general, and the descriptions of hell in particular, from Maimonides' discussion. In the *Commentary*, this is dictated by the Mishnaic discussion of the "share (*ḥeleq*) in the world to come," namely, the reward; but Maimonides seems immeasurably more concerned with paradise in all his writings, whereas hell hardly occupies his thoughts. In this, he is a typical philosopher (as opposed to *mutakallim*).

The subject matter of the discussion in the *Commentary* is "the felicity (*sa'āda*) which human beings attain from the performance of those precepts which God enjoined upon us by the hand of Moses."[19] Maimonides has a very clear notion of this felicity: "The final goal is the attaining to the world to come, and it is to it that the effort must be directed."[20] Before introducing his own concept of the hereafter, however, Maimonides feels obliged to disentangle the concept of the world to come from the three other, supposedly related concepts of *gan 'eden,* the days of the Messiah, and the resurrection of the dead. He first turns to define paradise:

> As for the Garden of Eden, it is a fertile spot on the earth's sphere, rich in streams and fruits. God will of a certainty disclose it to man one day, and will show him the path leading to it. Man will reap enjoyment within it, and there may possibly be found therein plants of a very extraordinary sort, great in usefulness and rich in pleasure-giving properties, in addition to those which are renowned with us. All this is not impossible nor farfetched. On the contrary, it is quite near possibility, and would be so even if the Torah failed to allude to it. How much more it is the case seeing that it has a clear and conspicuous place in the Torah.[21]

Maimonides demythologizes the term *gan 'eden,* the Adamic Eden, which, following Rabbinic tradition, is often identified with the eternal reward in paradise. As Maimonides curtly explains, the Garden of Eden, although as yet unidentified by geographers, is an earthly place. It is the place where Adam had lived; its location may one day be disclosed to us, when God finds us worthy of it, but it is not identical with the hereafter.[22]

[19] Introduction to *Pereq Ḥeleq,* 196; cf. Abelson's translation, "Maimonides on the Jewish Creed," 132.

[20] Abelson, "Maimonides on the Jewish Creed," 44.

[21] Ibid., 41.

[22] Of course, one would then have to ask what is the exact meaning of "the place where Adam had lived" for Maimonides, and how concrete can we take this place to be. See S. Klein-Braslavy, *Maimonides' Interpretation of the Adam Stories in Genesis: A Study of Maimomides' Anthropology* (Jerusalem, 1986), esp. 251–53 [Hebrew]. On closer scrutiny, Adam's original abode may well turn out to have a lot in common with the hereafter. For

In the Qur'ān, the same word (or words) is used for both the Adamic Eden and the hereafter. The interpretative approach that distinguishes between the two was therefore less easily accessible to Muslims. But even within the Jewish tradition Maimonides' approach stands out in its boldness.

As mentioned above, the Rabbis often identified the Garden of Eden with the ultimate reward, as did also some medieval Jewish theologians prior to Maimonides, for instance Muqammaṣ and, with some reserve, Saadya.[23] By rejecting this identification, Maimonides can eliminate a major component of the corporeal imagery of paradise, namely, its association with lush gardens. Maimonides is thus able to claim that the Jewish tradition never intended to identify the hereafter as paradise.

Maimonides then applies the same demythologizing approach to the Messianic times, which he describes as a specific historical period, albeit set in the future. It is a wondrous period, devoid of the troubles and toils of "regular" history, but a historical period nonetheless.[24]

The theme of the resurrection of the dead is treated by Maimonides as a Pandora's box, not to be opened. He accepts this belief as belonging to the basic Jewish creed, but refuses to discuss it any further (until forced to do so by popular uproar).[25] Even here the demythologizing approach is at work, to the best of Maimonides' ability. Although he cannot interpret this principle away, he limits it to the Messianic period, and insists that the resurrection is not for eternity: those risen from the dead will die again.[26]

This three-step demythologizing leaves the concept of the world to come as unrelated to the other concepts. It is not the Garden of Eden, nor is it identical with the Messianic times or the resurrection. It is not related to the earthly historico-mythical bliss, either past or future,[27] and it is not related to bodily reward. Maimonides can resort to this analysis

---

Maimonides, they both represent the ideal of intellectual humanity, the one in the form of what we could have been, the other in the form of what we can become.

[23]The ninth-century Dāwūd al-Muqammaṣ, who was probably influenced by Eastern Christian exegetes, says explicitly: "Paradise is the place where Adam was physically living and from which he was then driven out, and it is the abode of the just in the world to come;" see *Dāwūd ibn Marwān al-Muqammiṣ's Twenty Chapters,* 300. Saʿadya says that "the abode of the reward is called *gan ʿeden,* because in this world no place is nobler than that orchard, which God had made to be Adam's dwelling" (*Amānāt,* 274). This seems to mean that the Garden of Eden was an earthly place, and its name was borrowed to describe the hereafter, although the two are not necessarily identical.

[24]See Abelson, "Maimonides on the Jewish Creed," 42–44.

[25]On this, see chap. 6, below.

[26]Abelson, "Maimonides on the Jewish Creed," 42.

[27]See also *Hilkhot Teshuva* 8: 2, where Maimonides says that the world to come is not for the future, but rather exists now: "It was called 'the world to come' only because a person

because, unlike the Qur'ān, the Hebrew Bible does not identify the Garden of Eden with the hereafter. As mentioned above, neither does the Rabbinic tradition oblige him to identify the two, because of its frequent usage of the term "the world to come." Throughout his Arabic discussion of this question in the introduction *to Pereq Ḥeleq,* Maimonides uses the Hebrew terminology of the various aspects of paradise. By an analysis of the Hebrew terms Maimonides disengages the world to come (*ha-ʿolam ha-ba*) from the other three concepts, and by disengaging the world to come, he can move on to the philosophical, Arabic notion of reward. In other words, it is his participation in both worlds, that of Hebrew and that of Arabic culture, that allows him some freedom to maneuver between his religious and his philosophical traditions.

When Maimonides finally returns to "his original intention" of explaining the meaning of ultimate felicity, he is no longer focused on the Jewish tradition, and he sounds remarkably close to Avicenna, making the same argument and using identical terms:

> Know that just as a blind man can form no idea of colors, nor a deaf man comprehend sounds, nor a eunuch feel the desire for sexual intercourse, so the bodies cannot comprehend the delights of the soul. . . . Indeed, we have no pleasure in any way except what is bodily, and what the senses can comprehend of eating, drinking, and sexual intercourse. Whatever is outside these is non-existent to us. . . . For we live in a material world and the only pleasure we can comprehend must be material. But the delights of the spirit are everlasting and uninterrupted. . . . When after death the worthy from among us will reach that exalted stage, he will experience no bodily pleasure[s], neither will he have any wish for them, any more than would a king of sovereign power wish to divest himself of his imperial sway and return to his boyhood games with a ball in the street, although at one time he would without any doubt have set a higher worth upon a game with a ball than on kingly dominion . . . , just as we today rank the delights of the body above those of the soul.
>
> . . . And when you will give your consideration to the subject of these two pleasures, you will discover the meanness of the one and the high worth of the other. . . . Similarly, many a man prefers the obtaining of revenge over his enemies to many of the pleasures of the body. And many a man, again, shuns the greatest among all physical delights out of fear that it should bring him shame and [the] reproach (*ḥishma*) of men.[28]

reaches this (future) life after the life in this world of ours, where we live in both body and soul, and which universally precedes (the other life)."

[28] Introduction to *Pereq Ḥeleq,* 204: Abelson, "Maimonides on the Jewish Creed," 38; and see above, *apud* note 7.

Maimonides accompanies his argument with illustrations that we have seen used by Avicenna: the eunuch or the blind man, the little boy who does not understand the adults' pleasure, the person who prefers winning to material delights, and poverty to shame. On the basis of this passages Dov Schwartz has argued convincingly that "the relevant passages from Avicenna's *Kitāb al-Najāt* were known to Maimonides, either in their original form or in paraphrase, and that Maimonides shaped his doctrine of the intellect's or soul's experience in the afterlife in accordance with Avicenna."[29] Avicenna's way of handling the subject of paradise probably set for Maimonides the example of how to negotiate his way between philosophy and his own religious tradition.

Maimonides writes on a double linguistic and textual register. On the one hand, he has to interpret the Jewish texts, as understood by the Jewish tradition. On the other hand, he often writes in Arabic, and even when he writes in Hebrew, his philosophical frame of reference is that of Arabic philosophy. He can thus move from one language to the other, and give both tradition and philosophy their due.

In the most philosophical of his writings, the *Guide of the Perplexed,* Maimonides speaks little of the otherworldly paradise, and for more detailed discussions he refers the reader to his halakhic writings. What he does say, however, is highly significant.

To begin with, the *Guide* confirms Maimonides' care to distinguish between *gan ʿeden* and paradise in the sense of the hereafter. In his lengthy discussion of Adam's fall, Maimonides is careful to use the first, Hebrew concept. But in *Guide* 2.27, in the context of the question of the creation or pre-eternity of the world, he refers to the popular understanding of the hereafter, and there he uses the Arabic term *janna* (with a thinly veiled allusion to the Muslim descriptions of paradise):

> The same applies to the souls of the virtuous; for according to our opinion, they are created, but will never become non-existent. According to certain opinions of those who follow the literal sense of the *midrashim*, their bodies will also be in a state of perpetual felicity (*munʿama*) for ever and ever—an opinion resembling that of those whose belief as to the inhabitants of paradise (*al-janna*) is generally known.[30]

As could be expected, the *Guide* also confirms Maimonides' strict denial of a corporeal pleasure in the hereafter. But, more than the halakhic

[29] D. Schwartz, "Avicenna and Maimonides on Immortality," in R.L. Nettler, ed., *Medieval and Modern Perceptions on Jewish-Muslim Relations* (Luxembourg and Oxford, 1995), 188.

[30] *Guide* 2.27 (*Dalāla*, 233; Pines, 333).

writings, the *Guide* gives us a glimpse of a positive description of Maimonides' understanding of paradise.

Toward the end of the *Guide,* in what he calls "a kind of a conclusion," Maimonides turns to offer the reader a guide to the highest way of worship. This guide, he says, "makes known to him [that is, the reader] how providence watches over him in this habitation, until he is brought over to *the bundle of life (tsror ha-ḥayyim).*"[31] This last expression, taken from Abigail's words to David (1 Sam. 25:29), is interpreted in the Jewish tradition since the Talmud as referring to the world to come. This is also how Maimonides interprets this idiom, in his aforementioned introduction to *Pereq Ḥeleq*. True to his word, it is in this chapter 51 that Maimonides speaks most clearly of the lot of the perfect souls, at death and beyond it.

> The philosophers have already explained that the bodily faculties impede in youth the attainment of most of the moral virtues, and all the more that of pure thought, which is achieved through the perfection of the intelligibles that lead to passionate love of Him, may He be exalted.
>
> ... When a perfect man is stricken with years and approaches death, this apprehension increases very powerfully, joy over this apprehension and a great love for the object of apprehension become stronger, until the soul is separated from the body at that moment in this state of pleasure.
>
> ... The Sages ... followed the generally accepted poetical way of expression that call the apprehension that is achieved in a state of intense and passionate love for Him, may He be exalted, a kiss.
>
> ... After having reached this condition of enduring permanence, that intellect remains in one and the same state, ... And he will remain permanently in that state of intense pleasure.[32]

The individuals who have achieved the highest intellectual apprehension experience, in their death and beyond it, great joy and permanent intense pleasure. In this, Maimonides, like the other *falāsifa,* identifies the highest degree of the hereafter with the intellectual, noncorporeal bliss.

Like most *falāsifa*, Maimonides did not think of the bliss in the hereafter in terms of individual survival. He did not endorse Avicenna's personal immortality, and his express rejection of this theory developed by "a modern philosopher" may be directed specifically against Avicenna.[33] He also disagrees with Avicenna concerning the possibility of im-

[31] *Guide* 3.51 (*Dalāla,* 454; Pines, 618).
[32] *Guide* 3.51 *(Dalāla,* 462–63; Pines, 627–28).
[33] See Pines, "Translator's Introduction," ciii.

provement of the soul after death. Whereas Avicenna left room for the continuous development and elevation of some souls after death, Maimonides strongly believed in the constant, immovable state of the souls that have reached immortality. According to him, the possibility of change is a property of this world alone, and the point reached at death is incorrigible.[34] But in other respects he seems to have been greatly influenced by Avicenna's psychology and metaphysics.[35] Pines has suggested that Maimonides' discussion of "rational worship" in *Guide* 3.51 is reminiscent of Avicenna's concept of spiritual prayer.[36] Indeed, Avicenna's influence on Maimonides is evident in this chapter, especially in Maimonides' insistence on the passionate love (*ʿishq*) that the perfect individual feels toward the object of contemplation and that fills him with joy.[37]

Most of their contemporaries found the medieval philosophers' abstract, spiritual, and intellectual concept of the hereafter baffling. A typical reaction is recorded by the tenth-century Abū Ḥayyān al-Tawḥīdī: "Abū Sulaymān (al-Sijistānī) told us: A certain Christian described to us paradise, saying: 'There is no eating or drinking in it, nor copulating.' One of the (Muslim) theologians (*mutakallimūn*) heard it and said: 'What you describe is but sadness, sorrow and misery.' "[38] Those who found the philosophical hereafter incomprehensible often concluded that the philosophers' belief in paradise was insincere. From a different perspective, modern scholarship has witnessed the development of similar attitudes, particularly since the studies of Shlomo Pines, who suggested that Maimonides (following Fārābī and perhaps Ibn Bājja) did not believe in the human possibility of achieving metaphysical knowledge. According to Pines, these philosophers set for themselves the traditional

[34] *Commentary on the Mishnah, Avot* 4:22, 448–49.

[35] See H. Davidson, "Maimonides on Metaphysical Knowledge," *Maimonidean Studies* 3 (1992–93): 89.

[36] Pines, "Translator's Introduction," cii; and see *Risālat al-ṣalāt*, in *Jāmiʿ al-badāʾiʿ*, 2–14. See also S. Harvey, "Avicenna and Maimonides on Prayer and Intellectual Worship," in *Exchange and Transmission across Cultural Boundaries: Philosophy, Mysticism and Science in the Mediterranean* (Proceedings of a workshop in memory of Prof. Shlomo Pines, the Institute for Advanced Studies, Jerusalem; 28 February–2 March 2005), ed. H. Ben-Shammai, S. Shaked, and S. Stroumsa (forthcoming).

[37] On the Sufī context of this term in Maimonides's usage, see C.-A. Keller, *Die Religion der Gebildeten im Mittelalter: Averroes und Maimonides in Die Religion von Oberschichten* (Marburg, 1989), 49; and see S. Harvey, "The Meaning of Terms Designating Love in Judaeo-Arabic Thought and Some Remarks on the Judaeo-Arabic Interpretation of Maimonides," in N. Golb, ed., *Judaeo-Arabic Studies: Proceedings of the Founding Conference of the Society for Judaeo-Arabic Studies (Studies in Muslim-Jewish Relations* 3 (Reading, 1996), 175–96; D. Blumenthal, "Maimonides' Philosophical Mysticism", in idem, *Philosophic Mysticism: Studies in Rational Religion* (Ramat Gan, 2006), 128–51.

[38] *Al-Imtāʿ waʾl-muʾānasa*, 3: 192.

goal of apprehending the separate intellects, but did not actually think that this goal was attainable by humans. As a result, the highest attainable human perfection according to them was only civic and political happiness. In such a view, naturally, otherworldly happiness is non-existent, and indeed Fārābī is said to have expressed the opinion that the belief in the soul's immortality and the hereafter is nothing but myths, "old wives tales."[39] Pines examined Maimonides' writings closely, and came to the conclusion that "the only passage in the *Guide* which contains an apparently unambiguous affirmation of the survival of the intellect occurs at the end of 3.51."[40]

Pines's view has been strongly criticized by Davidson, who has attempted to show that Maimonides, like his two Muslim predecessors, "recognized the possibility of human thought with the active intellect itself as a permanent object, and he suggests that when the human intellect achieves such thought, it enters a state of permanent conjunction with the active intellect."[41] Concerning the same passage in *Guide* 3.51, Davidson concedes that its language "falls short of technical precision" but believes that it suggests a final conjunction with the incorporeal realm.

The lack of technical precision is indeed noteworthy and telling, but I believe it must be interpreted differently. Despite his insistence on the human inability to grasp this bliss or express it, Maimonides delves in this passage into untypical poetic descriptions.[42] Such descriptions are quite usual in the writings of Avicenna, but are rather rare in Maimonides' more sober rhetoric. In sharp contrast to his lukewarm, pursed-lipped admittance of the resurrection, his description of the bliss of the perfect souls rings with the exultation and rapture of the believer.

The goal that the philosophers set for themselves—apprehending the highest truth as a precondition to immortality—was an immensely daunting one. The examination of philosophical texts and rationalist analysis

[39] Pines, "The Limitations of Human Knowledge," 98; and see above, chap. 5, *apud* note 73.

[40] *Dalāla,* 463; (Pines, 628); Pines,"The Limitations of Human Knowledge," 95. On this chapter, see also Keller, "Die Religion der Gebildeten," 48–49.

[41] Davidson, "Maimonides on Metaphysical Knowledge," 98. Further on this question see, for example, B. S. Kogan, "'What Can We Know and When Can We Know It?' Maimonides on the Active Intelligence and Human Cognition," in E. L. Ormsby, ed., *Moses Maimonides and His Time* (Washington, D.C., 1989), 121–37; Avieze Ravitzky, "Maimonides: Esotericism and Educational Philosophy," in Seeskin, *The Cambridge Companion to Maimonides*, 316–17; G. Freudenthal, "The Biological Limitations of Man's Intellectual Perfection According to Maimonides," in Tamer, ed., *The Trials of Maimonides*, 137–49.

[42] A similar expansion can be seen in Maimonides' introduction to the *Guide,* where he describes the understanding of the perfect man as constant light.

led the philosophers to adhere to this theory, and they usually displayed confidence in their intellectual ability. Nevertheless, it is only natural that they would at times lose heart and lapse into skepticism. Their observations and analyses indicated to them that the attachment of the human intellect to the body was not a mere temporal obstacle, but a constant that defines humanity. Their statements about the possibility of immortality, therefore, vary in intensity, and sometimes even in content. It would be incorrect, in my view, to weigh these statements against each other and look for the single true belief, as opposed to the others that would be only a camouflage for the true skeptical view. In such cases as Maimonides' *Guide* 3.51 (or, for that matter, Avicenna's *Ishārāt*), where the philosopher abandons technical language to expand on his perception of the hereafter, the emotional language is a clear sign that what he says reflects exactly what he thinks at that moment, regardless of what he may have said before or after. It is a sincere expression of his confidence in the awaiting felicity.

Issues of Life and Death: The Controversy Regarding Resurrection

Among Maimonides' writings, *The Treatise on Resurrection* constitutes an enigma. Apologetic and yet aggressive, this treatise seems to reveal a personality quite different from the one reflected in his other works. It is not that he contradicts what he says in his previous writings: on the contrary, he repeats it. The sum total of these repetitions, however, creates a Maimonides who seems more orthodox in his concerns, and who is certainly more outspoken. The special character of this treatise accounts for the discomfort expressed by several scholars about it. Some scholars went as far as to reject its attribution to Maimonides altogether.[43] Its peculiarity, however, is recognized also by those who do not question its authenticity. For some, who note the bitter and disillusioned tone of this work, it reflects a compromise to which Maimonides was pushed as a result of a political situation within the Jewish community.[44] Davidson

[43] See J. L. Teicher, "A Literary Forgery in the Thirteenth Century: Maimonides' Epistle on Resurrection," *Melilah* 1 (1944): 81–92 [Hebrew]; N. L. Goldfield, *Moses Maimonides' Treatise on Resurrection: an Inquiry into its Authenticity* (New York, 1986); and see also J. L. Teicher, "Maimonides' Letter to Jospeh b. Jehudah—A Literary Forgery," *Journal of Jewish Studies* 1 (1948–49): 35–54.

[44] See R. Lerner, "Maimonides' Treatise on Resurrection," *History of Religions* 23 (1984): 140–55; Halkin and Hartmann, *Crisis and Leadership*, 246–47, 263; Lerner, *Maimonides' Empire of the Light*, 42, notes that "in none of his addresses to his public at large does Maimonides come so close to open despair as in the *Treateise on Resurrection*."

(who had no qualms in rejecting the authenticity of several other works generally attributed to Maimonides) goes beyond accepting its authenticity. For him, the *Treatise on Resurrection* represents the quintessential Maimonides; it is "the most personal of Maimonides' works," which "goes to the heart of his innermost beliefs."[45]

The heated debate that led Maimonides to compose this work is sometimes called "the first Maimonidean controversy." At the core of the controversy stood Maimonides' *Mishneh Torah*. Maimonides' opponents criticized him for having composed such a book, as well as for various specific halakhic points discussed in it. The sharpest criticism, however, was leveled against Maimonides because of his supposed denial of the resurrection of the dead. In his *Commentary on the Mishnah* Maimonides had listed the belief in the resurrection among the thirteen articles of faith that are central to Judaism. His detractors, however, blamed him for not mentioning this article of faith in the *Mishneh Torah*, or for playing it down, or for treating the resurrection as a mere metaphor; in either case, his attitude to the resurrection was taken to be a grave assault on the Jewish tradition.

Maimonides' *Treatise on Resurrection* is not a self-contained soliloquy. It represents his response to the extensive and protracted debate on resurrection, and its significance can be understood only when the other pieces of the debate are fitted together. The culmination of the debate is recorded in three "essays," published during a relatively short period (within about a year of each other, around 1191): a treatise by the Gaon Samuel ben Eli, titled *Treatise on Resurrection (Maqāla fī teḥiyyat ha-metīm)*;[46] a treatise by Joseph Ibn Shimʿon, entitled the *Silencing Epistle on the Resurrection of the Dead (Risālat al-iskāt fī ḥashr al-amwāt)*;[47] and Maimonides' treatise, bearing the same title as the Gaon's.[48]

One should first of all note that the discovery and publication of the two other components of the triad definitively puts to rest the idea of a misattribution of the *Treatise on Resurrection* to Maimonides. Joseph's *Silencing Epistle* quotes the Gaon's *Treatise on Resurrection* whereas Maimonides' *Treatise on Resurrection* shows his familiarity with the two

[45] Davidson, *Moses Maimonides*, 510.

[46] Only a medieval Hebrew translation of this text is extant; see Y. T. Langermann, "A New Codex of Medieval Jewish Philosophy" *Kiryat Sefer* 64 (1992–93): 1427–32 [Hebrew]; Idem, "Samuel ben Eli's Epistle on Resurrection," 66–82.

[47] Preserved in two incomplete Judaeo-Arabic manuscripts, as well as in a medieval Hebrew translation; see Stroumsa, *The Beginnings of the Maimonidean Controversy*.

[48] The Arabic text was edited and translated by J. Finkel, *PAAJR* 9 (1939); see also *Epistles*, 319–38; "The Essay on Resurrection," in Halkin and Hartmann, *Crisis and Leadership*, 211–31.

preceding publications.[49] Each of these works agrees with the style and theological position typical of its author. To postulate a forgery, one would thus have to imagine a whole industry of expertly fabricated texts. Furthermore, an essential element of the falsification theory was the claim that the *Treatise on Resurrection* can be understood in the context of Western Christianity better than in the oriental, Muslim context.[50] The other two essays, however, discuss issues of popular religiosity and of philosophy that are unmistakably couched in twelfth-century Baghdad. The third text must therefore also have been written as part of the discussion on resurrection that preoccupied religious thinkers in the Orient in that period. The explanation for any idiosyncrasies this text may contain should thus be sought in this oriental context.

The chronological order of the three essays is also clear from the available evidence. As noted already by Harkavy, Joseph's *Silencing Epistle* shows no familiarity with a response to the Gaon written by Maimonides.[51] A warm and close relationship had been established between Maimonides and Joseph, and it remained so after Joseph left for Aleppo. Not only does Maimonides call him "my son" (*beni*)—which, although affectionate, is a rather common Hebrew formula of address to younger persons—but he also calls him "my child" (*al-walad*), a more intimate form of address that seems to have been reserved for Joseph (and probably also for the younger biological son, Abraham). During the debate with the Gaon, Maimonides comforts both himself and his student by reminding Joseph of the bond between them: "Even if I did not find in my generation anyone [who would listen to me] except you alone, it would be enough."[52] He pleads with Joseph to continue writing to him, "since I have no better friend than [your letters]."[53]

In view of the intense and close correspondence between them, it is very unlikely that Joseph would have remained ignorant of Maimonides' response to the Gaon had it already been written, or that he would have refrained from quoting it. Furthermore, the nature of the relations between this disciple and his master makes it hardly thinkable that, after Maimonides' had had his say, Joseph would presume to have the last word on the same points or to add yet another elementary, step-by-step

[49] See further below.

[50] This, and not only issues of its consistency with Maimonides' other writings, was the mainstay of the falsification theory; cf. A. D. Friedberg, "Maimonides' Reinterpretation of the Thirteenth Article of Faith: Another Look at the *Essay on Resurrection*," *Jewish Studies Quarterly* 10 (2003): 245, note 3.

[51] See A. Harkavy, "Fragment einer Apologie des Maimonidischen *ma'amar teḥiyyat hametim*;" *Zeitschrift für hebräische Bibliographie* 1 (1897): 125–28, 181–88.

[52] *Epistles*, 293.

[53] Ibid., 313.

refutation to the response written by Maimonides, and which he had already described as "a superfluous repetition."[54] Indeed, Joseph's epistle responds, directly and passionately, to the only previously written component of the triad, the Gaon's treatise, whereas Maimonides' treatise represents the third and last stage of this literary debate.

Joseph was not the official target of Maimonides' treatise, and Maimonides does not mention him in it. As the following pages will attempt to show, however, Maimonides' treatise bears witness to his familiarity with Joseph's *Silencing Epistle*. It also indicates that in some ways, Joseph Ibn Shimʿon was a primary addressee of Maimonides' treatise, just as he was the primary addressee of the *Guide of the Perplexed*.[55]

As shown by both the text of Maimonides' *Treatise on Resurrection* and his correspondence with his student Joseph, Maimonides attempted to keep a restrained public tone as long as the debate remained confined to a more or less private discussion, reserving his more outspoken pronouncements to his private correspondence. It is only when the debate received a literary form and became highly visible that he felt obliged to respond and to defend himself in public.

As is often the case in theological debates, the origin of the dispute may have had little to do with theology. Baghdad had for centuries held the hegemony among Jewish communities around the Mediterranean. In the twelfth century, however, the city had lost much of its primacy, both as a Muslim metropolis and as an effective Jewish center. Ibn Jubayr, a Spanish Muslim traveler passing through Baghdad in 1185, was not much impressed by it. Compared to the thriving Cairo, which he had visited less than a year earlier, he found Baghdad to be a city that, intellectually and economically, lived on its past glory. At the same time, Ibn Jubayr remarked, the people of Baghdad still considered their city to be the center of the world: "You scarce can find among them any who do not affect humility, but who yet are vain and proud. Each conceives, in belief and thought, that the whole world is but trivial in comparison with his land, and over the face of the world they find no noble place of living save their own."[56] The deterioration of the status of the city as a spiritual and cultural center was still more perceptible regarding the Jewish community of Baghdad. Benjamin of Tudela, a Jewish traveler who visited the city only a few years earlier (around 1171), found 40,000 Jews in

[54] On the genre of Joseph's *Epistle*, see further below.

[55] On the close similarity of the *Treatise on Resurrection* to the *Guide*, see Lerner, "Maimonides' Treatise on Resurrection," 141; and see further below.

[56] See *Travels of Ibn Jubayr*, ed. W. Wright, rev. M. J. De Goeje (Leyden and London, 1907), 217–18; English translation in R.J C. Broadhurst, *The Travels of Ibn Jubayr* (London, 1952), 226 ff.

Baghdad, with ten functioning schools.[57] By the twelfth century, however, the renowned Jewish academic centers of Iraq, the *yeshivot,* had declined, and the incontestable political and spiritual leadership of the community had moved away from Mesopotamia. In particular, the personality of Maimonides commanded such respect that Egypt came to overshadow the more ancient center of Iraq.

The historical situation did not allow for a quiet shift of power. The Gaon Samuel ben Eli was also a strong personality, who regarded both Baghdad and himself as natural leaders for all Jewish communities.[58] Maimonides was keenly aware of the threat he represented to his opponent's authority, an awareness reflected in his admonitions to his student Joseph:

> How can you, my child, reproach this conceit in someone who was brought up from tender age to believe that no one in this generation is equal to him; whom old age, and high standing, and ancestry, and the absence of discerning people in that region, and his need to install in peoples' mind that accursed brew, namely the belief that they all [should] look up to him, to receive his *obiter dicta* issuing from the *Yeshiva*, or [to receive] an honorific title, and such ravings which became a second nature to them; how can my child expect him to reach the level of understanding that will make him recognize his shortcomings, and to undo his own honor and that of his ancestors?[59]

The close ties between Jewish communities, from Spain to the Yemen, contributed to the fact that the clash between the two leaders soon became a cause celèbre. The strife was not an openly political one; as Maimonides' authority became more firmly established and widespread, and as the Gaon continually tried to reassert his own authority, the discussion evolved around either legal matters or issues of dogma. Prime among the latter was the question of the resurrection of the dead.

It was the Gaon who opened the literary debate. For some time prior to his decision to compose a treatise, the debate had been going on in other contexts and taking various forms. During this first stage, the controversy retained an epistolary character in the strict sense of the word. The Jewish community in the Yemen (or, to be exact, several Yemenite

[57] Benjamin of Tudela, *Itinerary*, ed. and trans. A. Asher (New York, 1840–42), 54–56 (text), 93–105 (trans.).

[58] On the Gaon and on the rivalry between the two centers, see S. Assaf, "Letters of R. Samuel b. Eli and his Contemporaries," *Tarbiz* 1 (1930): 102–30; 2 (1931), 43–84; 3 (1932), 15–80 [Hebrew]; see also I. Yuval, "Moses *Redivivus*: Maimonides as the Messiah's Helper," *Zion* 72 (2007): 184.

[59] *Epistles*, 294.

Jewish communities) had been corresponding with the Gaon as well as with Maimonides, asking for clarifications regarding Maimonides' position on the resurrection of the dead, and receiving answers from both leaders.[60] There were also several public oral discussions of this issue. Maimonides mentions such a discussion that was held in Damascus, and Joseph Ibn Shimʿon recounts a heated debate he had held with the Gaon in Baghdad on the resurrection and on the soul's immortality. In medieval Arabic society, letters and public debates were standard, routine mechanisms of intellectual exchange. The redaction of a formal epistle or treatise, on the other hand, where the respective positions became fixed and were recorded in a systematic literary composition, represented a different stage, often an escalation of the polemic.

In his treatise, the Gaon refers to the correspondence with the Jews of Yemen, but as the immediate incentive for his decision to put pen to paper he mentions a question presented to him by a group of Baghdadi Jewish dignitaries. These people, he says, read what Maimonides had written,[61] and they have asked the Gaon "to compose an Arabic treatise on this subject, so that this should be understood by the elite as well as the general public."

The Gaon's treatise comprises a potpourri of arguments. It contains semi-philosophical arguments on the immortality of the soul, culled from various philosophical and theological sources, but the only philosophical source that he identifies by name is Saadia Gaon. Most of the treatise, however, is dedicated to the analysis of biblical verses as well as Talmudic and Midrashic passages. These verses and passages are intended to demonstrate in a definitive way that the resurrection of the dead is an integral part of the reward in the hereafter, a reward in which the body partakes as much as the soul.[62]

The publication of the Gaon's treatise did not remain unanswered. Joseph Ibn Shimʿon, whose home was in Aleppo, was at the time residing in Baghdad, whence he conducted his far-flung trade. He had participated in the debates mentioned by the Gaon, and was confident that he had

[60]The Yemenite correspondence with the Gaon was in Hebrew; the language of Maimonides' correspondence is not known to us.

[61]The Gaon refers to a "composition" (*ḥibbur*) by Maimonides, which suggests the *Mishneh Torah*; he also mentions "chapters" (*peraqim*) in this composition, and "a treatise" (*ma'amar*), which may indicate Maimonides' *Commentary on the Mishnah* and the introduction to *Pereq Ḥeleq*. Maimonides himself mentions the criticism regarding the *Mishneh Torah* (see *Epistles*, 293) as well as "their drivel" (*al-jamjama allatī yujamjimūhā*) regarding the *Commentary on the Mishnah* (*Epistles*, 295).

[62]For a summary of the Gaon's position, see Stroumsa, "Twelfth-Century Concepts of Soul and Body," 317–21; on the Gaon's sources, see Langermann, "Samuel ben Eli's Epistle on Resurrection," 54–61.

won the discussion. Much later, however, upon returning to Baghdad from one of his business travels, he discovered that the Gaon had published his treatise, in which he repeated the arguments he had presented in the oral debate. Joseph reacted by writing his *Silencing Epistle*, and by writing to Maimonides to inform him of this development. The epistle belongs to the genre of basic refutation in which lengthy paragraphs of the opponent's text are quoted and refuted.[63] Such works have an informative as well as a theological role, as they systematically present the opponent's claims. They tend, however, to be relatively unsophisticated, since their structure is not independent but determined by that of the refuted composition. In a protracted disputation, such works would usually represent the first stage, whereas later refutations of the same opponent could afford to stray further afield from the refuted work. This is indeed the case with Joseph's epistle, which was apparently sent to Maimonides immediately after it was written.[64] It presents quotations from the Gaon's text and endeavors to demonstrate Joseph's awareness of their absurdity as well as his indignation and his filial loyalty to Maimonides.

Maimonides' first reaction, still in private correspondence, was an attempt to calm his student down. He referred to his student's missive, expressing surprise that Joseph saw the necessity to send to him the Gaon's treatise as a proof of the latter's ignorance. For Maimonides this ignorance, typical of simple-minded preachers, required no proof.[65] He also promised to compose a comprehensive treatise on the subject, and to send the manuscript shortly to Joseph.[66] It is thus only after receiving his student's work, with the quotations from the Gaon's treatise that it contained, that he decided to react publicly, by dedicating an essay to the subject.

This sequence of events suggests that Maimonides' immediate reason for writing his *Treatise on Resurrection* was not the Gaon's treatise bearing the same title, but rather Joseph's epistle. This chronology is corroborated by the content of the text. Only a relatively short passage of Maimonides' treatise directly attacks the Gaon, and it does so rather mildly. Most of the treatise is devoted to theoretical and exegetical problems related to

[63] Such basic refutations often include in their titles either the words *al-radd ʿalā* . . . (literally: "A response to . . .), or (as is the case of Joseph's *Silencing Epistle*) belligerent words indicating their polemical intention, or both. See, for example, Abū Ḥusayn b. ʿUthmān al-Khayyāṭ, *Kitāb al-Intiṣār wa'l-radd ʿalā Ibn al-Rāwandī al-mulḥid (Le livre du triomphe et de la réfutation d'Ibn al-Rawandi l'hérétique)*, ed. A. N. Nader (Beirut, 1957).

[64] Joseph may have sent the *Epistle* to Maimonides shortly before making it public, but it is also possible that the publication of the *Epistle* was parallel to the correspondence.

[65] *Epistles*, 297, and see above, chap. 4, *apud* notes 160–61.

[66] *Epistles*, 298.

the resurrection, problems the discussion of which does not respond to the Gaon's treatise. In reading Maimonides' treatise in the context of the two other essays it becomes clear that Maimonides responds to his student's arguments at least as much as to the treatise the student was trying to refute. Moreover, even when Maimonides does react to the Gaon's text, he seems to know it only through Joseph's epistle. Several arguments raised by the Gaon are completely ignored by Maimonides.[67] On the other hand, all those arguments of the Gaon that Maimonides does refute are also quoted and refuted by Joseph in his epistle. In other words, Maimonides' treatise refers only to those parts of the Gaon's work that were quoted in the *Silencing Epistle*. There are no indications that, before writing his own treatise, Maimonides has seen the Gaon's treatise in any other form than through the extensive quotations in his student's work.[68] It therefore seems that when Maimonides mentions in his letter to Joseph the treatise of the Gaon that Joseph had sent him, he is actually referring only to the extensive quotations from this treatise that Joseph had included in his *Silencing Epistle*. Furthermore, even if we were to assume that Maimonides did read the Gaon's treatise in it's entirely, we must note the fact that he chose to respond to it only as it was reflected in his student's epistle.

This impression is further strengthened by the fact that Maimonides refers in his work to some positions of the Gaon that have left no trace in the Gaon's work, and that he could have derived solely from Joseph's epistle. For example, Maimonides states that in his treatise that the Gaon quotes Abū al-Barakāt al-Baghdādī's *al-Kitāb al-muʿtabar*, a text that, Maimonides adds with certain sarcasm, was written "in their place, in Baghdad (*ʿindahum fī baghdād*)." The Gaon, however, does not mention the source of the quotation, and it is only Joseph who identifies it in his epistle. Abū al-Barakāt's work was quite influential in contemporary Islamic philosophical circles, and in all likelihood, Maimonides could have

[67]For example, the Gaon claims that the suffering of the righteous in this world obliges us to believe that they will find their reward in the world to come, a reward that can only be given after the soul returns to the body (see Langermann, "Samuel ben Eli's Epistle on Resurrection," 71–72). Joseph repeats the biblical verses cited by the Gaon and reinterprets them. Maimonides, on the other hand, does not refer to any of these verses, and examines instead verses that seem to deny the idea of resurrection, and that are not cited by the Gaon or reexamined by Joseph.

[68]There is thus no need to postulate an additional document of marginal notes to the Gaon's treatise, written by Joseph and read by Maimonides, Joseph's treatise itself being, in fact, such marginal notes; cf. Langermann, "Samuel ben Eli's Epistle on Resurrection," 58; and Friedberg, "Maimonides' Reinterpretation," 245n3. Maimonides mentions in another (probably later) letter that he has already seen the Gaon's treatise, and that he had already responded by writing his own; see *Epistles*, 394.

identified it without his student's help.[69] His sarcastic remark, however, is very telling. In the *Silencing Epistle* Joseph records a disputation he had held with the Gaon regarding the witch of Ein Dor (2 Sam. 28). The Gaon has compared the witch's conjuring up the prophet Samuel to a divination by *mandal*. In this divination technique a young child, looking in a bright (usually liquid) surface, serves as the medium for conjuring up the souls of the dead. When Joseph disdainfully asked whoever has seen such mediums, the Gaon, unfazed, responded: "They can be found in our place, in Baghdad (*ʿindanā fī baghdād*)." Maimonides' sardonic expression "in their place, in Baghdad" seems to refer to this episode recorded by Joseph in his epistle.[70]

Moreover, in his epistle, Joseph claims that the Gaon's written text repeated the arguments he had presented in the preceding oral disputation. It is therefore possible that Maimonides had assumed the Gaon's treatise to include these words, which in fact belonged only to the oral disputation.

Technically, then, it seems that Maimonides' immediate trigger for writing his treatise was his student's epistle and the quotations it contained of the Gaon's treatise. But the ties that connect Maimonides' essay to his student's are not just technical. It should be stressed at this point that determining the order of composition of the three essays is significant not only for reasons of archival, chronological precision, but as a key to their correct interpretation. The sequence of events presented here suggests that the immediate reason for Maimonides' composition was not the Gaon's homiletic treatise but rather the urge to respond to his own chosen public, his disciple Joseph (just as the Gaon's immediate reason for writing was the wish to address his constituency, the dignitaries of Baghdad). In reading Maimonides' treatise we must therefore

[69] My working hypothesis being here, as throughout this book, that Maimonides was an avid reader, who took pains to remain abreast of contemporary scholarship in general and philosophical scholarship in particular; cf. Langermann, "Samuel ben Eli's Epistle on Resurrection," 53 and 58. On Abū al-Barakāt's place in Islamic philosophy, see S. Pines, "Etudes sur Awḥad al-Zamān Abu'l-Barakāt al-Baghdādī," *Revue des Etudes Juives* 8 (1937): note 4.

[70] Another example of this sort of veiled reference can be seen in Maimonides' insistence on his own style. In all his writings, he says, he attempts to be as brief as possible because "our purpose is not to add volume to our books (*takbīr aḥjām al-kutub*; *Epistles*, 331; Finkel, *Treatise*, 24). This declaration recalls the accusation of Joseph that the Gaon had introduced into his essay some elements that serve only to add volume to his treatise ("*li-yukbira ḥajm al-maqāla*"; see Stroumsa, *The Beginnings of the Maimonidean Controversy*, 35). In this last example, however, one could argue that it is the student who echoes Maimonides' wording rather than the other way around, whereas in the case of the *mandal* episode the primacy of Joseph's epistle is unquestionable.

remain attentive to those places where the treatise responds to the *Silencing Epistle*.

One example of this response may suffice. In the same sardonic passage referred to above, Maimonides states that the Gaon incorporated in his essay quotations from the *al-Kitāb al-muʿtabar* as well as from Avicenna's *maqālat al-maʿād*. In contradistinction to *al-Kitāb al-Muʿtabar* (which is indeed cited by the Gaon, although with no explicit identification of the book or its author), Avicenna is absent from the Gaon's treatise as we have it, and there is no indication that it had ever been cited in it.[71] In Joseph's *Silencing Epistle*, on the other hand, Avicenna is very present, although his name is never mentioned. Long excerpts from Avicenna are cited verbatim in order to prove Joseph's claim that the philosophers believe in the soul's immortality. Joseph's identification with Avicenna's view is so complete that when the latter says "in my opinion" Joseph copies these words, too, making Avicenna's view his own.

Neither the text of the Gaon's treatise as we have it nor Joseph's *Silencing Epistle* could have given Maimonides reason to believe that the Gaon had quoted Avicenna. It is therefore possible that, when Maimonides criticizes the Gaon's reliance on Avicenna, his criticism is addressed to the one who did rely on him, namely, his student.

A contextual reading of the three essays together reveals to what extent the *Silencing Epistle* could have displeased Maimonides. The Gaon's treatise is exactly what could have been expected from a traditional scholar who attempts to use a philosophical language. Maimonides regards him as a popular preacher (*darshan*), and mocks his philosophical pretensions.[72] In his correspondence, he deprecates "this poor man's rhetoric" and expresses regret that the Gaon did not confine himself to the *darshanim*'s bread-and-butter of Talmudic *midrashim*, rather than venture into discussions of the soul and the opinions of the philosophers. He notes that even people who are better than the Gaon indulge in such baseless ravings (*hadhayān*), and suggests that the Gaon undoubtedly transmitted the ravings of someone else.[73] The Gaon's excursions into philosophy are for Maimonides mere "ravings," an attempt to present nonscience as science.

In his treatise, however, Maimonides' condescending mockery of the Gaon is surprisingly free of either bitterness or anger. It is his own student, the one he affectionately calls "my child," who disappointed him. As already mentioned, Joseph's epistle is a polemical work in the genre of "*al-radd ʿalā* . . . ". Repeating the Gaon's arguments in order to refute them,

[71]Langermann, who notices this bewildering absence, assumes that the sole extant manuscript of the Gaon's treatise is incomplete; see "Samuel ben Eli's Epistle on Resurrection," 59.

[72]See Maimonides, *Epistulae* (Jerusalem, 1985), 650–66; *Epistles*, 325–26; Finkel, 12–14.

[73]*Epistles*, 297–98.

it does not manage to disengage itself from the text it seeks to refute. Its discourse is at times exegetical, at times apologetic, and even when it appeals to philosophical arguments these are derived from Avicennian texts that, as Maimonides reminds us, are not really philosophical as they are not addressed to real philosophers. The *Silencing Epistle* thus remains more theological than philosophical, a text of *kalām* rather than of *falsafa*. Such a work could not have pleased Maimonides, and his poorly disguised bitterness is grounded in this displeasure. In his letter to Joseph, Maimonides does not hide his disappointment: "I am astonished by the discourse of those who ask [that is, the Yemenite Jews] and their respondent [that is, the Gaon] as well as by what Your Honor [that is, Jospeh] say, that the Biblical verses concerning the resurrection should not be read allegorically. Who, pray, reads them in this way??!"[74]

Indeed, a significant part of Joseph's *Silencing Epistle* is dedicated precisely to this question and to this kind of interpretation. It is in this context, I submit, that Maimonides' promise to send to his student his own treatise in the near future should be seen.[75]

If so, the sequence of events sheds some light on how we should read the *Treatise on Resurrection* in the context of Maimonides' other works. In this context, one should read Maimonides' curious declaration, which he repeats several times, that the *Treatise on Resurrection* is only a "superfluous repetition" that requires no attentive reading.[76] When writing for philosophers, Maimonides always insists that nothing he writes is superfluous, that everything must be read and reread attentively. Scholars have therefore accepted Maimonides' declaration that the *Treatise on Resurrection* was written "only for the multitudes,"[77] and that it is "only a popular repetition and elaboration of things, only an additional explanation destined for women and for the ignorant."[78] This openly disdainful declaration, however, does not square with Maimonides' consistent style when addressing the general public. When writing for the multitudes, Maimonides is always encouraging, and he never tires of repeating what he has already said.[79] In the *Treatise on Resurrection*, on the other hand, Maimonides makes no attempt to hide his contempt for

[74] *Epistles*, 298.

[75] See note 66, above. See also Maimonides' allusion to the discussions (and perhaps more precisely, theological debates) that occurred between students (*waqaʿa fīhā al-kalām bayna al-ṭalaba*) in Damascus; see, for instance, *Epistles*, 326, 329 (Finkel, *Treatise*, 15, 21).

[76] *Epistles*, 326, 328, 331, 332, and 338 (Finkel, *Treatise*, 15, 19–20, 24, 26, and 37).

[77] *Epistles*, 338 (Finkel, *Treatise*, 37).

[78] *Epistles*, 326 (Finkel, *Treatise*, 15): "*tikrār maʿānī wa-taṭwīl jumhūrī lā ghayr wa-ziyādat bayān yafhamuhu al-nisāʾ wa'l-juhalāʾ lā gayr.*"

[79] In his *Letter on Astrology* he thus repeats what he has already said in his *Epistle to Yemen*, and in the *Epistle to Yemen* he repeats what he had said in the *Epistle on Forced Conversion*. See also his encouraging, solicitous style in the letter to Ibn Jābir.

those who, despite endless repetitions, "understand but little, comprehend but little, a smattering here and a smattering there."[80] This rudeness when addressing the public, so atypical of Maimonides, was also among the reasons that led some scholars to doubt the *Treatise* authenticity. Maimonides' declared impatience for the need to repeat may aim not at the general public, "the women and the ignorant" to whom the *Treatise* is supposedly addressed, nor the pretentious Gaon who writes homilies for them. Rather, the edge of impatience in his voice reveals another addressee of the *Treatise*: Maimonides' own beloved disciple, who should not have been tempted to play the *mutakallim*.

As is well known, medieval theological and philosophical epistles are often short monographs or treatises rather than letters. Even when they are addressed to real persons, the addressee serves often only as a literary device. The literary convention dictates this form in which a treatise on a well-defined topic, written in order to be published and read by a wider public, is formally addressed to a specific person.

The *Treatise on Resurrection* is usually listed among Maimonides' epistles, but its title describes it not as an epistle (*risāla*) but rather as a treatise (*maqāla*). Although *risāla* and *maqāla* are sometimes used as synonyms,[81] in this particular case the difference of these two terms seems to be significant. As I have tried to demonstrate, Maimonides did not write the *Treatise on Resurrection* as an epistle; indeed, almost the opposite is true. Using the fiction of a text addressed to the general public, he intended this text to be read more particularly by one specific person, and by the narrow class of people who resemble this person. Like the *Guide of the Perplexed* (also described by its author as a *maqāla*), the *Treatise on Resurrection* was primarily destined by Maimonides to correct and guide, yet again, his favorite student, Joseph Ibn Shimʿon.

This double destination may be observed, for example, in Maimonides' sour remark that the Gaon confuses the concepts soul and intellect. It is not only the Gaon, but also Maimonides' own disciple, who speaks too much of the soul and too little of the intellect. More than once in the *Silencing Epistle,* as Joseph was trying to navigate his way between tradition and philosophy, he was getting dangerously close to *kalām.* Maimonides' *Guide,* addressed explicitly to Joseph, was written for exactly this kind of person: one who is perplexed because of the seemingly contradictory messages of Jewish tradition and philosophy, and who is unsure as to the value of *kalām*'s arguments.[82] The *Silencing Epistle* shows us that several years after the completion of the *Guide,* Joseph was

[80] *Epistles*, 338 (Finkel, *Treatise*, 37–38).
[81] See A. Arazi and H. Ben-Shammai, art. *Risāla, EI,* 5: 549–57.
[82] See *Guide,* Dedicatory Epistle and Introduction (*Dalāla,* 1–11; Pines, 3–10).

still perplexed, at least concerning the soul and its states. Maimonides' *Treatise on Resurrection* testifies to his awareness of this continuing perplexity, as well as to his bitter disappointment.[83]

It has been argued that Maimonides' bitter tone in the *Treatise on Resurrection* results from his resentment at having had to retract his opinions.[84] On closer examination, however, it becomes obvious that he retracts nothing. Whereas, at first sight, Joseph's epistle seems to present a more "philosophic" and less traditional position than the *Treatise on Resurrection,* in fact the opposite is true. Joseph's *Silencing Epistle* is written in an emotional outburst, and is a one-dimensional composition; it says exactly what it purports to be saying. Maimonides' *Treatise on Resurrection*, on the other hand, reiterates the opinions of the *Guide* and is written in the same esoteric manner.

Leo Strauss has described the *Treatise on Resurrection* as "the most authentic commentary on the *Guide*."[85] This description follows from Strauss's general approach. Assuming a sharp dichotomy between what philosophers like Maimonides believed and what they could explicitly say, Strauss sees the esoteric discourse as a characteristic trait of Maimonides' writings. Strauss's insights were immensely useful in understanding medieval philosophy, and for a time were also widely accepted. The pendulum of scholarly fashion, however, now swings in the other direction.[86] This is due partly to the fact that Strauss's ideas were overused by Strauss himself, partly to their abuse by Strauss's disciples in the nonacademic world. Be that as it may, many readers today wince at the very suggestion of esoteric writing, and insist that, rather than scrutinize everything Maimonides says in search of its opposite meaning, we should listen to what he actually says. To be sure, one should not treat Maimonides as a disciple of Strauss; and indeed, one should listen to what Maimonides says in his own voice. This, however, includes Maimonides' repeated and unambiguous announcements that he intends to speak in an esoteric way.

Maimonides' esotericism is not a rigid, crafty, and manipulative political device. Rather, it reflects an unusual personality's awareness of his distinctiveness. It also reflects his sensitivity to the complex, rich, and multilayered

[83]The uncommonly frustrated and bitter tone of the treatise has already been noted by scholars. See, for instance, D. Hartmann, in Halkin and Hartmann, *Crisis and Leadership*, 248 and 263.

[84]See Hartmann, in ibid., 246–47.

[85]*Persecution and the Art of Writing*, 73.

[86]See, for instance, note 104, below; and see Seeskin, *Searching for a Distant God: The Legacy of Maimonides*, 177–88; Ravitzky, "Maimonides: Esotericism and Educational Philosophy," in Seeskin, *The Cambridge Companion to Maimonides*, 305; Guidi, "L'obscurité intentionnelle du philosophe."

fabric of human society in general and of his own audience in particular. Maimonides is a sharp observer of human nature, an open-eyed and realistic idealist. Like his namesake Moses, he may feel the urge to use his staff: to force the sea to give way, to make the rock let out the water of life. Moses' model, however, is also a cautioning reminder of the punishment for succumbing to impatience: being banned from entering the Promised Land. Maimonides therefore practices restraint in the use of his power, including the power of words. His supple writing meanders between saying and hinting, always aiming at the highest level his reader can reach, and then some, and always aware of his readers' potential as well as of their limits. A truly contextual reading of Maimonides must therefore be the reading of the historian, which takes into account the writer, the audience, and the way the moment works on both.

As I have argued above, I believe that Maimonides was familiar with Averroes's works. He mentions explicitly Averroes's commentaries, but his own work suggests that he also read Averroes's theological works. In his *Decisive Treatise*, Averroes argues that the Qur'ān speaks in different ways to the three levels of society: the multitudes, the theologians, and the philosophers, and that the spiritual leader or philosopher should try to follow this model. In his *Kashf al-adilla,* Averroes tries to some extent to show how this triple approach might work. Maimonides did not write any strictly philosophical book. The genre of writing on philosophy as commentaries was perfected in his time by Averroes, and Maimonides might have felt that the extensive works of the commentator Averroes made any addition superfluous. In the same way, we find him saying in the "Premise" (*muqaddima*) he introduces into *Guide* 2.2 that he has no intention of writing a scientific work, since there are enough such works, to which he has nothing original to add. His own original contribution was the attempt to show how Jewish sources work with philosophy, how one can be Jewish and yet at peace with one's rationality. Mutatis mutandis, one can say that Maimonides' major contribution was to write an extensive and full-blown Jewish version of the *Kashf*.

Like Averroes, Maimonides attempts to show the multiple voices of the religious tradition. This is not a "double truth," or the cunning speech of a politician speaking from the two sides of his mouth. The Straussian dichotomy of esoteric versus exoteric writing does not do justice to Maimonides' context-sensitive rhetoric, which covers a broad scale of tones.

With this understanding, we can go back to Strauss's above-mentioned observation, that the *Treatise on Resurrection* is "the most authentic commentary on the *Guide*." There are indeed several parallels between Maimonides' most philosophic work, the *Guide of the Perplexed*, and the *Treatise on Resurrection*, which is presented as the least philosophic.[87] Perhaps the most striking parallel is found in *Guide* 3.51, which Maimonides introduces as a chapter that "does not include additional matter over and above what is comprised in the other chapters."[88] Rather than labeling this repetition "superfluous," however, Maimonides describes it as "a kind of conclusion" (*shibh al-khātima*). Since it is followed by three dense and highly significant chapters, this description obviously does not refer to the chapter's place as the last chapter of the book. In categorizing this chapter as "a kind of conclusion" Maimonides was probably referring to its literary role, as a summary of the *Guide*'s main ideas and purpose.[89] In such a summary, one does not expect to find new ideas but a succinct presentation of the ones already discussed, and the repetition is not only acceptable but actually necessary. The parallelism of *Guide* 3.51 and the *Treatise on Resurrection* indicates their similar role, repeating and summing up ideas of primary importance. But while in the *Guide* these ideas have received their proper, refined elaboration before being summarized, the short treatise must present them curtly and crudely. The treatise's brevity leaves little room for the multilevel presentation that is essential for Maimonides' discourses, and flattens them to "a superfluous repetition."

Langermann (for whom Maimonides' treatise precedes his student's epistle) has suggested that in the *Mishneh Torah*, a book intended for the general public, Maimonides presented his sincere beliefs about the resurrection; and that after he saw the storm created by his words, he published his "so-called esoteric work," the *Guide of the Perplexed*, in which nothing is said concerning the issue that ignited polemics.[90] In other words, according to Langermann, Maimonides got cold feet from the storm, and therefore decided not to repeat his sincere belief in the resurrection (although this belief corresponded to the orthodox view). Such behavior would be as inexplicable as it is out of character; and it is indeed not supported by the evidence of what Maimonides does say in the *Guide* on this subject.

[87] See, for example, Maimonides' historical perception, in which God's divine condescendence plays a major role (*Guide* 3.32; *Epistles*, 335; Finkel, *Treatise*, 32); or the reference to the Sabians (*Guide* 3.29; *Epistles*, 335; Finkel, 31); and the insistence on the different levels of understanding of the public, with the very clear insinuation that Maimonides prefers to address a limited number of elite individuals rather than the thousands of the ignorant (*Guide*, Introduction, 11; Pines, 16; *Epistles*, 338; Finkel, *Treatise* 37).

[88] *Dalāla*, 454; Pines, 619.

[89] While introductions and their role in various literary contexts were extensively studied (see, for instance, J. D. Dubois and B. Roussel, eds., *Entrer en matière: les prologues* [Paris, 1998]), the function and conventions of conclusions or epilogues have received little scholarly attention.

[90] Langermann, "Samuel ben Eli's Epistle on Resurrection," 43–44.

Although in the *Guide* Maimonides never deals expressly with the resurrection, *Guide* 1.42, discussing the meaning of the word "living," is clearly related to our subject. In the course of this chapter Maimonides mentions the resurrection of a boy by the prophet Elisha (1 Kings 17:17), an event that Maimonides interprets as the resuscitation of a very sick child. He then cites the Talmudic saying, "The righteous are called living even when they are dead."[91] This saying may seem to refer to the resurrection, but Maimonides cites it in proximity to "the traditional interpretation" of Deut. 22:7: "That it may be well with thee and that you may live long." In Maimonides' understanding, the traditional interpretation of this last verse connects it to the world to come.[92] Whatever it was that Maimonides wanted his readers to understand by the resurrection of the dead, it may not have been very far from his understanding of the world to come. And the world to come, as we have already seen, was for him strictly incorporeal.

Maimonides' treatment of the resurrection of the dead stands in sharp contrast to his expansive style in describing the world to come.[93] When he had his choice, he said the strict minimum about the resurrection; and when forced to elaborate, rather than discussing the question systematically, he resorted to polemics and exegesis, which allowed him to divert the discussion. At no point in his discussion of the resurrection does one get the impression that the awaited resurrection aroused profound emotions in Maimonides.

We have seen above Maimonides' strict censoring of a corporeal image of God, a position that in his view no person, however limited intellectually, should be allowed to uphold. It is interesting to compare this attitude to the one he adopts regarding eschatology. When Joseph ibn Jābir asks him to explain the immortality of the soul in the world to come, Maimonides discourages him from trying to understand things beyond his ken, and says:

> It will not be detrimental to your religion to believe that the inhabitants of the world to come are bodies, until you clearly understand their existence. Even if you think that they eat, drink and procreate in the upper heaven or in ***Gan Eden***, as it was said—there is no

[91] BT *Berakhot* 8:2.

[92] See *Mishneh Torah, Hilkhot Teshuva* 10: 1; *Commentary on the Mishnah,* Introduction to *Pereq Ḥeleq*. 205: " 'That it may be well with thee'—in a world that is all good; 'and that you may live long'—in a world that is everlasting, which is the world to come"; and see also *Tosefta Ḥulin* 10.

[93] See above, *apud* note 32.

harm in that. There are worse things regarding which people are ignorant, without their ignorance being detrimental to them.[94]

Maimonides himself certainly did not think that the inhabitants of the world to come eat, drink, and procreate, yet he encouraged his correspondent to hold fast to this false belief. No wonder that in his letter to the same well-meaning and yet simple person, Maimonides flatly denies that he had ever denied the resurrection of the dead—that is to say, the return of the soul to the body—and refers his correspondent to the already written *Treatise on Resurrection*.[95]

Maimonides cares little for the body, whose only reason for existing is to provide tools for the soul. He also cares little for the soul as the vital principle of the body. Although he repeatedly uses the term "the immortality of the soul" (*baqāʾ al-nafs*), his aspirations focus on the immortality of the intellect. In the philosophers' language, this is referred to as the conjunction (*ittiṣāl*) of the human being with the Active Intellect. The individual, the person as a combination of body and soul, has no place in this blissful existence, for the conjunction annihilates the individuality of those who reach it. Maimonides here shares the views of his Muslim contemporary Averroes.

As we have seen above, there are indications that, at times, Fārābī and Maimonides doubted that it was possible for human beings to achieve this conjunction.[96] In this context, it is interesting to note Maimonides' reference to the "old wives tales" (*khurāfāt al-ʿajāʾiz*) that fill the heads of people who have pretensions to be the wise of Israel (a clear reference to the Gaon).[97] This is the exact expression that, according to Ibn Ṭufayl, was used by Fārābī in his lost commentary on the *Nichamachean Ethics*, where he is supposed to have denied the immortality of the soul.[98] Nevertheless, even if Maimonides and Fārābī doubted at times the possibility of intellectual conjunction, they still regarded this as the goal to which the philosopher must aspire.

In view of the analysis presented here, Maimonides' insistence on the obligatory belief in the resurrection of the dead appears like a baffling puzzle. One could understand that he would try to skirt a well-established article of faith that did not agree with his philosophical beliefs. Maimonides,

[94] *Epistles*, 414; see also chap. 1, above, *apud* note 72, and chap. 4, above, *apud* note 126.
[95] *Epistles*, 409–10.
[96] See Pines, "The Limitations of Human Knowledge"; and see above, *apud* note 39.
[97] *Epistle on Resurrection*, *Epistles*, 320 (Finkel, *Treatise* 3).
[98] Ibn Ṭufayl, *Ḥayy ibn Yaqẓān*, 112.

however, plays a double game: he skirts the article of faith and at the same time consolidates it. By Maimonides' time, the resurrection of the dead was assumed by most Jews to constitute an integral element of the Jewish faith, but Maimonides played an active and decisive role in upgrading it to a binding article of faith.[99] The tenth-century Saadya, for example, who discusses the resurrection at length in the seventh chapter of his *Book of Creeds and Beliefs*, does not mention the resurrection in any of his lists of articles of faith.[100] In the twelfth century, the Karaite Judah Hadassi counted resurrection as the eighth article of faith in his list of basic elements of belief (*ishur*), but there is no indication that he presented these articles as a legally binding Jewish dogma.[101] As noted above, in instituting a list of *legally binding* dogmas that define the boundaries of Judaism, Maimonides followed the example of the Almohads. In the case of this particular article, he also followed the example of the Almohads' source of inspiration, Ghazālī, who counted the denial of resurrection as one of the marks of the philosophers' heresy.[102] By including this belief in his credo, Maimonides canonized it as belonging to the basic Jewish creed, in conformity with what was universally accepted at the time as a mark of religiosity among Jews, Christians, and Moslems alike. If, as argued here, his philosophy did not support this belief, why did he canonize it?

Paradoxically, it is precisely Maimonides' philosophical background that suggested to him the definition of the resurrection as an article of faith (and *only* as an article of faith). Like Avicenna and Averroes, Maimonides adopted the position that the eschatological scene is dictated by the texts and should not be interpreted. By making this position into an article of faith, he relegated it to the "not-to-be-discussed-rationally" compartment.[103] Maimonides seems to have felt that by classifying the resurrection as a legally binding dogma, he established his credentials, as it were; in fact, he explicitly says that this is what he felt. The fact that he was pushed to repeat his credentials was for him a superfluous repetition, which he could not but resent. As his *Treatise on Resurrection* shows, forcing him to repeat did not bring him to elaborate. He could

[99] It is thus technically inaccurate to say that Maimonides reinterpreted the thirteenth article of faith, an article that he himself created; cf. Friedberg, "Maimonides' Reinterpretation of the Thirteenth Article."

[100] See H. Ben-Shammai, "Saadia Gaon's Ten Articles of Faith," *Daat* 37 (1996): 21 [Hebrew].

[101] See D. Lasker, "The Philosophy of Judah Hadassi the Karaite," *Jerusalem Studies in Jewish Thought* 7 (1988): 479 and note 9 [Hebrew].

[102] See note 11, above.

[103] On Maimonides' distinction between rational knowledge and belief, see chap. 3, note 77, above.

only reiterate his position: the resurrection of the dead is an article of faith, nothing less, nothing more.

"Gates for the Righteous Nation": The Philosopher as Leader

The controversy over resurrection exploded late in Maimonides' life, at the height of his career. As the controversy revealed, his intellectual reputation did not protect him from severe criticism (nor, after his death, did it protect his writings from being censored or even burned). The controversy was the direct result of his involvement in politics in the broad sense: the politics of community leadership as well as the politics of halakhic ruling. Maimonides could have avoided the unpleasantness had he remained within the domain of pure philosophical speculation. Neither his temperament, however, nor his philosophical education, allowed him to choose to remain completely aloof from political activity.

Muslim political thought, and its impact on Maimonides, has been extensively studied, and need not be repeated here.[104] The following pages will only seek to highlight some traits of this philosophy that seem peculiar to Maimonides.

Since Leo Strauss's early studies scholars have underlined the pivotal role of political philosophy in the medieval world of Islam. The Straussian approach, which underlines the cardinal role of political philosophy in the medieval Islamic world, raises it to the position of the most important aspect of philosophy. The importance of political philosophy can, however, be overemphasized. One example of such an overemphasis concerns the history of Islamic philosophy in al-Andalus, where historians were led to take the theory for reality. Since the philosophers have a political theory, and since they cooperate with the rulers, this cooperation is sometimes perceived as an application of the philosophers' political theory. The outcome is depicted as the realization of Plato's ideal republic, to the

[104] See, for instance, M. Galston, *Politics and Excellence: The Political Philosophy of Alfarabi* (Princeton, 1990); Ch. E. Butterworth, ed., *The Political Aspects of Islamic Philosophy: Essays in Honor of Muhsin Mahdi* (Cambridge, Mass., 1992); M. Mahdi, *Alfarabi and the Foundation of Islamic Political Philosophy* (Chicago, 2001); P. Crone, *God's Rule: Government and Islam: Six Centuries of Medieval Islamic Political Thought* (New York, 2004), 165–96; R. Brague, *La loi de Dieu: Histoire philosophique d'une alliance* (Paris, 2005), 205–9, 237–46; W. Z. Harvey, "Maimonides on Human Perfection, Awe and Politics," in I. Robinson, L. Kaplan and J. Bauer, eds., *The Thought of Moses Maimonides: Philosophical and Legal Studies* (Lewiston/Queenston/Lampeter, 1990), 1–15; M. Kellner, "Politics and Perfection: Gersonides vs. Maimonides," *Jewish Political Studies Review* 6 (1994): 49–58.

satisfaction of philosopher and king alike. When a discordant tone of alienation is discovered in the philosophers' writings, it is interpreted away as a local phenomenon, preparing the way for political activity. Such an interpretation, however, ignores the existence of a proclivity to alienation in the writings of the Islamic philosophers in general, in the East as well as in the West. Moreover, this alienation, far from being a mere afterthought, the result of frustrated political aspirations, is deeply ingrained in the philosophers' thought, to the point of being included in their theory.

In general, one can say that medieval philosophers, both Jews and Muslims, saw Plato's ideal republic, ruled by a philosopher and geared to nurture future philosophers, as their model. Notwithstanding the Platonic theory, however, not even a single historical case of a philosopher trying to overthrow the king and usurp his throne is documented, and there is never a suggestion in the *falāsifa*'s writings that a philosopher should do so. The fact that no philosopher has ever suggested the overthrow of an acting ruler shows the ambivalence in the philosophers' position. Without an understanding elite, the philosopher had no place in society, and thus, rather than becoming a philosopher-king, the *faylasūf* is found occupying the position of a compliant philosopher-courtier. A position in the court gave the philosopher a minimum of protection. Quite often (as the case of Avicenna demonstrates) it also gave him access to stupendous libraries. It allowed him to practice a dignified profession: he could be a physician or a judge, a scientist or *un intellectuel de métier*. And, in a society where readers were altogether scarce, it provided him with an audience of readers.[105]

Maimonides is known to have been an admirer of Fārābī, who in many ways had set the ground for Islamic political philosophy. In particular, Maimonides adopted Fārābī's idea that assimilated Plato's ruler of the perfect state, the philosopher-king, with the *imām*, or prophet, thus allowing for the integration of Islamic thought and the legacy of Hellenistic philosophy.

Maimonides often uses biblical verses as pithy pointers to his intention. Between the motto to the first part of the *Guide* (Is. 26:2: "Open ye the gates, that the righteous nation that keepeth faithfulness may enter in") and the last verse quoted before the conclusion of the book (Jer. 9:25: ". . . loving kindness, righteousness and judgment in the earth"), Maimonides strives to lay the foundation for the righteous, if not perfect, community.[106] He was also influenced, however, by Ibn Bājja and Ibn

[105] See further Stroumsa, "Philosopher-King or Philsopher-Courtier."

[106] See also Aviezer Ravitzky, "Contemplation and Leadership in Maimonides' Thought," *Daat* 57–59 (2006): 31–59 [Hebrew].

Ṭufayl, Andalusian philosophers like himself, in whose writings the more pessimistic, or perhaps realistic, streak is discernible. Although Ibn Bājja follows the well-paved Platonic tradition, he focuses on the imperfect state, where the philosopher is a stranger, living a secluded, withdrawn existence, and hoping for better times in the future. Ibn Ṭufayl, who develops Ibn Bājja's insights, examines, on the one hand, the option for the philosopher to become a ruler of an imperfect, but "good-enough" state, and the possibility of altogether withdrawing from human society, on the other.

As noted by Pines, some passages of the *Guide* show traces of the influence of Ibn Bājja's conception of the philosopher as isolated stranger in his own community. Speaking about the prophet, who has achieved intellectual perfection, Maimonides says:

> It is likewise necessary for the thought of that individual [that it] should be detached from the spurious kinds of rulership and that his desire for them should be abolished—I mean the wish to dominate or be held great by the common people and to obtain from them honor and obedience for its own sake. He should rather regard all people according to their various states with respect to which they are indubitably either like domestic animals or like beasts of prey. If the perfect man, who lives in solitude, thinks of them at all, he does so only with a view to saving himself from the harm that may be caused by those among them who are harmful if he happens to associate with them, or to obtaining an advantage that may be obtained from them if he is forced to it by some of his needs.[107]

As noted by Pines, this passage "may echo the conception or the vocabulary used by Ibn Bājja when dealing with these problems."[108] The perfect man lives in solitude, and his interaction with society consists mainly of protecting himself from it.

This defensive attitude, however, is only one option for the perfect man. The inner withdrawal described by Ibn Bājja, in which the philosopher travels in his mind to his own country, is also espoused by Maimonides. Maimonides attributes such a behavior to the patriarchs as well as to Moses. "Abraham our father" used his own judgment to arrive at true monotheism and rebelled against the Sabian religion surrounding him. Maimonides depicts him as standing alone, acting tirelessly to spread the word, "and he was traveling and preaching, and summoning people, going from city to the city and from kingdom to kingdom, until he reached the land of Canaan, where 'he called the name of the Lord, God of the

[107] *Guide* 2.36 (*Dalāla*, 262; Pines, 371–72).
[108] Pines, "Translator's Introduction," cvii.

World' (Gen. 21:35)."[109] Abraham had to suffer the violent reaction of his contemporaries, and he was rewarded with divine blessing, that in him "all the families of the earth be blessed" (Gen. 12:3). For Maimonides, Abraham is indeed the blessing for all the families of the earth, the father of monotheists past and present.[110] It is perhaps not accidental that Moses Maimonides chose to give this patriarch's name to his only son. An indication of Maimonides' identification with Abraham can be seen in his account of Abraham's sufferings, introducing it with a personal voice, as his own conjecture: "I have no doubt (*lā shakk ʿindī*) that in view of the fact that he, may peace be upon him, disagreed with the doctrine of all men, these erring men reviled, blamed and belittled him."[111] Abraham is thus the first activist prophet; and yet Maimonides also describes him, as well as the other patriarchs, as carrying on this activity while preserving an inner isolation, "performing these actions with their limbs only, while their intellects were constantly in His presence."[112] The option of keeping an inner isolation is best demonstrated in Maimonides' portrayal of Moses, whom Maimonides depicts as the emblematic philosopher-prophet-king. Maimonides praises the ability of some prophets to keep their minds on the contemplation of God while living in this world:

> And there may be a human individual who, through his apprehension of the true realities and his joy in what he has apprehended, achieves a state in which he talks with people and is occupied with his bodily necessities while his intellect is wholly turned toward Him, may He be exalted, while outwardly he is with people, in the sort of way described by the poetical parables that have been invented for these notions "I sleep, but my heart waketh." (Song of Songs, 5:2)[113]

Perhaps more than any Islamic philosopher, Maimonides, "the disciple of al-Fārābī," incorporates the notion of alienation into the philosophical ideal. While the Muslim philosophers present their alienation as a concession and justify their alienation as a response to a hostile society,

[109] See *Mishneh Torah, Hilkhot Avodat Kokhavim* 1:3. On Maimonides' use of this verse, see M. Schwarz's note in his Hebrew translation of *Guide of the Perplexed* (Tel-Aviv, 2002), 3n1.

[110] On Abraham as the first monotheist, see also Ravitzky, "Contemplation and Leadership in Maimonides' Thought." See also chap. 4, above, *apud* notes 6 and 124.

[111] *Guide* 3.29 (*Dalāla*, 375:14–15; Pines, 515).

[112] *Guide* 3.51 (*Dalāla*, 459:18–23; Pines, 624).

[113] *Guide* 3.51 (*Dalāla*, 459; Pines, 623). On this chapter, see Ravitzky, "Contemplation and Leadership in Maimonides' Thought," 46–52.

Maimonides makes room for the philosopher's withdrawal as central to his theory of the ideal state. Even the ideal philosopher-king must keep his inner alienation, otherwise he will not be a true philosopher. Being a king is only his chore.

The elitist approach of Maimonides is well attested. As we have seen above, most of society is for him incurably obtuse, "like domestic animals" and potentially dangerous "like beasts of prey," and the perfect man craves to remain aloof from them. The call of duty, however, does not allow him to do so: the perfect man is destined to lead the multitudes, to soften the edges of their brutality and, as much as possible, to inculcate in them true opinions. The internal conflict could be described as tragic, and at times must have felt so. Like various Muslim philosophers, Maimonides had his place at the court, as a court physician. Paradoxically, however, the fact of being the head of a minority community brought him closer to being "a king" than did any of the Muslim philosophers.[114] Judge and physician, arbitrator and educator, he was the effective ruler of the Jewish community. From this high vantage point, he could also better appreciate the limitations of the leader's power, as well as his vulnerability.

Already in Maimonides' lifetime, his admirers compared him to his revered namesake, and shortly after his death this comparison became canonized in the Hebrew dictum: "From Moses [the prophet] to Moses [Maimonides], there arose none like unto Moses" (*mi-Moshe le-Moshe lo qam ke-Moshe*). The popularity of the dictum may dull our senses to its audacity. It presents Maimonides as the one person who rendered Deut. 34:10 obsolete, saying in effect that "there arose not a prophet since in Israel like unto Moses, whom the Lord knew face to face"—that is, until Moses Maimonides, who did reach this rank.

Israel Yuval has suggested that Maimonides saw himself as a "Moses *redivivus*," and that his investment in building a better Jewish community should also be seen as preparing the way for the days of the Messiah.[115] Whether or not Maimonides harbored such aspirations, it is clear that his model of perfection was indeed "Moses, our Master and the master of all prophets."[116] One of the most challenging traits of this model, if not the most challenging one, was the need to balance communal responsibility with "the call of the noble soul" and its yearning

[114] See also chap. 3, above, *apud* note 110.

[115] Yuval, "Moses *Redivivus*: Maimonides as the Messiah's Helper."

[116] *Epistles*, 235; on Moses' prophecy, see Levinger, *Maimonides as Philosopher and Codifier*, 29–38.

"to discover prized words."[117] The career and literary output of Maimonides record the incessant move of his inner pendulum between the conflicting facets of his person: "from Moses," the leader who suffered his community, "to Moses" the philosopher, who sought the face of God.

[117]Eccles. 12:10; see *Guide*, Dedicatory Epistle (*Dalāla*, 1:20; cf. Pines, 4).

Conclusion

The preceding pages were dedicated to one major medieval thinker, Moses Maimonides, and to the examination of his thought in its context. The outcome of this examination bears first of all upon our understanding of Maimonides himself. The description presented here, of Maimonides as a Mediterranean thinker, is not meant to say that he was not also, and essentially, a Jewish thinker. Rather, it highlights and elucidates Maimonides' consistent interpretation of his own, Jewish tradition in contemporary terms, as they were shaped by his Mediterranean legacy.

Such an interpretation, which translates tradition into contemporary, more familiar terms, is in itself not an uncommon phenomenon: Rembrandt's Abraham, we know, looks distinctly Dutch. Maimonides' success in his interpretative effort is also not surprising: Maimonides' linguistic *diglossia* means not only that he switches easily from Hebrew to Arabic and back, but also that he thinks about the same issues in both Arabic and Hebrew. In each of these languages, words and phrases carry with them their own, mostly Muslim or mostly Jewish, conceptual and associative baggage. Maimonides' complex and nuanced thought is the product of his openness to his multiple cultural heritages, and of his talent to absorb and rework their riches. The reader who wishes to fathom the nuances of Maimonides' thought is thus challenged to be as open as he was, to constantly bear these legacies in mind, and to remain alert to their presence in Maimonides' work.

Beyond Maimonides, however, the results of the present study bear upon the methodology of medieval Jewish and Islamic thought. In studying Jewish philosophy in general, scholarly methods vary, and scholars disagree in their evaluation of the relevance of the non-Jewish context to the topic. Thus, while Shlomo Pines emphasizes the broader cultural circles that nurture Jewish philosophy, Eliezer Schweid views the development of Jewish philosophy as mainly an internal process, where Jewish thinkers carry on a dialogue with previous generations of Jewish scholars. Regarding the early medieval period, Schweid, like Pines, accepts the existence of direct influences of the immediate Muslim environment on Jewish thought, but he tends to play down their significance. The argument between scholars thus focuses on the scope and nature of Islamic influence. For Schweid, the Islamic world provides only the background to Jewish philosophy, within which we can distinguish "a continuous Jewish speculative literature, with a fair amount of internal influence."[1] Pines, on the other hand, states that in this period, "in the sphere of philosophical literature . . . Jewish thinkers had recourse primarily to the books of their Moslem counterparts," whereas "rare and of secondary significance is that relationship to the teaching of their Jewish predecessors."[2] Rather than admitting only occasional influences, Pines's approach, to which I subscribe, assumes medieval Jewish philosophy to have been shaped by the surrounding culture and impregnated by it. It would be impossible, according to this view, to correctly understand medieval Jewish philosophers outside the Islamic context—just as it would be impossible, of course, to understand them correctly if we ignored their Jewish identity.

The previous pages provide ample evidence to support the claim that Maimonides must be read within his broader cultural context of influences. Here, too, Pines's evaluation deserves to be quoted: "The fact that, relatively speaking, Maimonides had so little recourse to Jewish philosophy is significant. It implies *inter alia* that he had no use for a specific Jewish philosophic tradition. . . . *Qua* philosopher he had the possibility to consider Judaism from the outside."[3] The examination of Maimonides' work in other domains, however, demonstrates that Maimonides' ability "to consider Judaism from outside" was not limited to the field of philosophy. Maimonides emerges from the previous pages as a phenomenologist of religion who uses broad strokes of the brush to paint patterns of thought and behavior. He is a thinker who looks for absolute rules of the universe and humanity, an Aristotelian who tries to identify pure forms. He also emerges as a keen observer of human societies, a precursor of Ibn Khaldūn.

The consistent phenomenological stripe in Maimonides' work shows that, wholly immersed in the practice of Judaism as he was, Maimonides was nevertheless able to observe it "from the outside," beyond philosophy. In a way, this ability to distance himself from his own tradition, to put his own identity in brackets, is similar to his ability to withdraw into his inner world while carrying on the demanding task of a community leader. As a scientist and as a legal philosopher, as a sociologist or as a historian of religion, Maimonides integrated the "circles of influence" into his own thought.

Maimonides was an exceptional personality, and his integration of various legacies was no doubt also exceptionally successful. Nevertheless,

[1] E. Schweid, *Feeling and Speculation* (Ramat-Gan, 1970), 18–19 [Hebrew]. See also Aviezer Ravitzki, "On the Method of Studying Jewish Philosophy," *Jerusalem Studies in Jewish Thought* 1 (1981): 7–22 [Hebrew].

[2] See the preface, note 7, above.

[3] Pines, "Translator's Introduction," cxxxiv. For a reappraisal of Pines's statement, see Harvey, "Medieval Sources of Maimonides' *Guide*," 283–85.

the often seamless resulting synthesis could not have been achieved had he been a lone venturer. Maimonides honed and perfected methods that had been crafted by his Jewish medieval predecessors (who often remain unacknowledged by him). His originality and uniqueness do not lie in the very attempt to integrate legacies, but rather in the unusual scope, boldness, and authority of his synthesis. In order to account for this unique and original case, we must adopt the same integrative approach to the study of medieval Jewish thought in the broader world of Islam.

This claim, however, has implications beyond Jewish studies. Maimonides' erudition in subjects that are not typically Jewish could not have been achieved in a rarefied Jewish environment, without extensive, personal contacts with the non-Jewish world. It is from Muslims, as well as from Jews, that he bought and borrowed books, and also with Muslims that he discussed and debated ideas. The snippets of information provided by Muslim biographers as well as by Maimonides himself corroborate the existence of such extensive contacts. If, then, we assume that Maimonides met Muslim thinkers, and exchanged with them knowledge and ideas, by the same token we must assume that Muslim thinkers met with Maimonides, and exchanged with him knowledge and ideas.

Here again, the sources corroborate our assumption: unlike most Jewish thinkers, who, by and large, remained ignored by Muslims, Maimonides was read in Muslim circles and is quoted by Muslims.[4] Nevertheless, in the study of medieval Islamic thought, the evidence provided by Maimonides' writings is hardly ever adduced as part of the general argument, let alone the evidence of other Jewish thinkers. It goes without saying that, in a world defined, shaped, and ruled by Islam, the weight of Muslim thought is immeasurably greater than the intellectual contribution brought to it by the religious minorities. Ignoring this contribution altogether, however, or relegating it to a separate drawer, is likely to result in a skewed—flatter, monochromatic, and altogether poorer—picture of the rich tissue of medieval Islamic thought.

As a member of a minority, Maimonides was perhaps more sensitive to the options offered by Mediterranean culture, and more eager to avail himself of these options. Nevertheless, the portrait that emerges from the study of Maimonides in his cultural context indicates that, in this too, he should not be seen as sui generis, but rather as a superb example of a Mediterranean thinker.

[4]These quotations reflect his complex philosophical legacy, since it is not the Aristotelians (either his contemporaries, like Averroes, or subsequent generations of philosophers in the Orient), who quote him, but rather theologians and mystics. See Davidson, *Moses Maimonides*, 426; Schwarb, "Die Rezeption Maimonides' in der christlich-arabischen Literatur."

BIBLIOGRAPHY

Primary Sources

Abū Bakr al-Rāzī, *Rasā'il Falsafiyya*, ed. P. Kraus. Cairo, 1939; reprinted Beirut: *Dār al-āfāq al-jadīda*, n.d.

Avicenna—see Ibn Sīnā.

Abraham ibn Daud. The Book of Tradition (Sefer ha-Qabbalah), ed. G. D. Cohen. Philadelphia, 1967.

Badawī. ʿAbd al-Raḥmān. *Arisṭū ʿinda'l-ʿArab*. Cairo, 1947.

———. *Rasā'il falsafiyya li'l-kindī wa'l-Fārābī wa-ibn Bājja wa-ibn ʿAdī*. Benghazi, 1973.

———. *Manṭiq Arisṭū*. Cairo: *Maktabat al-nahḍa al-miṣriyya*, 1948.

Benjamin of Tudela. *Itinerary*, ed. and trans. A. Asher. New York, 1840–42.

Al-Bīrūnī, Abū Rayḥān. *al-Āṭār al-bāqiya ʿan al-Qurūn al-Khāliya*, ed. C. E. Sachau. Leipzig, 1878.

Al-Fārābī, Iḥṣā' al-ʿulūm, ed. ʿUthmān Amīn. Cairo, 1939.

Al-Filaḥa al-nabaṭiyya (L'agriculture nabatéenne), ed. T. Fahd. Damascus, 1993.

Al-Manṭiq ʿinda al-Fārābī, ed. Rafīq al-ʿAjam, vol. 3: *Kitāb al-jadal*. Beirut, 1986.

Ghāyat al-ḥakīm (Das Ziel des Weisen), ed. H. Ritter. Leipzig and Berlin, 1933.

Al-Ghazālī. *Iḥyā' ʿulūm al-dīn*. Beirut, 1994.

Al-Ghazālī Abū Ḥāmid. *The Incoherence of the Philosophers*. A parallel English-Arabic text, translated, introduced, and annotated by M. E. Marmura. Provo, Utah, 2000.

———. *Fayṣal al-tafriqa bayna al-islām wa-l-zandaqa*, ed. Sulaymān Dunyā. Cairo, 1961.

———. *Tahāfut al-Falāsifa*, ed. M. Bouyges. Beirut, 1927.

Ibn Bājja. *Shurūḥāt al-Samāʿ al-ṭabīʿī li-bn Bājja*, ed. Amīn Zīyādah. Beirut, 1978.

———. *Sharḥ al-Samāʿ al-ṭabīʿī li-arisṭuṭālis*, ed. Mājid Fakhrī. Beirut, 1974.

Ibn Dā'ūd, Avraham. *Sefer Emmunah Ramma*. Frankfurt, 1852; reprinted Jerusalem, 1967.

Ibn Kammūna, Saʿd Ibn Manṣūr. *Tanqīḥ al-abḥāth li-'l-milal al-thalāth. Saʿd Ibn Manṣūr Ibn Kammūna's* Examination of the Inquiries into the Three Faiths*: A Thirteenth-Century Essay in Comparative Religion*, ed. M. Perlmann. Berkeley and Los Angeles, 1967.

Ibn Khaldūn. *Kitāb al-ʿibar*. Beirut, 1959.

Ibn al-Jawzī. *Al-Muntaẓam fī ta'rīkh al-mulūk wa'l-umam*, ed. Muḥammad ʿAbd al-Qādir ʿAṭā and Muṣṭafā ʿAbd al-Qādir ʿAṭā. Beirut, 1992.

Ibn Jubayr. *Travels of Ibn Jubayr*, ed. W. Wright, rev. M. J. De Goeje. Leyden and London, 1907. (English translation in *The Travels of Ibn Jubayr*, trans. R.J.C. Broadhurst. London, 1952.)

Ibn al-Nadīm. *al-Fihrist*, ed. G. Flügel. Leipzig, 1872.

Ibn al-Qalānisī. *Dhayl ta'rīh Dimashq*, ed. H. F. Amedroz. Leiden, 1908.
Ibn al-Qifṭī. *Ta'rikh al-ḥukamā'*, ed. I. Lippert. Leipzig, 1903.
Ibn Rushd. *Bidāyat al-mujtahid wa-nihāyat al-muqtaṣid*. 2 vols. Cairo, n.d.
———. *al-Ḍarūrī fī'l-siyāsa—mukhtaṣar kitāb al-siyāsa li-Aflāṭūn*, ed. A. Shaḥlān. Beirut, 1998.
———. *al-Kashf 'an manāhij al-adilla fī 'aqā'id al-milla*, ed. M. 'A. al-Jābirī. Beirut, 1998.
———. *Talkhīṣ al-āthār al-'ulwiyya*, ed. Jamāl al-Dīn al-·Alawī. Beirut, 1994.
———. *al-Jawāmi' fī al-falsafa. Kitāb al-samā' al-ṭabī'ī*, ed. J. Puig. Madrid, CSIC 1983.
———. *Faṣl al-maqāl wa-taqrīr mā bayna al-sharī'a wa'l-'ikma min al-ittiṣāl*, ed. A. Nader. Beirut, 1973.
———. *Talkhīṣ mā ba'd al-ṭabī'a*, ed. 'Uṯmān Amīn. Cairo.
Ibn Ṣāḥib al-Ṣalāt. *al-Mann bi'l-imāma: ta'rīkh bilād al-maġrib wa-l-andalus fī 'ahd al-muwaḥḥidīn*, ed. 'Abd al-Hādī al-Tāzī. Beirut, 1964.
Ibn Ṣā'id Al-Andalusī. *Ṭabaqāt al-umam*, ed. Ḥ. Bū 'Alwān. Beirut, 1985.
Abū 'Alī b. Sīnā. *al-Najāt*. Cairo, 1321H.
Ibn Sīnā. *Kitāb al-shifā', Ilāhiyāt*, ed. G. Qanawātī et al. Cairo, 1960.
———. *De Anima*, ed. F. Rahman. London, 1959.
———. *Kitāb al-shifā', La logique: la sophistique (al-Safasṭa)*, ed. A. F. al-Ahwānī. Cairo, 1958.
———. *Rasā'il*, ed. Hilmi Ziya Ülken. Istanbul: Istanbul University, 1953.
———. *Risālat aḥwāl al-nafs wa-baqā'ihā wa-ma'ādihā*. Cairo, 1952.
———. *Al-mabda' wa'l-ma'ād*, ed. 'Abdallāh Nurānī. Tehran, I 343H.
Al-Subkī, Tāj al-Dīn Abū Naṣr 'Abd al-Wahhāb b/ 'Alī b. 'Abd al-Kāfī. *Ṭabaqāt al-shāfi'iyya al-kubrā*, ed. 'Abd al-Fattāḥ Muḥammad al-Ḥilū and Maḥmūd Muḥammad. Cairo, 1968.
Ibn Ṭufayl. *Risālat Ḥayy ibn Yaqẓān*, ed. Fārūq Sa'd. Beirut, 1980.
Ibn Tūmart: see Luciani, D.
Jāmi' al-badā'i', ed. Muḥyī al-Dīn Ṣabrī al-Kurdī. Cairo, 1917.
Judah Ha-Levi. *Kitāb al-radd wa'l-dalīl fī'l dīn al-dhalīl (al-Kitāb al-Khazarī)*, ed. D. H. Baneth and H. Ben-Shammai. Jerusalem, 1977.
Al-Jurjānī. *Kitāb al-ta'rīfāt*, ed. G. Flügel. Leipzig, 1845.
Al-Khayyāṭ, Abū Ḥusayn b. 'Uthmān. *Kitāb al-Intiṣār wa'l-radd 'alā Ibn al-Rāwandī al-mulḥid (Le livre du triomphe et de la réfutation d'Ibn al-Rawandi l'hérétique)*, ed. A. N. Nader. Beirut, 1957.
Al-Marrākushī, 'Abd al-Wāḥid. *al-Mu'jib fī talkhīṣ akhbār al-Maghrib*, ed. R. Dozy. Leiden, 1881; Spanish translation by A. Huici Miranda, *Colección de crónicas árabes de la Reconquista*, t. 4. Tétouan, 1955.
Al-Mas'ūdī. *Murūj al-dhahab*. C. Barbier de Meynard, *Maçoudi, Les Prairies d'or*. Paris, 1865.
———. 'Alī bn. al-Ḥusayn. *al-Tanbīh wa'l-ishrāf*, ed. 'Abdallāh Ismā'īl al-Ṣāfī. Cairo, n. d.
Moshe ben Maimon: see list of abbreviations.
Mūsā ben Maymūn: see list of abbreviations.
Al-Qirqisānī, Abū Ya'qūb. *Kitāb al-anwār wa'l-marāqib, Code of Karaite Law*, ed. L. Nemoy. New Haven, 1940–45.

Rabbi Yehuda Halevi, The Kuzari: In Defense of the Despised Faith, translated by N. Daniel Korobkin. Northvale, N.J., and Jerusalem, 1998.

Rasāʾil Ikhwān al-Ṣafāʾ wa-khillān al-wafāʾ. Beirut, n.d.

Al-Risāla al-jāmiʿa, ed. J. Ṣalība. Damascus, n.d.

Al-Rāzī, Abū Bakr. *Rasāʾil falsafiyya*, ed. P. Kraus. repr. Beirut, 1982.

———. *Risālat al-Bīrunī fī fihrist kutub Muḥammad b. Zakariyāʾ al-Rāzī. Epitre de Bīrunī contenant le répertoire des ouvrages de Muḥammad b. Zakarīyā ar-Rāzī*, ed. Paul Kraus. Paris, 1936.

Al-Rāzī, Abū Ḥātim. *Aʿlam al-nubuwwa (The Peaks of Prophecy)*, ed. Ṣalāḥ al-Sāwy. Teheran, 1977.

Saʿadya ben Yosef Fayyūmī. *Kitāb al-amānāt wa'l-iʿtiqādāt*, ed. Y. Qafiḥ. Jerusalem, 1970.

Al-Shahrastānī, Muaḥmmad. *Kitāb al-milal wa'l-niḥal, Book of Religious and Philosophical Sects*, ed. W. Cureton. Leipzig, 1923.

Al-Tahānawī. *Dictionary of Technical Terms (Kashshāf iṣṭilāḥāt al-funūn*. Cairo, 1963.

Tawḥīdī, Abū Ḥayyān. *Al-Muqābasāt*, ed. Ḥasan as-Sandūbī. Cairo, 1929.

———. *Kitāb al-imtāʿ wa'l-muʾānasa*, ed. Aḥmad Amīn and Aḥmad al-Zayn. Beirut, n.d.

Tisʿ rasāʾil fī al-ḥikma waʾl-ilāhīyyāt. Istanbul, 1298H.

Secondary Sources

al-Aʿsam, ʿAbd al-Amir. *Taʾrīkh Ibn al-Riwandī al-mulḥid* (=*History of Ibn ar-Riwandi the Heretic*). Beirut, 1975.

Abrahamov, B. "Al-Ghazālī's Supreme Way to Know God," *Studia Islamica* 77 (1993): 141–68.

———. "The Barāhima's Enigma: A Search for New Solution," *Die Welt des Orients* 18 (1987): 72–91.

Affifi, A. E. "The Influence of Hermetic Literature on Muslim Thought," *BSOAS* 13 (1951): 840–55.

Abelson, J. "Maimonides on the Jewish Creed," in *Eschatology in Maimonidean Thought: Messianism, Resurrection and the World to Come*, ed. J. I. Dienstang, 24–58. New York, 1979.

Abulafia, D. "Mediterraneans," in *Rethinking the Mediterranean*, ed. W. V. Harris. Oxford and New York, 2005.

Abun Nasr, Jamil M. *A History of the Maghrib in the Islamic Period*. Cambridge, 1987.

Aidi, Hishaam D. "The Interference of al-Andalus: Spain, Islam, and the West." *Social Text* 87 (2006): 67–88.

Akasoy, A. A. *Philosophie und Mystik in der späten Almohadenzeit: die Sizilanischen Fragen des Ibn Sabʿīn*. Leiden and Boston, 2006.

Anidjar, G. *"Our Place in al-Andalus": Kabbalah, Philosophy, Literature in Arab Jewish Letters* . Palo Alto, Cal., 2002.

Arkoun, M. *Min Faiṣal al-Tafriqa ilā Faṣl al-Maqāl: Ayna huwa l-fikr al-islāmī al-muʿāṣir*, trans. H. Ṣāli. London and Beirut, 1995.

Asín Palacios, M. "Le sens du mot '*tahāfot*' dans les œuvres d'el-Ghazalī et d'Averröes," *Revue Africaine* 261–62 (1906), reprinted in idem, *Obras Escogidas* (1946), 185–203.
Assaf, S. "On the History of the Karaites in the East," *Zion* 1 (1936): 208–51 [Hebrew].
———. "Letters of R. Samuel b. Eli and his Contemporaries," *Tarbiẓ* 1 (1930): 102–30; 2 (1931), 43–84; 3 (1932), 15–80 [Hebrew].
Assmann, J. *Moses the Egyptian: The Memory of Egypt in Western Monotheism.* Cambridge, Mass., 1997.
Averroes: see also Ibn Rushd.
Averroes. *The Book of the Decisive Treatise Determining the Connection between the Law and Wisdom; &, Epistle Dedicatory*, ed. and trans. C. E. Butterworth. Provo, Utah, 2001.
———. *Discours décisif*, trans. M. Geoffroy, with an introduction by A. de Libera. Paris, 1996.
———. *Tafsīr mā ba'd aṭ-ṭabī'at—"Grand commentaire" de la métaphysique*, ed. M. Bouyges. Beirut, 1986.
———. *Averroes' Commentary on Plato's Republic*, ed. E.I.J. Rosenthal. Cambridge, 1966.
Baneth, D. H. "Some Remarks on the Autographs of Yehudah Hallevi and the Genesis of the *Kuzari*," *Tarbiẓ* 26 (1956–57): 297–303 [Hebrew].
Bar-Asher, M. M. *Exegesis in Early Imami Shiism.* Jerusalem and Leiden, 1999.
Baron, S. W. "The Historical Outlook of Maimonides," *PAAJR* 6 (1935): 5–113. Reprinted in idem, *History and Jewish Historians,* 109–63. Philadelphia, 1964.
———. *Social and Religious History of the Jews*. New York, 1957.
Becker, A. H. *Fear of God and the Beginning of Wisdom: The School of Nisibis and Christian Scholastic Culture in Late Antique Mesopotamia*. Philadelphia, 2006.
Bello, I. A. *The Medieval Islamic Controversy between Philosophy and Orthodoxy: Ijmā' and Ta'wīl in the Conflict between al-Ghazālī and Ibn Rushd*. Leiden, 1989.
Benin S. D. *The Footprints of God: Divine Accommodation in Jewish and Christian Thought*. Albany, 1993.
———. "The 'Cunning of God' and Divine Accomodation," *Journal of the History of Ideas* 45 (1984): 179–91.
Ben-Sasson, C.-H. "The Singularity of the Jewish Nation as Seen in the Twelfth Century," *Peraqim* 2 (1969–74): 145–218 [Hebrew].
Ben-Sasson, M. "Maimonides in Egypt: The First Stage," *Maimonidean Studies* 2 (1991): 3–30.
Ben Shammai, H. "Maimonides and Creation *Ex Nihilo* in the Tradition of Islamic Philosophy," in *Maimónides y su época*, ed. C. del Valle et al., 103–20. Madrid, 2007.
———. "Major Trends in Karaite Philosophy and Polemics in the Tenth and Eleventh Centuries," in *Karaite Judaism: A Guide to Its History and Literary Sources*, ed. M. Polliack, 339–62. Leiden, 2003.

———. "Saadia Gaon's Ten Articles of Faith," *Daat* 37 (1996): 11–26.

———. "Between Ananites and Karaites: Observations on Early Medieval Jewish Sectarianism," *Studies in Muslim-Jewish Relations* 1 (1993): 19–29.

———. "Some Genizah Fragments on the Duty of the Nations to Keep the Mosaic Law," in *Geniza Research after Ninety Years: The Case of Judaeo-Arabic*, ed. J. Blau and S. C. Reif, 22–30. Cambridge, 1992.

Benedict, B. Z. "On the History of the Torah Center in Provence," *Tarbiẓ* 22 (1951): 85–109 [Hebrew].

Bergsträsser, G. "Ḥunain ibn Isḥāq über die syrischen und arabischen Galen-Uebersetzungen," *Abhandlungen für die Kunde des Morgenlandes* 17. Leipzig, 1925.

Berman, L. "Maimonides the Disciple of al-Fārābī," *IOS* 4 (1974): 154–78.

Bertolacci, A. "The Reception of Avicenna's 'Philosophia Prima' in Albert the Great's Commentary on the 'Metaphysics': The Case of the Doctrine of Unity." *Albertus Magnus zum Gedenken nach 800 Jahren: Neue Zugänge, Aspekte und Perspektiven*, ed. W. Senner et al., 67–78. Berlin, 2001.

Blau, J. " 'At Our Place in al-Andalus,' 'At Our Place in the Maghreb,' " in Kraemer, *Perpectives on Maimonides*, 293–94.

———. *The Emergence and Linguistic Background of Judaeo-Arabic: A Study of the Origins of Middle Arabic*. Jerusalem, 1981.

Blidstein, G. J. "Where Do We Stand in the Study of Maimonidean Halakhah?" in *Studies in Maimonides*, ed. I. Twersky, 1–30. Cambridge, Mass., 1990.

Blumenthal, D. R. "Maimonides' Philosophical Mysticism," *Philosophic Mysticism: Studies in Rational Religion*. Ramat Gan, 2006.

———. "Maimonides: Prayer, Worship and Mysticism," in *Approaches to Judaism in Medieval Times*, ed. D. R. Blumenthal, 3. Atlanta, 1988.

———. "Maimonides' Intellectual Mysticism and the Superiority of the Prophecy of Moses," *Approaches to Judaism in Medieval Times* 1 (1984): 27–51.

Booth, E. *Aristotelian Aporetic Ontology in Islamic and Christian Thinkers*. Cambridge, 1983.

Bos. *Maimonides On Asthma*: see list of abbreviations.

Bos, G. "Maimonides' Medical Works and Their Contribution to His Medical Biography," *Maimonidean Studies* 5 (2008): 243–66.

Bouretz, P. "A la recherche des lumières médiévales: la leçon de Maïmonide," in *Critique* 64, no. 728–29 (Jan.–Feb. 2008): *Philosophie et Judaïsme*, ed. J. Baumgarten, P. Birnbaum, and M. Kriegel: 28–41.

Bowersock, G. W. *Hellenism in Later Antiquity*. Ann Arbor, 1990.

Brague, Rémi. "La ruse divine (*talaṭṭuf*); quelques textes nouveaux," in T. Langermann and J. Stern, eds., *Adaptations and Innovations: Studies on the Interaction between Jewish and Islamic Thought and Literature from the Early Middle Ages to the Late Twentieth Century, Dedicated to Professor Joel L. Kraemer*, 17–26. Paris, Louvain, and Dudley, 2007.

———. *Au moyen du Moyen Age: Philosophies médievales en chrétienté, judaïsme et islam*. Chatou, 2006.

———. *La loi de Dieu: Histoire philosophique d'une alliance*. Paris, 2005.

———. *Maïmonide, Traité d'éthique—"Huit chapitres,"* traduction, presentation, et notes par R. Brague. Paris, Desclée de Brouwer, 2001.

Braudel, Fernand. *La Méditerranée et le monde méditerranéen à l'époque de Philippe II*. Paris, 1949. (=*The Mediterranean and the Mediterranean World in the Age of Philip II*, trans. S. Reynolds. New York, 1976).

Brock, S. "Aspects of Translation Technique in Antiquity," *Greek, Roman and Byzantine Studies* 26 (1979): 69–89.

Brunschvig, R. "Averroès juriste," in *Etudes d'Orientalisme dédiées à la mémoire de Lévi-Provençal*, 1: 35–68. Paris, 1962; reprinted in idem, *Etudes d'Islamologie*, ed. by A. M. Turki, 2: 167–200. Paris, 1976.

———. "Encore sur la doctrine du Mahdī Ibn Tūmart," *Folia Orientalia* (1970): 33–40.

———. "Sur la doctrine du Mahdī Ibn Tūmart," *Arabica* 2 (1955): 137–49.

Bujis, Joseph. A., ed. *Maimonides: A Collection of Critical Essays*. Notre Dame, 1988.

Burman, Thomas E. *Religious Polemic and the Intellectual History of the Mozarabs, c.1050–1200*. Leiden and New York, 1994.

Burnett, C.S.F. "Arabic, Greek and Latin Works on Astrological Magic Attributed to Aristotle," in *Pseudo-Aristotle in the Middle Ages: The* Theology *and Other Texts*, ed. Jill Kraye et al., 84–96. London, 1986.

Butterworth, C. E., ed. *The Political Aspects of Islamic Philosophy: Essays in Honor of Muhsin Mahdi*. Cambridge, Mass., 1992.

———. "Ethics and Classical Islamic Philosophy: A Study of Averroes' *Commentary on Plato's Republic*," in *Ethics in Islam*, ed. R. Hovannisian, 17–45. Malibu, 1985.

Cameron, A. "The Last Days of the Academy at Athens," *Proceedings of the Cambridge Philological Society* 195 (n.s. 15) (1969): 7–30 (reprinted in idem, *Literature and Society in the Early Byzantine World*. London, 1985).

Chiat, M. J., and K. L. Reyerson, eds. *The Medieval Mediterranean: Cross-Cultural Contacts*. St. Cloud, Minn., 1988.

Chwolsohn, D. *Die Ssabier und der Ssabismus*, 2 vols. St. Petersburg, 1856.

———. "Über die Überreste der altbabylonischen Literatur in arabischen Übersetzung," *Mémoires des savants étrangers*, 8. St. Petersburg, 1850.

Cohen, Carmiel. "The Correct Meaning of an Autobiographical Note Attributed to Maimonides," *Tarbiẓ* 76 (2006–2007): 283–87 [Hebrew].

Cohen, Mark C. "Geniza for Islamicists, Islamic Geniza, and 'the New Cairo Geniza,'" *Harvard Middle Eastern and Islamic Review* 7 (2006): 129–45.

Cohen, M. R. *Jewish Self-Government in Medieval Egypt: The Origins of the Office of the Head of the Jews, ca. 1065–1126*. Princeton, 1980.

Conrad, L. I. "Through the Thin Veil: On the Question of Communication and the Socialization of Knowledge in Ḥayy b. Yaqẓān," in *The World of Ibn Tufayl: Interdisciplinary Perspectives on Ḥayy b. Yaqẓān*, ed. L. I. Conrad, 238–66. Leiden, 1996.

———, ed. "The World of Ibn Ṭufayl," in *The World of Ibn Ṭufayl: Interdisciplinary Perspectives on Ḥayy ibn Yaqẓān*, ed. L. I. Conrad, 1–37. Leiden, 1996.

Constable, O. R. *Trade and Traders in Muslim Spain: The Commercial Realignment of the Iberian Peninsula, 900–1500*. Cambridge and New York, 1994.

Cook, M. *Commanding Right and Forbidding Wrong in Islamic Thought*. Cambridge, 2000.

———. "The Origins of Kalam," *BSOAS* 43 (1980): 32–43.

Corbin, H. "Rituel sabéen et exégèse ismaélienne du rituel," *Eranos Jahrbuch* 19 (1950): 194–394.

Corcos, D. *Studies in the History of the Jews of Morocco*. Jerusalem, 1976.

Cressier, P. et al., eds. *Los Almohades: Problemas y Perspectivas*. 2 vols. Madrid, 2005.

Crone, P. *God's Rule: Government and Islam: Six Centuries of Medieval Islamic Political Thought*. New York, 2004.

Crone, P., and M. Cook. *Hagarism: The Making of the Islamic World*. Cambridge, 1977.

Cruz-Hernández, M. *Abû-l-Walīd Muḥammad Ibn Rushd (Averroes): Vida, obra, influencia*. Cordova, 1997.

Daftary, F. *The Ismāʿīlīs—Their History and Doctrines*. Cambridge, 1990.

Dahan, G. "Maïmonide dans les controverses universitaires du XIIIe siècle," in *Maïmonide: philosophe et savant*, ed. T. Lévy and R. Rashed, 367–93.

D'Ancona Costa, C. "Commenting on Aristotle: From Late Antiquity to the Arab Aristotelianism," in *Der Kommentar in Antike und Mittelalter: Beitäge zu seiner Erforschung*, ed. W. Geerlings and C. Schulze, 201–51. Leiden, Boston, and Köln, 2002.

Davidson, H. A. *Moses Maimonides: The Man and His Works*. Oxford, 2005.

———. "The Authenticity of Works Attributed to Maimonides," in *Me'ah Sheʿarim: Studies in Medieval Jewish Spiritual Life in Memory of Isadore Twersky*, ed. E. Fleischer et al., 111–33. Jerusalem, 2001.

———. "Maimonides' Putative Position as Official Head of the Egyptian Jewish Community," in *Hazon Nahum*, ed. N. Lamm, 115–28. New York, 1998.

———. "Maimonides on Metaphysical Knowledge," *Maimonidean Studies* 3 (1992–93): 49–103.

Davis, N. Z. *Trickster Travels: A Sixteenth-Century Muslim between Worlds*. New York, 2006.

De Blois, F. C. "The 'Sabians' (*Ṣābiʿūn*) in Pre-Islamic Arabia," *Acta Orientalia* (1995): 39–61.

———. "Ṣābī," *EI*, 8: 672–75.

De Libera, A. *Penser au Moyen Age*. Paris, 1999.

Dienstang, J. I., ed. *Eschatology in Maimonidean Thought: Messianism, Resurrection and the World to Come*. New York, 1979.

Dreyfus, F. "La condescendance divine (*synkatabasis*) comme principe herméneutique de l'Ancien Testament dans la tradition juive et dans la tradition chrétienne," *Supplements to Vetus Testamentum* 36: 96–107.

Drijvers, H. "The Persistence of Pagan Cults and Practices in Christian Syria," in *East of Byzantium: Syria and Armenia in the Formative Period; Dumbarton Oaks Symposium, 1980*, ed. N. Garsoïan et al., 35–43. Washington D.C., 1987.

Drory, J. "The Early Decades of Ayyūbid Rule," in *Perspectives on Maimonides*, ed. J. K. Kraemer, 295–302.

Dubois, J. D., and B. Roussel, eds. *Entrer en matière: les prologues*. Paris, 1998.

Dunlop, D. M. "Al-Farabi's Introductory *Risāla* on Logic," *Islamic Quarterly* 4 (1957): 224–35.

Efros, I. "Maimonides' Arabic Treatise on Logic," *PAAJR* 34 (1966): 9–62 [Hebrew].

———. "Maimonides' Treatise on Logic," *PAAJR* 8 (1938).

Eliyahu, A. "Genizah Fragments from the Hermetic Literature," *Ginzei Kedem* 1 (2005): 9–29 [Hebrew].

Endress, Gerhard. "Der Islam und die Einheit des mediterraneen Kulturraums in Mittelalter," in *Das Mittelmeer—die Wiege der europäischen Kultur*, ed. C. Rozen, 270–95. Bonn, 1998.

Eran, A. "Al-Ghazālī and Maimonides on the World to Come and Spiritual Pleasures," *JQR* 8 (2001): 137–66.

Ess, van J. "Disputationpraxis in der islamischen Theologie: Eine vorläufige Skizze," *Revue des études Islamiques* 44 (1976): 23–60.

Fahd, T. "Retour à Ibn Waḥshiyya," *Arabica* 16 (1969): 83–88.

Fattal, Antoine. *Le statut légal des non-musulmans en pays d'Islam*. Beirut, 1995.

Faur, J. *'Iyunim be-Mishneh Torah leha-Rambam: Sefer ha-Mada'*. Jerusalem, 1978 [Hebrew].

Fenton, P. B. "Une source arabe du *Guide* de Maïmonide: L'agriculture nabatèenne d'Ibn Waḥshiyya," in *Maïmonide philosophe et savant*, ed. T. Lévy and R. Rashed, 303–33.

———. *Deux traités de mystique juive : Obadyah b. Abraham b. Moïse Maïmonide (Le traité du puits=al-Maqāla al-Ḥawḍiyya), David b. Josué, dernier des Maïmonides (Le guide du détachement=al-Murshid ilā t-Tafarrud)*. Lagrasse, 1987.

———. "Jewish Attitudes to Islam: Israel Heeds Ishmael," *Jerusalem Quarterly* 29 (1983): 84–102.

———. "A Meeting with Maimonides," *BSOAS* 45 (1982): 1–4.

———. *Obadiah ben Abraham Maimonides, The Treatise of the Pool=al-Maqāla al-Ḥawdiyya*. London, 1981.

Fierro, M. "Ill-Treated Women Seeking Divorce: The Qur'ānic Two Arbiters and Judicial Practice among the Malikis in al-Andalus and North Africa," in *Dispensing Justice in Islam: Qadis and their Judgement,* ed. M. Kh. Masud, R. Peters, and D. Powers, 323–47. Leiden and Boston, 2006.

———. "Proto-Mālikīs, Mālikīs and Reformed Mālikīs in al-Andalus, " in *The Islamic School of Law: Evolution, Devolution, and Progress*, ed. P. Bearman, R. Peters, and F. E. Vogel, 57–76. Cambridge, Mass., 2005.

———. "Revolución y tradición: algunos aspectos del mundo del saber en al-Andalus durante las épocas almorávide y almohade," in *Biografías almohades*, ed. M. L. Avila and M. Fierro, 2: 131–65. Madrid-Granada, 2000.

———. "Spiritual Alienation and Political Activism: The *Ghurabā'* in al-Andalus during the Sixth/Twelfth Century,"*Arabica* 47 (2000): 230–60.

———. "The Legal Policies of the Almohad Caliphs and Ibn Rushd's *Bidāyat al-Mujtahid*," *Journal of Islamic Studies* 10 (1999): 226–48.

———. "La religión," in *El retroceso territorial de al-Andalus: Almorávides y almohades, Siglo XI al XIII: Historia de España fundada por R. Menéndez Pidal y dirigida por J. M. Jover*, coord. M. J. Viguera, vol. 8:2, 435–546. Madrid, 1997.

———. "Bātinism in al-Andalus. Maslāma b. Qāsim al Qurṭubī (d.353/964), author of the *Rutbat al-Ḥakīm* and the *Ghāyat al-Ḥakīm (Picatrix)*," *Studia Islamica* 84 (1996): 7–112.

———. "Ibn Ḥazm et le Zindīq juif," *Revue du Monde Musulman et de la Mediterrannée* 63–64 (1992): 81–89.

Finkel, J. *Maimonides' Treatise on Resurrection (Maqāla fī tehiyyat ha-metim)*. New York, 1939.

Fletcher, M. "Ibn Tūmart's Teachers: The Relationship with al-Ghazāli." *Al-Qanṭara* 18 (1997): 305–30.

Fraenkel, C. F. *From Maimonides to Samuel ibn Tibbon: The Transformation of Dalalat al-Ha'irin into the Moreh ha-Nevukhim*. Jerusalem, 2007 [Hebrew].

Frank, D. H. "Humility as a Virtue: A Maimonidean Critique of Aristotle's Ethics," in *Moses Maimonides and His Time*, ed. E. L. Ormsby, 89–99.

Freudenthal, G. "The Biological Limitations of Man's Intellectual Perfection According to Maimonides," in *The Trials of Maimonides*, ed. G. Tamer, 137–49.

———. "Maimonides' Philosophy of Sceince," in *The Cambridge Companion to Maimonides*, ed. G. Tamer, 134–66.

Friedberg, A. D. "Maimonides' Reinterpretation of the Thirteenth Article of Faith: Another Look at the *Essay on Resurrection*," *Jewish Studies Quarterly* 10 (2003): 244–57.

Friedman, M. A. *Maimonides: The Yemenite Messiah and Apostasy*. Jerusalem, 2002 [Hebrew].

Friedmann, Yohanan. *Tolerance and Coercion in Islam: Interfaith Relations in the Muslim Tradition*. Cambridge and New York, 2003.

Fricaud, E. "La place des *Çalaba* dans la société almohad mu'minide," in *Los Almohades*, ed. P. Cressier et al., 525–45.

———. "Les *Ṭalaba* dans la société almohade. (Le temps d'Averroès)," *Al-Qanṭara* 18 (1997): 331–88.

Funkenstein, A. *Perceptions of Jewish History*. Berkeley, 1993.

———. *Theology and the Scientific Imagination: From the Middle Ages to the Seventeenth Century*. Princeton, 1986.

———. "Gesetz und Geschichte: Zur historisierenden Hermeneutik bei Maimonides und Thomas von Aquin," *Viator* 1 (1970): 147–78.

Gabrieli, F. "Le origini del movimento almohad in una fonte storica d'Oriente," *Arabica* 3 (1956): 1–7.

García-Arenal, M. M. *Messianism and Puritanical Reform: Mahdīs of the Muslim West*. Leiden, 2006.

———. "La práctica del precepto de *al-amr bi-l-ma'rūf wa-l-nahy 'an al-munkar* en la hagiografía maghrebí," *Al-Qanṭara* 13 (1992): 143–65.

———. "Rapports entre les groupes dans la peninsule ibérique. La conversion des juifs à l'Islam (XIIe–XIIIe)," *RMMM* 63–64 (1992): 91–101.

Gauthier, L. *La théorie d'Ibn Rochd (Averroès) sur les rapports de la religion et de la philosophie*. Paris, 1983.

Galston, M. *Politics and Excellence: The Political Philosophy of Alfarabi*. Princeton, 1990.

Garden, K. *Al-Ghazālī's Contested Revival: "Iḥyā' 'ulūm al-dīn" and Its Critics in Khorasan and the Maghrib*. Ph.D. Diss., University of Chicago, 2005: UMI.

Gellman, J. I. "Maimonides' 'Ravings,'" *Review of Metaphysics* 45 (1991): 309–28.

Gellner, E. *Muslim Society*. Cambridge and New York, 1981.

Genequand, Ch. *Alexander of Aphrodisias on the Cosmos*. Leiden, Boston, and Köln, 2001.

Gil, M., and E. Fleischer. *Yehuda ha-Levi and His Circle—55 Geniza Documents*. Jerusalem, 2001 [Hebrew].

Gil'adi, A. "A Short Note on the Possible Origin of the Title *Moreh Ha-Nevukhim*," *Tarbiẓ* 48 (1979): 346–47 [Hebrew].

Geoffroy, M. "A propos de l'almohadisme d'Averroès: L'anthropomorphisme (*taǧsīm*) dans la seconde version du *Kitāb al-kašf ʿan manāhiǧ al-adilla*," in *Los Almohades*, ed. P. Cressier et al., 853–94.

———. "L'almohadisme théologique d'Averroès (Ibn Rushd)," *Archives d'Histoire Doctrinale et Littéraire du Moyen Age* 66 (1999): 9–47.

———. "Ibn Rušd et la théologie almohadiste: une version inconnue du *Kitāb al-kašf ʿan manāhiǧ al-adilla* dans deux manuscrits d'Istanbul," *Medioevo* 26 (2001): 328–56.

Gevaryahu, H.M.Y. "Paganism According to Maimonides," in *Tzvi Karl Memorial Volume*, ed. A. Weiser and B. Z. Lourie, 353–60. Jerusalem, 1960 [Hebrew].

Goitein, S. D. *A Mediterranean Society: The Jewish Communities of the Arab World as Portrayed in the Documents of the Cairo Geniza*, 6 vols. Berkeley, 1967–93.

———. "The Moses Maimonides-Ibn Sanāʾ al-Mulk Circle (A Deathbed Declaration from March 1182)," in *Studies in Islamic History and Civilization, in Honour of Professor David Ayalon*, ed. M. Sharon, 399–405. Jerusalem and Leiden, 1986.

———. *Letters of Medieval Jewish Traders*. Princeton, 1974.

———. "The Biography of Rabbi Judah Ha-Levi in Light of the Cairo Geniza Documents," *PAAJR* 28 (1959): 41–56.

———. *Jews and Arabs: Their Contacts through the Ages*. New York, 1955.

Goldfield, N. L. *Moses Maimonides' Treatise on Resurrection: An Inquiry into Its Authenticity*. New York, 1986.

Goldziher, I. Introduction to D. Luciani, ed., *Le Livre de Mohammed Ibn Toumert, Mahdi des Almohades*. Algiers, 1903.

Goldziher, I. *The Ẓāhirīs: Their Doctrine and Their History: A Contribution to the History of Islamic Theology*. Leiden, 1971.

Goodman, L. E. "Maimonides' Philosophy of Law," *Jewish Law Annual* 1 (1978): 72–107.

Gouguenheim, S. *Aristote au mont Saint-Michel: Les racines greques de l'Europe chrétienne*. Paris, 2008.

Goodman, L. E. *Jewish and Islamic Philosophy: Crosspollinations in the Classic Age*. Edinburgh, 1999.

Graetz, H. *Die Konstruktion der jüdischen Geschichte*. Berlin, 1936 (=*The Structure of Jewish History and Other Essays*, trans. I. Schorsch. New York, 1975).

Greene, T. M. *The City of the Moon God: Religious Traditions of Harran*. Leiden, 1992.

Griffel, F. "Ibn Tūmart's Rational Proof for God's Existence and Unity, and His Connection to the Niẓāmiyya *Madrasa* in Baghdad," in *Los Almohades*, ed. P. Cressier et al., 753–813.

———. *Apostasie und Toleranz im Islam: Die Entwicklung zu al-Gazālis Urteil gegen die Philosophie und die Reaktionen der Philosophen*. Leiden, 2000.

Griffith, S. H. *The Church in the Shadow of the Mosque: Christians and Muslims in the World of Islam*. Princeton and Oxford, 2007.

Guichard, P. *Al-Andalus, 711–1492: Une histoire de l'Andalousie arabe*. Paris, 2000.

Guidi, A. "L'obscurité intentionnelle du philosophe: thèmes néoplatoniciens et Farabiens chez Maïmonide," *Revue des études juives* 166 (2007): 129–45.

Gutas, D. "The 'Alexandria to Baghdad' Complex of Narratives: A Contribution to the Study of Philosophical and Medical Historiography among the Arabs," *Documenti e studi sulla tradizione filosofica medievale* 10 (1999): 155–93.

———. *Greek Thought, Arabic Culture: The Graeco-Arabic Translation Movement in Baghdad and Early ʿAbbāsid Society (2nd–4th/8th–10th Centuries)*. London and New York, 1998.

———. *Avicenna and the Aristotelian Tradition: Introduction to Reading Avicenna's Philosophical Works*. Leiden, 1988.

———. "Plato's *Symposion* in the Arabic Tradition," *Oriens* 31 (1988): 36–60.

Hämeen-Anttila, J. *The Last Pagans of Iraq: Ibn Waḥshiyya and His Nabatean Agriculture*. Leiden, 2006.

Halbertal, M. "*Sefer Ha-Mizvot* of Maimonides—His Architecture of *Halakha* and Theory of Interpretation," *Tarbiẓ* 59 (1990): 457–80 [Hebrew].

Halbertal, M., and A. Margalit. *Idolatry*, trans. N. Goldblum. Cambridge, Mass., 1992.

Halkin, A. I. *Igeret Teman*. New York, 1952.

Halkin, A., and D. Hartmann. *Crisis and Leadership: Epistles of Maimonides*. Philadelphia, New York, and Jerusalem, 1985.

Halm, H. *The Fatimids and Their Traditions of Learning*. London, 1997.

Harkavy, A. "Fragment einer Apologie des Maimonidischen *ma'amar teḥiyyat ha-metim*," *Zeitschrift für hebräische Bibliographie* 1 (1897): 125–28, 181–88.

Harris, J. M., ed. *Maimonides after 800 Years: Essays on Maimonides and His Influence*. Cambridge, Mass., 2007.

Harris, William V., ed. *Rethinking the Mediterranean*. Oxford and New York, 2005.

Harvey, L. P. *Muslims in Spain: 1500 to 1614*. Chicago and London, 2005.

Harvey, S. "Avicenna and Maimonides on Prayer and Intellectual Worship," in *Exchange and Transmission across Cultural Boundaries: Philosophy, Mysticism and Science in the Mediterranean* (Proceedings of a workshop in memory of Prof. Shlomo Pines, the Institute for Advanced Studies, Jerusalem; 28 February–2 March 2005), ed. H. Ben-Shammai, S. Shaked, and S. Stroumsa (forthcoming).

———. "Alghazali and Maimonides and their Books of Knowledge," in *Be'erot Yitzhak: Studies in Memory of Isadore Twersky*, ed. J. M. Harris, 99–117. Cambridge, Mass., 2005.

———. "Medieval Sources of Maimonides' *Guide*," *Bulletin de Philosophie Médiéval* 46 (2000): 283–87.

———. "Averroes' Use of Examples in his Middle Commentary on the Prior Analytics, and Some Remarks on His Role as Commentator," *Arabic Sciences and Philosophy* 7 (1997): 91–113.

———. "The Meaning of Terms Designating Love in Judaeo-Arabic Thought and Some Remarks on the Judaeo-Arabic Interpretation of Maimonides," in *Judaeo-Arabic Studies: Proceedings of the Founding Conference of the Society for Judaeo-Arabic Studies* (*Studies in Muslim-Jewish Relations*), ed. N. Golb, 3: 175–96. Reading, 1996.

Harvey, W. Z. "On Maimonides' Allegorical Readings of Scripture," in *Interpretation and Allegory: Antiquity to the Modern Period*, ed. J. Whitman, 181–88. Leiden, Boston, and Köln, 2000.

———. "Why Maimonides Was Not a Mutakallim," in *Perspectives on Maimonides: Philosophical and Historical Studies*, ed. J. L. Kraemer, 105–14. Oxford, 1991.

———. "Maimonides on Human Perfection, Awe and Politics," in *The Thought of Moses Maimonides*, ed. I. Robinson, L. Kaplan, and J. Bauer, 1–15.

———. "Averroes and Maimonides on the Duty of Philosophical Contemplation (*iʿtibār*)," *Tarbiẓ* 58 (1989): 75–83 [Hebrew].

———. "The Obligation of Talmud on Women According to Maimonides," *Tradition* 19 (1981): 122–30.

Hasnawi, A. "Réflexions sur la terminologie logique de Maïmonide et son contexte farabien: Le *Guide des perplexes* et le *Traité de logique*," in *Maimonide: philosophe et savant*, ed. T. Lévy and R. Rashed, 39–78.

Hasselhoff, G. K. *Dicit Rabbi Moyses: Studien zum Bild von Moses Maimonides im lateinischen Western vom 13. bis zum 15. Jahrhundert*. Würzburg, 2004.

Hasselhoff, G., and O. Fraisse. *Moses Maimonides (1138–2004): His Religious, Scientific and Philosophical Wirkungsgeschichte in Different Cultural Contexts*. Würzburg, 2004.

Hauber, A. "Ṭomṭom (Ṭimṭim)=Dandamis=Dindymus," *ZDMG* 63 (1909): 457–72.

Heinemann, I. "Maimuni und die arabischen Einheitslehrer," *Monatsschrift für Geschichte und Wissenschaft des Judentums* 79 (1935): 102–48.

Heinemann, Y. "Judah Halevi's Historical Perception," *Zion* 9 (1949): 147–77 [Hebrew].

Hirschberg, H. Z. (J. W.). *A History of the Jews in North Africa*, second revised ed., trans. from Hebrew. Vol. 1. *From Antiquity to the Sixteenth Century*. Leiden, 1979.

Hjärpe, J. *Analyse critique des traditions arabes sur les sabéens ḥarraniens*. Uppsala, 1972.

Hopkins, J.F.P. *Medieval Muslim Government in Barbary until the Sixth Century of the Hijra*. London, 1958.

Hopkins, S. "The Languages of Maimonides," in *The Trials of Maimonides*, ed. G. Tamer, 85–106.

Horden, P., and N. Purcell. *The Corrupting Sea: A Study of Mediterranean History*. Oxford, 2000.

Hourani, G. F. "Maimonides and Islam," *Studies in Islamic and Judaic Traditions*, ed. W. N. Brinner and S. D. Ricks, 153–65. Atlanta, 1986.

———. "Averroes: The Decisive Treatise, Determining What the Connection Is between Religion and Philosophy," in *Medieval Political Philosophy*, ed. R. Lerner and M. Mahdi, 163–85. Ithaca, 1963.

Huici Miranda, A. *Historia Politica del Imperio Almohade* 2 vols. Tetouan, 1956–57.

Husain, Adnan A., and K. E. Fleming, eds. *A Faithful Sea: The Religious Cultures of the Mediterranean, 1200–1700*. Oxford, 2007.

Hymann, A. "Interpreting Maimonides," in *Maimonides: A Collection of Critical Essays*, ed. J. A. Bujis, 19–29. Notre Dame, 1988.

Ibn Rushd. *The Distinguished Jurist's Primer—Bidāyat al-Mujtahid wa Nihāyat al-Muqtaṣid*, trans. Imran Ahsan Khan Nyazee. Reading, 2000.

Idris, H. R. "Les tributaires en occident musulman médiéval d'aprés le 'Miʿyār' d'al-Wanšarīsī," in *Mélanges d'islamologie: Volume dédié à la mémoire d'Armand Abel par ses collègues, ses élèves et ses amis*, ed. P. Salmon, 172–96. Leiden, 1974.

Ivry, A. L. "The Guide and Maimonides' Philosophical Sources," in *The Cambridge Companion to Maimonides*, ed. K. Seeskin, 58–81.

———. "Maimonides' Relation to the Teachings of Averroes," *Sefunot*, n.s. 8 (2003): 60–74 [Hebrew].

———. "The Utilization of Allegory in Islamic Philosophy," in *Interpretation and Allegory: Antiquity to the Modern Period*, ed. J. Whitman, 153–80. Leiden, Boston, and Köln, 2000.

———. "Ismāʿīlī Theology and Maimonides' Philosophy," in *The Jews of Medieval Islam: Community, Society and Identity*, ed. D. Frank, 271–99. Leiden, 1995.

———. "Neoplatonic Currents in Maimonides' Thought," in *Perspectives on Maimonides*, ed. J. L. Kraemer, 115–40.

———. *Al-Kindī's Metaphysics*. Albany, 1974.

Jolivet, J. "Esquisse d'un Aristote arabe," in *Penser avec Aristote*, ed. A. Sinaceur, 179–85. Toulouse, 1991.

Jolivet, J., ed. *Multiple Averroès*. Paris, 1978.

Joose, N. P. "An Example of Medieval Arabic Pseudo-Hermetism: The Tale of Salāmān and Absāl," *Journal of Semitic Studies* 38 (1993): 289–90.

Keller, C.-A. *Die Religion der Gebildeten im Mittelalter: Averroes und Maimonides in Die Religion von Oberschichten*. Marburg, 1989.

Kellner, M. "Philosophical Misogyny in Medieval Jewish Philosophy—Gersonides v. Maimonides," in *Joseph Baruch Sermoneta Memorial Volume* (Jerusalem Studies in Jewish Thought 14), ed. Aviezer Ravitzky, 113–28. Jerusalem, 1998 [Hebrew].

———. "Politics and Perfection: Gersonides vs. Maimonides," *Jewish Political Studies Review* 6 (1994): 49–58.

Kennedy, H. *Muslim Spain and Portugal: A Political History of al-Andalus*. Edinburgh, 1996.

Klein-Braslavy, S. *Maimonides' Interpretation of the Story of Creation*. Jerusalem, 1988 [Hebrew].

———. *Maimonides' Interpretation of the Adam Stories in Genesis: A Study of Maimomides' Anthropology*. Jerusalem, 1986 [Hebrew].

Kluxen, W. "Maïmonide et l'orientation philosophique de ses lecteurs latins," in *Maïmonide: philosophe et savant*, ed. T. Lévy and R. Rashed, 395–409.

Kogan, Barry S. "'What Can We Know and When Can We Know It?' Maimonides on the Active Intelligence and Human Cognition," in *Moses Maimonides and His Time*, ed. E. L. Ormsby, 121–37.

J. L. Kraemer. "How (Not) to Read the *Guide of the Perplexed*," *JSAI* 32 (2006): 350–409.

———. "Moses Maimonides: An Intellectual Portrait," in *The Cambridge Companion to Maimonides*, ed. K. Seeskin, 10–57. Cambridge, 2005.

———. "Maimonides' Intellectual Milieu in Cairo," *Maïmonide: philosophe et savant*, ed. T. Lévy and R. Rashed, 1–37.

———. "The Islamic Context of Medieval Jewish Philosophy," in *The Cambridge Companion to Medieval Jewish Philosophy*, ed. D. H. Frank and O. Leaman, 38–69. Cambridge, 2003.

———. *Maimonides: The Life and World of One of Civilization's Greatest Minds*. New York, 2008.

———. "Maimonides and the Spanish Aristotelian Tradition," in *Christians, Muslims and Jews in Medieval and Early Modern Spain—Interaction and Cultural Change*, ed. M. M. Meyerson and E. D. English, 40–68. Notre Dame, 1999.

———. "The Influence of Islamic Law on Maimonides: The Case of the Five Qualifications," *Te'udah* 10 (1996): 225–44 [Hebrew].

———. *Humanism in the Renaissance of Islam: The Cultural Revival during the Buyid Age*. Leiden, New York, and Köln, 1992.

———. "Maimonides on the Philosophic Sciences in His *Treatise on the Art of Logic*," in *Perspectives on Maimonides*, ed. J. L. Kraemer, 77–104. Oxford, 1991.

———, ed. *Perspectives on Maimonides: Philosophicnl and Historical Studies*. Oxford, 1991.

———. "Maimonides on Aristotle and Scientific Method," in *Moses Maimonides and His Time*, ed. E. L. Ormsby, 53–88.

———. "On Maimonides' Messianic Posture," in *Studies in Medieval Jewish History and Literature,* vol. 2, ed. I. Twersky, 109–42. Cambridge, Mass., and London, 1984.

Kraus, P. "Raziana," *Orientalia* n.s. 4 (1935): 300–304; 5 (1936): 35–56, 358–78.

———. "Beiträge zur islamischen Ketzergeschichte, das Kitāb al-Zumurrud des Ibn al-Rāwandī," *Revista degli Studi Orientali* 14 (1933–34): 93–129, 335–79.

Kreisel, H. "Judah Halevi's Influence on Maimonides: A Preliminary Appraisal," *Maimonidean Studies* 2 (1991): 95–121.

Kriegel, M. "Messianisme juif, dissidence chrétienne et Réformes: les usage d'une thèse de Maïmonide," *Pardès* 24 (1998).

Lameer, J. "From Alexandria to Baghdad: Reflection on the Genesis of a Problematical Tradition," in *The Ancient Tradition in Christian and Islamic Helle-*

nism: Studies on the Transmission of Greek Philosophy and Sciences, Dedicated to H. J. Drossart Lutlofs on His Ninetieth Birthday, ed. G. Endress and R. Kruk, 181–91. Leiden, 1997.

Langermann, Y. T. "L'œuvre médicale de Maïmonide: Un aperçu général," in *Maimonide: philosophe et savant,* ed. T. Lévy and R. Rashed, 275–302.

———. "Another Andalusian Revolt? Ibn Rushd's Critique of Al-Kindī's Pharmacological Computus," in *The Enterprise of Science in Islam—New Perspectives*, ed. J. P. Hogendijk and A. I. Sabra. Cambridge, Mass., and London, 2003.

———. "Maimonides and the Sciences," in *The Cambridge Companion to Jewish Philosophy*, ed. D. H. Frank and O. Leaman, 157–75. Cambridge, 2003.

———. "Samuel ben Eli's Epistle on Resurrection," *Qobez al Yad: Minora Manuscripta Hebraica*, n.s. 15 (2001): 39–94 [Hebrew].

———. "Science and the *Kuzari*," *Science in Context* 10 (1997): 495–522.

———. "Arabic Writings in Hebrew Manuscripts: A Preliminary Listing," *Arabic Science and Philosophy* 6 (1996): 137–60.

———. "A New Codex of Medieval Jewish Philosophy" *Kiryat Sefer* 64 (1992–93): 1427–32 [Hebrew].

———. "The 'True Perplexity': *The Guide of the Perplexed,* Part II, Chapter 24," in *Perspectives on Maimonides*, ed. J. L. Kraemer, 159–74.

———. "The Mathematical Writings of Maimonides," *JQR* 75 (1984): 57–65.

Lasker, D. "Karaism in Twelfth-Century Spain," *Jewish Thought and Philosophy* (1992): 179–95.

———. "Judah Halevi and Karaism," in *From Ancient Israel to Modern Judaism: Intellect in Quest of Understanding: Essays in Honor of Marvin Fox*, ed. J. Neusner et al., 3: 11–123. Atlanta, 1989.

———. "The Philosophy of Judah Hadassi the Karaite," *Jerusalem Studies in Jewish Thought* 7 (1988): 477–92 [Hebrew].

Lay, J. "L'Abrégé de l'Almageste: un inédit d'Averroès en version hébraïque," *Arabic Sciences and Philosophy* 6 (1966): 23–61.

Lazarus-Yafeh, H. "Was Maimonides Influenced by al-Ghazālī?" In *Tehillah le-Moshe: Biblical and Judaic Studies in Honor of Moshe Greenberg*, ed. M. Cogan et al., 163–93. Winona Lake, 1997.

———. *Intertwined Worlds: Medieval Islam and Bible Criticism*. Princeton, 1992.

Leicht, R. *Astrologumena Judaica: Untersuchungen zur Geschichte der astrlogischen Literatur der Juden*. Tübingen, 2006.

Lerner, R. *Maimonides' Empire of the Light: Popular Enlightenment in an Age of Belief*. Chicago and London, 2000.

———. "Maimonides' Treatise on Resurrection," *History of Religions* 23 (1984): 140–55.

———. *Averroes on Plato's Republic*. Ithaca and London, 1974.

Lerner, R., and M. Mahdi, eds. *Medieval Political Philosophy: A Sourcebook*. Ithaca, 1963.

Levine, H., and R. S. Cohen, eds. *Maimonides and the Sciences*. Dordrecht, Boston, and London, 2000.

Lévy, T. "Maïmonide et les science mathématiques," *Maimonide: philosophe et savant,* ed. T. Lévy and R. Rashed, 219–52.

Lévy, T., and R. Rashed, eds. *Maïmonide: philosophe et savant.* Leuven, 2004.

Levinger, J. "Was Maimonides 'Rais al-Yahud' in Egypt?" in *Studies in Maimonides,* ed. I. Twersky, 83–93. Cambridge, Mass., 1990.

Levinger, J. S. *Maimonides as Philosopher and Codifier.* Jerusalem, 1989 [Hebrew].

Lewis, B. D. "Maimonides and the Muslims," *Midstream* 25, no. 9 (1979): 16–22.

———. "Jews and Judaism in Arab Sources," *Metsudah* 3–4 (1945): 171–80 [Hebrew].

Libson, G. "Parallels between Maimonides and Islamic Law," in *The Thought of Moses Maimonides,* ed. Robinson, Kaplan, and Saver, 209–48.

———. "Interaction between Islamic Law and Jewish Law during the Middle Ages," in *Law in Multicultural Societies: Proceedings of the International Association of Law Libraries. Jerusalem, July 21–26, 1985,* ed. E. I. Cuomo, 95–100. Jerusalem, 1989.

Lieber, E. "The Medical Works of Maimonides: A Reappraisal," in *Moses Maimonides: Physician, Scientist, and Philosopher,* ed. F. Rosner and S. S. Kottek, 13–24.

Liebes, Y. *Elisha's Sin: The Four Who Entered Pardes and the Nature of Talmudic Mysticism.* Jerusalem, 1990 [Hebrew].

Luciani, D., ed. *Le Livre de Mohammed Ibn Toumert, Mahdi des Almohades.* Algiers, 1903.

Mahdi, M. *Alfarabi and the Foundation of Islamic Political Philosophy.* Chicago, 2001.

———. "The Arabic Text of Alfarabi's against John the Grammarian," *Medieval and Middle Eastern Studies in Honor of Aziz Suryal Atiya,* ed. S. A. Hanna, 268–84. Leiden, 1972.

———. "Alfarabi against Philoponus," *Journal of Near Eastern Studies* 26 (1967): 233–60.

Marquet, Y. *La philosophie des Iḫwān al-ṣafā.* Algiers, 1973.

Maïmonide. *Le Guide des égarés: traité de théologie et de philosophie par Moïse ben Maimoun dit Maïmonide,* trad. S. Munk. Paris, 1881.

Maimonides: see list of abbreviations

Makkī, M. ʿA. "Contribución de Averroes a la ciencia juridica musulmana," in *Al encuentro de Averroes,* ed. Andrés Martinez Lorca, 15–38. Madrid, 1993.

Malti-Douglas, F. "Ḥayy Ibn Yaqẓān as Male Utopia," in *The World of Ibn Ṭufayl: Interdisciplinary Perspectives on Ḥayy Ibn Yaqẓān,* ed. L. I. Conrad, 52–68. Leiden, 1996.

———. *Woman's Body, Woman's Word: Gender and Discourse in Arabo-Islamic Writing.* Princeton, 1992.

Al-Manūnī, M. "*Iḥyāʾ ʿulūm al-dīn fi manẓūr al-gharb al-islāmī ayyām al-murābiṭin wa-l-muwaḥḥidin,*" in *Abū Ḥāmid al-Ghazālī, Dirāsāt fi fikrihi wa-ʿaṣrihi wa-taʾthīrihi,* 125–37. Rabat, 1988.

Marín, M. *Mujeres en al-Andalus.* Madrid, 2000.

Marsden, M. "Evangelical and Fundamental Christianity," in *The Encyclopedia of Religion,* ed. M. Eliade, 5: 190–97. New York and London, 1987.

Marx, A. "Texts by and about Maimonides," *JQR* n.s. 25 (1934–35): 374–81.

Massé, H. "La profession de foi (*ʿaqīda*) et les guides spirituels (*morchida*) du Mahdi Ibn Toumart," in *Mémorial Henri Basset*, 105–21. Paris, 1928.
Mazor, A. "Maimonides' Conversion to Islam: New Evidence," *Peʿamim* 110 (2007): 5–8 [Hebrew].
McAuliffe, J. D. "Exegetical Identification of the Ṣābi'ūn," *Muslim World* 72 (1982): 95–106.
Mehren, M.A.F. *Traités mystiques d'Abou Alī al-Hosain b. Abdallah b. Sīnā ou d'Avicenne.* Leiden, 1889–99.
Melamed, A. "Maimonides on Women: Formless Matter or Potential Prophets?" in *Perspectives on Jewish Thought and Mysticism: Proceedings of the International Institute of Jewish Studies University College London, 1994, . . . Dedicated to the Memory . . . of . . . Alexander Altmann,* ed. A. L. Ivry, E. R. Wolfson, and A. Arkush, 99–134. Amsterdam, 1998.
Menocal, M. R. *The Ornament of the World: How Muslims, Jews, and Christians Created a Culture of Tolerance in Medieval Spain.* Boston, 2002.
Meyerhof, M. "The Medical Works of Maimonides," in *Essays on Maimonides: An Octocentennial Volume*, ed. S. W. Baron, 265–99. New York, 1941.
Michot, J. R. "Eschatologie" = J. R. Michot, "L'eschatologie d'Avicenne selon F. D. al-Rāzī," *Revue Philosophique de Louvain* 87 (1989): 235–63.
———. "L'eschatologie d'Avicenne selon F.D. al-Rāzī," *Revue Philosophique de Louvain* 87 (1989): 235–63.
———. "La destinée de l'homme selon Avicenne: Le retour à Dieu (*maʿād*) et l'imagination," *Académie Rayale de Belgique, Classe des Lettres,* "Fonds René Draguet, t. V." Louvain, 1986.
Molénat, J.-P. "Sur le rôle des Almohades dans la fin du christianisme local au Maghreb et en al-Andalus," *Al-Qanṭara* 18 (1997): 389–413.
Morata, N. "La presentación de Averroes en la corte almohade," *La Ciudad de Dios* 153 (1941): 101–22.
Munk, S. *Mélanges de philosophie juive et arabe.* Paris, 1859; reprinted Paris, 1988.
———. *Des principaux philosophes arabes et de leur doctrine.* Paris: Vrin, 1982.
———. "Notice sur Joseph ben Iehoudah," *Journal Asiatique* 14 (1842): 5–70.
Muntner, S., ed. *Maimonides' Medical Writing.* 3 vols. Jerusalem, 1961,
Nagel, T. "La destrucción de la šarīʿa por Muhammad b. Tūmart," *al-Qanṭara* 18 (1997): 295–304.
———. *Im Offenkundigen des Verborgene, Die Heilszusage des sunnitischen Islams.* Göttingen, 2002.
Nasr, Seyyed Hossein, and Oliver Leaman, eds. *History of Islamic Philosophy.* London and New York, 1996.
Nöldecke, Th. "Noch Einiges über die 'nabatäische Landwirtschaft,'" *ZMDG* 29 (1875): 445–55.
Nomanul Haq, Sayed. *Names, Natures and Things: The Alchemist Jābir b. Hayyān and his* Kitāb al-aḥjār *(Book of Stones).* Dordrecht and Boston, 1994.
Nyberg, H. S. "Amr ibn ʿUbayd et Ibn al-Rawendi, deux reprouvés," in *Classicisme et déclin culturel dans l'histoire de l'Islam*, ed. R. Brunschvig and G. E. Von Grunebaum, 125–39. Paris, 1977.
———. "Introduction," in al-Ḥayyāṭ, *Kitāb al-intisār.* Cairo, 1925.

Ormsby, E. L., ed. *Moses Maimonides and His Time*. Washington, 1989.

Parens, J. *Metaphysics as Rhetoric: Alfarabi's Summary of Plato's "Laws."* Albany, 1995.

Pedersen, J. "The Criticism of the Islamic Preacher," *Die Welt des Islams* 2 (1953): 215–31.

———. *"The Ṣābians," A Volume of Oriental Studies Presented to Edward G. Browne on His Birthday*, ed. T. W. Arnold and R. A. Nicholson, 383–91. Cambridge, 1922.

Peters, F. E. "The Origins of Islamic Platonism: The School Traditions," in *Islamic Philosophical Theology*, ed. P. Morewedge, 14–45. Albany, 1979.

"Picatrix": Das Ziel des Weisen von Pseudo-Majrīṭī, trans. H. Ritter and M. Plessner. London, 1962.

Pines, S. "A Lecture on the *Guide of the Perplexed*," *Iyyun* 47 (1998): 115–28 [Hebrew].

———. "Scholasticism after Thomas Aquinas and the Teachings of Ḥasdai Crescas and His Predecessors," trans. A. L. Ivry, *Proceedings of the Israel Academy of Science and Humanities* 1, no. 10 (1967); reprinted in *The Collected Works of Shlomo Pines, 5: Studies in the History of Jewish Thought*, ed. W. Z. Harvey and M. Idel, 489–589. Jerusalem, 1997.

———. "La 'philosophie orientale' d'Avicenne et sa polémique contre les Baghdadiens," *Archives d'Histoire Doctrinale et Littéraire du Moyen-Age* 19 [année 27] (1952): 5–37 (reprinted in *The Collected Works of Shlomo Pines*, vol. 3, *Studies in the History of Arabic Philosophy*, ed. S. Stroumsa, 301–33. Jerusalem, 1996).

———. "Some Traits of Christian Theological Writing in Relation to Muslim Kalām and to Jewish Thought," *Proceedings of the Israel Academy of Sciences and Humanities* 5 (1976): 104–25 (reprinted in *The Collected Works of Shlomo Pines*, vol. 3, *Studies in the History of Arabic Philosophy*, ed. S. Stroumsa, 79–99. Jerusalem, 1996).

———. "On the Term *Ruḥaniyyot* and Its Origin and on Judah Halevi's Doctrine," *Tarbiẓ* 57 (1988): 511–40 [Hebrew].

———. "Shiʿite Terms and Conceptions in Judah Halevi's Kuzari," *JSAI* 2 (1980): 248–51.

———. "Ibn Khaldūn and Maimonides, a Comparison between Two Texts," *Studia Islamica* 32 (1979): 265–74 (reprinted in *The Collected Works of Shlomo Pines*, vol. 5: *Studies in the History of Jewish Thought*, ed. W. Z. Harvey and M. Idel, 383–96. Jerusalem, 1996).

———. "La conception de la conscience de soi chez Avicenne et chez Abū'l Barakāt al-Baghdādī," *Archives d'Histoire Doctrinale et Littéraire du Moyen-Age* 21 (1954): 21–98 (reprinted in S. Pines, *Collected Works*, vol. 1, *Studies in Abūl-Barakāt al-Baghdādī, Physics and Metaphysics*, 181–259. Jerusalem and Leiden, 1979).

———. "The Limitations of Human Knowledge According to Al-Fārābī, Ibn Bājja, and Maimonides," in *Studies in Medieval Jewish History and Literature*, ed. I. Twersky, 82–109. Cambridge, Mass., 1979.

———. "Contributions to the Study of Averroes' Political Theory," in idem, *Studies in the History of Jewish Philosophy—the Transmission of Texts and Ideas*, 84–102. Jerusalem, 1977 [Hebrew].

———. "Philosophy," s.v., *The Cambridge History of Islam*, ed. P. M. Holt et al. Cambridge, 1970.

———. "Translator's Introduction: The Philosophic Sources of the *Guide of the Perplexed*," in *Moses Maimonides, The Guide of the Perplexed*, trans. Sh. Pines, lvii–cxxxiv. Chicago and London, 1963.

———. "Etudes sur Awḥad al-Zamān Abu'l-Barakāt al-Baghdādī," *Revue des Etudes Juives* 8 (1937): 1–33 (reprinted in *The Collected Works of Shlomo Pines*, vol 1:, *Studies in Abu'l-Barakāt al-Baghdādī Physics and Metaphysics*. Jerusalem, 1979).

Pirenne, H. *Mahomet et Charlemagne*. Paris, 1937.

Plessner, M. "Al-Farabi's Introduction to the Study of Medicine," in *Islamic Philosophy and the Classical Tradition: Essays Presented by His Friends and Pupils to Richard Walzer on His Seventieth Birthday*, ed. S. M. Stern et al., 307–14. Oxford, 1972.

Poonawala, I. K. "Ismāʿīlī *ta'wīl* of the Qur'ān," in *Approaches to the Qur'ān*, ed. G. R. Hawting and A. A. Shareef, 199–222. London and New York, 1993.

Puig Montada, J. "El proyecto vital de Averroes: explicar y interpretar a Aristóteles," *Al-Qanṭara* 23 (2002): 12–52.

Rawidowicz, S. "Maimonides' *Sefer Ha-mitswoth* and *Sefer Ha-madda*," *Metsudah* 3–4 (1945): 185 [Hebrew].

Rahman, F. *Avicenna's Psychology: An English Translation of Kitāb al-Najāt*, book 2, chap. 6. London, 1952 (reprinted in *Philosophy in the Middle Ages*, ed. A. Hyman and J. J. Walsh, 255–263).

Rashed, R. "Philosophie et mathématique selon Maimonide. Le modèle andalou de rencontre philosophique," in *Maimonide: philosophe et savant*, ed. T. Lévy and R. Rashed, 253–73.

———, and J. Jolivet. *Œuvres philosophiques et scientifiques d'al-Kindī*, vol. 2, *Métaphysique et cosmologie*. Leiden, 1998.

Ravitzky, Aviezer. "Contemplation and Leadership in Maimonides' Thought," *Daat* 57–59 (2006): 31–59 [Hebrew].

———. "Maimonides: Esotericism and Educational Philosophy," in *The Cambridge Companion to Maimonides*, ed. K. Seeskin, 300–23.

———. " 'As Much as Is Humanely Possible'—The Messianic Era in Maimonides' Teaching," in *Messianism and Eschatology*, ed. Z. Baraz, 191–220. Jerusalem, 1981 [Hebrew].

———. "On the Method of Studying Jewish Philosophy," *Jerusalem Studies in Jewish Thought* 1 (1981): 7–22 [Hebrew].

Reif, S. C. *The Cambridge Genizah Collections: Their Contents and Significance*. Cambridge, 2002.

———. *A Jewish Archive from Old Cairo: The History of Cambridge University's Genizah Collection*. Richmond and Surrey, 2000.

Rescher, N. "Al-Farabi on Logical Tradition," *Journal of the History of Ideas* 24 (1963): 127–32 (reprinted in idem, *Studies in the History of Arabic Logic*, 13–27. Pittsburgh, 1963).

Rigo, C. "Zur Rezeption des Moses Maimonides im Werk des Albertus Magnus," in *Albertus Magnus zum Gedenken nach 800 Jahren: Neue Zugänge, Aspekte und Perspektiven*, ed. W. Senner et al., 29–66. Berlin, 2001.

Robinson, I., L. Kaplan, and J. Bauer, eds. *The Thought of Moses Maimonides: Philosophical and Legal Studies*. Lewinston, Queenston, and Lampeter, 1990.

Rosenthal, F. "Maimonides and a Discussion of Muslim Speculative Theology," in *Jewish Tradition in the Diaspora*, ed. M. Maswari Caspi, 109–12. Berkeley, 1981.

———. *The Classical Heritage in Islam*. Berkeley and Los Angeles, 1975.

———. *Knowledge Triumphant: The Concept of Knowledge in Medieval Islam*. Leiden, 1970.

———. "The Prophecies of Bābā the Ḥarrānian," in *A Locust's Leg: Studies in Honour of S. H. Taqizadeh*, ed. W. B. Henning and E. Yarshater, 220–32. London, 1962.

———. *The Technique and Approach of Muslim Scholarship*. Rome, 1947.

———. *Aḥmad ibn at-Ṭayyib al-Saraḫsī*. New Haven, 1943.

Rosner, F., and S. S. Kottek, eds. *Moses Maimonides: Physician, Scientist, and Philosopher*. North Vale, N.J., 1993.

Roth, N. *Jews, Visigoths and Muslims in Medieval Spain: Cooperation and Conflict*. Leiden, 1994.

Rowson, E. K. *A Muslim Philosopher on the Soul and Its Fate: Al-ʿĀmirī's Kitāb al-Amad ʿalā l-abad*. New Haven, 1988.

Russell, H. M., and Rabbi J. Weinberg. *The Book of Knowledge from the Mishneh Torah of Maimonides*. New York, 1983.

Rustow, M. *Rabbanite-Karaite Relations in Fatimid Egypt and Syria: a Study Based on Documents from the Cairo Geniza*. Ph.D. Dissertation, Columbia University, 2004.

Sabra, A. I. "The Andalusian Revolt against Ptolemaic Astronomy: Averroes and al-Bitrūji," in *Transformation and Tradition in the Sciences: Essays in Honor of Bernard Cohen*, ed. E. Mendelsohn, 133–53. Cambridge, 1984 (reprinted in *Optics, Astronomy and Logic: Studies in Arabic Science and Philosophy*, ed. A. I. Sabra. Norfolk, 1994).

Safrey, H.-D. "Le chrétien Jean Philopon et la survivance de l'école d'Alexandrie au VIe siècle," *Revue des Etudes Grecques* 67 (1954).

Schacht, J., and M. Meyerhof. "Maimonides against Galen, on Philosophy and Cosmogony," *Bulletin of the Faculty of Arts of the University of Egypt* 5 (1937): 53–88.

Shatzmiller, M. "*al-Muwaḥḥidūn*," *EI*, 7: 801–7.

Schlosberg, E. "Maimonides' Attitude to Islam," *Pe'amim* 42 (1990): 38–60 [Hebrew].

Schwarb, G. "ʿAlī Ibn Ṭaybughā's Commentary on Maimonides' *Mishneh Torah, Sefer Ha-Madaʿ, Hilkhot Yesodei Ha-Torah* 1–4: *A Philosophical 'Encyclopaedia' of the 14th Century*" (forthcoming).

———. "Die Rezeption Maimonides' in christlisch-arabischen Literatur," *Judaica* 63 (2007): 1–45.

Schwartz, Dov. "Avicenna and Maimonides on Immortality," in *Medieval and Modern Perceptions on Jewish-Muslim Relations*, ed. R. L. Nettler, 185–97. Luxembourg and Oxford, 1995.

Schwartz, Merlin L. *Astral Magic in Medieval Jewish Thought*. Ramat Gan, 1999 [Hebrew].

———. *Ibn al-Jawzī's Kitāb al-Quṣṣāṣ wa'l-mudhakkirīn*. Beirut, 1969.

Schwarz, Michael. "*Al-fiqh*, a Term Borrowed from Islam Used by Maimonides for a Jewish Concept in His *Sefer ha-Mitzwoth* and in *The Guide of the Perplexed*," in *Adaptations and Innovations: Studies on the Interaction between Jewish and Islamic Thought and Literature from the Early Middle Ages to the Late Twentieth Century, Dedicated to Professor Joel L. Kraemer*, ed. Y. Tzvi Langermann and J. Stern, 349–53. Paris, Louvain, and Dudley, 2007.

———. *Maimonides, The Guide of the Perplexed. Annotated Hebrew Translation from the Arabic.* 2 vols. Tel-Aviv, 2002.

———. "Who Were Maimonides' *Mutakallimūn*? Some Remarks on *Guide of the Perplexed*, Part 1, Chapter 73," *Maimonidean Studies* 1 (1991): 159–209; 3 (1992–93): 143–72.

Schwartz, Y. "Meister Eckharts Schriftauslegung als maimonidisches Projekt," in *Moses Maimonides (1138–2004): His Religious, Scientific and Philosophical Wirkungsgeschichte in Different Cultural Contexts*, ed. Hasselhoff and Fraisse, 173–208.

Schweid, E. *Feeling and Speculation*. Ramat Gan, 1970 [Hebrew].

Seeskin, K., ed. *The Cambridge Companion to Maimonides*. Cambridge, 2005.

———. *Searching for a Distant God: The Legacy of Maimonides*. New York and Oxford, 2000.

Sela, S. "Queries on Astrology Sent from Southern France to Maimonides: Critical Edition of the Hebrew Text, Translation and Commentary," *Alef* 4 (2004): 89–190.

Serrano, D. "Por qué llamaron los almohades antropomorfistas a los almorávides?" in *Los Almohades*, ed. P. Cressier et al., 815–52.

Silver, D. J. *Maimonidean Criticism and the Maimonidean Controversy 1180–1240*. Leiden, 1965.

Soloveitchik, H. "*Mishneh Torah*: Polemic and Art," in *Maimonides after 800 Years*, ed. Jay Harris, 327–43. Cambridge, Mass., 2007.

Sonne, I. "Maimonides's Epistle to Samuel Ibn Tibbon," *Tarbiẓ* 10 (1939): 135–54 [Hebrew].

Steinschneider, M. *Die hebräischen Übersetzungen des Mittelalters und die Juden als Dolmetscher*. Berlin, 1893 (reprinted Graz, 1956).

———. *Al-Farabi (Alfarabius): Des arabischen Philosophen Leben und Schriften*. St. Petersburg, 1869.

———. *Al-Farabi, des arabischen Philosophen Leben und Schriften*, Mémoires de l'Académie Impériale des Sciences de Saint-Pétersbourg, VIIe série, t. 13, no. 4 (1869): 248b–249a.

———. "Zur pseudepigraphischen Literatur, insbesondere der geheimen Wissenschaften des Mittelalters aus hebräischen und arabischen Quellen," *Wissenschaftlische Blätter aus der Veitel Heine Ephraim'schen Lehranstalt (Beth Ha-Midrasch) in Berlin I* 3. Berlin, 1862.

Stern, J. "The Fall and Rise of Myth in Ritual: Maimonides versus Nahmanides on the *Huqqim*, Astrology and the War against Idolatry," *Journal of Jewish Thought and Philosophy* 6 (1997): 185–263 (reprinted in S. Stern, *Problems and Parables of Law: Maimonides and Nahmanides on Reasons for the Commandments* [Taʿamei Ha-Mitzvot], 109–60. Albany, 1998.)

Strauss, L. "Note on Maimonides' 'Book of Knowledge,'" in idem, *Studies in Platonic Political Philosophy*, 192–204. Chicago and London, 1983.
———. *Persecution and the Art of Writing*. Glencoe, Ill., 1952.
Strohmaier, G. "Die ḥarrānischen Sabier bei Ibn an-Nadīm und al-Bīrūnī," in *Ibn al-Nadīm und die mittelalterliche arabische Literatur: Beiträge zum 1. Johann Wilhelm Fück Kolloquium. Halle, 1987*, 1–56. Wiesbaden, 1996.
———. "Von Alexandrien nach Baghdad—eine fiktive Schultradition," *Aristoteles, Werk und Wirkung, Paul Moreaux gewidmet*, ed. J. Weisner, 2: 380–89. Berlin, 1987.
Stroumsa, G. G. *A New Science: The Discovery of Religion in the Age of Reason*. Cambridge, Mass. (forthcoming).
Stroumsa, S. "The Barāhima in Early Kalām," *JSAI* 6 (1985): 229–43.
———. "The Muslim Context of Medieval Jewish Philosophy," in *The Cambridge History of Jewish Philosophy: From Antiquity through the Seventeenth Century*, ed. S. Nadler and T. Rudavsky, 39–59. Cambridge, 2009.
———. "Philosophy as Wisdom: On the Christians' Role in the Translation of Philosophical Material to Arabic," in *Exchange and Transmission across Cultural Boundaries: Philosophy and Science in the Mediterranean: Proceeding of a Workshop in memory of Prof. Shlomo Pines, the Institute for Advanced Studies, Jerusalem; 28 February–2 March 2005*, ed. H. Ben-Shammai, S. Shaked, and S. Stroumsa (forthcoming).
———. "The Literary Corpus of Maimonides and Averroes," *Maimonidean Studies* 5 (2008): 193–210.
———. "Soul-Searching at the Dawn of Jewish Philosophy: A Hitherto Lost Fragment of al-Muqammaṣ's *Twenty Chapters*," *Ginzei Qedem* 3 (2007): 137–61.
———. "Maimonides' Auffassung vom jüdischen *Kalām*: sein Wahrheitsgehalt und seine geschichtliche Wirkung." *Judaica: Beiträge zum Verstehen des Judentums* 61 (2005): 289–309.
———. "Philosophes almohades? Averroès, Maïmonide et l'idéologie almohade," in *Los Almohades*, ed. P. Cressier et al., 1137–1162.
———. "Sabéens de Harran et Sabéens de Maïmonide," in *Maïmonide: philosophe et savant*, ed. T. Lévy and R. Rashed, 335–52.
———. "Philosopher-King or Philosopher-Courtier? Theory and Reality in the *Falāsifa*'s Place in Islamic Society," in *Identidades Marginales*, ed. Cristina De la Puente. Estudios Onomàstico-Biogràficos de al-Andalus. 13, 433–60. Madrid, 2003.
———. "Entre Ḥarrān et al-Maghreb: la théorie maïmonidienne de l'histoire des religions et ses sources arabes," in *Judios y musulmanes en al-Andalus y el Magreb—Contactos intelectuales*, ed. M. Fierro, 153–64. Madrid, 2002.
———. "Islam in the Historical Consciousness of Jewish Thinkers of the Arab Middle Ages," in *The Intertwined Worlds of Islam: Essays in Memory of Hava Lazarus-Yafeh*, ed. N. Ilan, 443–58. Jerusalem, 2002 [Hebrew].
———. *Saadia Gaon: A Jewish Thinker in a Mediterranean Society,* ed. M. A. Friedmann. Jewish Culture in Muslim Lands and Cairo Geniza Studies. Tel-Aviv, 2001 [Hebrew].

———. "Citation Traditions: On Explicit and Hidden Citations in Judaeo-Arabic Philosophical Literature," in *Heritage and Innovation in Medieval Judaeo-Arabic Culture: Proceedings of the Sixth Conference for Judaeo-Arabic Studies*, ed. J. Blau and D. Doron, 167–78. Ramat Gan, 2000 [Hebrew].

———. *The Beginnings of the Maimonidean Controversy in the East: Yosef Ibn Shim'on's* Silencing Epistle Concerning the Resurrection of the Dead. Jerusalem, 1999 [in Hebrew, with English introduction].

———. *Freethinkers of Medieval Islam: Ibn al-Rāwandī, Abū Bakr al-Rāzī, and Their Impact on Islamic Thought*. Islamic Philosophy and Theology 35. Leiden, 1999.

———. " 'True Felicity': Paradise in the Thought of Avicenna and Maimonides," *Medieval Encounters* 4 (1998): 51–77.

———. "Twelfth-Century Concepts of Soul and Body: The Maimonidean Controversy in Baghdad," in *Self, Soul and Body in Religious Experience*, ed. A. Baumgarten et al., 313–34. Leiden, 1998.

———. "Elisha Ben Abuya and Muslim Heretics in Maimonides' Writings," *Maimonidean Studies* 3 (1995): 173–93.

———. "Habitudes religieuses et liberté intellectuelle dans la pensée arabe médiévale," in *Monothéisme et Tolérance: Actes du Colloque du Centre International de Recherche sur les Juifs du Maroc, 1-4 Octobre, 1996*, ed. M. Abitbol and R. Assaraf, 57–66. Paris, 1997.

———. "The Blinding Emerald: Ibn al-Rāwandī's *Kitāb al-zumurrud*," *JAOS* 114, no. 2 (1994): 163–85.

———. "Al-Fārābī and Maimonides on Medicine as a Science," *Arabic Sciences and Philosophy* 3 (1993): 235–49.

———. "Al-Fārābī and Maimonides on the Christian Philosophical Tradition: A Re-evaluation," *Der Islam* 68 (1991): 263–87.

———. "The Impact of Syriac Tradition on Early Judaeo-Arabic Bible Exegesis," *Aram* 3 (1991): 83–96.

———. "A Note on Maimonides' Attitude to Joseph Ibn Ṣadīq," *Shlomo Pines Jubilee Volume*, part 2. *Jerusalem Studies in Jewish Thought* 8, 210–15. Jerusalem, 1990 [Hebrew].

———. *Dāwūd ibn Marwān al-Muqammiṣ's Twenty Chapters ('Ishrūn Maqāla)*. Etudes sur le judaïsme médiéval 13. Leiden, 1989.

———. "From Muslim Polemics to Jewish Muslim Heresy: Ibn al-Rāwandī's *Kitāb al-Dāmigh*. *JAOS* 107 (1987): 767–72.

Talbi, M. "Le christianisme magrébin de la conquête musulmane à sa disparition: une tentative d'explication," in *Conversion and Continuity: Indigenous Christian Communities in Islamic Lands, Eighth to Eighteenth Centuries*, ed. M. Gervers and R. J. Bikhazi, 313–51. Toronto, 1990.

Tamer, G., ed. *The Trials of Maimonides: Jewish, Arabic and Ancient Cultures of Knowledge*. Berlin, 2005.

Tardieu, M. *Les paysages reliques: routes et haltes syriennes d'Isidore à Simplicius*. Louvain and Paris, 1990.

———. "Ṣābiens coraniques et Ṣābiens de Ḥarrān," *Journal Asiatique* 274 (1986): 1–44.

Teicher, J. L. "Maimonides' Letter to Jospeh b. Jehudah—A Literary Forgery," *Journal of Jewish Studies* 1 (1948–49): 35–54.

———. "A Literary Forgery in the Thirteenth Century: Maimonides' Epistle on Resurrection." *Melilah* 1 (1944): 81–92 [Hebrew].

Teixidor, J. *Bardesane d'Edesse, la première philosophie syriaque.* Paris, 1992.

Türker, M. "*Al-maqāla fī ṣināʿat al-manṭiq* de Mūsā Ibn Maymūn." *Review of the Institute of Islamic Studies* 3 (1959–60): 55–60, 87–110.

Turki, A. "La place d'Averroès juriste dans l'histoire du malikisme et de l'Espagne musulmane," in *Multiple Averroès*, ed. J. Jolivet, 33–43. Paris, 1978.

Twersky, I. "Did R. Abraham Ibn Ezra Influence Maimonides?" in *Rabbi Abraham Ibn Ezra: Studies in the Writings of a Twelfth-Century Jewish Polymath,* ed. I. Twersky and J. M. Harris, 21–48. Cambridge, Mass., 1993.

———, ed. *Studies in Maimonides.* Cambridge, Mass., 1990.

———. *Introduction to the Code of Maimonides (Mishneh Torah).* New Haven and London, 1980.

———, ed. *Studies in Medieval Jewish History and Literature.* Cambridge, Mass., 1979.

———. "The *Mishneh Torah* of Maimonides." *Proceedings of the Israel Academy of Sciences and Humanities* 5 (1976): 265–95.

———, ed. *A Maimonides Reader.* New York and Philadelphia, 1972.

Ullmann, M. *Natur-und Geheimwissenschaften im Islam.* Leiden, 1972.

Urbach, E. E. *The Sages, Their Concepts and Beliefs.* Jerusalem, 1975.

Urvoy, D. *Averroès: Les ambitions d'un intellectuel musulman.* Paris, 1998.

———. "La pensée almohade dans l'œuvre d'Averroès," in *Multiple Averroès*, 45–53.

———. *Pensers d'al-Andalus: La vie intellectuelle à Séville et Cordoue au temps des empires berbères (fin XIe siècle–début XIIIe siècle).* Toulouse, 1990.

Vajda, G. "A propos d'une citation non identifiée d'al-Fārābī dans le *Guide des égarés,*" *Journal asiatique* 253 (1965): 43–50.

Van Bladel, K. *The Arabic Hermes* (forthcoming).

Verrycken, K. "The Development of Philoponus' Thought and Its Chronology," in *Aristotle Transformed*, ed. R.R.K. Sorabji, 233–74. London, 1990.

von Gutschmid, A. "Die nabatäische Landwirtschaft und ihre Geschwister," *ZDMG* 15 (1861): 1–110.

Walker, P. E. *Early Philosophical Shiism: The lsmaili Neoplatonism of Abū Yaʿqūb al-Sijistānī.* Cambridge and New York, 1993.

Walzer, R. *Greek into Arabic.* Oxford: B. Cassirer, 1962.

Wasserstrom, S. M. *Between Muslim and Jew: The Problem of Symbiosis under Early Islam.* Princeton, 1995.

Watt, W. Montgomery. "Philosophy and Theology under the Almohads." *Actas del Primer Congresso de Estudios Arabes e 1slàmicos. Córdoba 1962*, 101–7. Madrid, 1964.

———. "Ḥanīf," *EI*, 3: 165–66.

Watts, E. J. *City and School in Late Antique Athens and Alexandria.* Berkeley, 2006.

Wéber, E.-H. "Un thème de la philosophie arabe interprété par Albert le Grand," in *Albertus Magnus zum Gedenken nach 800 Jahren: Neue Zugänge, Aspekte und Perspektiven*, ed. W. Senner et al., 79–90. Berlin, 2001.

Weiss, R. L., and Ch. E. Butterworth. *Ethical Writings of Maimonides*. New York, 1975.

Westernick, L. G. *Anonymous Prolegomena to Platonic Philosophy*. Amsterdam, 1962.

Yahalom, Y. " 'Sayeth Tuviyyah ben Ẓidkiyyah': The *Maqama* of Joseph ben Simeon in Honor of Maimonides," *Tarbiẓ* 66 (1997): 543–77.

Yuval, I. "Moses *Redivivus*: Maimonides as the Messiah's Helper," *Zion* 72 (2007): 161–88 [Hebrew].

———. Yuval, "*Two Nations in Your Womb": Perceptions of Jews and Christians*. Tel Aviv, 2000 [Hebrew].

INDEX

Abraham (Patriarch), 185–86
Abraham ibn Daud, 36
Abū Ya'qūb Yūsuf (Almohad ruler), 80
afterlife, 122. *See also* hereafter
Alexander of Aphrodisias, 14–15
Alexandrian Academy, Fārābī's concentration on, 29
Alexandrian school, Christianization of, 28
al-Filāḥā al-nabaṭiyya, 100
Almohads, 8–10, 53–59; and astronomy, 80–82; and legal methodology, 61–70; and philosophy, 80–82; and theology, 70–79
Almoravids, 8, 54
'Amiri, Abū al-Ḥasan al-, 136–37, 143
anachronism, 30
Andalusians, 36
anthropomorphism, 54, 70–72
Arabic language, 19–22
Aristotelian philosophy, 15, 44, 51, 97
Aristotelian physics, 80–83
Aristotelian tradition, Arabic, 14–15, 30, 34
Aristotle, 14–15, 132, 149
astrology, 96, 114, 140, 146; distinguished from astronomy, 141
astronomy, 80–82, 113–14, 125, 141
Averroes (Ibn Rushd), 14, 16, 19, 67–70, 73–75, 80, 92n41, 116, 124, 154, 182; *Bidāyat al-mujtahid,* 68
Avicenna (Ibn Sīnā), 16, 18–19, 145, 154, 160–64, 174, 182; *Epistle Against Astrology,* 146–47
Avot (tractate), 11
Ayyūbids, 9, 17

Baghdad, 86, 168
Baghdādī, Abū al-Barakāt al-, 18, 172
Baghdādī, 'Abd al-Laṭif al-, 20
Baron, Salo W., 33, 41n59
Baṣīr, Yūsuf al-, 35
Benjamin of Tudela, 168–69
Berman, Lawrence, 103
Bible (Hebrew), and hereafter, 156
biblical references: Ezekiel 17:3, 1; Jeremiah 2:25, 60; Psalms 94:8–9, 51
Bīrūnī, Abū Rayḥān al-, 143
Biṭrīq, Yaḥyā al-, 30, 30n24
Boethusians, 42
Book of Commandments (Maimonides), 21
Braudel, Fernand, 3–4
Byzantium, Christian, 106

Cairo, 168
Cairo Geniza, 3, 100n80, 151n123
censorship, 183
Christianization, of Alexandrian philosophy, 28
Christian *kalām,* 26–38
Christians: and Aristotelianism, 15; Byzantine, 122; Greek and Syriac, 29; and intellectual history of Muslim Spain, xiii–xiv; Oriental, 96; as protected minority, 56; and transmission of Hellenic culture to Arabs, 32; use of Greek philosophy, 28
Chwolsohn, Daniel, 90, 91n33, 103
Code (Maimonides). See *Mishneh Torah*
Commentary on the Mishnah (Maimonides), 11, 21, 38, 43, 45, 71–72, 107, 150–51, 157, 166
comparisons, systematic, 101
convivencia, 5–6
Cordoba, 8
cultural biography, xii
cultural influence, 32–33

darshan, 122
David ben Judah Leon, 83
divinations, 113
divine accommodation, 105
divine economy, 92
Dunash ben Tamim, 36

Egypt: ascendance over Iraq as Jewish center, 169; Ayyūbid, 9; Fāṭimid, 8–9
Egyptians: as Sabians, 91

Elisha Ben Abuya, 43–45, 49, 137
Epistle on Astrology (Maimonides), 45, 140–41
Epistle on Forced Conversion (Maimonides), 60
Epistles of the Pure Brethren, The, 100
Epistle to Yemen (Maimonides), 25, 27, 41, 120–21
Equivalence of Proofs, 50n89
exegesis, 73–78

Fārābī, Abū Naṣr al-, 16, 28–29, 29n19, 31, 33, 91n34, 106, 127, 135–36, 164, 184; *On the Changing Beings,* 28; *Commentary on the Nicomachean Ethics,* 140; *Discourse,* 28–29; *Encyclopedia,* 134; *Epistle on Medicine,* 134
Fāṭimids, 9, 16–17
Fez, 8, 59–60
forced conversion, 16
forgeries, examination of, 166–79
fundamentalism, 58
Funkenstein, Amos, 104

Galen, 135–36
Garden of Eden, as earthly place, 158
Ghāyat al-ḥakīm, 100
Ghazālī, Abū Ḥāmid al-, 9–10, 25, 44, 54, 69, 123–24; *al-Munqidh min al-ḍalāl,* 25–26; *Intentions of the Philosophers,* 156
Goitein, Shlomo Dov, 3, 5–6, 13
Graetz, Heinrich, 104
Greek philosophy, 12, 28
Guide of the Perplexed (Maimonides), 20, 24, 37–38, 45, 70, 73, 90–91, 99, 107–10, 139, 142, 149, 161, 179, 184–85

hadhayān, 145–49
Halevi, Judah, 25, 36, 40, 98, 101n86, 108–9; *Kuzari,* 25
Ḥarrān, 86–88
Hebrew language, 19–22
hereafter, demythologizing of, 159–60
heresies, Islamic, 38–52
heresies, Jewish, 38–52
heresy, 39, 121
heretic: *min,* 38–52; zindīq, 38–52
Hippocrates, 133, 135
Hourani, G. F., 106
Husik, Isaac, 33

Ibn ʿAbbās, 12
Ibn Abī Uṣaybiʿa, 30n24, 60, 129; *Classes of Physicians,* 28
Ibn ʿAdī, Yaḥyā, 29–31
Ibn al-Jawzī, 144
Ibn al-Qifṭī, 126, 128–31, 133
Ibn al-Rāwāndī, 45–48, 144
Ibn Bājja, 15–16, 95, 184–85
Ibn Ezra, Abraham, 98, 108
Ibn Ḥazm, 144
Ibn Qurra, Ṭābit, 88
Ibn Qutayba, 12
Ibn Rushd, Abū'l-Walīd. *See* Averroes (Ibn Rushd)
Ibn Ṣaddīq, Joseph, 27, 36
Ibn Sanā' al-Mulk, 129
Ibn Shimʿon, Joseph, 14, 18, 36–37, 57n18, 170; *Silencing Epistle on the Resurrection of the Dead,* 166–79
Ibn Tibbon, Samuel, 24, 27, 30, 97, 151
Ibn Ṭufayl, 16, 184–85
Ibn Tūmart, Muḥammed, 53–55, 61, 68, 77, 81
idolatry, 93–95, 93n44, 114
immortality of soul, 154–61
influences, importance of, xiii
intellect, 154; permanence of, 164
Iran, Sassanian, 106
Islamic, use of term, 7n25
Islamic context, of Judaeo-Arabic philosophy, xii
Islamic heretics, 45–48
Islamic *kalām* (theology), 17, 24–38; *Ashʿariyya,* 34–35; *Muʿtazila,* 32, 34–35
Islamic law, 9–10, 14; *fiqh,* 14; *madhhab,* 9
Islamic political thought, 183
Israeli, Isaac, 27, 49–50; *Book of Definitions,* 143; *Book of Elements,* 143

Jesus, 43
Jewish *kalām,* 26–38; Karaite, 26 (*see also* Karaite heresy); Rabbanite, 26 (*see also* Rabbanite Jews)
Jewish law *(halacha),* xii, 13–14

Jewish philosophy, 26; and interpretation of Islam, 107–11
Jewish world, development and transformation of, 18–22
Jews, as protected minority, 56
Judah the Prince, Rabbi, 65
Judaism: and Aristotelian thought, 36; and biblical heritage, 26; development of, 95; and emergence of Islam, 106; and Talmudic heritage, 26
Judeo-Arabic language, 19–22

Kalām, 26–38, 47, 69, 176; Ashʿarite, 54; Ashʿarriyya, 26; Muʿtazila, 26
Karaite heresy, 39–43
Karaite Jews, 17, 32
Kindī, al-, 12
king, duties of, 78
knowledge, transfer of, 19
Kraemer, Joel, 66, 78

language, use of, 19–22
Leo Africanus (alias Yuḥanna al-Asad), 129
Letter on Astrology (Maimonides), 101
Letter to Ibn Tibbon (Maimonides), 14–15, 24, 49, 142
Letter to Obadia the Proselyte (Maimonides), 109–11
living, use of term, 180
logic, importance of, 126

Maghrebi-Andalusian intellectual tradition, 95
Mahdi, Muhsin, 31n28
Maimonides: and Almohads, 59–83; as Andalusian, 6–7; as architect of ideas, 11; as Aristotelian philosopher, 14; and Averroes, 73–75; correspondence of, 10; criticism of *kalām,* 32, 36–38; decision to feign conversion, 57n18; and development of religion, 92; as disciple of al- Fārābī, 186; as educator, 113; and forced conversion, 59; and hereafter, 153–65; as historian of religion, 106–11; and Islamic law, 65–70; as Islamic thinker, 1; as Jewish leader, 1, 10; as Mediterranean thinker, 6–12; and Neoplatonic philosophy, 16–17; as phenomenologist of religion, 84–125; as philosopher, 37; philosophic origins, 13–17; as physician, 9, 125; as political philosopher, 183–88; on pseudo-science, 138–52; as scientist, 125–52; and Talmud, 62–65; theory of religion, 14; use of Hebrew, 20–21; use of Judaeo-Arabic, 19–20; and women, 117–18
Maimonides, works: *On Asthma,* 131; *Book of Commandments,* 21; *Commentary on the Mishnah,* 11, 21, 38, 43, 45, 71–72, 107, 150–51, 157, 166; *Epistle on Astrology,* 45, 140–41; *Epistle on Forced Conversion,* 60; *Epistle to Yemen,* 25, 27, 41, 120–21; *Guide of the Perplexed,* 20, 24, 37–38, 45, 70, 73, 90–91, 99, 107–10, 139, 142, 149, 161, 179, 184–85; *Letter on Astrology,* 101; *Letter to Ibn Tibbon,* 49, 142; *Letter to Obadia the Proselyte,* 109–11; *Mishneh Torah,* 18, 20–21, 62–64, 108, 114, 166, 179; *Treatise on Logic,* 126–28; *Treatise on Resurrection,* 165–83
Maimonides scholarship, inflation of, 1–2, 1n1
Mālikī law, 9–10, 55, 66
Mandeans, 87
Manicheans, 87, 143
Marrākushī, al-, 57
Marzūqī, 144
Masʿūdī, al-, 86, 88–89, 97
medical training, 129
medicine, 125–38
Mediterraneanism, 3–7, 23
Messiah, 78, 158
Messianic era, as parable, 77
milla, 91
Mishneh Torah (Maimonides), 18, 20–21, 62–64, 108, 114, 166, 179
monotheism, 71
Moses, as Philosopher-Prophet-King, 186
Muʾmin, ʿAbd al-, 53
Muqammas, Dāwūd al-, 34, 96, 98, 159
Murābiṭūn. *See* Almoravids
Muslim, use of term, 7n25. *See also under* Islamic
Muslims, and Torah, 109
mutakallim, 31, 35, 37, 176
muwaḥḥidūn, 54. *See also* Almohads

Nabateans, 97, 100
Neoplatonism, 16–17, 27, 88, 143
Nuʿmāī, Muḥammad al-, 105n102

On Asthma (Maimonides), 131

Palestine, 8
persecution of religious minorities, 58
phenomenology, 105
Philo, 26n10
Philoponus, John, 15, 28, 28n15, 29, 29n19
philosophers: Hellenistic, 11–12; Muslim, 11–12
philosophy: Andalusian, 80; Aristotelian, 15, 44, 51, 97; Greek, 12, 28; harnessed to religion, 30–32; Jewish, 26, 107–11
physicians, 49–52
physics, Aristotelian, 80–83
Pines, Shlomo, xiii, 14, 24–25, 28, 47, 52n94, 73, 87n15, 91n34, 92n41, 96, 98, 100, 149, 163–64, 185, 189
Pirenne, Henri, 3
Plato, *Republic,* 116, 183–84
Platonism, 78, 153, 183–85
Plotinus, 15
political theory, 79
prophets, denial of, 44
pseudo-science, 138–52
Ptolemaic astronomy, 80–83
Ptolemy, 80

Qirqisānī, 35, 98
Qur'an, and concept of hereafter, 153, 156

Rabbanite Jews, 32
"ravings," 138–52
Rāzī, Abū Bakr Muḥammad b. Zakariyyā al-, 50–51, 51n92, 135, 144; *Divine Things,* 142–46
reason and truth, 120
religion: development of, 92; popular, 111–24
resurrection, 165–83; and resuscitation, 180

Saadia Gaon (Saʿadia ben Yosef Fayyūmī), 23, 108, 119, 159, 170
Sabian calendar, 85
Sabian literature, 16
Sabians, 13, 49n88, 84–105, 139, 150, 179n87, 185; and Arabic sources, 84–91; Maimonides on, 91–105
Sadducees, 42
sages, 150; Talmudic, 118–19
Samuel ben ʿEli (Gaon of Baghdad), 18, 157, 169; *Treatise on Resurrection,* 166–79
Samuel ibn Tibbon, 14–15
science, 16, 125–38. *See also* astronomy; pseudo-science
Seville, 8
Shahrastānī, 86, 98
Shiʿur Qoma, 71–72, 150
soul: immortality of, 154–61, 170; improvement after death, 162–63; survival of, 154
sources, identification of, 24
Steinschneider, Moritz, 33, 83, 100, 103, 127
Strauss, Leo, 37, 77, 177–79, 183
Sufism, 17
symbiosis (Goitein), 5

Talmud: and hereafter, 156; on heresy, 42–43
Tawḥīdī, Abū Ḥayyān al-, 30n24, 163
Ṭayyib, Ibn al-, 30
Themistius, 14–15
theology, 70–72
thought, Maimonides' definition of, xi
Torah, Muslims and, 109
translations, 19–22
Treatise on Logic (Maimonides), 126–28
Treatise on Resurrection (Maimonides), 165–83; authenticity of, 165–66
truth, 12; quest for, 28; and reason, 120

understanding, limits of, 148, 148n115
uṣūl, 55, 58–59, 64, 67, 78, 82–83

whirlpool effect, xiv
wine, Muslim, 110, 112
world, eternity of, 44

Yaḥyā b. ʿAdī, 15, 145

Ẓāhirī school, 80–81
Zoroastrians, as Sabians, 91